GUIDE TO REFERENCE BOOKS FOR ISLAMIC STUDIES

GUIDE TO REFERENCE BOOKS FOR ISLAMIC STUDIES

C. L. Geddes

BIBLIOGRAPHIC SERIES No. 9

AMERICAN INSTITUTE OF ISLAMIC STUDIES
Denver, Colorado

Published in the United States of America by
The American Institute of Islamic Studies, Inc.
P.O. Box 10398
Denver, Colorado 80210

Library of Congress Cataloging-in-Publication Data

Geddes, C. L. (Charles L.), 1928-
Guide to reference books for Islamic studies

(Bibliographic series, ISSN 0065-8847 / American Institute of Islamic Studies ; no. 9)
Includes index.
1. Islam--Bibliography. 2 Civilization, Islamic--Bibliography. 3. Islamic countries--Bibliography. I. Title. II. Series: Bibliographic series (American Institute of Islamic Studies)
Z7835.M6A54 no. 9 016.909 s [016.909'097671] 85-13558
[BP161.2]
ISBN 0-933017-00-6

Printed and bound in the United States of America

To the Memory of

Rashād ᶜAbd al-Muṭṭālib
Friend, Scholar, Teacher

PREFACE

This is a guide to more than 1,200 books, articles, tables, and charts, both classical and modern, for the study of the history, culture, society, and faith of the Muslim peoples. It covers the geographical expanse from Spain to China, and chronologically from the time of Muhammad to the abolition of the caliphate in 1924. Limited to this last date the *Guide* excludes reference materials on the contemporary politics, modern states, and related subjects of the Middle East and North Africa; for this it is suggested that Reeva S. Simon's *The Modern Middle East: a guide to research tools in the social sciences* be consulted.

Because of the vast size of the literature on some subjects a certain amount of selectivity has had to be employed. Thus, the listings of bibliographies is severly limited to those the compiler believes are of particular importance for each subject from amongst the thousands which have been published. In addition, although to date a complete listing of the commentaries upon the Qurʾān has not been made only a few which are generally regarded as the most important have been included; this same selectivity has been employed as well for the collections of the traditions, primarily, although not exclusively limited to the six "canonical" collections of the Sunnīs and the four books of the Shīʿites. Also, because of the large numbers of language dictionaries in the primary languages of the Muslim world - Arabic, Farsi, Turkish, and Urdu - a strict limitation has been placed with reference made to those bibliographies of dictionaries which have been published. To have attempted to be more comprehensive would have delayed the publication of this *Guide* even more than it has been and, in addition, would have resulted in a multi-volumed work. Despite this required selectivity no reference tool has been excluded because of language.

Because of the very nature of a work of this kind it has been considered imperative that all titles should be printed in their original scripts. Except for those in the languages of western Europe, all titles have, in addition, been translated into English, unless a translation into French or German has been provided by the original author. In this case the two titles have been separated by a slanted line (/). The translations made by the compiler have been included within brackets ([ ]). In every case the translation is as close to the meaning of the original as possible and still make sense. This has often resulted in some very interesting titles because of the interest of many classical Arabic and Persian authors in alliterative or rhyming phrases rather than in seeking clarity. At the request of librarians primary titles in alphabets other than Latin have been transliterated into a short-title form. The transliteration systems employed are those of the Library of Congress.

Approximately ninety-percent of the main entries are annotated; these vary in nature according to the work. It is within these annotations that translations, abridgements, supplements, continuations, and indices are included. This arrangement, it is believed, will be of greater use than to have placed them as separate entries. Furthermore, the annotations frequently include the dates and locales of additional printings, reprints, and other editions. No attempt was made, however, to be all inclusive. In this regard the edition employed for the main entry was that most readily available at the time, although a serious effort was made to employ that generally regarded as the best to date.

Included is an addenda for materials which either had not been released from the press or did not otherwise become available until after the body of the text had been typed. These are, however, included within the index and their numbers, ending with the letter "a", follow the arrangement of the *Guide*.

The compilation of the *Guide* has extended over a quarter of a century and has been conducted in numerous libraries in Africa, Asia, Europe, and the United States, including several private collections.

To the responsible officials and individuals, some now deceased, go my appreciation and heartfelt thanks for their many kindnesses. Also, I am extremely grateful to the numerous friends, scholars, and publishers who have provided me with copies of their publications as well as for suggestions and assistance. Finally, I wish to express my thanks to my colleague, Professor Peter Golas, for transcribing the Chinese and Japanese titles for use within the *Guide*.

No one is more aware of the imperfections, both in commission and omission, of this work than I. There is the Muslim adage that only Allāh can create perfection and I must, perforce, fall back upon this. It is hoped, however, that the *Guide* may, at the least, indicate those reference materials which we do possess, and that it may, as well, illustrate those which are still required for the advancement of the field. Suggestions, corrections, and additions for the improvement of this work will be most gratefully received.

Denver, Colorado
July 1985

ABBREVIATIONS

cir.: *circa*
dbl. col.: double column
ed.(s): editor(s)
GAL: Carl Brockelmann, *Geschichte der arabischen Literatur*
inc.: incorporated
lith.: lithographed
Mushār: Khān Bābā Mushār, *Muʾallifīn Kutub Chāpī Fārsī wa ʿArabī...*
p. (pp): page(s)
Sarkīs: Yūsuf Alyān Sarkīs, *Muʿjam al-Maṭbūʿāt al-ʿArabīya...*
Storey: Charles A. Storey, *Persian Literature:...*
trans.: translation; translator(s)

CONTENTS

CONTENTS

BIBLIOGRAPHY A

GENERAL

A1
^{c}ABD al-RAḤMĀN, ^{c}Abd al-Jabbār.
دليل المراجع العربية و المعربة، فهرست ببليوغرافى يعرف و يقيم المراجع العربية و المعربة فى مختلف الموضوعات، و المراجع الاجنبية التى تحث عن شؤون العرب/
Guide to Arabic Reference Books: an annotated bibliography of books in Arabic and books in western languages dealing with the Arabs. Basra, Dār al-Ṭabā^{c}a al-Ḥadītha, 1970. 12, 556 + 5 p.
With Arabic and English introductions.
Title transliterated: Dalīl al-Marāji^{c} al-^{c}Arabīya wa al-Mu^{c}arraba...

A2
al-AMĪN, ^{c}Abd al-Karīm *and* Zāhida, Ibrāhīm.
Guide to Arabic Reference Books/دليل المراجع العربية
Baghdad, Maṭba^{c}a Shafīq, 1970- .
Title transliterated: Dalīl al-Marāji^{c}al-^{c}Arabīya.

A3
DAQQĀQ, ^{c}Umar.
مصادر التراث العربى فى اللغة و المعاجم و الادب و التراجم
[Sources of the Arab Legacy in Language, Lexicons, Belles-lettres, and Biographies]. Aleppo, Al-Maktaba al-^{c}Arabīya, 1968. 331 p.
Title transliterated: Maṣādir al-Turāth al-^{c}Arabī fī al-Lugha...

A4
ETTINGHAUSEN, Richard, *ed.*

A Selected and Annotated Bibliography of Books and Periodicals in Western Languages Dealing with the Near and Middle East: with special emphasis on medieval and modern times (completed Summer 1951). Washington, D.C., The Middle East Institute, 1952. vii + 111 p. [dbl. col.].

Classified listing with brief annotations of 1,721 books, maps, and serial titles on the ancient, Islamic, and modern history and culture of the Near East and North Africa, including Moghul India, selected by 48 American scholars. Reissued in 1954 with a 23 page supplement containing 253 additional items to December 1953. Although now out-of-date it is still useful for quick reference.

Contents: I. Near East in General; II. The Ancient Near East; III. Islamic Civilization to the Early 1800's; IV. The Modern Near East. Author index.

A5
GAY, Jean.

Bibliographie des Ouvrages Relatifs à l'Afrique et l'Arabie: catalogue méthodique de tours les ouvrages français & des principaux en langues étrangéres traitant de la géographie, de l'histoire, du commerce, des arts de l'Afrique & de l'Arabie. San Remo, J. Gay & Fils, 1875. XI + 312 p. [dbl. col.].

Classified list with occasional annotations of 3,696 books in western European languages published to *cir.* 1875.

Contents: I. Afrique et Arabie; II. Afrique en Générale: ouvrages concernant plusiers états de l'Afrique; III. Afrique septentrionale; IV. Afrique centrale; V. Afrique méridionale; VI. Arabie - Arabes. Author index. Each region is further subdivided by country and subject.

Reprinted in Amsterdam in 1961.

A6
GRIMWOOD-JONES, Diana, *ed.*

Middle East and Islam: a bibliographical introduction. *2nd ed.* Zug, Switzerland, Inter Documentation Company AG, 1979. IX + 429 p.

Bibliotheca Asiatica 15.

Published on behalf of the Middle East Libraries Committee of the United Kingdom.

Classified listing of 41 separate bibliographies by 31 individuals. The result is unevenness of treatment in the various topics. Some have good annotations, others have none at all. Full bibliographic details are lacking throughout.

Contents: 1. Reference- General and Special Bibliographies and Reference Works; Islamic and Middle Eastern Periodicals; Oriental, Arabic and Islamic Studies. 2. History and Islamic Studies- Islamic History; Modern Middle Eastern History; Muslim Spain; The Maghrib; Islamic Law; Islamic Art, Architecture and Archaeology; Arms, Armour and Armies; Islamic Religion; Islamic Theology; Islamic Philosophy; Arabic Mathematics and Astronomy; Arabic/Islamic Medicine; The World of Islam: a note. 3. Subject Bibliographies: Middle Eastern Anthropology; The Geography of the Middle East; Middle Eastern Politics; The Recent Economic History of the Middle East 1800 - 1967; Middle Eastern Oil; Official Publications. 4. Regional Bibliographies: Arabia; Egypt; Islam in Indonesia; Iraq: Modern Political, Social and Economic History; North Africa; Turkey; Palestine-Israel/Jordan/The Palestinians; Pre-Qajar Persia; The Iranian Economy; Persian Periodicals and Newspapers; The Sudan; Syria and Lebanon. 5. Language and Literature: Classical Arabic Literature; Modern Arabic Literature; Arabic Periodicals and Newspapers; Dialect Studies; Berber Studies. Author index.

A7
ḤAMĀDA, Muḥammad Māhir.

[Arabic and Arabized Sources]. N.P., Muʾassasa al-Risāla, 1392/1972. 335 p. المصادر العربية و المعرّبة

A guide to reference books in Arabic with some annotations. Although the compiler proudly states that he has a doctorate in library science many of the entries lack some or all publication data and there is no index. Errata sheet included.

Title transliterated: Al-Maṣādir al-ʿArabīya...

A8
KĀTIB ČELEBI, Muṣṭafā ibn ʿAbd Allāh (d. 1067/1657).

[Book of كتاب كشف الظنون عن أسامي الكتب و الفنون. Removing the Uncertainties on the Names of the Books and Sundries]. *Ed. & trans.* Gustav Flügel, *Lexicon bibliographicum et encyclopaedicum a Mustafa ben Abdallah Katib Jelebi dicto et nomine Haji Khalfa.* Leipzig and London, Oriental Translation Fund, 1835-58. 8 vols.

Bibliography of all of the Arabic, Persian, and Turkish books known to the author arranged alphabetically by title.

The *Kashf* was also printed in two volumes in Bulaq, 1274/1857, and has been reprinted twice in Turkey, the latest being in 1971-72, in two volumes.

Ismāʿil ibn Muḥammad Amīn al-Baghdātlī (d. 1920) compiled a supplement, *Īḍāḥ al-Maknūn fī Dhayl ʿalā Kashf al-Ẓunūn (Keşf-el-Zunun Zeyli), ed.* Ş. Yaltkaya and K. R. Bilge. Istanbul, Millî Eğitim Bakanliği, 1945-47. 2 vols. This edition was reprinted in 1972.

A9
MARTIN, Aubert.

Eléments de Bibliographie des Etudes arabes. Paris, Publications Orientalistes de France, 1975. [ii] + 235p.

A classified listing of books in Arabic and western European languages regarding, primarily, the classical period intended for students. Written in essay form with the works mentioned listed in greater detail at the end of each chapter.

Contents: I. Revues et Périodiques, Collections et Séries; II. Bibliographie; III. Catalogues de Manuscrits arabes - Paléographie; IV. Biographies et Généalogies; V. Encyclopédies; VI. Histoire littéraire; VII. Morceaux choisis: anthologies, chrestomaties; VIII. Muḥammad - Qurʾān - Ḥadīṯ - Tafsīr; IX. Islamologie, Civilisation, Institutions; X. Histoire; XI. Géographie, Voyages; XII. Etude de la Langue classique; XII. Arabe dialectal; XIV. Droit; XV. Philosophie; XVI. Les Arts: architecture, musique, peinture, arts mineurs; XVII. Quelques Traductions arabes d'Oeuvres de la Littérature occidentale (principalement française); XIX. Bibliographies de Quelques Grands Arabisants. Index of authors, editors, and translators.

A10
MEISELES, Gustav.
Reference Literature to Arabic Studies: a bibliographic guide. Tel-Aviv, University Publishing Projects Ltd., 1978. xiv + 250 p.

An unannotated, classified listing of books and some articles in European, Arabic, and Hebrew languages for Arabic studies from the classical period to modern times. The Arabic and Hebrew materials are presented in their original scripts without transliteration or translation, while those in Russian are given only in transliteration. The guide is particularly strong in Arabic language and literature, but weak in other fields. Indices of authors and titles in the Latin script and in Arabic and Hebrew. Includes many introductory works.

Contents: 1. General; 2. Arabic Studies; 3. Bibliographies; 4. Bio-bibliographic Sources for Arabic Literature; 5. Biographical Onomastic & Genealogical Sources; 6. Encyclopaedias and Related Reference Works; 7. Arabic Paleography and Manuscripts; 8. Arabic Language and Lexicography; 9. Reference Works for the Study of the Qurʾān and Ḥadīth; 10. Historical and Geographical Sources; 11. Islamic Art; 12. Periodicals. Appendices.

A useful feature is Appendix II: "Common Abbreviations in Arabic Books (general, dictionaries, ḥadīth and adab, traditionalists, Qurʾānic texts)".

A11
al-NADĪM, Muḥammad ibn Isḥāq (d. 380/990-91).
[Book of the Index]. كتاب الفهرست
Trans. Bayard Dodge, *The Fihrist of al-Nadīm: a tenth century survey of Muslim culture.* New York, Columbia University Press, 1970. 2 vols.

Records of Civilization: Sources and Studies, LXXXIII.

An attempt by the author to list the works of every known scholar to his own time.

It is generally acknowledged that there is no definitive text of the *Fihrist*, although it has been printed numerous times since it was first published by Gustav Flügel in 1871. Professor Dodge's translation, upon which he worked for many years, based upon eleven manuscripts, together with his numerous notes, is as close to an exact text yet published.

Title transliterated: Kitāb al-Fihrist.

A12

PAKISTAN. National Book Centre of Palistan.

اردو میں حوالی کی کتابیں: انسائیکلوپیڈیا، لغت اور دیگر کتب حواله.

[Urdu Reference Books: encyclopaedias, language, and other reference books]. Karachi, National Book Centre of Pakistan, 1965. 67 p.

Listing of Urdu and English language books relating to Urdu materials and arranged according to the International Dewey Decimal System. Headings in English and Urdu. No index.

Title transliterated: Urdū men Ḥawāla kī Kitābīn...

A13

PEARSON, James D.

Oriental and Asian Bibliography: an introduction with some reference to Africa. London, Crosby Lockwood & Son Ltd., 1966. xvi + 261 p.

An introductory handbook primarily for students in essay form. Often lacks full bibliographic details. The index is very limited.

Contents: Part I: Producers of the Literature; Part II: The Literature and its Controls; Part III: Storehouses of the Literature. Contains in Appendix A a list of booksellers in Asia, compiled by K. B. Gardner.

A14

SIMON, Reeva S.

The Modern Middle East: a guide to research tools in the social sciences. Boulder, Colorado, Westview Press, 1978. xv + 283 p.

Westview Special Studies on the Middle East.

Selection of reference sources in both oriental and western languages, with emphasis upon those in English, for the study of the history, politics, sociology, and anthropology, with less emphasis upon the geography, economics, psychology, and education of the Middle East in the nineteenth and twentieth centuries. "The Middle East is defined as encompassing the present day countries of the Arab East and the Arab West, plus Afghanistan, Iran, Israel, and Turkey." *[Intro.]*.

Contents: A. Bibliography; B. Periodicals; C. Primary Source Materials; D. Reference Sources; E. Report Literature. Each section is further subdivided by subject and each has a brief introductory paragraph.

Based upon the collections of Columbia University and the New York Public Library.

A15
TERNAUX-CAMPANS, H.
Bibliothéque asiatique et africaine: ou catalogue des ouvrages relatifs à l'Asie et à l'Afrique qui ont parus depuis la découverte de l'imprimerie jusqu'en 1700. Paris, Chez Arthus Bertrand Librarie, MDCCCXLI. vj + 347p.

Chronological listing of 3,184 books published between 1473 and 1700 in the languages of western Europe. Those in languages other than French are listed in the original and provided with French translations. Subject and author indices. Important for early materials which might not be listed in other bibliographies. Reprinted in Amsterdam in 1968.

A16
ZENKER, J. Th.
Bibliotheca orientalis: manuel de bibliographie orientale. *2nd ed*. Leipzig, G. Engelmann, 1846-61. 2 vols.

Retrospective, classified listing, with occasional annotations, of 8,831 oriental language books and of translations from or into the languages of western Europe printed between the beginning of printing to *cir*. 1857. The first edition was so savagely reviewed that Zenker brought out this second edition in an attempt to meet the criticisms of his attackers.

Contents: T. I: 1. Les Livres arabes, persans et turcs Imprimés depuis l'Invention de l'Imprimerie jusqu'à Nos Jours, tant en Europe qu'en Orient, disposés par Ordre de Matières; 2. Table des Auteurs, des Titres orientaux et de Editeurs; 3. Un Aperçu de la Littérature orientale. T. II: 1. Supplément du Premier Volume. 2. Littérature de l'Orient chrétien; 3. Littérature de l'Inde; 4. Littérature des Parsis; 5. Littérature de l'-Indo-Chine et de la Malaise; 6. Littérature de la Chine; 7. Littérature du Japan; 8. Littérature mantchoue, mongole et tibétaine; 9. Table des Auteurs, des Titres orientaux et des Editeurs. Reprinted in Amsterdam in 1966 in one volume.

SERIAL BIBLIOGRAPHIES

A17

"Wissenschaftliche Jahresberichte." 1846-47, 1849-67, 1876-81. Leipzig, Deutsche Morgenländische Gesellschaft, 1846-81.

Annual report, with bibliographical footnotes, on the scholarly activities of the members of the society and on the advancement of oriental studies in general. Published occasionally as supplements to the *Zeitschrift der Deutsche Morgenländische Gesellschaft*, but more usually as an integral part of the journal.

A18

FRIEDERICI, Charles.

Bibliotheca orientalis: or a complete list of books, papers, serials and essays published in 1876[-83] in England and the colonies, Germany and France on the history, languages, religions, antiquities, literature and geography of the east. Leipzig, Otto Schulze, 1877-84. 8 pts.

Annual classified bibliography of the materials published during the preceding year. Friederici began his list when the "Wissenschaftliche Jahresberichte" failed to appear for several years. An index was lacking in the first issue, thereafter included annually. For 1877 American periodical literature began to be included. For 1879 and after purely geographical books were omitted. Publication of the *Bibliotheca* ceased upon the appearance in 1883 of Johannes Klatt's "Bibliographie." Title varies between English and German and is occasionally in both.

Friederici's annual list was superior to both its predecessor and its successor in that it was published in separate annual installments with indices and it provided publisher and price for each book.

Contents: General Philology; Comparative Mythology; General History, Geography; China; Japan and Corea; Australia and Polynesia; Indian Archipelago and Malacca; Indo-China; India; Afghanistan; Persia; Armenia; Caucasus; Northern and Central-Asia, Thibet; Asia Minor, Turkey, Osmanli; Semitic Philology; Mesopotamia. Cuneiform. Inscriptions; Palestine and Syria; Arabia; Africa; Egypt; Abyssinia; East-Africa; South-Africa; Central-Africa; West-Africa and Marocco; Algeria; North Africa. As required each section further subdivided by subject. Reprinted in one volume in Amsterdam in 1967.

A19
KLATT, Johannes.
"Bibliographie. 1882[-86]." *Literatur-Blatt für Orientalische Philologie*, I-IV, 1883-88.

Annual classified listing of books, articles, and reviews published during the preceding year on Africa and the Orient. Begun in opposition to Friederici's list and was in turn supplanted by the *Orientalische Bibliographie*.

Issuance: Vol. I (1883-84): 1882-83, pp. 33-42, 72-116, 253-378; Vol. II (1884-85): 1883-84, pp. 97-371; Vol. III (1885-87): 1885, pp. 1-261; Vol. IV (1887-88): 1886, pp. 1-192.

Contents: Allgemeines; Malayisch-polynesisches Sprachgebeit; China; Japan; Hinterindien; Tibetisch, Mandschu, Mongolisch.-Central-Asien; Uralaltaische Sprachen.-Nord-Asien; Osmanisch.-Türkei; Indo-germanisch; Vorderindien; Alt-Iran; Neu-Iran; Afghanistan; Belutschistan; Kafiristan, Pamir; Armenien. Kaukasusländer; Kleinasien; Semitisch; Keilinschriften; Palaestina und Syrien; Hebraeisch.

Altes Testament; Rabbinica und Judaica; Aramäisch; Arabisch. Islam; Abessinien; Africa; Aegypten. "Alphabetisches Register zu Band I-IV," IV, pp. 193-222.

A20
ORIENTALISCHE BIBLIOGRAPHIE. 1887-1911.

Annual classified listing of books, pamphlets, articles, reviews, etc., published, at first, during the preceding year on Africa, the Orient, and Oceania. Appeared regularly until 1906, those for 1906-07-08 were published in 1908-10, and those for 1909-10 did not appear until 1912-15. For 1911 the volume was not published until 1922. Fifteen years were then skipped and an attempt was made to bring out a volume for 1926 in 1928, but only two sections were completed. Contents vary.

A21
BECKER, Carl H. *and* GRAEFE, Erich.
"Bibliographie." *Der Islam*, I-III, 1910-12.

Tri-annual author listing of books and articles on Islam and the Muslim world in an attempt to fill the gap left by the faltering *Orientalische Bibliographie*.

Issuance: Vol. I (1910), pp. 103-104, 200-203, 393-396; Vol. II (1911), pp. 115-116, 299-304, 414-418; Vol. III (1912), pp. 207-212, 319-322, 414-418.

A22
"Abstracta Islamica." 1927- .

Annual classified listing of books, pamphlets, articles, etc. published in European and oriental languages during the preceding period and printed as a supplement to *Revue des Etudes Islamiques*, I-1927- . Most items include short, signed, annotations and for books locations of reviews. Author index in each issue. Over the years the organization has varied considerably.

A23
"Recent Publications." 1947- . *The Middle East Journal*, I- , 1947- .

Quarterly listing of recent books in European and oriental languages on the Near East and North Africa. Organization varies upon occasion.

A24
"Abstracta Iranica." 1978- . *Studia Iranica*, I- , 1978- .

Selective, classified listing, with annotations, of books and articles published on pre-Islamic and Islamic Iran, Afghanistan, and the "Indo-Aryan" world.

BIBLIOGRAPHIES OF BIBLIOGRAPHIES

Africa

A25
BESTERMAN, Theodore.
A World Bibliography of African Bibliographies. Revised and brought up to date by J. D. Pearson. Totowa, New Jersey, Rowman and Littlefield, 1975. 241 cols. [including the introductory pages].

Based upon the fourth edition of Besterman's *A World Bibliography of Bibliographies* (1965-66) which extends to 1963, with additional material to 1973. Includes only materials published in western languages. Arranged by region and by country, although, strangely, does not include Egypt. No annotations. Index of authors and titles.

A26
ROBINSON, A. M. Lewin.
A Bibliography of African Bibliographies Covering Territories South of the Sahara. *4th ed.* Cape Town, South African Public Library, 1961. IV + 79 p. [dbl. col.].

Grey Bibliographies No. 7.

Subject listing of bibliographies published both separately and as parts of special studies, first printed in *South African Libraries* in 1942-43. Excludes the northern tier - Morocco, Algeria, Tunisia, Libya, and Egypt. Author, title, and subject index.

A27

SCHEVEN, Yvette.
Bibliographies for African Studies, 1970-1975. Los Angeles, Crossroads Press, 1978. 2 vols.
Annotated, classified listing of 993 items restricted to sub-Saharan Africa.
Supplements: 1976-1979 [809 entries].

Egypt

A28
GEDDES, Charles L.
An Analytical Guide to the Bibliographies on Modern Egypt and the Sudan (1798-1972). Denver, American Institute of Islamic Studies, 1972. [ii] + 78 p.
Bibliographic Series No. 2.
Alphabetical listing of 135 bibliographies by author with detailed annotations and analysis of contents. Index of authors, titles, journals, institutions, and subjects.

Asia

A29
BESTERMAN, Theodore.
A World Bibliography of Oriental Bibliographies. Revised and brought up to date by J. D. Pearson. Totowa, New Jersey, Rowman and Littlefield, 1975. 727 cols.
Based upon the fourth edition of Besterman's *A World Bibliography of Bibliographies* (1965-66) which extends to 1963, with additional material to 1973.
Arranged by region (General; Asia: General; West Asia; South Asia; South-east Asia; East Asia, Far East) and then arranged by country, people, topic, etc. Weak on bibliographies published in languages other than western European and contains a number of errors and duplications. Incomplete in bibliographical details and no annotations. Author and title index.

Arabian Peninsula

A30
GEDDES, Charles L.
Analytical Guide to the Bibliographies on the Arabian Peninsula. Denver, American Institute of Islamic Studies, 1974. [i] + 50 p.

Bibliographic Series No. 4.

Annotated author listing of 70 bibliographies published in western European languages and Russian.

Central Asia

A31

BISNEK, A. G. *and* SHAFRANOVSKIĬ, K. I.

Библиография Библиографий Средней Азии. [Bibliography of Bibliographies of Central Asia]. Moscow, Izdatel'stvo Akademii Nauk SSSR, 1936. 48 p. [dbl. col.].

Listing by type and location of 289 bibliographies, with annotations, published between 1852 and 1935 on and in the Karakalpak, Kirghiz, Tajik, Turkmen, and Uzbeg republics of the Soviet Union. Author index.

Previously published in **Библиография Востока**, 1936, nos. 8-9, pp. 152-194.

Fertile Crescent

A32

GEDDES, Charles L.

An Analytical Guide to the Bibliographies on the Arab Fertile Crescent (with a section on the Arab-Israeli conflict). Denver, American Institute of Islamic Studies, 1975. [x] + 131 p.

Bibliographic Series No. 8.

Alphabetical author listing, with detailed annotations, of 217 bibliographies published in western and eastern European languages (including Russian) and in Arabic. Indices in Arabic, Russian, and Latin alphabets.

Southeast Asia

A33

NUNN, G. Raymond.

South and Southeast Asia: a bibliography of bibliographies. Honolulu, East-West Center, University of Hawaii, 1966. iv + 59 p. [one side only].

Occasional Papers No. 4.

Listing by country, and then by date of publication, of 350 bibliographies and catalogues available in the collections of the University of Hawaii or listed in the published catalogues of six American and British institutions. Location is noted for each item. Those materials in oriental languages are given only in English translation. No annotations.

Contents: Asia; Southern Asia; Afghanistan; Ceylon; India; Nepal; Pakistan; Southeast Asia; Burma; Cambodia; Indochina and Vietnam; Indonesia; Laos; Malaysia; Philippines; Thailand. Index of subjects and authors.

A34
TOKYO. The Centre for East Asian Cultural Studies. A Survey of Bibliographies in Western Languages Concerning East and Southeast Asian Studies. Tokyo, The Centre for East Asian Cultural Studies, 1966-68. 2 pts.

Bibliographies Nos. 4 & 5.

"In this volume [part 1] are listed bibliographies in western languages of East and Southeast Asian studies in the fields of social sciences and humanities and their neighbouring fields. The listing is limited to those published in book form, several important bibliographies published in journals and circulated separately, catalogues and lists of publications of libraries and research institutes specialized in East and Southeast Asian studies, catalogues of maps and paintings and auction catalogues of collections of eminent scholars in these fields of study." [Intro. Remarks]. Part 2 contains bibliographies published in journals through 1968. Arranged by country.

Indonesia

A35
TAIRAS, J. N. B.
Indonesia: a bibliography of bibliographies/ Daftar Karya Bibliografi Indonesia. *Rev. ed.* New York, The Oleander Press, 1975. 123 p.

A mimeographed list produced in Indonesia of 661 annotated books and articles in Indonesian and western European languages. Index of authors, titles, and subjects. No table of contents. Provides library location for each item.

Contents: General; Indexes, Abstracts, etc.; Library Catalogues; Publishers' Catalogues; Periodicals & Newspapers; Manuscripts; Religion; Social Sciences: General; Politics & Government; Economics; Law; Government Publications; Education; Language & Literature; Natural Sciences; Geology & Mining; Medicine; Agriculture; Technology/Industries; Geography & Maps; Regional Bibliographies; History; Personal Author; Theses, etc., Miscellany. Author, title, and subject index.

PUBLICATION & PRINTING

Retrospective Catalogues

Arabic

A36
SARKĪS, Yūsuf Aliyān.
معجم المطبوعات العربية و المعربة و هو شامل لاسماء الكتب المطبوعة الاقطار الشرقية و العربية مع ذكر اسماء مؤلفيها و لمعة من ترجمتهم و ذلك من يوم ظهور الطباعة الى نهاية السنة الهجرية ١٣٣٩ الموافقة لسنة ١٩١٩ ميلادية/
Dictionary of Arabic Printed Books: from the beginning of Arabic printing until the end of 1339 A.H. = 1919 A.D. Cairo, Maṭbaᶜa Sarkīs bi-Miṣr, 1346/1928. 2 vols.

Bio-bibliographical survey of books published in Arabic in the Near East and Europe. Each author is listed in alphabetical order by the name by which he is best known, followed by his full name and dates, either *hijra* or Christian, of his birth and death. For most authors there is a brief biographical sketch. Titles of his printed works are provided with place and date of printing, with number of pages. The second volume contains the author and title indices.

Supplements: Bulletin جامع التصانيف الحديثة/ bibliographique: [I] Cairo, Maṭbaᶜa al-ᶜArabī, 1345/1927. 163 + iv p. [for period 1920-26]; [II] Cairo, Maṭbaᶜa Sarkīs, [1928?]. 60 + i p. [for 1927].

Title transliterated: Muᶜjam al-Maṭbūᶜāt al-ᶜArabīya wa al-Muᶜarraba...

A37
SCHNURRER, Christian Frideric de.
Bibliotheca arabica: actum nunc atque integram. *2nd ed.* Halae ad Salam, I. C. Hendelii, MDCCCXI. XXI + 529 p.

Classified, annotated bibliography of Arabic books printed in Europe and the Near East between 1505 and 1810. Titles and some notes in Arabic. No index.

Reprinted in Amsterdam in 1968. The reprint includes the useful "Table alphabetique de la *Bibliotheca arabica*" by Victor Chauvin published in the fourth volume of his *Bibliographie des ouvrages arabes* (Liège, 1892).

Persian

A38
MUSHĀR, Khānbābā.
[Index of Persian Print- فهرست کتابهای چاپی فارسی Books]. Tehran, Majmūᶜaᵓ Īrānshanāsī, 1337-42/ 1958-63. 2 vols.

Title catalogue of books printed in Farsi in the Near East, India, and Europe from the beginning of Persian printing to 1960. Index of authors in volume two.

Title transliterated: Fihrist Kitābhā-ī Chāpī Fārsī.

Supplements: Karāmat Raᶜnā-Ḥusaynī, فهرست کتابهای چاپی فارسی : ذیل فهرست مشار/ Bibliography of Persian Printed Books: the supplement of Mushār's bibliography. Tehran, Anjuman Kitāb, 1349/1970. 67 p.

Khānbābā Mushār, فهرست کتابهای چاپی فارسی [Bibliography of Persian Printed Books]. Tehran, N.P., 1350-55/1971-76. 5 vols. Mushār's own additions to and continuation of his bibliography. Unfortunately, there is no index.

A39
TEHRAN. Bungā-ha Tarjama-ha wa Nashr Kitāb.
فهرست کتابهای چاپی فارسی از آغازتا آخر سال ١٣٤٥

[Index of Persian Printed Books from the Beginning (of printing) to the End of the Year 1345/1967]. Tehran, Bungā-ha Tarjuma-ha wa Nashr Kitāb, 1352/1973. 3 vols.

Intashārāt Bungā-ha Tarjuma-ha wa Nashr Kitāb, 409/Majmūᶜa-ha Īrānshanāsī, 61.

A listing based, to a great extent, upon Khānbābā Mushār's bibliography.

Title transliterated: Fihrist Kitābhā-ī Chāpī Fārsī...

Turkish

A40

ÖZEGE, M. Seyfettin.

Eski Harflerle Basılmış Türkçe Eserler Kataloğu [Catalogue of Old Printed Turkish Works]. Istanbul, Fatih Yayınevi Matbaası, 1971- .

Alphabetical listing by title of Ottoman Turkish books up to the introduction of the new script in 1928. Provides full bibliographic information as to location of publication, publisher, date (Muslim and Christian), number of pages, and size of page. Issued in fascicules. Titles in modern Turkish only.

Urdu

A41

KARACHI. Anjuman Taraqqi-e Urdū Pākistān.

قاموس الكتب اردو [Dictionary of Urdu Books]. *Ed.* Mawlawī ᶜAbd al-Haqq. Karachi, Anjuman Taraqqi-e Urdū Pākistān, 1961- [all published?]

Subject listing of Urdu printed books to *cir.* date of compilation. Provides author, title, number of pages, date and place of publication.

Contents: Vol. I: *Muzhabiyat* [Religion].

Title transliterated: Qāmūs al-Kutub Urdū

National Bibliographies

Afghanistan

A42

NAᵓĪL, Ḥusayn.

فهرست كتب چاپی دری أفغانستان/ The Catalogue of Dari Printed Books in Afghanistan. Kabul, Anjuman Taᵓrīkh-ī Afgānistān, 1356/1977. [ii] + 276 p.

Numbar Musalsal 120.

Author listing of 1,268 books published since the early 19th century, with full bibliographical data, including size of book. Title index. A fine catalogue.

Title transliterated: Fihrist Kutub Chāpī Darī Afghānistān

A43
STWODAH, Mohammad Ibrahim.
National Bibliography of Afghanistan Pushto Books: Kabul University profesors' *[sic]* works, students' papers. Kabul, Kabul University Library, 1975. v, 52, 73 + 4 p.

Library Series No. 6.

Pushto printed books and pamphlets published in Afghanistan between 1891 and 1975. Entries in Pushto with English translations. Title also in Pushto.

Algeria

A44
MASSE, Henri.
"Les Etudes arabes en Algérie (1830-1930)." *Revue Africaine*, LXXIV, 1933, pp. 208-258, 458-505.

Classified listing of Arabic books published since the French invasion and occupation.

Iran

A45
MUSHĀR, Khānbābā.
فهرست کتابهای چاپی عربی ایران: از آغاز چاپ تا کنون سایر کشورها: بشتیر از سال ١٣٤٠ هـ بعد
[Index of Arabic Books Printed in Iran from the Introduction of Printing to 1340 A.H.]. Tehran, Dār Chāp Rangīn, 1344/1965. [18 p.], 1014 dbl. cols. + 109 p.

Title listing, with full bibliographical details, of the Arabic language books published up to 1961.

Title transliterated: Fihrist Kitābhā-ī Chāpī ᶜArabī Īrān:...

Iraq

A46
ᶜABD AL-RAḤMĀN, ᶜAbd al-Jabbār.
فهرست المطبوعات العراقية ١٨٥٦ ــ ١٩٧٢ : شبت بليوغرافى للكتب العربية التى او نشرها العراقيون منذ دخول الطباعة العراق حتى عام ١٩٧٢. مرتبة حسب الموضوعات
[Index of Iraqi Publications 1856-1972:...]. Basra and Baghdad, Wizāra al-Thaqāfa wa al-Funūn, 1398-1402/1978-82. 3 vols.

Silsila al-Muᶜajim wa al-Faharis, 18, 27, 51.

The first two volumes comprise a classified listing of Arabic books either written by Iraqis and published elsewhere or published in Iraq since the introduction of printing. Volume 3 is the index.

Title transliterated: Fihrist al-Maṭbūᶜāt al-ᶜIraqīya 1856-1972:...

Mosul

A47
MAḤMŪD, ᶜAṣān Muḥammad *and* al-LĀWAND, ᶜAbd al-Ḥalīm.
مطبوعات الموصل منذ سنة ١٨٦١ ــ ١٩٧٥م / Mosul Printed from 1861-1970. Mosul, Maṭbaᶜa al-Jumhūr, 1971. 156 p.

Lists the names and histories of 30 publishing houses, with 80 newspapers published between 1885-1970, periodicals between 1902-1970, and the titles of books between 1861-1970. Author index.

The English title appears only on the paper cover.

Title transliterated: Maṭbūᶜāt al-Mawṣil mundh sana 1861-1970.

Najaf

A48
al-AMĪNĪ, Muḥammad Hādī.
معجم المطبوعات النجفية : منذ دخول الطباع الى النجف حتى الاذ
[Dictionary of Najafīya Printed Materials; from the introduction of printing into Najaf to the present]. Najaf, Maṭbaᶜa al-Nuᶜmān, 1386/1966. 399 p., illus.

Alphabetical listing by title of 1,815 books, with full bibliographical details, and illustrated with eight plates of authors and title pages. No index.

Title transliterated: Muᶜjam al-Maṭbūᶜāt al-Najafīya:...

Morocco

A49

BEN CHENEB, M. *and* LEVI-PROVENÇAL, E.

Essai de Répertoire chronologique des Editions de Fès. Algiers, Jules Carbonel, 1921. 62 p.

Chronological listing of 356 works printed between 1126/1714 and 1337/1919. Subject index. The *Répertoire* was reprinted from *Revue Africaine*, LXII, 1921, pp. 158-173, 275-290; LXIII, 1922, pp. 170-185, 333-347.

Author index in: H. Pérès and A. Sempéré, "Répertoire alphabétique des auteurs publiés à Fès de 1126 H. à 1337 H.," *Bulletin des Etudes Arabes*, VII, 1947, pp. 63-70.

Turkey

A50

BIANCHI, Thomas-Xavier de.

Catalogue des Livres turcs, arabes et persans, Imprimés à Constantinople, Depuis l'Introduction de l'Imprimére, en 1726-27, Jusqu'en 1820; avec notice sur le premier ouvrage d'anatomie et de médecine, imprimé en turc, à Constantinope, en 1820, intitulé *Miroir des Corps dans l'Anatomie d l'Homme*. Paris, Imprimére de L. T. Cellot, 1821. 40 + [vii] p.

Lists on pages 33-40, by date, 68 works. No index.

A51

HAMMER-PURGSTALL, Joseph von.

"Liste der osmanischen Literatur des 18ten und 19ten Jahrhunderts," *Geschichte des Osmanischen Reiches*, Bd. 7, "Erläuterungen zum siebenten Bande," pp. 583-595. Pest, C. A. Hartleben, 1827-35. 10 vols.

Chronological listing of 98 works published by the Imperial press in Constantinople from 1728 to 1830.

¶ The lists of both Bianchi and Hammer-Purstall were supplemented in various journals by themselves and others covering publications of short periods of time until 1890.

NEWSPAPERS & PERIODICALS

Directories

General

A52
AMAN, Mohammed M.
Arab Periodicals and Serials: subject bibliography. New York, Garland Publishing, Inc., 1979. x + 252 p.
Garland Reference Library of Social Science, 57.
"... a guide to serials and periodicals in Arabic, English, French and other European languages published in the Arab countries or in the Western hemisphere, both current and cessations." *[Intro.]*.
Classified listing of 2,711 journals and other serials which, in most instances, provides the name of the issuing organization (if such exists), editorial address, periodicity, dates, and subscription price. Arabic titles in transliteration. No index. The list is, however, quite imcomplete.
Contents: Agriculture; Arabs Abroad; Archaeology; Art and Architecture; Banking and Finance; Bibliographies; Biological Sciences; Building and Construction; Business and Industry; Chemistry; Children and Youth; Christianity; Communications; Computer Sciences; Criminology and Law Enforcement; Earth Science; Economics; Education; Electricity and Electrical Engineering; Engineering and Technology; General Periodicals; Humanities, History, Philosophy; Indexes and Abstracts; Islam; Labor and Industrial Relations; Law; Library, Archives, and Information Science; Linguistics; Literature; Management; Mathematics; Medical Sciences; Meteorology; Middle East Studies; Military Science; Motion Picture Industry; Music; Official Gazettes; Petroleum; Physics; Political Science; Population Studies; Psychology; Public Administration; Science; Social Science and Sociology; Social Services; Sports; Statistics; Trans-

portation; Travel and Tourism; Water, Water Resources and Oceanography; Women.

A53
LJUNGGREN, Florence *and* HAMDY, Mohammed.
Annotated Guide to Journals Dealing with the Middle East and North Africa. Cairo, The American University in Cairo Press, 1964. viii + 107 p.

Alphabetical listings of 283 journals in western European languages (including modern Turkish) and 78 in Arabic being published at time of compilation which deal, partly or wholly, in the social sciences and humanities in the Middle East and North Africa from antiquity to the present. Attempts to provide for each journal its frequency of publication, year begun, price, name and address of issuing body, and notes concerning its special features, subject fields, etc. Those in Arabic are listed in transliteration and translation with a separate listing of their titles in the Arabic script. Indices of subjects and of publishing bodies. Now partially out of date.

Arabic

A54
AHMED-BIOUD, Abdelghani; HANAFI, Hassan *and* FEKI, Habib.
3200 ٣٢٠٠ مجلة و جريدة عربية ١٨٠٠ ــ ١٩٦٥/
Revues et Journaux arabes de 1800 à 1965. Paris, Bibliothèque Nationale, 1969. XV + 252 p. [dbl. col.].

Alphabetical list in Arabic script, with transliteration of 3,258 periodicals and newspapers printed in the Arabic language throughout the world. Notes years that publication began, but not year ceased if no longer in publication, subjects, editors and/or founders, and cities of publication. Indication of periodicity is lacking. Supplemental list of 230 Tunisian newspapers and serials not included in main work. Index of transliterated titles.

A55
TARRĀZĪ, Fīlīb dī [Philip de Tarrazi].

[History of Arabic Journalism]. تاريخ الصحافة العربية Beirut, Al-Maṭbaᶜa al-Adabīya, 1913-33. 4 vols.

The fourth volume contains the important indices and tables of 3,023 Arabic language newspapers and periodicals published in Africa, Asia, Europe, and North and South America between December 6, 1800 and December 1929. The names of the journals, their founders, and dates of first issue appear in both Arabic and English on opposite pages. The lists and indices are very detailed. Reprinted in two volumes in Baghdad, 1967.

Title transliterated: Taʾrīkh al-Ṣiḥāfa al-ᶜArabīya.

Geographic

Africa - General

A56

TRAVIS, Carole *and* ALMAN, Miriam.

Periodicals from Africa: a bibliography and union list of periodicals published in Africa. Boston, G. K. Hall & Co., 1977. xvii + 619 p. [dbl. col.].

Lists by country, excluding Egypt, some 15,000 periodicals with holdings of 60 British libraries. Excluded are newspapers and government reports. Periodical title index.

Published under the auspices of the Standing Conference on Library Materials on Africa.

Egypt

A57

MAUNIER, René.

"Liste chronologique des Revues Publiées en Egypte de 1798 à 1916," in his *Bibliographie Economique, Juridique et Sociate de l'Egypte moderne (1798-1916)*. Cairo, Société Sultanieh d'Economie Politique, de Statistique et de Législation, 1918.

Lists 64 European language journals.

Tunisia

A58

VAN LEEUWEN, A.
"Index des Publications périodiques Parues en Tunisie (1874-1954)," *IBLA [Institut des Belles Lettres Arabes]*, XVIII, 1955, pp. 153-167.

Classified, annotated listing of 90 newspapers, periodicals, annuals, etc., published during the period.

Contents: 1.- Revues de Langue arabe (63); 2.- Alamanachs, Annuaires, Bulletins annuels (16); 3.- Publications assimilées aux Revues (7); 4.- Revues tunisiennes en Langue français (4).

A59
ZAWADOWSKI, G.
"Index de la Presse indigène de Tunisie," *Revue des Etudes Islamiques*, 1937, pp. 357-389, table.

Classified, annotated listing of 247 newspapers published in Arabic, French, and Hebrew between 1861 and 1937.

Contents: I. Presse arab en Langue arabe (161); II. Presse arabe en Langue française (13); III. Presse judéo-arabe (73); IV. Sous-titres français des Journaux arabes et juifs.

Asia

A60
SHAW, G. W. *and* QURAISHI, S.
The Bibliography of South Asian Periodicals: a union list of periodicals in South Asian languages. Harvester Press, 1982. 192 p.

Catalogue of the oriental language newspapers and serials for Afghanistan, India, Pakistan, Bangladesh, Nepal, and Sri Lanka, published anywhere in the world between 1800 and 1979.

Afghanistan

A61
BERTEL'S, E. Ė.
"Афганская Пресса," Библиография Востока ["Afghanistan Press," *Bibliography of the East*], V-VI, 1934, pp. 9-26.

Discussion of the development of the Afghan press since 1874, with an examination of 35 newspapers and journals.

Title transliterated: Afganskaîà Pressa

India

A62
ṢIDDĪQĪ, Rafīᶜ al-Dīn.

[Urdu Periodicals of Pakistan]. پاکستان میں اردو رسائیل Karachi, Akṭar Maḥmūd Ḥusayn Laɔbrīrī, Karāchī Ūnīwursitī, 1975. [xii] + 187 p.

Rather than confined to Pakistan this is a detailed listing of 1,178 Urdu language newspapers and serials published in the Indian sub-continent since the 19th century.

Title transliterated: Pākistān men Urdū Rasāɔīl

¶ For a list of 341 English and bi-lingual Eng-and Indian language and 251 Indian language newspapers published during the period 1750-1950 see: Margaret H. Case, *South Asian History 1750-1950: a guide to periodicals, dissertations, and newspapers* [J67].

Iran

A63
RABINO, H. L.

صورت جرائد ایران و جرائدی کی درخارج ایران بزبان فارسی طبع شدهاست

[List of Iranian Newspapers and Persian Language Newspapers of Iran Printed Outside]. Resht, Maṭbaᶜa ᶜUrwat al-Wuthqā, 1329/1911. 30 p.

Alphabetical listing of the Persian language newspapers printed in Iran and elsewhere from *cir.* 1848 to 1911 and those in other languages (Armenian, Arabic, French, and Ottoman Turkish) printed in Iran during the same period. The place of publication, periodicity, method of printing (lithography, type, or ditto), dates of inception and conclusion, political leaning, and name of proprietor or editor are provided for each.

Translated by L. Bouvat, "La Presse persans Depuis ses Origins Jusqu'à nos Jours," *Revue du Monde Musulman*, 22, 1913, pp. 287-315.

Edward G. Browne, in his *The Press and Poetry of Modern Persia* (Cambridge, The University Press, 1914, pp. 1-166), published, with annotations, an English translation of an unprinted supplement to Rabino by Mirza Muḥammad ᶜAlī Khān "Tarbiyat" in which he listed an additional 371 newspapers.

Title transliterated: Ṣūrat Jarāᵓid Īrān...

A64
ṢADRA HĀSHAMĪ, Sayyid Muḥammad.
تاريخ جرائد و مجلات ايران (تاشـــهريـــون ١٣٢٠)
[History of the Journals and Revues of Iran (to September 1320/1940)]. Isfahan, N.P., 1322-26/1943-47. 4 vols.

Alphabetical listing by title of 1,186 newspapers, journals, and periodicals published in Iran from 1895 to 1940. Provides detailed information on the editors, publishers, dates, and places of publication.

Title transliterated: Taᵓrīkh Jarāᵓid wa Majalāt Īrān...

Iraq

A65
al-ḤASĀNĪ, ᶜAbd al-Razzāq.
[History of the Iraqi Press]. تاريخ الصحافة الاراقية Najaf, Maṭbaᶜa al-Gharī, 1353/1935. 111 p. ill.

Annotated catalogue of the serial publications of Iraq to the end of 1933.

Title transliterated: Taᵓrīkh al-Ṣiḥāfa al-Irāqīya.

Lebanon

A66
DĀGHIR, Yūsuf Asᶜad.
س الصحافة اللبنانية، ١٨٥٨ ــ ١٩٧٤: و هو معجم
رف و يؤرخ للصحف و الدوريات التى اصدرها
بنانيون فى لبنان و الخارج /
Dictionnaire de la Presse libanaise, 1858-1974: répertoire alphabét et signalement de 2500 periodiques divers fondés des Libanais au Liban ou à l'étranger. Beirut, A

Jāmiʿa al-Lubnānīya, 1978. 526 + 25 p.

Title transliterated. Qamūs al-Ṣiḥāfa al-Lubnānīya, 1858-1974:...

Malaya

A67
ROFF, William R.

Guide to Malay Periodicals 1876-1941, with details of known holdings in Malaya. Singapore, Eastern Universities Press Ltd., 1961 [ix] + 46 p.

Papers on Southeast Asian Subjects, No. 4 [Department of History, University of Malaya].

Chronological listing with details concerning place of origin, frequency, dates of publication, editor(s), and known holdings in Malaya, primarily the library of the University of Malaya, of 147 Malayan language and six English language newspapers and serials published in the Peninsula during the period. Those in the modified Arabic script (Java) have been transliterated. Index of titles. Appendix A contains an annotated list of 14 Malayan language periodicals published overseas but circulated within the Peninsula.

This brief guide is a very important reference for any study of Islam in the Malay Peninsula.

A68

Bibliography of Malay and Arabic Periodicals Published in the Straits Settlements and Peninsular Malay States 1876-1941: with an annotated union list of holdings in Malaysia, Singapore and the United Kingdom. London, Oxford University Press, 1972. 74 p.

London Oriental Bibliographies, Vol. 3.

Turkey

A69
NÜZHET, Selim.

Türk Gazeteciliği 1831-1931 [Turkish Newspapers 1831-1931]. Istanbul, Devlet Matbaası, 1931. 92 + [lxvii] p., ill.

Bibliographic essay on the development of newspapers in the Ottoman Empire and the Turkish Republic during the century. Interestingly illustrated with reproductions of 73 front pages.

A70
TURKEY. Millî Kütüphane. Bibliyografya Enstitüsü. Eski Harfli Türkçe Süreli Yayınlar Toplu Kataloğu. (Muvakkat Basım). [Descriptive Catalogue of Published Serials in the Old Turkish Language. (Preliminary Edition)]. Ankara, Millî Kütüphane Cilt ve Basım Atelyesi, 1963. Pp. unnumbered.

Detailed catalogue of the 1,816 Ottoman Turkish serials and periodicals published in the Arabic script between 1729 and 1928. Listed in alphabetical order according to the modern Turkish alphabet.

Holdings Lists

Egypt

A71
EGYPT. Dār al-Kutub.
فهرست الدوريات العربية التى تقتنيها الدار
[Index to the Arabic Periodicals Preserved in the House (Library)]. *Comp.* Maḥmūd Ismāʿīl ʿAbd Allāh. Cairo, Maṭbaʿa Dār al-Kutub, 1961-63. 2 vols. [continuous pagination].

Alphabetical listing by title of newspapers, journals, and other periodicals. Provides full bibliographical details, including shelf numbers. Author or editor, places of publication, dates, and subject indices, with statistical tables. The Egyptian National Library undoubtedly has the single largest collection of these materials.

Title transliterated: Fihrist al-Dawrīyāt al-ʿArabīya ...

France

A72
PARIS. Ecole Pratique des Hautes Etudes, Centre Russe. Catalogue des Microfilms des Périodiques musulmans

en Russie et des Périodiques Publiés à l'Etranger par des Musulmans russes émigrés, avant 1920, se Trouvant au Centre Russe de l'Ecole Pratique des Hautes Etudes. Paris, Centre Russe, Ecole Pratique des Hautes Etudes, N.D. 76 p.

"Notre catalogue comprend 76 titres de périodiques, dont: 30 en azeri, 22 en tatar de Kazan, 7 en tatar de Crimée, 6 en turc (osmanly), 3 en uzbek, 3 en arabe, 2 en kazah, 2 en persan, 1 en turkmène. 68 périodiques ont été publiés en Russie, 8 à l'étranger - 7 en Turquie, I en Allemagne -."

Provides title in transliteration and translation, language, periodicity, place of publication, location of surviving numbers, and numbers on microfilm in the Centre.

India

A73
INDIA. National Library.
Catalogue of Periodicals, Newspapers and Gazettes. *Comp.* Benoy Sen Gupta. Calcutta, Government of India Press, 1956. vi + 285 p.

Covers the serial publications of India of the 18th and 19th centuries.

Indonesia

A74
JAKARTA. Museum Pusat, Perpustakaan.
Katalogus Surat-kabar: koleksi Perpustakaan Museum Pusat, 1810-1973 [Catalogue of Newspapers: collection of the Pusat Museum Library, 1810-1973]. Jakarta, Perpustakaan Museum Pusat, 1973. xxix + 131 p.

Iran

A75
IRAN. Kitābkhānah Millī Īrān.
فهرست روزنامههای موجود در کتابخانه ملی ایران
[Index to the Newspapers Held in the Iranian National Library]. *Comp.* Bīzhan Sartīpzādah *and* Khubra

Khudāparast. Tehran, Kitābkhānah Millī Īrān, 2536/1977. 247 p.

Alphabetical listing by title of 479 Farsi newspapers dating from approximately 1895. Index of editors, publishers, and places of publication. Full bibliographical details are provided.

Title transliterated: Fihrist Rawznāmah-hā-ī Mawjūd Dar Kitabkhānah Millī Īrān.

A76

---. ---.

فهرست مجاه های موجود در کتابخانه ملی ایران

[Index to the Journals Held in the Iranian National Library]. *Comp.* Bīzhan Sartīpzādah *and* Khubra Khudāparast. Tehran, Kitābkhānah Millī Īrān, 1357/2537/1978. [vi] + 324 p.

Alphabetical listing by title of 525 serials other than newspapers in Farsi with full bibliographical details. Indices.

Title transliterated: Fihrist Majallah-hā-ī Mawjūd Dar Kitabkhānah Millī Īrān.

Netherlands

A77

AMSTERDAM. Koninklijk Vereeniging "Koloniaal Instituut", Centrale Boekerij.

Catalogus van Tijdschriften en Periodisch Verschijnende Publicaties Aanwezig in de Centrale Boekerij van de Koninklijk Vereeniging "Koloniaal Instituut" te Amsterdam. Amsterdam, De Bussy, 1928. 112 p.

United States

A78

UNITED STATES. Library of Congress, African and Middle Eastern Division.

Arab-World Newspapers in the Library of Congress. *Comp.* George Dimitri Selim. Washington, D.C., Library of Congress, 1980. v + 85 p.

Near East Series.

"The list is arranged alphabetically first by language and then by country, city and title. Arabic titles are transliterated according to the Library of Congress transliteration system. The dates given show the Library's holdings. ... This publication includes three indexes: two title indexes (one for Arabic-language titles, the other for Western-language titles) and a place-name index." *[Preface]*.

A79
---. ---. ---.

Persian and Afghan Newspapers in the Library of Congress, 1871-1978. *Comp.* Ibrahim V. Pourhadi. Washington, D.C., Library of Congress, 1979. xiv + 101 p.

Alphabetical listing by title, according to the Latin alphabet, of 326 Farsi language newspapers, and 23 Dari, Farsi, and Pushto newspapers published in Afghanistan, during the century. Titles are transliterated only. Provides full bibliographic information for each, extent of the Library's holdings, and a descriptive annotation. Chronological index and index of places of publication.

Union Lists

Germany

A80
BLOSS, I. *and* SCHMIDT-DUMONT, M.
Zeitschriften verzeichnis Moderner Orient/Union List of Middle Eastern Periodicals, Stand 1979/Up to 1979. Hamburg, Deutsches Orient-Institut, Dokumentations-Leitstelle Moderner Orient, 1980. xxviii + 657 p.

Dokumentationsdienst Moderner Orient: Reihe B, Bd. 1.

United Kingdom

A81
AUCHTERLONIE, Paul *and* SAFADI, Yasin H.
Union Catalogue of Arabic Serials and Newspapers in British Libraries. London, Mansell Information/Publishing Ltd., 1977. xvi + 147 p. [dbl. col.].

Published for Middle East Libraries Committee.

Indices to Periodicals

Western Language

A82
ASAMANI, J. O.
Index Africanus. Stanford, Hoover Institution Press, 1975. xiii + 659 p. [dbl. col.].
Hoover Institution Bibliographies, 53.

An important listing of 24,694 articles which appeared in approximately 200 periodicals, 20 volumes of *festschriften*, 20 proceedings of congresses, etc. between 1885 and 1965, not including Russian language materials. For this it will be necessary to consult S. L. Mili͡avskai͡a and I. E. Sinit͡syna's **Библиографя Африки** [J18]. Arranged by region (Africa General; Central Africa; East Africa; North Africa; West Africa; Southern Africa), then by political subdivision, and finally by subject. Items specifically on Islamic culture are excluded. Author index. The table of contents, unfortunately for a reference book, is virtually useless, and there are no page headings.

A83
"Bibliography of Periodical Literature" [1947-]. *The Middle East Journal*, I- , 1947- .

Quarterly classified listing of articles and book reviews on the past and present Middle East and North Africa published in approximately 340 journals, including Arabic, Hebrew, Persian, Russian, and Turkish language serials. Kept fairly well up to date.

Contents: Geography; History (Medieval); History and Politics (Modern); Economic Conditions; Social Conditions; Science; Philosophy and Religion; Language; Literature and Arts; Law; Biography; Bibliography; Book Reviews.

Cumulations: P. M. Rossi. *Articles on the Middle East 1947-1971: cumulation of the bibliographies from* The Middle East Journal. Ann Arbor, Michigan, Pierian Press, 1980. 4 vols. Indices in vol. 4.

A84

PEARSON, James D., *ed.*
Index Islamicus 1906-1966: a catalogue of articles on Islamic subjects in periodicals and other collective publications. Cambridge, W. Heffer & Sons Ltd., 1958. xxxvii + 897 p. [dbl. col.].

Classified listing of 26,076 articles in western languages, including Russian, published in 510 periodical titles, 120 *festschriften*, and 70 volumes of congress proceedings.

Supplements:

Index Islamicus Supplement 1956-1960. Cambridge, W. Heffer & Sons Ltd., 1962. xxviii + 316 p [dbl. col.]. 7,296 articles catalogued.

Index Islamicus Supplement 1961-1965. Cambridge, W. Heffer & Sons Ltd., 1967. xxx + 342 p. [dbl. col.]. 8,023 articles catalogued.

Index Islamicus Third Supplement 1966-1970. London, Mansell Information/Publishing Ltd., 1972. xxxvi + 384 p. [dbl. col.]. items unnumbered.

Index Islamicus Fourth Supplement 1971-1975. London, Mansell Information/Publishing Ltd., 1977. xlii + 429 p. [dbl. col.]. items unnumbered.

Index Islamicus Fifth Supplement 1975-1980. London, Mansell Information/Publishing Ltd., 1982. xliii + 539 p. [dbl. col.]. 14,187 items.

Beginning in January 1977 *The Quarterly Index Islamicus: current books, articles and papers on Islamic studies* began to be issued by Mansell which are then cumulated to form the quintennial supplements.

A85
REGAZZI, John J. *and* HINES, Theodore C.
A Guide to Indexed Periodicals in Religion. Metchuen, New Jersey, Scarecrow Press, 1975. xiv + 314 p.

A listing by title and by key-word of approximately 2,700 western language journals of religion which are abstracted or indexed by 17 religiously oriented services, thus not including the more commonly used *Reader's Guide to Periodical Literature*, *Social Sciences & Humanities Index*, etc.

A86
"Survey of Periodicals" [1911-]. *The Muslim World*,

I- , 1911- .

Quarterly classified listing of articles, primarily of religious interest, on Islam and Islamic studies published during the period in more than 160 western language periodicals. No accumulations. Some duplication with *The Middle East Journal* "Bibliography of Periodical Literature," and *The Quarterly Index Islamicus*. Arrangement varies.

¶ Margaret H. Case, *South Asian History 1750-1950* [J67], has catalogued 351 periodicals and 26 *festschriften* on Indian history for the period.

Oriental Language

Chinese

A87
SINGAPORE. Nanyang University, Institute of Southeast Asia.
南洋研究中文期刊資料索引 /
Index to Chinese Periodical Literature on Southeast Asia 1905-1966. Singapore, Institute of Southeast Asia, Nanyang University, 1968. [x], 363 + [ii] p. [dbl. col.]. [all published].

Arranged by country and then by subject. Includes nearly 10,000 articles appearing in more than 500 journals. Entirely in Chinese. Important source for Islam in Malaysia and Indonesia.

Farsi

A88
AFSHĀR, Īraj.
فهرست مقالات فارسی، جلد اول : ۱۳۲۸ ـ ۱۳۳۸/
Index Iranicus: répertoire méthodique des articles persans concernant les études iranologiques, publiés dans les périodiques et publications collectives, volume I: 1910-1958. Tehran, Groupe Bibliographique National Iranien, 1961. [li], 984 + [vi] p.

Groupe Bibliographique National Iranien No. 3/ Publication de l'Université de Tehran No. 697.

Classified listing of 5,993 articles from Farsi journals, with indices.

Supplements:

فهرست مقالات فارسی، ۲: ۱۳۳۹ ـ ۱۳۴۵/

Index Iranicus, II: 1959-1966. Tehran, Dānishkāha Tihrān, 1347/1969. 708 p. 4,642 articles catalogued.

فهرست مقالات فارسی، ۳: ۱۳۴۶ ـ ۱۳۵۰/

Index Iranicus, III: 1967-1971. Tehran, Sharkat Sahāmī Kitābhā-ī Jībī, 2535/1977. [xxxiv] + 382 p. [dbl. col.]. 5,456 articles catalogued.

Turkish

A89

TURKEY. Millî Kütüphane. Bibliyografya Enstitüsü. Türkiye Makaleler Bibliyografyası/Bibliographie des Articles Parus dans les Périodiques turcs. Istanbul, Millî Eğitim Basımevi, 1952- .

Issued quarterly with an index of authors in each issue.

Urdu

A90

NEW DELHI. Indian Institute of Islamic Studies. "Bibliography of Urdu Periodicals" [1970-]. *Studies in Islam*, VIII- , 1971- .

Annual (more or less) classified and annotated listing of articles published in Urdu language periodicals in India and Pakistan during the preceding period.

Indices to Book Reviews

A91

BEHN, Wolfgang H.
Islamic Book Review Index [1980-]. Berlin, Adıyok, 1982- .

Annual index of reviews of books on both Islamic and contemporary Middle Eastern subjects published in European, Arabic, Persian, and Turkish languages. In the 1983 issue 156 journals, including those in oriental languages, were surveyed. Reviews are listed by author or title.

¶ An index to book reviews is also published quarterly in the "Bibliography of Periodical Literature" of *The Middle East Journal*, which, as of Vol. 37, 1983, surveyed 242 journals in oriental and western languages.

OFFICIAL PUBLICATIONS

General

A92
GREGORY, Winifred.
List of the Serial Publications of Foreign Governments, 1815-1931. New York, The H. W. Wilson Co., 1932. [viii] + 720 p.

"This list includes only the serial publications of national governments, and of such of their states as are to some extent self-governing; ... . The arrangement is alphabetical by country, under which is grouped their dependent sub-divisions. Dominions, colonies, protectorates are entered under their own names. ... Under each country, entries are arranged alphabetically under the department, bureau or ministry responsible for their publication." *[Explanations]*.

Although comprehensiveness is not claimed this is a very important source as it is more than an union list for governmental publications in western languages. Those in oriental languages are transliterated. Wherever possible holdings in approximately 85 American public and university libraries are indicated. Not included are publications of colleges, universities, or learned societies even though they might receive support from a government.

Compiled for the American Council of Learned Societies, American Library Association, and the National Research Council.

Africa

A93
UNITED STATES. Library of Congress, General Reference and Bibliography Division.
French-speaking Central Africa: a guide to official publications in American libraries. *Comp.* Julian W. Witherell. Washington, D.C., Library of Congress,

1973. xiv + 314 p. [dbl. col.].

"It includes documents of former Belgian and French possessions from the beginning of the colonial rule to the time of independence... ." *[Preface]*. Most of the documents date from the later period. Author, title, and subject index.

A94

---. ---. ---.

Spanish-speaking Africa: a guide to official publications. *Comp.* Susan Knoke Rishworth. Washington, D.C., Library of Congress, 1973. xiii + 66 p. [dbl. col.].

"... this guide lists published official records of Spanish-speaking Africa from the 19th century to the present, including publications issued by the Spanish Government about or on behalf of its African territories. For the purpose of this bibliography, Spanish-speaking Africa will include Equatorial Guinea, Spanish Sahara, Ifni, and that part of northern Morocco known as the Spanish Zone until it was united with the rest of the country when Morocco became independent from France in 1956." *[Preface]*.

Lists 640 items by author or title under five geographic headings. Index of subjects and personal authors.

Tunisia

A95

PILIPENKO, Hélène *and* ROUSSET DE PINA, Jean. Récapitulation des Périodiques officiels Parus en Tunisie de 1881 à 1955. Tunis, Bibliothèque Nationale de Tunisie, MCMLVI. 108, [ii] + 10 [Arabic] p.

A very important listing, by ministry or other official body, of 101 journals and series issued in French during the occupation of the country. The list is greatly enhanced by the very detailed annotations provided for each title. Title index.

DISSERTATIONS

General

A96
PARIS. Association Française des Arabisants.
Dix Ans de Recherche universitaire française sur le Monde arabe et islamique de 1968-69 à 1979. Paris, Editions Recherche sur les Civilisations, 1982. 438 p. [dbl. col.].

Classified listing by subject, university, and then by author of 5,807 theses and dissertations presented during the ten year period to the universities of France.

A97
MONTAGUE, Joel.
"French Doctoral Dissertations on the Near East and North Africa. Part I: Thesis *[sic]* submitted 1970-1974." *Middle East Studies Association Bulletin*, X, February 1976, pp. 26-35.

Arranged by country and within country alphabetically by author.

A98
SCHWARZ, Klaus.
Verzeichnis deutschsprachiger Hochschulscriften zum islamischen Orient (1885-1970). Deutschland-Österreich-Schweiz. Freiburg-im-Breisgau, N.P. 1971. 280 p.

A99
SIMS, Michael.
United States Doctoral Dissertations in Third World Studies, 1869-1978. Los Angeles, Crossroads Press, 1981. 450 p.

A geographic listing of some 19,000 doctoral dissertations on North Africa, Sub-Saharan Africa, Asia, the Middle East, Latin America, and the Caribbean. Information includes author's name, year of completion, and institution. Subject, place name, personal name, language, and ethnic group index.

A100
SLUGLETT, Peter.
Theses on Islam, the Middle East and North-West Africa 1880-1978. London, Mansell, 1983. 200 p.

Lists over 3,000 theses submitted to British

and Irish universities between 1880 and 1978 arranged alphabetically by author, by region, country, and subject. Subject and author index. Incomplete in that Islam is not confined in Africa to the Mediterranean coast.

Africa

A101
DINSTEL, Marion *and* HERRICK, Mary Darrah.
List of French Doctoral Dissertations on Africa, 1884-1961. Boston, G. K. Hall & Co., 1966. v + 336 p. [dbl. col.].

Regional and country-by-country listing of 2,923 theses submitted during the period to universities in France and dependencies. Photographic reproduction of the card catalogue maintained in the African Document Center, African Studies Program, Boston University with 10 entries to the page. Author, area/country, and subject indices. The last is quite inadequate considering the importance of the list.

A102
GREAT BRITAIN. Standing Conference on Library Materials on Africa.
Theses on Africa Accepted by Universities in the United Kingdom and Ireland. Cambridge, W. Heffer & Sons, Ltd., 1964. x + 74 p.

Listing of 1,142 theses and dissertaions for the bachelor's, master's, and doctoral degrees during the period 1920 through 1962. Arranged in broad groups of north, west, east, and south Africa and within these by country and then by subject. Index of authors only.

A103
KÖHLER, Jochen.
Deutsche Dissertationen über Afrika: ein verzeichnis für die Jahre 1918-1959. Bonn, K. Schroeder, 1962. pp. unnumbered.

Published for the Deutsche Afrika-Gesellschaft, the list contains 795 entries arranged by geographical area. Separate section of linguistic studies. Author and subject indices.

A104
McISWAINE, J. H. St. J.
Theses on Africa 1963-1975 Accepted by Universities in the United Kingdom and Ireland. London, Mansell Information/Publishing Ltd., 1980. xvi + 123 p. [dbl. col.].

Published for the Standing Conference on Library Materials on Africa in continuation of their earlier list [A103].

Listing of 2,231 theses and dissertaions for the bachelor's, master's, and doctoral degrees arranged by region and country, and then by subject. Includes an appendix of an additional 124 supplemental items not included in the earlier list. Author index only.

A105
SIMS, Michael *and* KAGAN, Alfred.
American & Canadian Doctoral Dissertations & Master's Theses on Africa, 1886-1974. Waltham, Massachusetts, African Studies Association, 1976. [x] + 365 p.[dbl. col.].

A listing by country and then by subject of 6,070 theses and dissertaions updating the earlier lists on Africa and the Arab world published by the Library of Congress in 1961, 1967, and 1969. Subject and author indices.

Apparently this list replaces an earlier one published by the Association in 1973 edited by Michael Bratton and Anne Schneller, *American Doctoral Dissertations on Africa, 1886-1972*.

A106
UNIVERSITY MICROFILMS INTERNATIONAL.
Egypt, North Africa, and Sub-Saharan Africa: a dissertation bibliography. Ann Arbor, Michigan, University Microfilms International, 1978(?). [iii] + 53 p. [triple col.].

Lists 2,633 doctoral dissertations, 88 master's theses, and 5 advanced research papers submitted to American and Canadian universities between 1969 and 1978. Arranged by subject. Author index. Primarily a sales catalogue.

A107

---.
Africa: a catalogue of doctoral dissertations. Ann Arbor, Michigan, University Microfilms International, 1982. [iv] + 29 p. [triple col.].

Contains the titles of 1,262 dissertations submitted to American and Canadian universities between 1978 and 1981 in continuation of the earlier listing [A107]. Arranged by country. No index.

¶ A listing of doctoral and candidate dissertations presented to universities in the Soviet Union during the period 1941-1961 is to be found in the appendix to S. L. Mili͡avskai͡a and I. E. Sinit͡syna's Библиография Африки, pp. 234-239 [J18].

Asia

A108
BLOOMFIELD, B. C.
Theses on Asia Accepted by Universities in the United Kingdom and Ireland 1877-1964. London, Frank Cass & Co., Ltd., 1967. xi + 127 p. [dbl. col.].

Regional and subject listing of 2,571 theses accepted for advanced degrees covering the area from the Middle East through Oceania. Reproduced from typescript.

Supplements are published periodically in the *Bulletin of the Association of British Orientalists.*

Middle East

A109
FINKE, Detlev; HANSEN, Gerda *and* PREISBERG, Rolf-Dieter
Deutsche Hochschulshriften über de Modernen islamischen Orient/German Theses on the Islamic Middle East. Hamburg, Deutsches Orient-Institut, Dokumentations-Leitstelle Moderner Orient, 1973. viii + 177 p.

A110
ʿIZZ al-DĪN, Inshād Maḥmūd *and* BISHĀY, ʿĀdil Bashīlī.
دليل رسائل الماجستر و الدكتوراه المتعلقة بالشرق

[Guide to الاوسط التى اجيزت بالجامعات المصرية Master's and Doctoral Dissertations Relating to the Middle East Submitted to Egyptian Universities]. Cairo, Maṭbaᶜa Jāmiᶜ ᶜAyn Shams, 1977. 122 p.

Jāmiᶜa ᶜAyn Shams, Markaz Buḥūth al-Sharq al-Awsaṭ.

Title transliterated: Dalīl Rasāʾil al-Māzhistīr wa al-Duktūrāh al-Mutaᶜalliqa bi-al-Sharq al-Awsaṭ...

A111
SCHWARZ, Klaus.
Der Vordere Orient in den Hochschulschriften Deutschlands, Österreichs und der Schweiz: eine bibliographie von dissertationen und habilitationsschriften (1885-1978). Freiburg-im-Breisgau, Klaus Schwarz Verlag, 1980. XXIII + 721 p.

Islamkundliche Materialien, Bd. 5.

Detailed classified listing of 5,050 theses and dissertations covering the period from pre-historic times to the present.

A112
SELIM, George Dimitri.
American Doctoral Dissertations on the Arab World 1883-1968. Washington, D.C., Library of Congress, 1970. xvii + 103 p. [dbl. col.].

Lists 1,032 dissertations by author on all subjects pertaining to the Middle East and Islam accepted by universities in the United States and Canada. Detailed subject index.

Supplement: George Dimitri Selim, *American Doctoral Dissertations on the Arab World 1975-1981.* Washington, D.C., Library of Congress, 1983. xiii + 200 p.

A113
UNIVERSITY MICROFILMS INTERNATIONAL.
Middle East & Southwest Asia: a dissertation catalog. Ann Arbor, Michigan, University Microfilms International, 1980. [ix] + 17 p. [dbl. col.].

A listing by country of doctoral dissertations submitted to universities in the United States and Canada 1978-1980.

Supplement: University Microfilms International

Current Research on the Middle East: a catalog of doctoral dissertations - culture, economics, education, politics. Ann Arbor, Michigan, University Microfilms International, 1982. [v] + 31 p. [dbl. col.]. 584 titles submitted 1980-1982. Arranged by country.

Turkey

A114
SUZUKI, Peter T.
French, German, and Swiss University Dissertations on Twentieth Century Turkey: a bibliography of 593 titles, with English translations. Wiesbaden, N.P., 1970. II, v + 138 p.

In alphabetical order by author, with title in original language and in English translation, date of submission, university, number of pages, and, if published, in what form. Includes German dissertations from 1900 to 1965, French from 1900 to 1967, and Swiss from 1900 to 1968. Also includes some dissertations submitted to the universities of Graz and Vienna. Subject index.

Southeast Asia

A115
SARDESAI, D. R. *and* SARDESAI, Bhanu D.
Theses and Dissertations on Southeast Asia: an international bibliography in social sciences, education and fine arts. Zug, Switzerland, Inter Documentation Co. AG, 1970. IV + 176 p. [dbl. col.].

Bibliotheca Asiatica, 6.

Classified listing of 2,814 M.A. and Ph.D., or their equivalents, theses and dissertations covering Southeast Asia in general, Burma, Indonesia, Laos, Cambodia, Vietnam, Malaysia, Singapore, The Philippines, and Thailand since the 1920's. "We feel the present volume includes titles of most of the work submitted for the doctorate in the United States, Soviet Union, British Isles, Malaysia, Singapore, Australia, New Zealand, the Philippines, the Netherlands, Czechoslovakia and Japan. The coverage of research in France, Germany, Thailand, India and Canada is not as extensive." *[Preface].*

Contents: Anthropology, Sociology, Religion and Folklore; Economics; Education; Fine Arts; Geography; History and Archeology; Linguistics and Literature; Political Science and International Affairs. Index of authors.

A116

UNIVERSITY MICROFILMS INTERNATIONAL.

Current Research on Southeast Asian History: a catalog of doctoral dissertations - culture, education, politics, religions. Ann Arbor, Michigan, University Microfilms International, [1981]. [v] + 25 p. [dbl. col.].

"Carefully selected through a comprehensive search of all the titles on the history of southeast Asia, these 802 titles were completed between 1937 and 1981." *[Intro.]*.

Arranged by country.

A117

---.

Southeast Asia: a dissertation bibliography. Ann Arbor, Michigan, University Microfilms International, 1980. 41 p. [dbl. col.].

Lists 2,128 doctoral dissertations submitted to American and Canadian universities from 1938 to 1980. Arranged by country and then by author.

¶ For a list of 650 doctoral dissertations on the history of India 1750-1950 presented to American, British, and Indian universities see: Margaret H. Case, *South Asian History 1750-1950: a guide to periodicals, dissertations, and newspapers* [J67].

LIBRARIES & ARCHIVES B

DIRECTORIES

Institutes

B1
LJUNGGREN, Florence *and* GEDDES, Charles L.
An International Directory of Institutes and Societies Interested in the Middle East. Amsterdam, Djambatan, 1962. 159 p.

Detailed listing of 353 societies, institutes, university programs, etc. throughout the world which have a scholarly interest in the ancient, Islamic, and modern Middle East and North Africa, geographically arranged. Provides titles of periodicals and publication series issued by these. Indices of names and titles. Now seriously out of date.

B2
ISTANBUL. Research Centre for Islamic History, Art and Culture.
Addresses of Cultural Institutions in O.I.C. Countries. Istanbul, Organisation of Islamic Conference, Research Centre for Islamic History, Art and Culture, 1402/1982. XII, [iv], 149 + 5 [Arabic text] p.

A directory in English of learned societies and research institutes, libraries and archives, museums, and university and educational institutions in member states of the Organisation of the Islamic Conference. Preface in Arabic, English, and French. No index.

The Centre has announced that it has under preparation a world-wide guide which should replace that of Ljunggren and Geddes.

Libraries

Africa

B3
DADZIE, E. W. *and* STRICKLAND, J. T.
Directory of Archives, Libraries and Schools of Librarianship in Africa. Paris, UNESCO, 1965. 112 p.
Brief details, obtained through questionnaires, of 508 institutions in the countries of Africa south of the Sahara.
Contents: I. Archives; II. Schools and Courses on Librarianship; III. Libraries and Documentation Centres. Within each section arrangement is by country in alphabetical order, with the material in English or French.

Egypt

B4
BADR, Ahmad.
Directory of Archives, Libraries, Documentation Centres and Bibliographical Institutions in Arabic Speaking States. Cairo, UAR National Commission for UNESCO, 1965. 104 p.
Despite its title the *Directory* is primarily confined to Egypt, with some information concerning the archives in Morocco.

Libya

B5
WARD, Philip.
A Survey of Libyan Bibliographical Resources. *2nd ed.* Tripoli, Libyan Publishing House, 1965. 44 + 43 [Arabic] p.
Basically a listing by city of the libraries of the country.

Middle East

B6
DAGHER, Joseph.
Répertoire des Bibliothèques du Proche et du Moyen-Orient. Paris, UNESCO, 1951. XI + 182 p.

An invaluable, if dated, directory to most public, university, and research libraries in Aden, Saʿūdī Arabia, Egypt, Iraq, Israel, Jerusalem, Lebanon, Iran, Syria, Turkey, and the Yemen. Provides information regarding addresses, means of classification employed, numbers of books, manuscripts, and journal titles received, means of access, hours, etc.

Turkey

B7
KUT, Günay.
"Manuscript Libraries in Istanbul." *Middle East Studies Association Bulletin*, XVI, July, 1982, pp. 24-43.

B8
TURKEY. Millî Kütüphane. Bibliyografya Enstitüsü. Türkiye Kütüphaneleri Rehberi/Répertoire des Bibliothèques de Turquie. Ankara, Millî Kütüphane Basim ve Ciltevi, 1957. x + 243 p.

Europe

United Kingdom

B9
COLLISON, Robert *and* MOON, Brenda E.
Directory of Libraries and Special Collections on Asia and North Africa. Hamden, Connecticut, Archon Books, 1970. x + 123 p.
Published on behalf of the Standing Conference of National and University Libraries of Great Britain.
Alphabetical listing by city of the libraries in the United Kingdom and Ireland which have recognizable holdings of western and oriental language materials. Included is a very useful "Index of Names of Libraries and Special Collections" within libraries. Subject index.

B10
NETTON, Ian Richard.
Middle East Materials in United Kingdom and Irish

Libraries: a directory. London, Library Association Publishing, 1983. 136 p.

Subtitle: "A MELCOM Guide to Libraries and other Institutions in Britain and Ireland with Islamic and Middle Eastern Books and Materials."

"... a directory of libraries and institutions in Britain and Ireland with large or small collections of Middle Eastern books, manuscripts and materials." *[Preface]*. Brief, detailed information on each library and its holdings listed by town.

As the directory was based upon a questionnaire the list of those not responding (Appendix Two) is fairly extensive and they are therefore not included in the body of the guide.

CATALOGUES OF PRINTED BOOKS

Egypt

Cairo

Dār al-Kutub al-Miṣrīya

B12

Egypt: subject catalogue. *3rd ed.* Cairo, Egyptian National Library Press, 1957. XII + 413 p. [dbl. col.].

Classified catalogue of the books in western languages on Egypt held by the national library and accessioned to 1956. No index.

B13

قائمة بأوائل المطبوعات العربية المحفوظة بدار الكتب حتى سنة ١٨٦٢م

[Catalogue of the First Arabic Printed Books Contained in the National Library until the Year 1862 A.D.]. *Comp.* Muḥammad Jamāl al-Dīn al-Shawrabijī. Cairo, Maṭbaᶜa Dār al-Kutub, 1383/1963. [ii] + 403 p.

Detailed catalogue of 851 Arabic language books printed in Europe and the Middle East between 920/1514 and 1280/1862. In addition to the usual bibliographic data also provides the library's shelf-number. Indices of titles, printers, and authors.

Title transliterated: Qā'ima bi-Aw'il al-Maṭbū^cāt al-^cArabīya...

B14
فهرست الكتب الموجودة بالكتبخانة الخديوية المصرية
[Index to the Books Found in the Egyptian Khedivial Library]. Cairo, Kutubkhāna al-Khidīwīya al-Miṣrīya, 1289/1872. 333 + 3 p.

Summary catalogue of the Arabic, Persian and Turkish printed books in the national library.

Title transliterated: Fihrist al-Kutub al-Mawjūda bi-al-Kutubkhāna al-Khidīwīya al-Miṣrīya.

B15
فهرست الكتب العربية المحفوزة بالكتبخانة الخديوية
[Index to the Arabic Books Preserved in the Khedivial Library]. Cairo, Maṭba^ca ^cUthmān ^cAbd al-Razzaq 1301-08/1884-91. 7 vols.

Subject catalogue of both printed books and manuscripts preserved in the national library. Vol. I was reprinted in 1310/1893.

Title transliterated: Fihrist al-Kutub al-^cArabīya al-Maḥfūza bi-al-Kutubkhāna al-Khīdiwīya.

B16
[Index to the فهرست الكتب العربية الموجودة بالدار Arabic Books Preserved in the House]. Cairo, Maṭba^ca Dār al-Kutub, 1342-61/1924-42. 8 vols.

Catalogue of Arabic printed books and manuscripts acquired following the publication of the first catalogue [B15].

Title transliterated: Fihrist al-Kuṭub al-^cArabīya al-Mawjūda bi-al-Dār.

B17
فهرست الكتب الفارسية الموجودة بالكتبخانة الخديوية
[Index to the Persian Books Preserved in the Khedivial Library]. Cairo, Maṭba^ca ^cUthmān ^cAbd al-Razzaq 1306/1889. 153 p.

Title transliterated: Fihrist al-Kutub al-Fārsīya al-Mawjūda bi-al-Kutubkhāna al-Khidīwīya.

B18
فهرست الكتب التركية الموجودة بالكتبخانة الخديويـة المصرية
[Index to the Turkish Books Preserved in the Khedivial Library of Egypt]. Cairo, Maṭbaʿa ʿUthmān ʿAbd al-Razzaq, 1306/1889. 406 p.

Title transliterated: Fihrist al-Kutub al-Turkīya al-Mawjūda bi-al-Kutubkhāna al-Khidīwīya al-Miṣrīya.

France

Paris

Bibliothèque Nationale

B19
Catalogue général des Livres Imprimés: auteurs. Paris, Imprimerie Nationale, 1900-77. 227 vols.

Unlike the British Museum's *Catalogue of Printed Books* that of the French national library includes books in oriental languages, printed in their respective scripts. Listed by author only to Wuzel.

B20
Catalogue général des Livres Imprimés: auteurs, collectivités- auteurs, anonymous 1960-1969. Série 2- Caractères non latins: T. 4- Caractères arabes. Paris, Bibliothèque Nationale, 1978. [vii], 968 [dbl. col.] + vi p.

"La première partie de ce volume du Catalogue comprend uniquement les livres en langue arabe et en caracterès arabes, entrés et catalogués du ler janvier 1960 au 31 décembre 1969." *[Intro.]*.

Première partie- Ouvrages arabes; Deuxième partie- Ouvrages persans. Each part has title index in Arabic script and author index in transliteration.

Ecole des Langues Orientales Vivantes, Bibliothèque

B21

Catalogue de la Bibliothèque de l'Ecole des Langues Orientales Vivantes. Tome Premier: Linguistique: I: Philologie. II. Langue arabe. *Comp.* E. Lambrecht. Paris, Imprimerie Nationale, MDCCCXCVII. VII, [v] + 621 p. [all published].

Classified catalogue of the Arabic printed books. Within each section the items are listed by title which, in most cases, are printed in the Arabic script with transliteration and a short sentence regarding subject matter. Details regarding bibliographical data, including shelf-number. Indices of titles in transliteration, Arabic script, and authors.

Germany

Strassburg

Kaiserliche Üniversitäts- und Landesbibliothek

B22
Katalog der Kaiserliche Üniversitäts- und Landesbibliothek in Strassburg: arabische literature. *Comp.* J. Euting. Strassburg, Verlag Karl J. Trübner, 1877. 110 p. [all published].

Catalogue of Arabic books and western language materials on Arabic literature and grammar.

India

Bankipore

Khuda Bakhsh Oriental Library

B23
[The Beloved محبوب الالباب فى تعريف الكتب و الكتّاب Collection in the Knowledge of Books and Writers]. *Comp.* Khuda-Bakhsh Khan. Hyderabad, Maṭbaᶜa Dāᵓira al-Maᶜārif al-Niẓamīya, 1314/1897. ii, ii, lii, xl + 858 p.

Author catalogue of the Arabic and Persian printed books and manuscripts in the library of this noted Indian Muslim barrister and scholar, with notices of the authors.

Title transliterated: Maḥbūb al-Labāb fī Taᶜrīf al-Kutub wa al- Kuttāb.

Calcutta

Asiatic Society of Bengal, Library

B24
A Catalogue of the Arabic Books and Manuscripts in the Library of the Asiatic Society of Bengal. *Comp.* Shamsul-l ᶜUlama Mirza Ashraf ᶜAli. Calcutta, Asiatic Society of Bengal, 1899-1904. 153 p.

Classified and annotated list, with shelf-numbers. Title and author indices. Issued in fascicules.

B25
Author-catalogue of the Ḥaidarābad Collection of Manuscripts and Printed Books. Calcutta, Asiatic Society of Bengal, 1913. iv + 62 p.

Catalogue of the collection of Arabic, Persian, and Urdu works presented to the Society in 1907 by Nawwāb Azīzjang Bahādur of Hyderābad. No index.

B26
Catalogue of Persian Printed Books in the Library of the Asiatic Society. *Comp.* Maulvi Mutier Rahman. Calcutta, The Asiatic Society, 1967. 175 p. [dbl. col.].

Author list of 1,072 books accessioned to April 30, 1967. Title and subject indices.

Replaces the earlier catalogue of Persian books compiled by Maulavi Mirza Ashraf Alī published in 1890-95 and a part of the catalogue of the Hyderabad collection.

Al-Madrasa al-ᶜĀlīya, Maktaba

B27
فهرست الكتب العربية و الفارسية و الهندى الموجودة بمكتبة المدرسة العالية
[Index to the Arabic, Persian, and Hindi (Urdu) Books Preserved in the Library of

the ᶜĀlīya Madrasa]. Calcutta, Al-Madrasa al-ᶜĀlīya, 1928. vii + 381 p.
Title transliterated: Fihrist al-Kutub al-ᶜArabīya wa al-Fārsīya wa al-Hindī...

National Library

B28
Catalogue of Arabic, Persian and Urdu Books in the Imperial Library. Calcutta, Superintendent Government Printing, 1915. i, 1, 11 + [i] p. [all printed].
The Arabic part only printed.

Hyderabad

Maktaba Āṣafīya

B29
[Index to the فهرست کتب ی عربی، فارسی و اردو Arabic, Persian, and Urdu Books]. Hyderabad, Maktaba Āṣafīya, 1914-28. 3 vols.
Title transliterated: Fihrist Kutubī ᶜArabī, Fārsī wa Urdū.

Indonesia

Djakarta

Centraal Kantoor voor de Statistiek, Bibliotheek

B30
Catalogus der Boekwerken Betreffende Nederlandsch-Indië Aanwezig in de Bibliotheek van het Centraal Kantoor voor de Statistiek (bijgewerket tot 18 November 1938). Batavia, Centraal Kantoor voor de Statistiek, 1938. XVIII + 309 p.
Classified list of books about Indonesia.

Iran

Mashad

Kitābkhāna-ī Āstāna-ī Quds-ī Riḍawī

B31
فهرست کتب کتابخانهٔ مبارکه آستانه قدس رضوی
[Index to the Books in the Library of the Holy Shrine of Riḍa]. Mashad, Chāpakhāna Ṭūsī, 1305-29/ 1926-51. 5 vols.

Classified, annotated catalogue of the Arabic and Persian printed books and manuscripts in this large and important library.

Title transliterated: Fihrist Kutub Kitābkhā-nah-ī...

Madrasah-ī Fāḍilīya, Kitābkhānah-ī

B32
فهرست کتب کتابخانهٔ مدرسهٔ فاضلیه
[Index to the Books in the Library of the Fāḍilīya Madrasa]. Mashad, Chāpakhāna Khurasān, 1309/1930. 265 p.

Classified, annotated catalogue of the Arabic and Persian printed books and manuscripts.

Title transliterated: Fihrist Kutub Kitābkhā-nah-ī Madrasah-ī Fāḍilīya.

Iraq

Baghdad

Jāmiʿa Baghdād, al-Maktaba al-Markazīya

B33
Classified Catalogue of Materials About Iraq Available in the Central Library - University of Baghdad. Baghdad, Central Library, University of Baghdad, 1968. 28 + [viii]. p.

Subject listing of books, articles, and chapters in books about Iraq in western European languages.

B34
فهرست موضوعی بالكتب العربية عن العراق الموجودة في المكتب المركزية لجامعة بغداد
[Subject Index of Arabic Books About Iraq Contained in the Central Library of the University of Baghdad]. Baghdad, Al-Maktaba al-Markazīya li-Jāmiʿa Baghdād, 1968. 105 + 32 p.

With classification numbers and author and

title index.
Title transliterated: Fihrist Mawḍūʿī bi-al-Kutub al-ʿArabīya...

Japan

Tokyo

Tōyō Bunko, Institute of Central Asian and Islamic Studies

B35 東洋文庫所蔵アラビア語文献
および関係書誌目録
فهرست الكتب العربية فى دار الكتب الشرقية بطوكيو
[Index to the Arabic Books in the Oriental Library of the Tōyō Bunko]. Tokyo, Tōyō Bunko, 1974. 138 + 5 p.

Classified listing, in Japanese, of 9,035 Arabic books, in Arabic script. Two author indices.
Title transliterated: Tōyō Bunko Shozo Arabiago Bunken oyobi Kandei Shoshi Mokuroku.

B36 東洋文庫所蔵トルコ語オスマン
語文献および関係書誌目録
Türkçe-osmanlica Kitapları Katalogu [Catalogue of Ottoman Turkish Books]. Tokyo, Tōyō Bunko, 1974. 8 + 163 p.

Classified listing, in Japanese, of Turkish books on the Ottoman Empire contained in the Toyo Bunko, with shelf-numbers. Author index.
Title transliterated: Tōyō Bunko Sho-zō Torokoso Osuman Gobunken yobi Kandei Shoshi Moku-Roku.

B37
Union Catalogue of Printed Books in Persian Language, from Selected Libraries of Japan. Tokyo, Tōyō Bunko, 1984. 780 p.

Early lithographed and modern printed books and pamphlets, newspapers, and journals housed in 58 public and private university libraries.

Morocco

Rabat

Khizāna al-Malakīya

B38
Catalogues of the Royal فهرست الخزانة الملكية/ Library. Rabat, N.P., 1980- .
Vol. I. History and Travel. *Comp.* Muḥammad ᶜAbd Allāh ᶜAnnān.
Title transliterated: Fihrist al-Khizāna al-Malakīya.

Tetwan

Biblioteca General del Protectorado

B39
Catálogo de Autores y Títulos de la Biblioteca General del Protectorado (Sección árabe). *Comp.* Ahmed Mohammed Mekinasi. Tetwan, Editoria Marroquí, 1952. 603 p.

B40
Catálogo de Materias (obras relativas al-Islam y Africa) de la Biblioteca General del Protectorado. *Comps.* Guillermo Guastavimo Gallent *and* Carlos Rodríquez Joulia Saint-Cyr. Tetwan, Editoria Marroquí, 1952. 609 p. [dbl. col.].
Subject listing, subdivided by country, of 5,810 books and pamphlets. Subject, author, and geographical indices.

Netherlands

Amsterdam

Molukken Instituut, Bibliotheek

B41
Overzicht van de Literatuur betreffende de Molukken. *Comps.* W. Ruinen *and* A. B. Nalthenius. Amsterdam, Molukken-Instituut, 1928-35. 2 vols.
Classified and annotated listing of over 4,570 books, pamphlets, articles, and maps printed be-

tween 1550 and 1933 preserved in the library of the institute.

Vol. I, by W. Ruinen, catalogues works published between 1550 and 1921. Vol. II, by A. B. Tutein, lists those printed between 1922 and 1933. Author and title indices in each volume.

The Hague

Koninklijk Instituut voor de Taal- , Land- en Volkenkunde van Ned. Indië en het Indisch Genootschap, Bibliotheek

B42

Catalogus der Koloniale Bibliotheek van het Kon. Instituut voor de Taal-, Land- , en Volkenkunde van Ned. Indië en het Indisch Genootschap. *Comps.* G. P. Rouffaer *and* W. C. Muller. 's-Gravenhage, Martinus Nijhoff, 1908. IX + 1053 p.

Classified catalogue of the books and periodicals in western and oriental languages received up to 1907.

Supplements:

Catalogus der Koloniale Bibliotheek...: Eerste supplement. *Comp.* W. C. Muller. 's-Gravenhage, Martinus Nijhoff, 1915. VIII + 426 p. Additions received during the years 1908-13.

Catalogus der Koloniale Bibliotheek...: Tweede supplement. *Comp.* W. C. Muller. 's-Gravenhage, Martinus Nijhoff, 1927. VIII + 458 p. Additions received during the years 1914-25.

Catalogus der Koloniale Bibliotheek...: Derde supplement. *Comp.* W. J. M. Buch. 's-Gravenhage, Martinus Nijhoff, 1937. VIII + 438 p. Additions received during the years 1926-36.

Catalogus van de Bibliotheek van het Koninklijk Instituut...: [Vierde] supplement... . *Comp.* P. Voorhoeve. 's-Gravenhage, Martinus Nijhoff, 1966. IX + 801 p. Additions received during the years 1936-59.

Pakistan

Lahore

Punjab Public Library

B43
[Supplement- مكمّل فهرست كتب (فارسى) بلحاظ مضامين ary Catalogue of Books (Persian) by Subject]. Lahore, Punjab Public Library, 1942. 58 p.

A catalogue of the Persian collection at that time with works listed by subject. All published.

Title transliterated: Mukammal Fihrist Kutub (Fārsī) bi-Laḥāẓ Maḍāmīn.

Sudan

Khartoum

Jāmiᶜa al-Kharṭūm, Maktaba

B44
الفهرست المصنف لمجموعة السودان بمكتبة جامعة الخرطوم / The Classified Catalogue of the Sudan Collection in the University of Khartoum Library. Khartoum, Maktaba Jāmiᶜa al-Kharṭūm, 1971. pp. unnumbered. 50 p. of index.

Photoreproduction of the card catalogue containing 5,114 books, pamphlets, theses, photocopies, etc. Arranged by subject and issuing body. Author and "relative" indices in Latin and Arabic scripts.

Turkey

Ankara

Millî Kütüphane

B45
Millî Kütüphanede Mevcut Arap Harfli Türkçe Kitaplarin Muvakkat Kataloğu. Ankara, Millî Kütüphane Cilt ve Basımevi, 1964- . I- .

Alphabetical author listing of the Ottoman Turkish books printed in the Arabic script between 1729 and 1928 preserved in the national library of Turkey. Authors and titles are given only in modern Turkish transliteration.

Istanbul

İstanbul Üniversitesı, Kütüphane

B46
İstanbul Üniversitesı Kütüphanesi Arapça Basmalar Kataloğu [Catalogue of the Arabic Printed Books in Istanbul University Library]. *Comp.* Fehmi Edhem Karatay. Istanbul, İstanbul Üniversitesı, 1953. 857 p.

Author catalogue.

B47
İstanbul Üniversitesı Kütüphanesi Farşca Basmalar Kataloğu [Catalogue of Persian Printed Books in Istanbul University Library]. *Comp.* Fehmi Edhem Karatay. Istanbul, İstanbul Üniversitesı, 1949. VII + 200 p.

List of works written in Farsi, translations from and into Farsi, and about Iran.

B48
İstanbul Üniversitesı Kütüphanesı: Turkçe Basmalar Alfabe Kataloğu [Catalogue of Turkish Printed Books in Istanbul University Library]. *Comp.* Fehmi Edhem Karatay. Istanbul, İstanbul Üniversitesı, 1956. 2 vols.

Alphabetical catalogue of the Ottoman Turkish books printed between 1729 and 1928. Titles are printed in both the Arabic script and in modern Turkish. Provides full bibliographical data. Indices of titles (in Arabic script) and of subjects.

Union of Soviet Socialist Republics

Leningrad

Akademii͡a Nauk, Instituta Vostokovedenii͡a

B49
"Catalogue des Ouvrages arabes, persans et turcs Publiés à Constantinople, en Egypte et en Perse qui se trouvent au Musée asiatique de l'Académie." *Comp.* Bertram Dorn. *Bulletin de l'Académie Imperiale des Sciences de St. Pétersbourg*, X, 1866, pp. 168-213.

The library was absorbed by the Institute of Oriental Studies, Academy of Sciences (Instituta Vostokovedenii͡a, Akademii͡a Nauk), in 1930.

B50
Каталог Литографированных Книг на Персидском Языке в Собрании Ленинградского Отделения Института Востоковедения ан СССР [Catalogue of Lithographed Books in the Persian Language in the Assembly of the Leningrad Branch of the Oriental Institute of the U.S.S.R.]. *Comp.* O. P. Shcheglova. Moscow, Izdatel'stvo "Nauka" Glavnai͡a Redaktsii͡a Vostochnoĭ Literatury, 1975. 2 vols.

Classified listing of a total of 1,923 books on all subjects lithographed from the early part of the 19th century in Persia and India. Each is given in the Persian script and transliterated into Russian with brief annotations and the library's shelf-number. Author and transliterated title indices.

Title transliterated: Katalog Litografirovannyt͡s Knig na Persidskom I͡azke...

United Kingdom

London

British Library

B51
Catalogue of Arabic Books in the British Museum. *Comp.* A. G. Ellis *and* A. S. Fulton. London, Trustees of the British Museum, 1894-1905. 3 vols. [dbl. cols.].

Author catalogue of Arabic books, translations from the Arabic, and works in western languages on Arabic literature received by the Museum up to 1894. Indices, by A. S. Fulton, are contained in volume III. Reprinted, with corrections, in 1967.

Supplements:

Supplementary Catalogue of Arabic Printed Books in the British Museum. *Comps.* Alexander S. Fulton *and* A. G. Ellis. London, Trustees of the British Museum, 1926. 1188 dbl. cols. Materials received between 1894 and 1925.

Second Supplementary Catalogue of Arabic Printed Books in the British Museum. *Comps.* Alexander S. Fulton *and* Martin Lings. London, Trustees of the British Museum, 1959. viii p. + 1132 dbl. cols. Materials received between 1925 and 1957.

Third Supplementary Catalogue of Arabic Printed Books in the British Museum, 1958-69. *Comps.* Martin Lings *and* Y. H. Safadi. London, British Library, Reference Division, 1977. 4 vols. Vols. 1-2: Authors; Vol. 3: Titles; Vol. 4: Subject index. Reproduction of typewritten cards with bad Arabic writing. Not up to the standards of the British Museum, and at an exorbitant price!

B52

Catalogue of Hindustani Printed Books in the Library of the British Museum. *Comp.* J. F. Blumhardt. London, British Museum, 1889. vi + [ii]p. + 458 dbl. cols. + [iii] p.

Descriptive catalogue of the Urdu printed books acquired through 1888.

Supplement: A Supplementary Catalogue of Hindustani Books in the Library of the British Museum Acquired During the Years 1889-1908. *Comp.* J. F. Blumhardt. London, British Museum, 1909. vi + [ii] p. + 678 dbl. cols. + [i] p.

B53

A Catalogue of the Persian Printed Books in the British Museum. *Comp.* Edward Edwards. London, Trustees of the British Museum, 1922. viii p. + 968 cols.

Annotated author listing of printed books in the Farsi script, European translations from the Farsi, and works in western languages on Persian literature. Author's names are only in transliteration. Titles in the Farsi script, in transliteration, and in translation. Indices to subjects and titles.

B54

Catalogues of the Hindi, Panjabi, Sindhi, and Pushtu Printed Books in the Library of the British Museum. *Comp.* J. F. Blumhardt. London, British Museum, 1893. 4 pts.

Supplement: Panjabi Printed Books in the British Museum: a supplementary catalogue. *Comp.* L. D. Barnett. London, British Museum, 1961. viii + 121 p. Descriptive list of approximately 1,100 Panjabi and Multani printed books received since 1893.

India Office Library

B55

Catalogue of the Library of the India Office. Vol. II, Pt. VI: Persian books. *Comp.* Arthur J. Arberry. London, Secretary of State for India, 1937. 571 p.
Annotated alphabetical list. No index.

Royal Asiatic Society, Library

B56

Catalogue of Printed Books Published Before 1932, in the Library of the Royal Asiatic Society. London, Royal Asiatic Society, 1940. vii, 541 + [i] p.

Replaces the earlier catalogue published in 1893.

Includes books in the various oriental languages held in the Library.

Royal Empire Society, Library

B57

Subject Catalogue of the Library of the Royal Empire Society, formerly Royal Colonial Institute. *Comp.* Evans Lewin. London, Royal Empire Society, 1930-37. 4 vols.

"The present catalogue does not entirely supersede that of 1901, and it is not exhaustive. In practice, however, few publications of any present use or importance have been omitted... ." *[Preface]*.

Vol. I: The British Empire generally, and Africa; IV: The Mediterrranean Colonies, the Middle East, India, Burma, Ceylon, Malaya, East Indies, and the Far East.

During World War II a considerable portion of the library was destroyed by enemy action.

University of London, School of Oriental and African Studies, Library

B58
Library Catalogue of the School of Oriental and African Studies. Boston, G. K. Hall & Co., 1963. 13 vols.

Excludes the Chinese catalogue.

Supplements:

Library Catalogue of the School of Oriental and African Studies. First Supplement. Boston, G. K. Hall & Co., 1968. 6 vols.

Library Catalogue of the School of Oriental and African Studies. Second Supplement. Boston, G. K. Hall & Co., 1973. 6 vols.

Library Catalogue of the School of Oriental and African Studies. Third Supplement. Boston, G. K. Hall & Co., 1979. 8 vols.

United States of America

Cambridge

Harvard University, Libraries

B59
Catalogue of Arabic, Persian, and Ottoman Turkish Books. Cambridge, Harvard University Library, 1968. 5 vols.

Reproduction of the catalogue cards in greatly reduced size.

Vols. I-III: Arabic; IV: Persian and Turkish; V: Topical subject index.

The Arabic portion of this catalogue has been superseded by the following.

B60
Catalog of the Arabic Collection, Harvard University. Boston, G. K. Hall Library Catalogs, 1983. 6 vols.

Considerably updated and expanded catalogue reproducing some 90,000 catalogue cards of books and serials in the Widener Library, the Houghton and Law School libraries, the Countway Library of Medicine, and the Andover-Newton Theological Library.

Chicago

University of Chicago, Oriental Institute, Library

B61
Catalogue of the Oriental Institute Library. Boston, G. K. Hall & Co., 1970. 16 vols.

Dictionary catalogue of one of the finest collections of orientalia, particularly rich in Islamic materials.

Supplement: First Supplement: I. Catalogue of the Middle Eastern Collection. Boston, G. K. Hall & Co., 1977. 962 p.

New Haven

American Oriental Society, Library

B62
Catalogue of the Library of the American Oriental Society. *Ed.* Elizabeth Strout. New Haven, Yale University Library, 1930. vii, [i] + 308 p.

Subject listing of the printed books and manuscripts of the library housed in the Sterling Memorial Library of Yale University. Pages 116-241 have the works arranged by language family and then by individual languages. General index.

New York

New York Public Library

B63
Dictionary Catalogue of the Oriental Collection. Boston, G. K. Hall & Co., 1960. 16 vols.

Alphabetical dictionary catalogue of all materials contained in the Oriental Division, plus works relating to the Orient housed in other parts of the library. Photoreproduction of 318,000 cards, including approximately 15,000 cards for indexed periodical articles. The catalogue contains more than 5,000 subject and form headings. The Oriental Division's holdings are extensive in Arabic language works and on Islam.

Supplement: Dictionary Catalogue of the Oriental Collection. First Supplement. Boston, G. K. Hall & Co., 1976. 8 vols.

Salt Lake City

University of Utah, Aziz S. Atiya Library

B64
University of Utah Middle East Library Catalogue Series I: Arabic Collection; Aziz S. Atiya Library for Middle East Studies. Salt Lake City, University of Utah Press, 1968. xv + 841 p. [dbl. col.].

Photoreproduction of the catalogue cards, classified by subject.

Supplements:

Middle East Library Catalogue Series: Supplement One to Volume I: Arabic Collection. Salt Lake City, University of Utah Press, 1971. x + 470 p. [dbl. col.]. Includes a list of periodical holdings and indices of authors and titles.

Middle East Library Catalogue Series: Supplement Two to Volume I: Arabic Collection. Salt Lake City, University of Utah Press, 1979. 896 p. [dbl. col.].

Stanford

Stanford University, Hoover Institution on War Revolution, and Peace, Library

B65
The Library Catalogs of The Hoover Institution on War, Revolution, and Peace, Stanford University: catalog of the Arabic collection. Boston, G. K. Hall & Co., 1969. xi + 902 p. [triple col.].

Photoreproduction of the card catalogue in dictionary form (authors, titles, and subjects). Includes uncatalogued materials, government documents and society publications, serials, and newspapers.

B66
The Library Catalogs of The Hoover Institution on War, Revolution, and Peace, Stanford University:

Catalogs of the Turkish and Persian collections. Boston, G. K. Hall & Co., 1969. xi + 670 p. [triple col.].

Photoreproduction of the card catalogues in dictionary form with authors, titles, and subjects interfiled. Includes uncatalogued materials, government documents, society publications, serials, and newspapers.

Contents: Turkish, pp. 1-626; Persian, pp. 627-670.

Washington, D.C.

Library of Congress

B67

The National Union Catalogue Pre-1956 Imprints: a cumulative author list representing Library of Congress printed cards and titles reported by other American libraries. *Comp. & ed.* Library of Congress *and* National Union Catalog Subcommittee of the Resources Committee of the Resources and Technical Services Division, American Library Association. London, Mansell Information/Publishing Ltd., 1968-1981. 754 vols. [triple col.] [with supplement].

Although a general catalogue of books and serials held by the Library of Congress and other American libraries it is, because it contains works in oriental languages an excellent reference for Arabic, Persian, Turkish, and Urdu printed books.

Supplements:

Library of Congress and National Union Catalog Author Lists, 1942-1962: a master cumulation. Detroit, Gale Research Co., 1969-71. 152 vols.

The Library of Congress Catalogs, The National Union Catalog: a cumulative author list representing Library of Congress printed cards and titles reported by other American libraries 1963-1967. Ann Arbor, J. W. Edwards Publisher, Inc., 1969. 59 vols.

The Library of Congress Catalogs, The National Union Catalog: ... 1968-1972. Ann Arbor, J. W. Edwards Publisher, Inc., 1973. 104 vols.

Library of Congress Catalogs, National Union Catalog 1973-1977. Totowa, New Jersey, Rowman and

Littlefield, 1978. 135 vols.

Library of Congress Catalogs, National Union Catalog 1978. Washington, D.C., Library of Congress, 1979. 16 vols.

Library of Congress Catalogs, National Union Catalog 1979. Washington, D.C., Library of Congress, 1980. 16 vols.

Library of Congress Catalogs, National Union Catalog 1980. Washington, D.C., Library of Congress, 1981. 18 vols.

Library of Congress Catalogs, National Union Catalog 1981. Washington, D.C., Library of Congress, 1982. 15 vols.

Library of Congress Catalogs, National Union Catalog 1982. Washington, D.C., Library of Congress, 1983. 8 vols. + 12 pts. [All published].

Middle East Institute, Library

B68

Catalog of the Middle East Institute Library. Boston, G. K. Hall & Co., 1984. 4 vols.

Photoreproduction of the card catalogue with approximately 48,000 entries divided into author/title and subject sections. Although most of the works are in western European languages (predominantly English) books in oriental languages, in transliteration, are included.

MANUSCRIPT DIRECTORIES

General

B69

PEARSON, J. D.

Oriental Manuscripts in Europe and North America: a survey. Zug, Switzerland, Inter Documentation Co., AG, 1971. 595 p.

Bibliotheca Asiatica, 7.

Detailed description of the collections of manuscripts in Asian languages with listings of published and unpublished catalogues available.

For the United Kingdom replaces his earlier *Oriental Manuscript Collections in the Libraries of Great Britain and Ireland* (London, Royal Asiatic Society, 1954).

North America

B70
MARTIN, Thomas J.
North American Collections of Islamic Manuscripts. Boston, G. K. Hall & Co., 1977. xx + 96 p.

Brief guide to 109 institutions in Canada and the United States with holdings of manuscripts in Arabic, Persian, and Ottoman Turkish. Provides details regarding each collection.

Arabic

B71
HUISMAN, A. J. W.
Les Manuscrits arabes dans le Monde: un bibliographie des catalogues. Leiden, E. J. Brill, 1967. x + 99 p.

List of the printed catalogues of the manuscripts preserved in private collections and in institutional and public libraries. Arranged by country, city, and library with index of authors, cities, and libraries. Now requires a supplement for catalogues published during the last seventeen years.

Replaces the older list compiled by Georges Vajda, *Répertoire des Catalogues et Inventaires de Manuscrits arabes* (Paris, 1949).

B72
al-MUNAJJID, Ṣalāḥ al-Dīn.
معجم المخطوطات المطبوعة بين ١٩٥٤ ـ ١٩٦٠/
A Dictionary of Arabic Manuscripts Edited Between 1954-1960. Beirut, Dār al-Kitāb al-Jadīd, 1962-70. 3 vols.

Title transliterated: Muᶜjam al-Makhṭūṭāt al-Maṭbūᶜa...

Persian

B73
AFSHAR, Īraj.
كتابشناسى فهرست نسخهاى خطى فارسى دركتابخانه هاى دنيا /
Bibliographie des Catalogues des Manuscrits persans. Tehran, Université de Tehran, 1337/1958. [x], 88 + [iv] p.

Publications de l'Université de Tehran, No. 485.
List of 222 catalogues in Farsi and western languages by country, with annotations in Farsi. Indices of libraries and authors. Requires updating.
Title transliterated: Kitābshināsī Fihrist-hā-ī Nuskha-hā-ī Khaṭṭī Fārsī...

¶ Lists of academic centers, libraries, research institutes, etc., in Iran and throughout the world for Iranian studies are to be found in Iraj Afshar's *A Directory for Iranian Studies* [J4].

C ENCYCLOPAEDIAS

This listing contains encyclopaedias of a general nature only. Specific encyclopaedias and handbooks will be found in those sections in which they properly belong.

GENERAL

C1

Encyclopaedia of Islām: a dictionary of the geography, ethnology and biography of the Muhammadan peoples. Leiden, E. J. Brill/ London, Luzac & Co., 1908-38. 4 vols. + suppl., illus.

Detailed, scholarly articles on the persons, places, and subjects of importance in Islam and the Muslim world written by numerous contributors. Appended to each article is a short bibliography of the most important primary and secondary references in western and oriental languages. The articles are in dictionary form according to the Arabic, Persian, Turkish, etc., name in transliteration. The cross-references to articles are inadequate, and there is no index. The supplementary volume was issued for articles of importance omitted from the main work and for the revision of those rendered obsolete by advancing scholarship. Issued in English, French, and German editions. Now being replaced by the second edition.

Translations:

Arabic: دائرة المعارف الاسلامية فى ترجمة عربية [Islamic Encyclopaedia in Arabic Translation]. *Trans.* Muḥammad Thābit al-Fandī *and* Ibrāhīm Zakī Khurshid. Cairo, N.P., 1933. 15 pts. An incomplete translation of the first edition only through the letter ᶜ*ayn*. Reprinted in Baghdad in 1970 and again in Tehran (N.D.).

Turkish: İslâm Ansiklopedisi: İslâm âlemi coğrafya, etnoğrafya ve biyografya lûgati [Encyclopaedia of Islam: dictionary of the world of Islam geography, ethnography, and biography]. Istanbul, Maarif Matbaası, 1940- [10 vols. to date]. In this translation the articles on the Turks and the Ottoman Empire have either been entirely rewritten or corrected. Beginning with fascicule 90 (1960) publication was assumed by the Millî Eğitim Basımevi.

Urdu: [Urdu Encyclopaedia of Islam]. اردو دائره معارف اسلاميه Lahore, University of the Panjab, 1959- . I- [in progress], illus. Translation being made under the auspices of the Dānish Gāh Panjāb. Articles from the first and second editions with additions and corrections.

C2

Encyclopaedia of Islam. New edition. Leiden, E. J. Brill/ London, Luzac & Co., 1954- . I- [in progress], illus.

In this second edition the articles from the first have either been revised or replaced, and new articles added so that the new edition will be comprised of six volumes. Cross-references have been improved, although still far from adequate. Issued slowly in fascicules, doubled early on, the first double fascicule of the *Supplement* has already been issued (1980), and a "Preliminary List of Articles" for the supplement to the first three volumes has also been published (1974).

Fortunately, from the beginning, an index was planned and the index to volumes I-III, compiled by H. & J. D. Pearson (edited by E. van Donzel), was published in 1979.

Issued only in English and French editions some German scholars have refused to contribute.

Beginning with volume IV E. J. Brill became the sole publisher. Usually abbreviated as *E.I.*^{2}.

C3

KREISER, Klaus; DIEM, Werner *and* MAJOR, Hans Georg, *comps*.

Lexicon der islamischen Welt. Stuttgart, Verlag W. Kuhlhammer, 1974. 3 vols.

Articles on both historical and contemporary subjects treated in comparatively brief form for more popular use with no index. Published in small format.

C4
RONART, Stephen *and* Nancy.
Concise Encyclopaedia of Arabic Civilization. Amsterdam, Djambatan/ New York, Frederick Praeger, 1959-66. 2 vols., illus., maps.
Short popularized handbook in dictionary form on the cultural, economic, and political developments in the Arabic-speaking world from the rise of Islam to modern times. Written by and for non-specialists.
Contents: Vol. I: The Arab East; II: The Arab West [North Africa and Spain].
A revised German translation, by Fritz Hofer and Walter W. Müller, has been published in one volume, *Lexikon der arabischen Welt: ein historisch- politisches nachschlagewerk* (Zurich, Artemis Verlag, 1972. xv + 1085 p.).

ARABIC

C5
ᶜATĪYA ALLĀH, Aḥmad, *ed.*
[Dictionary of Islam]. القموس الاسلامى
Cairo, Maktaba al-Nahḍa al-Miṣrīya, 1963- , I- , illus.
Dictionary of the history and culture of Islam, based upon, although not a translation of, *The Encyclopaedia of Islam.*
Title transliterated: Al-Qamūs al-Islāmī.

C6
ṬĀSHKUBRĪZĀDA, Aḥmad ibn Muṣṭafā (d. 968/1561).
مفتاح السعادة و مصباح السيادة فى موضوعات العلوم
[The Felicitous Key and the Lamp of Authority in the Subject of Knowledge]. *Ed.* Kāmil Kāmil Bakrī *and* ᶜAbd al-Wahāb Abī al-Nūr. Cairo, Dār al-Kutub al-Ḥadītha, 1968. 3 vols.
A general encyclopaedia of the arts and sciences, first published, according to Sarkīs, in Hyderabad-Deccan in 1328/1910. Translated by his son, Mu-

ḥammad ibn Aḥmad, into Turkish مضوعات العلوم and printed in Istanbul, 1313/1895-96.

Title transliterated: Miftaḥ al-Saᶜāda wa Misbāḥ al-Siyāda fī Mawḍūᶜāt al-ᶜUlūm.

GEOGRAPHICAL

AFRICA

C7

OLIVER, Roland *and* CROWDER, Michael, *eds.*
Cambridge Encyclopedia of Africa. Cambridge, Cambridge University Press, 1981. 492 p., illus., maps.

Articles on the history, political economy, political relations, societies, and religions of Africa from pre-historic to modern times.

INDIA

C8

BALFOUR, Edward Green.
Cyclopaedia of India and of Eastern and Southern Asia, commercial, industrial, and scientific; products of the mineral, vegetable, and animal kingdom; useful arts and manufactures. *3rd ed.* London, B. Quaritch, 1885. 3 vols.

INDONESIA

C9

PAULUS, J. *and* GRAAF, S. de, *et. al.*
Encyclopaedie van Nederlandsch- Indië. *2nd ed.* 's-Gravenhage, Matinus Nijhoff, 1917-40. 4 vols. + 4 suppls.

IRAN

C10

YARSHATER, Ehsan, *ed.*
Encyclopaedia Iranica. London, Routledge & Kegan Paul, 1983-, I- [in progress].

Articles on all aspects of Iranian history and society from pre-history to the present. Issued in fasciculi.

The editor instituted a similar *Encyclopaedia of Iran and Islam* based upon *The Encyclopaedia of Islam* in Farsi (Tehran, The Royal Institute of Translation and Publication, 1976) which, following the issuance of only three fasciculi ceased publication with the Iranian Revolution. The present work is entirely in English.

RELIGION & PHILOSOPHY D

GENERAL

Bibliographies

Bibliographies of Bibliographies

D1

GEDDES, Charles L.

An Analytical Guide to the Bibliographies on Islām, Muḥammad, and the Qur'ān. Denver, American Institute of Islamic Studies, 1973. [ii] + 78p.

Bibliographic Series, No. 3.

A preliminary annotated listing of 211 books and articles in oriental and western (including Russian) languages which have been published between 1658 and 1972 arranged by author. Author, title, and subject index.

Bibliographies

D2

ḤAMĪDULLĀH, Muḥammad.

Qur'ān in Every Language. القرآن فى كلّ لسان/

3rd ed. Hyderabad-Deccan, 1947.

This title is listed as one of his publications by the author in his *Muslim Conduct of State* (6th ed. Lahore, 1973). However, no copy of this bibliography has been found to date in any library in the United States, nor in any library in Great Britain. Full publication details are therefore not presently available. Fourth edition reportedly published in *France-Islam,* 1967- , also not located.

D3

D6

JUWAYNĪ, Muṣṭafā al-Ṣāwī.
[Guide to أعلام الدراسات القرآنية فى خمسة عشر قـرنـا Qurʾānic Studies over Fifteen Centuries]. Alexandria, Munshaʾa al-Nāshir al-Maʿārif, 1982. 381 + [ii] p.

Kutub al-Dirāsāt al-Qurʾānīya, 7.

Bio-bibliographical survey of Arabic studies concerning the Qurʾān arranged by century.

Title transliterated: Aʿlām al-Dirāsāt al-Qurʾanīya fī Khamsa ʿAshr Qarnan.

D4

KHAN, Muin ud-Din Ahmad.
"A Bibliographical Introduction to Modern Islamic Development in India and Pakistan 1700-1955." *Journal of the Asiatic Society of Pakistan*, IV, 1959, vii + 170 p.

Publication of the compiler's M.A. thesis submitted to McGill University as an appendex to the journal.

Classified listing of 869 books and articles.

D5

LOEWENTHAL, Rudolf.
"Russian Materials on Islam and Islamic Institutions: a selective bibliography." *Der Islam*, XXXII, 1957, pp. 280-309.

Subject listing of 381 books, pamphlets, and articles published between approximately 1850 and 1950. Russian titles are transliterated and provided with English translations. Author, person, and subject index.

D6

PFANNMÜLLER, Gustav.
Handbuch der Islam-Literatur. Berlin, Verlag von Walter de Gruyter & Co., 1923. VIII + 436 p.

A very detailed bibliographic essay of books and articles in oriental and western languages published up to the time of publication. Although not confined to religious studies the greatest part of the work is devoted to that subject. Now sixty years old and therefore to a large extent out of date it is still of value for its essays.

Contents: I. Die Bibliographie des Islams im

Allgemeinen; II. Länder und Völker des Islams; III. Politische Geschichte und Kulturgeschichte des Islams; IV. Die Religion des Islams; V. Die Philosophie des Islams; VI. Die Kunst des Islams; VII. Die Literatur der Araber, Perser und Türken. Index of authors.

D7

Religious Books 1876-1982. New York, R. R. Bowker Co., 1983. 4 vols. [quadruple col.].

Subject index of nearly all books published or distributed in the United States in western languages (predominantly in English) on all aspects of religion. Provides full bibliographical details, Library of Congress number, and often a brief annotation. Islam, further subdivided by subject, is to be found in Vol. 2, cols. 1921-1927.

Arrangement: Vol. 1 - A-B; Vol. 2 - C-J; Vol. 3 - M-Z; Vol. 4 - Author and title indices.

D8

SHINAR, Pessah.

Essai de Bibliographie sélective et annotée sur l'Islam maghrebin contemporain: Maroc, Algérie, Tunisie, Libye (1830-1978). Paris, Centre National de la Recherche Scientifique, 1983. XXIV + 506 p.

Recherches sur les Sociétés Mediterranéennes.

Annotated listing of 2,025 books and articles in Arabic, French, English, German, Italian, and Spanish arranged by country and then by subject. Indices of authors' names, subjects, names of persons, names of places.

D9

YENER, Enıse.

Türkiye Dinler Tarihi ve İslâm Dinime Ait: bir bibliyografya denemesi (1928-1960) [Turkish Religious History and the Islamic Faith: a provisional bibliography (1928-1960)]. Ankara, Ankara Fakültesi Basımevi, 1963. 32 p.

İlâhiyat Fakültesi Yayınlarından, XLVI.

Alphabetical listing by author of 454 books, pamphlets, and articles on religious history and Islam in general published in Turkey since the reform of the alphabet. Although primarily in Turkish there are a few titles in English and French.

D10

UNITED STATES. Library of Congress, African Section. Islam in Sub-Saharan Africa: a partially annotated guide. *Comp.* Samir M. Zoghby. Washington, D.C., Library of Congress, 1978. [vi] + 317 p. [dbl. col.].

Chronological, regional, and subject listing, with occasional annotations, of 2,682 books, articles, unpublished lectures, etc. to the end of 1974 in Arabic and western European languages. Author, title, and subject index.

D11

---. ---.

Library of Congress Catalogue of Printed Cards: Religion. Chicago, Bibliography Press, 1975. 9 vols.

Reprinting in new type of all Library of Congress printed cards covering that institution's classification BL - BX (religion) for the period 1898-1974 with 192,000 entries. Arranged according to the L.C. classification number. Post 1974 accessions are issued monthly with an annual cumulative volume. Non-Roman alphabet titles have been transliterated. Index volume includes author, title, series, L.C. numbers, and L.C. subject headings.

Under the L.C. classification system Islam is BP1-199, to be found in volume three of this set.

Serial Bibliographies

D12

International Bibliography of the History of Religions. Leiden, E. J. Brill, 1954- .

Published under the auspices of The International Association for the History of Religions.

Annual bibliography, from 1952, of books and articles in western languages. Arrangement varies.

¶ Attention should also be given to the serial listings in the various indices to periodical literature, most of which have sections on Islam.

¶ The Research Centre for Islamic History, Art and Culture of the Organisation of the Islamic Conference reports that it has under preparation "A Bibliography of the Translations of the Meaning of the Holy Quran" (1983).

Biographies

D13

Biographic Encyclopedia of Religion. Chicago, World Biography Press, 1976. 11 vols.

Alphabetically arranged biographical dictionary of 8,060 religious personalities from the earliest times to the present throughout the world, including those of classical and contemporary Islam, with numerous illustrations and maps. Each entry includes bibliographical references. The eleventh volume is an index and study guide. Prepared for student and general public use.

¶ See also the specialized biographical dictionaries within each subsequent division of this section as well as biographical articles within the encyclopaedias.

Encycopaedias & Handbooks

D14

Bibliographic Encyclopedia of Religion. Chicago, World Biography Press, 1976- [in progress], illus.

Alphabetically arranged encyclopaedia of the religions of the world from the earliest times to the present with proper names, individuals, concepts, etc., in 8,060 signed articles ranging in length from 500 to 3,500 words. Each includes a brief bibliography. Illustrated with maps and 4,253 photographs and drawings. Vol. 11 contains a detailed index and a word curriculum oriented study guide.

D15

GIBB, H. A. R. *and* KRAMERS, J. H., *eds.*

Shorter Encyclopaedia of Islam. Leiden, E. J. Brill, 1963. viii + 671 p. [dbl. col.] , illus.

Reprinting of the articles on religion and jurisprudence from the first edition of *The Encyclo-*

paedia of Islam with corrections, revisions, and additions.

D16

HUGHES, Thomas Patrick.

A Dictionary of Islam: being a cyclopaedia of the doctrines, rites, ceremonies and customs, together with the technical and theological terms, of the Muhammadan religion. London, W. H. Allen & Co., 1885. v, [iii] + 750 p. [dbl. col.], illus.

Written by a Christian missionary to India many of the articles were both sceptical and critical of Islam. Nevertheless, it remains, despite its age, an interesting and useful handbook. It has undergone several photographic reprintings. In that of the Premier Book House, Lahore, N.D., the statements considered derogatory to Islam have either been expunged or rewritten.

D17

International Encyclopedia of Religion and Philosophy. New York, Worldwide Reference Books, 1976. 13 vols., illus.

Popularized encyclopaedia on all major religions and philosophies arranged by region. Each article is accompanied by an annotated bibliography. The thirteenth volume contains a cumulative index, a study guide, and a bibliography for the set.

Arrangement: I: Canada; II. Latin America; III. Europe; IV: Europe; V. Europe; VI. U.S.S.R.; VI: Middle East; VIII: Africa; IX: South Asia; X: East Asia; XI: Southeast Asia; XII: Australia and New Zealand; XIII: Index.

D18

WENSINCK, A. J. *and* KRAMERS, J. H., *eds.*

Handwörterbuch des Islam. Leiden, E. J. Brill, 1941. 847 p. [dbl. col.].

Articles, with correction, additions, and revisions, on the faith and jurisprudence of Islam taken from the German edition of *The Encyclopaedia of Islam*. Index.

Holidays & Festivals

D19
GRUNEBAUM, Gustav E. von.
Muhammadan Festivals. New York, Schuman, 1951. viii + 107 p., illus.
A brief survey of Muslim religious observances.

¶ See also V. Grumel, *Traité d'Etudes Byzantines: I. Chronologie*. The third part, "Tableaux chronologiques," contains a section entitled "Principales fêtes musulmanes." [J225].

Rituals

D20
BOUSQUET, G. H.
Les Grandes pratiques Rituelles de l'Islâm. Paris, Presses Universitaires de France, 1949. VIII + 134 p.
Mythes et Religions, vol. 24.
Although written for the intelligent layman, this is a good, brief examination of each of the "Five Pillars" by the late professor of North African sociology and comparative Muslim law in the Faculté de Droit d'Alger.
Contents: I. Introduction à l'Etude du Rituel orthodoxe de l'Islâm; II. La Profession de Foi, la Pureté Rituelle et la Circoncision; III. La Prière: 1. Généralités; Prières quotidiennes; IV. La Prière: 2. De la Mosquée et de Prières; V. Le Jeûne; VI. Le Pèlerinage; VII. Conclusions. Le Culte musulman, ses caractères sociologiques généraux; son avenir. No index.

D21
GHAFOORI, Ali, *Ayatullah.*
The Ritual Prayer of Islam. Tehran, The Hamdami Foundation, [1982]. 167 p., illus.
Provides the required prelude acts to prayer (intention, ablution, etc.), the postures in prayer, and the phrases in the Arabic script, in transliteration, and in English translation for the daily and congregational prayers as well as for special observances.

D22
KAMAL/AHMAD.
The Sacred الرحلة المقدسة الى بيت الله الحرام/ Journey, being pilgrimage to Makkah. New York, Duell, Sloan and Pearce, 1961. xx, 108, ix + 115 p. [Arabic text].

Secondary title: *The Traditions, Dogma, and Islamic Ritual that Govern the Lives and the Destiny of More Than Five Hundred Million Who Call Themselves Muslim: one seventh of mankind.*

An explanation of the "Fifth Pillar" of Islam presented in a readable form by a Muslim of Central Asian extraction. Published originally in 1952 in Baghdad and presented here in both Arabic and English texts.

Contents: Part 1: The Sacred Journey to Makka; Part 2: The Sacred Journey to Madinah and Jerusalem.

D23
ṢAWWĀF, Muḥammad Maḥmūd.
The Muslim Book of Prayer. Doha, Qatar, Tabaᶜ bi-Muwāfiqa al-Muʾallif ᶜala Nafaqa al-Shuʾūn al-Dīnīya bi-Dawla Qaṭar, 1980. x + 70 p.

D24
PADWICK, Constance E.
Muslim Devotions: a study of prayer-manuals in common use. London, S.P.C.K., 1961. xxix + 313 p.

A study of common devotions through a detailed examination of readily available small prayer-manuals, many of which are of classical Islamic origin.

Contents: Part 1: Type-names for Devotions; Part 2: On the Threshold of the Prayer-rite; Part 3: Within the Prayer-rite; Part 4: Outside the Prayer-rite. Appendices. Index.

Islam & Other Religions

D25
CASPAR, R.
"Bibliographie du Dialogue Islamo-chrétien." *Islamochristiana* [Rome], I, 1975, pp. 125-181; II, 1976, pp. 187-249; III, 1977, pp. 255-286; IV, 1978, pp. 247-267; V, 1979, pp. 299-317; VI, 1980,

pp. 259-299.

A running bibliography of books and articles in western languages, primarily in English and French.

For an earlier bibliography see: Jean Déjeux *and* Robert Caspar, "Bibliographie sur le Dialogue Islamo-chrétien," *Proche Orient Chrétien* [Jerusalem], XVI, 1966, pp. 179-182.

D26

GALANTE, Abraham.

Documents officiels turcs Concernant les Juifs de Turquie: recueil de 114 lois, règlements, firmans, bérats, ordres et décisions de tribunaux, traduction française avec résumés historiques, annotations et un appendice avec sept autres documents. Istanbul, Etablissements Haim, Rozio & Co., 1931. iii + 255 p.

An important collection arranged by subject concerning the relations of a large and powerful community with the Ottoman government and the Muslim community from the 16th century to the abolition of the caliphate. Appendix of terms employed in the documents.

D27

MONNOT, G.

"Les Ecrits musulmans sur les Religions non-bibliques." *Mélanges de l'Institut Dominicain d'Etudes Orientales*, XI, 1972, pp. 5-49.

D28

STEINSCHNEIDER, Moritz.

"Polemische und apologetische Literatur in arabischer Sprache, zwischen Muslimen, Christen und Juden, nebst Anhängen verwandten Inhalts." *Abhandlungen für die Kunde des Morgenlandes*, VI, 3, 1877. XII + 456 p.

Classified listing of unpublished and published, including translations, materials with various subject, title, and author indices.

Although now out of date still a useful compilation.

D29

WISMER, Don.
The Islamic Jesus: an annotated bibliography of sources in English and French. New York, Garland Publishing, Inc., 1977. xix + 305 p.

Alphabetical listing by author of 726 books and articles published in the two languages and of works written in an oriental language translated into English or French, with lengthy, detailed annotations, often with quotations from the authors. Periodical, short-title, and subject indices.

Folklore

D30
AWWAD, Kurkis.
"الآثار المخطوطة و المطبوعة في الفولكلور العراق"
["Manuscript and Published Works on Iraqi Folklore"]. *Majalla al-Ṭurāth al-Shaᶜbī*, I, 1963, pp. 1-16.

Arabic and western language materials. Those in Arabic are listed by subject; those in western languages (p. 16) are in alphabetical order.

Title transliterated: "Al-Athār al-Makhṭūṭa wa al-Maṭbūᶜa fī al-Fūlklūr al-ᶜIrāq."

D31
DONALDSON, Bess Allen.
The Wild Rue: a study of Muhammadan magic and folklore in Iran. London, Luzac & Co., 1938. 216 p.

A detailed study by the wife of a long-term Christian missionary resident in the holy city of Mashad.

"Most of the material has been collected within the provice of Khorasan, but since pilgrims come to the 'sacred city' of Meshed from all over Iran, many of them to remain for the rest of their lives, its population is after all a representative group." [*Preface*].

Fairly detailed index.

D32
GUPTA, Sankar *and* PARMAR, Shyam.
A Bibliography of Indian Folklore and Related Subjects. Calcutta, Indian Publications, 1967. 196 p. [dbl. col.].

Indian Folklore Series No. 11.

A catalogue of publications in English arranged by subject. Although predominantly Hindu the bibliography does include some Muslim materials.

Contents: A. General Folklore; B. Prose Narratives; C. Folk Music, Ballad, Song, Dance and Drama; D. Art, Craft and Architecture; Proverb, Parable, Epigram; Riddle; Language and Grammar; M. Material Culture; Totem, Taboo, Belief Superstition; Social & Cultural Anthropology; Village Studies; Marriage; Medicine; Mankind; Blood Group; Miscellaneous; Reports. Author index.

D33
IBN AZZUZ, Mohammad.
Diccionarío de Supersticiones y Mitos marroquíes. Madrid, Consejo Superior de Investigaciones Científicas, Instituto de Estudios Africanos, 1958. 61 p.

D34
KIRKLAND, Edwin Capers.
A Bibliography of South Asian Folklore. Bloomington, Indiana University Press, 1966. xxiv + 291 p. [dbl. col.].

Folklore Institute Monograph Series, 21.

Author listing of 6,852 books and articles in European and Asian languages on the folklore of India, Pakistan, Nepal, Tibet, Ceylon, Bhutan, and Sikkim. As it does not include any items for countries east of India or west of Pakistan the title is misleading.

Subject index includes 73 items, unhappily under "Mohammedan," and 10 items under Pakistan. Appropriate regions, *e.g.* Bengal, Punjab., etc., and languages, Urdu, Bengali, etc., should also be consulted.

D35
MONIRUZZAMAN, Mohammad.
Baṃlādeśe loka Saṃskṛti Sandhāna, 1941-71/ Manirujjāmāna. Dacca, Bāṅalā Ekāḍemī, 1982. 11 + 256 p.

An index to the articles and studies on Bengali folklore published in Bengali periodicals, 1941-71.

D36

PRESTON, W. D.

"A Preliminary Bibliography of Turkish Folklore." *Journal of American Folklore*, LVIII, 1945, pp. 245-51.

Classified listing of 130 books and articles in western languages.

Contents: Journals and Series; General; Folk-tale; Folksong; Folk-Theatre; Folk-Book; Anecdotes; Riddles; Related Literature.

D37

TURKEY. Millî Folklor Enstitüsü.

Türk Folklor ve Etnografya Bibliyografyası [Bibliography of Turkish Folklore and Ethnology]. Ankara, Başbakanlık Basımevi, 1971. XXVI + 521 p.

Millî Folklor Enstitüsü Yayınları: 5.

Classified listing in great detail of 5,219 books and articles in Turkish. Author and title indices and a very detailed subject index.

D38

WESTERMARCK, Edward Alexander.

Ritual and Belief in Morocco. London, Macmillan & Co., 1926. 2 vols.

An extremely detailed study of the folklore and magic of Morocco by a noted sociologist who spent seven years in the country studying the popular beliefs of the inhabitants. Both the table of contents and the index are paragons of scholarship. Makes for fascinating reading. Reprinted in 1968.

QURʾĀN

Introductions

D39

BLACHERE, Régis.

Introduction au Coran. Paris, Editions G. P. Maison-Neuve, 1947-51. 3 vols.

The above is the title given on the title-page. However, to make things confusing the title on the paper covers is *Le Coran: traduction selon un essai de reclassement des sourates*.

An important modern translation with an attempt to reorganize the *sūras* chronologically, similar to that attempted by Bell. The introductory essay (second edition, 1959) dealing with the problems attendant upon the death of Muḥammad to collect and edit the verses, the variant readings, the history of the text, etc., occupies the entire first volume.

D40
GÄTJE, Helmut.
Koran und Koranexegese. Zurich/Stuttgart, Artemis Verlag, 1971. 400 p.
Die Bibliothek des Morgenlandes, MCMLXXI.
A detailed study by subject of the Arabic commentaries upon the Qur◌ān.

D41
JEFFERY, Arthur, *ed.*
Materials for the History of the Text of the Qur◌ān, the Old Codices: the *Kitāb al-Maṣāḥif* of Ibn abī Dāwūd together with a collection of the variant readings from the codices of Ibn Maᶜsūd, Ubai ᶜAlī, Ibn ᶜAbbās, Anas, Abū Mūsā and other early Qur◌ānic authorities which present a type of text anterior to that of the canonical text of ᶜUthmān. Leiden, E. J. Brill, 1937. X, 327 + 223 p. [Arabic text].

D42
KHALIFA, Mohammad.
The Sublime Qur◌ān and Orientalism. London, Longman Group Ltd., 1983. xviii + 262 p.
An introduction to the internal make-up of the Qur an and to its basic teachings by a Muslim scholar to counter some of the arguments of non-Muslim Islamists.

D43
PARET, Rudi.
Der Koran: kommentar und konkordanz. Stuttgart, Verlag W. Kohlhammer, 1971. 559 p.
Notes and comments on each verse of each *sura* according to the standard arrangement.
Appendices: 1. Verbesserungen der Übersetzung; 2. Namen und Abkürzungen von Suren: I. Register der Surennamen und -abkürzungen, angeordnet nach Reihenfolge der Suren; II. Register der Suren-

namen und -abkürzungen, angeordnet nach dem Alphabet.

D44
SHIḤĀTA, ʿAbd Allāh Maḥmūd.
[History of the Qurʾān and the Commentaries]. تاريخ القرآن و التفسير Cairo, Al-Haiʾa al-Miṣrīya al-ʿĀmma li-l-Kitāb, 1972. 198 p.
A modern introduction.
Title transliterated: Taʾrīkh al-Qurʾān wa al-Tafsīr.

D45
WATT, W. Montgomery.
Bell's Introduction to the Qurʾān. Edinburgh, Edinburgh University Press, 1970. xi + 258 p.
Islamic Surveys 8.
A completely revised and enlarged edition of Richard Bell's *Introduction to the Qurʾān* (Edinburgh, 1953) which brings into account more modern interpretations with a less Christian bias. This edition includes the important table for converting the verse numbers in Gustav Flügel's edition of the Qurʾān and the official Egyptian edition. Included for the first time is a "Table of Sūras" providing for each *Sūra*: "(1) usual title in Arabic; (2) title in English; (3) the number of verses in the official Egyptian text, followed ... by the number in Flügel's text where the two differ; (4) the length as shown by the number of lines in Redslob's edition of Flügel's text...; (5) the initial letters where they occur...; and (6) the chronological order according to Muir, Nöldeke, Grimme and the official Egyptian text."
Professor Watt also includes a new English index to the Qurʾān which is of value as no complete index to the English translation has yet been compiled.

Companions

D46
---.
Companion to the Qurʾān Based On the Arberry Translation. London, George Allen and Unwin Ltd., 1967.

355 p.

Explanation of certain obscure passages of the Qurʾān *Sūra* by *Sūra* based upon Arthur J. Arberry's *The Koran Interpreted* (London, 1955). "Index to Proper Names in the Qurʾān," "Index to the Commentary."

Commentaries *(Tafsīr)*

From among the numerous commentaries upon the Qurʾān, both classical and modern, only the four major ones of the former are here listed, and only one of the latter, particularly because it is in a western language and is based upon the major earlier works representing a variety of schools of interpretation.

D47

al-BAYḌĀWĪ, ʿAbd Allāh ibn ʿUmar (d. 685?/1286?).

[The Gifts of the Revelation and the Secrets of the Interpretation]. انول التنزيل و اسرار التأويل Cairo, Al-Maṭbaʿa al-ʿĀmira, 1317-20/1899-1902. 6 vols.

Title transliterated: Anwāl al-Tanzīl wa Asrār al-Taʾwīl.

D48

al-RĀZĪ, Muḥammad ibn ʿUmar (d. 606/1210).

[Keys to the Hidden in the Great Commentary]. مفاتيح الغيب بالتفسير الكبير Cairo, Al-Maṭbaʿa al-Khayrīya, 1307/1889. 8 vols.

Index: Daud Rahbar, *Indices to the Verses of the Qurʾān in the Commentaries of al-Ṭabarī and al-Rāzī*. Hartford, Hartford Seminary Foundation, 1962. iv + 106 p.

Title transliterated: Mufātīḥ al-Ghayb bi-al-Tafsīr al-Kabīr.

D49

al-ṬABARĪ, Muḥammad ibn Jarīr (d. 310/923).

[Book of Comprehensive Clearness in the Interpretation of the Qurʾān]. من كتاب جامع البيان فى تفسير القرآن Cairo, Al-Maṭbaʿa al-Kubrā al-Amīrīya, 1323-29/1905-11. 30 vols. in 10.

Index: Daud Rahbar, *Indices to the Verses of*

the Qurɔān in the Commentaries of al-Ṭabarī and al-Rāzī. Hartford, Hartford Seminary Foundation, 1962. iv + 106 p.

Title transliterated: Min Kitāb Jāmiᶜ al-Bayān fī Tafsīr al-Qurɔān.

D50
al-ZAMAKHSHARĪ, Maḥmūd ibn ᶜUmar (d. 538/1144).

الكشاف عن حقائق التنزيل و عيون الاقاويل فى وجوه التاويل

[The Discoverer About the Truths of the Revelation and the Sources of Statements in the Intentions of the Interpretation]. Cairo, Al-Maṭbaᶜa al-Miṣrīya, 1281/1864. 2 vols.

Title transliterated: Al-Kashāf ᶜan Ḥaqāɔiq al-Tanzīl... .

D51
AYOUB, Mahmoud M.

The Qurɔān and Its Interpreters. Albany, State University of New York Press, 1984- [in progress].

"This volume is the first of a series that will cover the entire Qurɔān. I have long dreamed of a work in English that would present the Qurɔān to western readers and non-Arabic-speaking Muslims as Muslims have understood it throughout their long history. ... To ensure that the primary aim of this work is fulfilled, I have carefully chosen my sources so as to represent all the major trends in Islamic thought from the classical period to the present." *[Preface]*.

A verse by verse commentary based upon 13 Sunnī and Shīᶜite scholars.

Contents: Vol. I: *Suras* one and two, *i.e.*, al-Fātiḥah and al-Baqarah.

Dictionaries & Glossaries

General

D52
DIETERICI, Friedrich Heinrich.

Arabisch-deutsches Handwörterbuch zum Koran und Thier und Mensch vor dem König der genien. *2nd ed.* Leipzig, J. C. Hinrichs, 1894. iv + 183 p.

D53
EGYPT. Majma^c al-Lugha al- ^cArabīya.
[Dictionary of the Holy معجم الفاظ القرآن الكريم Qur>ān]. Cairo, Maṭba^ca al-Amirīya, 1953-70. 2 vols.

An Arabic-Arabic dictionary arranged by verbal root prepared and published by the Egyptian academy of the Arabic language.

Title transliterated: Mu^cjam al-Fāẓ al-Qur>ān al-Karīm.

D54
al-MIṢRĪ, ^cAbd al-Ra>ūf ibn Rizq Ismā^cīl.
معجم القرآن: و هو قاموس مفردات القرآن و غريب فيه تفسير، لغة، علم اجتماع، فلسفة اصول الكلمات و دلالاتها، و تاريخ الكتب السماوية و الاديان، و بعض الاعلام
[Dictionary of the Qur>ān: a lexicon of terms...]. Cairo, Maṭba^ca Ḥijāzī, 1327/1948. 2 vols.

An attempt to provide a comprehensive dictionary of the difficult and foreign words, history of the text, philosophy, etc.

Title transliterated: Mu^cjam al-Qur>ān:... .

D55
al-DIMĀSHQĪ, Muḥammad Munīr.
[The ارشاد الراغبين فى الكشف عن آى القرآن المبين Desired Guidance in the Illumination of the Verses of the Qur>ān]. Cairo, Idāra al-Tabā^ca al-Munīrīya, 1346/1928. 261 p.

Title transliterated: Irshād al-Rāghibīn fī al-Kashf ^can āy al-Qur>ān al-Mubīn.

D56
IBRĀHĪM, Muḥammad Ismā^cīl.
[Dictionary of Qur>ānic معجم الالفاظ و الاعلام القرآنية Terms and Proper Names]. *2nd ed.* Cairo, Dār al-Fikr al- ^cArabī, 1969. 2 vols. in 1.

First edition published in 1958.

Title transliterated: Mu^cjam al-Alfāẓ wa al-A^clām al-Qur>ānīya.

D57
MAKHLŪF, Ḥasanayn Muḥammad.

[The Words of the Qurʾān, كلمات القرآن، تفسير و بيان Explained and Clarified]. Cairo, Muṣṭafā al-Bābā al-Ḥalabī, 1965. 526 p.

Title transliterated: Kalimāt al-Qurʾān, Tafsīr wa Bayān.

D58
NAṢṢĀR, Ḥusayn.

معجم آيات القرآن، فهرس تفصيلى مرتب على حروف الهجاء.
[Dictionary of the Verses of the Qurʾān: a minutely organized index according to the words as spelled]. Cairo, Al-Bābā al-Ḥalabī, 1965. 279 p.

Title transliterated: Muʿjam Āyat al-Qurʿān:...

D59
NĀẒIM, Ṣāliḥ.

[Guide for the دليل الحيران فى الكشف عن آيات القرآن Perplexed in the Illumination of the Verses of the Qurʾān]. Cairo, Muḥammad ʿAlī Ṣabīḥ, 1965. 288 p.

First edition published in Istanbul, 1284/1867-68, as ترتيب زيبا.

Title transliterated: Dalīl al-Ḥayrān fī al-Kashf ʿan Āyāt al-Qurʾān.

D60
PENRICE, John.

A Dictionary and Glossary of the Kor-ân; with copious grammatical references and explanations of the text, Arabic-English. London, Henry S. King & Co., 1873. [iv] + 166 p. [dbl. col.].

A student's dictionary arranged by verbal root in the Arabic script and according to the Arabic alphabet. Provides the form of the word as employed in the Qurʾān. Based upon Gustav Flügel's edition. Two recent photographic reprints of the work have been issued in Great Britain and Lebanon.

D61
SHAH, Ahmed.

Miftah-ul-Quran: concordance & complete glossary of the Holy Qurʾān. Benares, E. J. Lazarus & Co., 1906. 2 vols.

Vol. I- Concordance. Gives the word in Arabic

script as it appears in the Qurʾān (*not* by verbal root), a Latin transliteration, the root of the word, and the *Sūra* (by number and title), the number of the verse, and the number of the *ruku*.

Vol. II- Glossary. Provides an alphabetical listing of all words employed in the Qurʾān with all forms from the same root listed together. Provides an English and Urdu translation for each.

Reprinted recently in Lahore without date.

Verse-endings

D62

KAZIM, Syed *and* ALI, Hashim Amir.

Rhythmic Verse-endings of the Qurʾan. Hyderabad-Deccan, N.P., 1969. 5 + 76 p.

This fascinating little volume, a true labor of love, was printed privately in a limited edition, probably 500 copies. It lists, in transliteration, the final rhyme word of each verse, totaling 6,236, of the Qurʾān according to the official Egyptian edition. Part I lists the verse endings by *sūra* and verse number; part II arranges the verse endings in alphabetical order according to the Arabic alphabet, with reference to *sūra* and verse.

The compilation of the work is of Syed Kazim alone. The cover of the volume (there is no title page) gives the publication date as 1969, whereas the introduction has the date January 1971.

Foreign Words

D63

ʿABD AL-BĀQĪ, Muḥammad Fuʾād.

معجم غريب القرآن: مستخرجا من صحيح البخارى و فيه ما ورد من ابن عباس من طريق ابن ابى طلحة خاصة

[Dictionary of Foreign Words in the Qurʾān: elucidations from the *Ṣaḥīḥ* of al-Bukhārī and interpretations of what Ibn ʿAbbās gave to Ibn abī Ṭalḥa Khāṣa]. [Cairo?], Dār Ahyaʾi al-Kutub al-ʿArabīya, [1950?]. XXV + 296 p.

Title transliterated: Muʿjam Gharīb al-Qurʾān...

D64

JEFFERY, Arthur.

The Foreign Vocabulary of the Qurᵓān. Baroda, Oriental Institute, 1938. XV + 311 p.

Gaekwad's Oriental Series, No. LXXIX.

An examination of what are to be believed are the non-Arabic loan words listed in alphabetical order according to, and in, the Arabic script, with transliteration, translation, *sūra* and verse, and detailed discussion.

D65
al-SUYŪTĪ, ᶜAbd al-Raḥmān ibn abī Bakr (d. 910/1505).
المتوكلى فيما ورد فى القرآن باللغة الحبشيسة و الفارسية و الهندية و التركية و الزنجية و النبطية و السريانية و العبرانية و الرومية و البر بريـــة
[The Reliant Regarding What Appears in the Qurᵓān of the Abyssinian, Persian, Hindu, Turkish, African, Nabatean, Syriac, Hebrew, Latin, and Berber Languages]. Damascus, Maktaba al-Qudsī wa al-Badīr, 1348/1929-30. 20 p.

The first 13 pages consist of a list of foreign words in the Qurᵓān and on pages 14-20 are original meanings of some of the Arabic words.

Translation: William Y. Bell, *The Mutawakkili of as-Suyuti, a translation of the Arabic text with introduction, notes, and indices.* Cairo, Printed at the Nile Mission Press, 1926. 71 p.

Title transliterated: Al-Mutawakkilī fīmā Warada fī al-Qurᵓān bi-al-Lugha...

D66
---.
[The Teacher المهذب فيما وقع فى القرآن من المعرب Regarding What Occurs in the Qurᵓān from the Non-Arabic]. *Ed.* Al-Tihāmī al-Rājī al-Hāshimī. N.P., N.D. 275 p.

Includes index.

Title transliterated: Al-Muhadhdhib fīmā Waqaᶜ fī al-Qurᵓān min al-Muᶜarrab.

Unusual Words

D67
al-DAMAGHĀNĪ, al-Ḥusayn ibn Muḥammad.
[Explanation اصلاح الوجوه و النظائر فى القرآن الكريم

of the Semblence and the Similar in the Holy Qur-ān]. *Ed.* ᶜAbd al-ᶜAzīz Sayyid al-Ahl. Beirut, Dār al-ᶜIlm li-l-Malāyīn, 1970. 512 p.

Dictionary of the unusual words in the Qur-ān listed by root with the phrase in which each appears followed by explanation and other usages.

Title transliterated: Iṣlāḥ al-Wujūh wa al-Naẓā-ir fī al-Qur-ān al-Karīm.

D68
al-HARAWĪ, Aḥmad ibn Muḥammad (d. 402/1011).

كتاب الغريبين، غريبى القرآن و الحديث [Book of the Two Obscure: unusual (words) in the Qur-ān and the Traditions]. *Ed.* Maḥmūd Muḥammad al-Ṭabāhī. Cairo, N.P., 1970- [all published?].

Al-Majlis al-Aᶜlā li-l-Shuᶜūn al-Islamīya.

Author occasionally listed under his *kunya* - Abū ᶜUbayd al-Harawī.

Dictionary of difficult words found in the Qur-ān and the major collections of traditions.

Title transliterated: Kitāb al-Gharībayn, ...

D69
al-IṢFAHĀNĪ, al-Ḥusayn ibn Muḥammad (d. 502/1108-9).

المفردات فى غريب القرآن [Unusual Words in the Qur-ān]. *Ed.* Muḥammad Sayyid Kīlānī. Cairo, Muṣṭafī al-Bābī al-Ḥalabī, 1961. 556 p.

Translation [Urdu]: Muḥammad ᶜAbdu al-Falāḥ al-Fīrūzpūrī. Lahore, Al-Maktaba al-Qāsimī, 1963. 1040 p.

Title transliterated: Al-Mufradāt fī Gharīb al-Qur-ān.

D70
al-MIṢRĪ, Muḥammad.

تفسير غريب القرآن، المعروف بقاموس اوضح التبيان فى حل الفاظ القرآن [Explanation of the Unusual (Words) of the Qur-ān]. Cairo, Maktaba al-Hillāl, 1934. 127 p.

Title transliterated: Tafsīr Gharīb al-Qur-ān.

D71
QAMḤAWĪ, Muḥammad al-Ṣādiq.

[Lexicon of Strange Words in the قاموس غريب القرآن Qurʾān]. Cairo, Maktaba wa Maṭbaʿa Muḥammad ʿAlī Ṣabīḥ, 1970. 217 + [xxi] p.

Title transliterated: Qāmūs Gharīb al-Qurʾān.

Military Terms

D72

KHAṬṬĀB, Maḥmūd Shīt.

[Military Technical Terms in the Holy Qurʾān]. المصطلحات العسكرية في القرآن الكريم Beirut, Dār al-Fatah al-Ṭabaʿ wa al-Nashr, 1966-67. 2 vols.

Title transliterated: Al-Muṣṭalaḥāt al-ʿAskarīya fī al-Qurʾān al-Karīm.

Indices & Concordances

Arabic

D73

ʿABD AL-BĀQĪ, Muḥammad Fuʾād.

[Index to the Holy Qurʾān]. المعجم المفهرس لالفاظ القرآن الكريم Cairo, Maṭbaʿa Dār al-Kutub al-Miṣrīya, 1364/1945. xiii + 782 p. [dbl. col.].

Concordance to the "official" Egyptian edition arranged by verbal root. Each word in the Qurʾān is listed under the root as it appears, with full vowel markings, together with the phrase or sentence in which it appears, the number of the verse, and the name and number of the *sūra*. This is generally regarded as the best concordance yet produced.

Title transliterated: Al-Muʿjam al-Mufharis li-al-Fāẓ al-Qurʾān al-Karīm.

D74

al-ANṢĀRĪ, Ibrāhīm ibn ʿAbd Allāh.

[Guidance for the Perplexed to the Knowledge of the Verses of the Qurʾān]. ارشاد الحيران لمعرفة آى القرآن [Doha, Qatar], N.P., N.D.

Title transliterated: Irshād al-Ḥayrān li-Maʿrifa Āy al-Qurʾān.

D75

BARAKĀT, Muḥammad Fāris.

[Correct Path المرشد الى آيات القرآن الكريم و كلماته to the Verses of the Holy Qurʾān and Its Words]. Damascus, Al-Maktaba al-Ḥāshimīya, 1358/1939. 11 + 653 p.

Title transliterated: Al-Murshid ila Āyāt al-Qurʾān al-Karīm wa Kalimātahu.

D76
FLÜGEL, Gustav.

Concordantiae Corani arabicae: ad litterarum ordinem et verborum radices diligenter disposuit. Leipzig, C. Tauchnit, 1842. XII + 219 p.

Based upon his edition of the Qurʾān, first printed in 1834, whose verse numberings do not coincide with the "official" Egyptian edition.

Concordance to all the words, including personal pronouns, in the Qurʾān according to the verbal root. The name and number of the *sūra* and the number of the verse is provided in which that form of the word appears, but, unlike ʿAbd al-Bāqī's concordance, does not give the relevant phrase or sentence in which it occurs to provide context.

The work has been reprinted numerous times, the last in 1965.

D77
NUKHĀBĪ, Ibrāhīm Sūrī.

[Index to the Verses of the Qurʾān]. كشف آيات القرآن Cairo, Dār Iḥyāʾ al-Kutub al-ʿArabīya, 1920. 416 p.

Title transliterated: Kashf Āyāt al-Qurʾān.

D78
al-SHĀFIʿĪ, Ḥusayn Muḥammad Fahmī.

[The Perfect Guide الدليل الكامل لأيات القرآن الكريم to the Verses of the Holy Qurʾān]. Cairo, Al-Majlis al-Aʿilī li-al-Shuʾūn al-Islāmīya, 1972. 15 + 475 p.

Title transliterated: Al-Dalīl al-Kāmil li-Āyāt al-Qurʾān al-Karīm.

¶ The first volume of Ahmad Shah's *Miftah-ul-Quran* [D61] is a concordance to each word in the Qurʾān as it appears rather than by verbal root.

English

D79
KASSIS, Hanna E.
A Concordance of the Qurʾan. Berkeley, University of California Press, 1984. 1486 p.

An index and a concordance in two parts, each divided into two parts - "The Divine Name" and "The Remaining Vocabulary." Based upon Arthur Arberry's translation, *The Koran Interpreted*, the words are listed in Arabic alphabetical order, in transliteration, by root and are then provided with an indication as to part of speech, and English translation, the verse and *sūra* in which each appears, and the translation of the line(s) in which each is used.

D80
KHERIE, Al-Haj Khan Bahadur Altaf Ahmad.
A Key to the Holy Quran: index-cum-concordance for the Holy Quran. Karachi, The Holy Quran Society of Pakistan, 1974- [in progress?].

To be completed in two volumes.

Index in English, according to Abullah Yusuf Ali's edition and English translation, of the Qurʾān whereby all verses have been keyed to practical religious and sociological-juridical subjects.

Contents: Part I: Biblical Equivalents of Proper Names; List of *Sīpāras* (parts) of the Holy Qurān; List of *Sūras* (chapters) of the Holy Qurān, in Serial Order; *Sūras* Arranged in Chronological Order; Table Showing the Numbers of the *Āyat* in each *Rukūʿ* of the Various *Sūras*; List of Verses on Recital Whereof Prostration is Required; Abbreviated Letters (*Muqaṭṭaʿt*). Part II: 1. Allah; 2. Angels; 3. Allah's Books; 4. Prophets and Apostles Other Than the Holy Prophet; 5. The Holy Prophet; 6. The Hereafter; 7. Divine Worship; 8. Commandments and Prohibitions; 9. The Good; 10. The Bad; 11. Man and the Universe; 12. Certain Persons, Peoples, Places, etc.; General Index.

Each chapter is subdivided into sections by subject with *sūra* and *āyat* numbers and either a partial translation or paraphrasing of the verse provided.

D81

PEERMAHOMED EBRAHIM TRUST.

Subjectwise Index of English Quran. Karachi, Peermahomed Ebrahim Trust, 1393/1973. iii + 152 p.

Alphabetically arranged with the verse numberings based upon the translation made by Janab S. V. Mir Ahmad Ali Sahib.

¶ W. Montgomery Watt has included an index to the English translation in his *Bell's Introduction to the Qurʾān* [D45] although he does not state whose translation he has used.

Urdu

D82

MUẒHAR AL-DĪN MULTĀNĪ, Muḥammad.

مفتاح القرآن : مشتمل بر حوالجات جمل الفاظ قرآن/

Mifta-ul-Qurʾan: concordance of the Holy Qurʾan. Lahore, Daftar Bayt al-Qurʾān, 1970. 524, 112 + 2 p.

A concordance in Urdu based upon the Urdu translation.

Title transliterated: Miftāḥ al-Qurʾān:...

Biographies

Personalities

D83

ᶜUMAYRA, ᶜAbd al-Raḥmān.

[Men Referred to by God in the Qurʾān]. رجال آنزل الله فيهم قرآنا Riyad, Dār al-Liwāʾ li-Nashr wa al-Tawzīᶜ, 1976-.

Multi-volumed biographical dictionary of individuals and peoples mentioned in the Qurʾān.

Title transliterated: Rijāl Anzal Allāh fīhim Qurʾānan.

Commentators (Mufassirīn)

D84

al-DĀWŪDĪ, Muḥammad ibn ᶜAlī (d. 945/1538).

[Classes of the Commentators]. طبقات المفسرين *Ed.* ᶜAlī Muḥammad ᶜUmar. Cairo, Maktaba Wahba, 1972. 2 vols.

Title transliterated: Ṭabaqāt al-Mufassirīn.

D85
al-SUYŪṬĪ, ᶜAbd al-Raḥmān ibn abī Bakr (d. 911/1505).
[Book of the Classes of the Commentators]. كتاب طبقاط المفسرين *Ed.* A. Meursinge, *Specimen e Litteris orientalibus, exhibens Sojutií* Librum de Interpretibus Korani,... . Leiden, S. & J. Luchtmans, 1839. 2 vols.

Title transliterated: Kitāb Ṭabaqāt al-Mufassirīn.

Memorizers (Ḥuffāẓ)

D86
al-DHAHABĪ, Muḥammad ibn ᶜUthmān (d. 748/1348).
[Reminder of the Memorizers]. تذكرة الحفّاظ Hyderabad-Deccan, Dā᾿ira al-Maᶜārif al-Niẓāmīya, 1333/1914. 4 vols. in 2.

Biographical dictionary arranged by decades.

Title transliterated: Tadhkira al-Ḥuffāẓ.

Appendices & continuations:

The following appendices to this work were edited, with notes and indices, by Muḥammad Zāhid al-Kawtharī, ذيل تذكرة الحفّاظ الخ. Damascus, Maṭbaᶜa Ḥasām al-Dīn al-Qudsī, 1347/1928. iii + 454 p.:

1. Muḥammad ibn ᶜAlī al-Ḥusaynī (d. 765/1364), (pp. 11-67), التنبيه و الايقاظ في ذيل تذكرة الحفّاظ
2. Muḥammad ibn Muḥammad ibn Fahd al-Makkī (d. 871/1466), (pp. 69-344), لحظ اللاحظ بذيل طبقات الحفّاظ
3. ᶜAbd al-Raḥmān ibn abī Bakr al-Suyūṭī (d. 911/1505), (pp. 345-82), ذيل طبقات الحفّاظ

Al-Suyūṭī's abridgement and continuation was previously published by Ferdinand Wüstenfeld, *Liber classium virorum qui Korani et Traditienem cognitione ercelluerunt...* (Gottingen, 1833-34).

Another modern scholar, Aḥmad Rāfī al-Ṭahṭāwī, published his own corrections and additions to al-Dhahabī under the title, التنبيه و الايقاظ لما فى ذيول تذكرة الحفّاظ Damascus, Maṭbaᶜa al-Qudsī, 1348/1929. ii + 166 p.

Reciters (Mashhūrīn)

D87
IBN AL-JAZARĪ, Muḥammad ibn Muḥammad (d. 833/1429).

[Book of the Ultimate End in the Classes of the Reciters] كتاب غاية النهاية فى طبقات القرّاء. *Ed.* Gotthelf Bergsträsser *and* Otto Pretzl, *Das biographische Lexikon der Koranlehrer*. Cairo, Maṭbaᶜa al-Saᶜāda, 1933-37. 4 vols.

Bibliotheca Islamica, VIII.

Biographical dictionary of the noted Qurᵓānic memorizers and reciters to *cir.* 1400, in continuation of al-Dhahabī's طبقات القرّاء المشهورين.

First part edited by Bersträsser, second part and indices (in volume four) edited and prepared by Pretzl. Photographic reprint by Maktaba al-Muthanna (Baghdad, 1973).

Title transliterated: Kitāb Ghāya al-Nihāha fī Ṭabaqāt al-Qurrāᵓ.

PHILOSOPHY

Bibliographies

D88

MENASCE, P. J. de.

Arabische Philosophie, *in* I. M. Bochenski, *ed.*, *Bibliographische Einführungen in das Studium der Philosophie*, No. 6. 49 p. Bern, A. Francke AG. Verlag, 1948.

A very detailed classified listing of books and articles. Index of names.

Dissertations

D89

ANN ARBOR. University Microfilms International.

Philosophy, Religion and Theology: a catalogue of current doctoral dissertation research. Ann Arbor, University Microfilms International, 1983. iv + 39 p. [dbl. col.].

Listing by topic of more than 2,000 doctoral dissertations and masters' theses completed between 1978 and 1983 submitted to U.S. and Canadian universities.

See esp: Islamic and Jewish Philosophy, p. 25.

Dictionaries

D90

AFNAN, Soheil Muhsin.

A Phil- واژنامهٔ فلسفی / قاموس فلسفي فارسي – عربي / osophical Lexicon in Persian and Arabic. Beirut, Dār al-Mashriq, 1969. 332 p.

With introductions in Farsi and English.

Title transliterated: Vāzha-nāma-yi Falsafī/ Qāmūs Falsafī Fārsī - ᶜArabī.

D91

SHEIKH, M. Saeed.

A Dictionary of Muslim Philosophy. Lahore, Institute of Islamic Culture, 1970. vii + 146 p.

Dictionary of Arabic philosophical terms with English equivalents and explanations.

MUḤAMMAD

Bibliographies

D92

PĀNĪPATĪ, Shaykh Mubārak Maḥmūd.

[Biographies of the Prophet]. سيرت رسول Lahore, National Book Centre of Pakistan, 1973. 52 p.

Author listing of Urdu books, including translations into that language, published in Pakistan between 1947 and 1972. Author and title index.

Title transliterated: Sīrat Rasūl.

D93

SHĀH, Iftikhār Ḥusayn.

Armughan-e-Haq: ارمغان حق : ١٤٠٠هـ· كتب سيرت (an annotated bibliography of books about the life of the Holy Prophet). Multan, Bahaɔ al-Dīn Zakarīya Ūnīwursitī, 1981. 2 vols.

Annotated listing by language of 2,713 biographies of the Prophet in celebration of the fourteenth millennium of Islām. Those in languages of the sub-continent are listed first. This is probably a fairly complete list. Those in western languages are to be found at the end of the second volume, which is less complete. In most instances full bibliographical information is provided. Unfortunately, there is no index of authors.

The English title is provided only on the paper wrappers.

Biographies of the Companions

D94
al-ᶜASQALĀNĪ, Aḥmad ibn ᶜAlī ibn Ḥajar (d. 852/1449).
[Acuteness of Mind in the الاصابة فى تمييز الاصحابة Distinction of the Companions]. Cairo, Maṭbaᶜa Muṣṭafā Muḥammad, 1358/1939-40. 4 vols.

An extensive biographical dictionary of persons who knew Muḥammad. Printed together with a biographical dictionary of Muḥammad's Companions by Yūsuf ibn ᶜAbd Allāh ibn ᶜAbd al-Barr al-Qurṭubī (d. 463/1071), كتاب استيعاب فى اسماء الاصحاب. Al-Asqalānī's dictionary occupies the top half of the page and al-Qurṭubī's the bottom half.

The *Iṣāba* was first published in parts by the Asiatic Society of Bengal in its *Bibliotheca Indica, XX*, 1856-93. Another edition, with al-Qurṭubī's *Istīᶜāb* on the margins, was printed in Cairo in 1328/1910 in four volumes.

Title transliterated: Al-Iṣāba fī Tamyīz al-Aṣḥāba.

D95
al-DHAHABĪ, Muḥammad ibn ᶜUthmān (d. 748/1348).
[The Successful in الاصابة فى تجريد اسماء الصحابة Uncovering the Names of the Companions]. Bombay, Sharaf al-Dīn al-Kutubī, 1969- .

In alphabetical order.

Title transliterated: Iṣāba fī Tajrīd Asmāᵓ al-Ṣaḥāba.

D96
---.
[The Confusion المشتبه فى الرجال : اسمائهم و انسابهم Among the Companions: their names and their nisbas]. *Ed.* ᶜAlī Muḥammad al-Bajāwī. Cairo, ᶜĪsā al-Bābī al-Ḥalabī, 1962. 2 vols.

Previously edited by P. de Jong, *Al-Moschtabih* ... (Leiden, 1863-81).

Title transliterated: Al-Mushtabih fī al-Rijāl:.

D97
IBN AL-ATHĪR, ᶜAlī ibn Muḥammad (d. 630/1233).
[Lions of the Thicket اسد الغابة فى معرفة الصحابة in the Knowledge of the Companions]. Bulaq,

1285-87/1869-71. 5 vols.

A compendium from earlier biographical dictionaries of the Companions.

Title transliterated: Usd al-Ghaba fī Maᶜrifa al-Ṣaḥāba.

D98

al-NAWAWĪ, Yaḥyā ibn Sharaf (d. 676/1277).

[Book of Education of the Names]. كتاب تهذيب الاسماء. *Ed.* Ferdinand Wüstenfeld, *The Biographical Dictionary of Illustrious Men, chiefly at the beginning of Islamism.* Göttinggen, Printed for the London Society for the Publication of Oriental Texts, 1842-47. 878 p.

Includes only the first part of the text.

Title transliterated: Kitāb Tahdhīb al-Asmāʾ.

¶ Additional sources for the biographies of the Companions are the *Kitāb Ṭabaqāt al-Kabīr* by Ibn Saᶜd [D145] and Ibn Khayyaṭ's *Ṭabaqāt* [D144]. Ibn Qunfudh [D152] prepared a book of the death dates of the Companions and the tradionists.

TRADITIONS

Bibliographies

D99

DENFFER, Ahmad von.

Literature on Hadith in European Languages: a bibliography. Leicester, The Islamic Foundation, 1981. 94 p.

Simple author listing of 559 books, articles, and essays primarily in English, French, and German. Subject index.

Guides & Handbooks

D100

AZAMI, Muhammad Mustafa.

Studies in Hadīth Methodology and Literature. Indianapolis, American Trust Publications, 1977. iii + 122 p.

An introduction to the very important study of the traditions by the Professor of Science of Hadith, University of Riyadh, Saudi Arabia.

D101
al-KHAWLĪ, Muḥammad ᶜAbd al-ᶜAzīz
[Key to the Sunna, مفتاح السنة او تاريخ فنون الحديث or a History of the Science of the Traditions]. Cairo, Maṭbaᶜa al-Manār, 1339/1921. viii + 173 p.
Title transliterated: Miftāḥ al-Sunna aw Taᵓrīkh Funūn al-Ḥadīth.

D102
SIDDIQI, Muhammad Zubayr.
Hadīth Literature: its origin, development, special features and criticism. Calcutta, Calcutta University Press, 1961. xxviii + 211 p., illus.
"This little book has been composed in order to present to the English-reading public, Muslim as well as non-Muslim, the viewpoint of orthodox Islām with regard to Ḥadīth literature, its origin and development, and its criticism by the Muslim doctors." *[Preface]*.

Collections

Sunnī

"The Six Books"

D103
ABŪ DAᵓŪD, Sulaymān ibn al-Ashᶜath (d. 275/888).
[The Path of Abū Daᵓūd]. سنن ابو داود
Ed. Aḥmad Saᶜd ᶜAlī. Cairo, Muṣṭafā al-Bābī al-Ḥalabī, 1952. 2 vols.
Arranged by legal subject with approximately 4,800 traditions. See Addenda.
Title transliterated: Sunan Abū Daᵓūd.

D104
al-BUKHĀRĪ, Muḥammad ibn Ismāᶜīl (d. 256/870).
[The Truth of Ibn ᶜAbd Allāh al-Bukhārī]. صحيح ابو عبد الله البخارى Cairo, Al-Maṭbaᶜa al-Bahīya al-Miṣrīya, 1933-62. 25 vols.
Title transliterated: Ṣaḥīh Abī ᶜAbd Allāh al-Bukhārī.
Translations:
1. O. Houdas *and* W. Marçais. *El-Bokhari. Les Traditions islamiques, traduites de l'Arab*

avec notes et index. Paris, Imprimerie Nationale, 1903-14. 4 vols. The index to the Arabic text by Krehl and Juynboll and the above French translation was published by Oskar Rescher. *Sachindex zu Bokhari, nach der Ausgabe Krehl-Juynboll (Leiden, 1862-1908) und der Übersetzung von Houdas-Marçais (Paris, 1903-1914)*. Stuttgart, N.P., 1923. iii + 52 p.

2. Muḥammad Muḥsin Khān. *The Translation of the Meanings of Saḥīḥ al-Bukhārī. 3rd rev. ed.* Chicago, Kazi Publications, 1976. 9 vols. Provides the Arabic text with English translation in parallel columns.

D105
IBN MĀJA, Muḥammad ibn Yazīd (d. 273/887).
[The Path]. السنن
Ed. Muḥammad Fuʾād ʿAbd al-Bāqī. Cairo, Dār Iḥyāʾ al-Kutub al-ʿArabīya, 1952-53. 2 vols.

The last of the six canonical collections containing about 4,000 traditions in 150 chapters.

Title transliterated: Al-Sunan.

D106
MUSLIM IBN AL-ḤAJJĀJ (d. 261/875).
[The Truth of Muslim]. الصحيح مسلم
Cairo, Maktaba wa Maṭbaʿa Muḥammad ʿAlī Ṣabīh wa Awladahu, 1963. 8 vols.

Collection of 3,033 traditions divided into 52 books without further subdivision into chapters.

Title transliterated: Al-Ṣaḥīḥ Muslim.

Translation: ʿAbdul Ḥamid Ṣiddiqī. *Ṣaḥīh Muslim: being traditions of the sayings and doings of the Prophet Muhammad as narrated by his companions and compiled under the title* al-Jāmiʿ-uṣ-Ṣaḥīh, *by Imām Muslim*. Lahore, Sh. Muhammad Ashraf, 1971-75. 4 vols.

D107
al-NASĀʾĪ, Aḥmad ibn Shuʿayb (d. 303/915).
[Book of the Great Path]. كتاب السنن الكبر
Cairo, Al-Maṭbaʿa al-Maymunīya, 1312/1894. 2 vols.

Printed together with al-Suyūṭī's زهر الربا، a commentary upon the collection.

A new edition, by ʿAbd al-Samad Sharaf al-Dīn,

has been printed in Bhiwandi, India, by al-Dār al-Qayyama, 1972.
Title transliterated: Kitāb al-Sunan al-Kubrā.

D108
al-TIRMIDHĪ, Muḥammad ibn ᶜĪsā (d. *cir.* 279/892-93).
[The Comprehensive of the Truth]. جامع الصحيح
Bulaq, 1292/1875. 2 vols.
Title transliterated: Jāmiᶜ al-Ṣaḥīh.

Additional Collections of Importance

D109
al-ᶜASQALĀNĪ, Aḥmad ibn ᶜAlī (d. 852/1449).
[The Highest Authority in Increasing the Eight Authorities]. المطالب العالية بزوائد المسانيد الثمانية
Ed. Ḥabīb al-Raḥmān al-Aᶜzamī. Cairo, Wizāra al-Awqāf wa al-Shuᵓūn al-Islāmīya, 1973. 4 vols.
Collection of an additional 4,702 traditions not found in the Six Books or in Mālik ibn Anas or Ibn Ḥanbal.
Title transliterated: Al-Muṭālib al-ᶜĀlīya bi-Zawāᵓid al-Musānīd al-Thamānīya.

D110
al-DĀRIMĪ, ᶜAbd Allāh ibn ᶜAbd al-Raḥmān (d. 255/869).
[The Collected Traditions]. المسند الجامع
Ed. Muḥammad ᶜAbd al-Rashīd Kashmīrī. Cawnpore, (litho.), 1293/1876. x, xx + 447 p.
Although not regarded as one of the Six Books this is held in high esteem. Arranged by subject.
Title transliterated: Al-Musnad al-Jāmiᶜ

D111
IBN ḤANBAL, Aḥmad ibn Muḥammad (d. 241/855).
[The Authority]. المسند
Cairo, Dār al-Maᶜārif, 1955-57. 7 vols.
Title transliterated: Al-Musnad.

D112
MĀLIK IBN ANAS IBN MĀLIK (d. 179/795).
[The Footsteps of Imām Mālik]. الموطئ الامام مالك
Ed. Muḥammad Fuᵓād ᶜAbd al-Bāqī. Cairo, Dār Iḥyāᵓ al-Turāth al-ᶜArabī, 1951. 2 vols.
Title transliterated: Al-Muwāṭṭaᵓ Imām Mālik.

Translation: ᶜAʾisha ᶜAbdarahman al-Tarjumana *and* Yaᶜqub Johnson. *Al-Muwatta Imam Malik*. Norwich, Diwan Press, 1982. xlix + 549 p. [dbl. col.] English translation with glossary and index.

D113
al-SUYŪṬĪ, ᶜAbd al-Raḥmān ibn abī Bakr (d. 911/1505). [The Collection جمع الجوامع، المعروف بالجامع الكبير of the Collections, the Knowledge of the Great Comprehensive (Collections)]. Cairo, Majmaᶜ al-Buḥūth al-Islāmīya, 1970-78. 3 vols.

Alphabetical compilation by text word or transmitter's name of about 100,000 traditions found in all of the recognized collections. Edited by a committee of scholars under the auspices of the Academy of Islamic Research.

Title transliterated: Jamᶜ al-Jawāmiᶜ,...

D114
al-ṬAYĀLISĪ, Sulaymān ibn Daʾūd (d. 203/818-19). [Traditions of Abī Daʾūd al-Ṭayālisī] مسند ابى داود الطيالسى. Hyderabad/Deccan, Maṭbaᶜ Majlis Dāʾira al-Maᶜārif al-Niẓāmīya, 1321/1904. 392, 2, 11 p.

Contains 2,767 traditions over the entire field.

Title transliterated: Musnad Abī Daʾūd al-Ṭayālisī.

D115
al-TIBRĪZĪ, Muḥammad ibn ᶜAbd Allāh (d. 737/1337). [Niche for the Lamp]. مشكاة المصابيح *Ed.* Muḥammad Muᶜaẓẓam *and* Abū Muḥammad ᶜAbd al-Wahhāb. Delhi, (litho.), 1307/1890. viii + 576 p.

A revision, with additions of مصابيح السنة by Al-Ḥusayn al-Baghawī (d. 516/1122) which was a collection of 4,719 traditions, largely from al-Bukhārī and Abū Muslim, with others, from which the chains of authority were omitted, to serve as a guide to the Muslims. Al-Tibrīzī's revision, completed in 737/1336-37, added 1,511.

Title transliterated: Mishkāt al-Maṣābīḥ.

Translations: James Robson. Mishkat al-Masabih, *English translation with explanatory notes*. Lahore, Sh. Muhammad Ashraf, 1975. 2 vols. The purpose of the translation has been to provide in English a very popular work among Muslims.

In addition to the explanatory notes Professor Robson has also provided biographical notices of persons mentioned or quoted in the text. An earlier English translation was made by A. N. Mathews, *Mishcàt-ul-Maṣábìḥ, or a collection of the most authentic traditions,...*, Calcutta, 1809. 2 vols.

Shīᶜī

"The Four Books"

D116
IBN BĀBAWAYH, Muḥammad ibn ᶜAlī (d. 381/991).
[Book of the Hopeful Sign for the Learned]. *Ed.* Muḥammad ᶜAlī al-Kashānī. Tehran (litho.), 1300/1883. v + 402 p. كتاب امالي علامة العلماء
The second in point of time of the major collections reportedly containing 9,044 traditions. The compiler is often termed "Shaykh-i Ṣadūq".
Title transliterated: Kitāb Amālī ᶜAlāma al-ᶜUlamāᵓ.

D117
al-KULĪNĪ, Muḥammad ibn Yaᶜqūb (d. 329/941).
[The Sufficiency in Faith]. Tehran (litho.), 1281/1864. 494 p. الكافي في الدين
The author, whose name contemporary Shīᶜite authors transliterate as "al-Kulaynī", was a Shīᶜite jurist of Baghdad who first collected and organized the Shīᶜite traditions. The work is said to contain 16,099 *ḥadīth* and has been reprinted numerous times. Khānbābā Mushār gives it the title الكافي الفقه.
Title transliterated: Al-Kāfī fī al-Dīn.

D118
al-ṬŪSĪ, Muḥammad ibn al-Ḥasan (d. 460/1068).
[Emendation of the Ordinances]. Tehran, N.P., 1316-17/1898-1900. 2 vols. تهذيب الاحكام
Reportedly contains 13,590 traditions.
Title transliterated: Tahdhīb al-Aḥkām.

D119
---.
[Book of Inves- كتاب الاستبصار فيما اختلف من الاخبار

tigation in the Diversity of the News]. Lucknow, (litho.), 1307/1890. 3 vols.

The fourth of the standard collections which is a shortened version of the *Tahdhīb*, particularly eliminating those which appear to be discrepant. Reportedly contains 5,511 traditions. Lithographed and printed many times.

Title transliterated: Kitāb al-Istibṣār fīmā Ikhtalaf min al-Akhbār.

Later Collections

D120
FAYD KĀSHANĪ, Muḥammad ibn Murtaḍā (d. 1091/1680).
[The Complete]. الوافى
Tehran, (litho.), 1310-14/1892-97. 2 vols.

Compendium of the traditions found in the four major collections, eliminating the duplications, with explication of the more difficult texts. Khānbābā Mushār lists four additional printings.
Alternate title: كتاب الجامع الوافى

Title transliterated: Al-Wāfī.

D121
al-ḤURR AL-ᶜĀMILĪ, Muḥammad ibn al-Ḥasan (d. 1104/-1692-93).
تفصيل وسائل الشيعة الى تحصيل الشريعة
[The Detailed Shīᶜite Instrument to Studying the Issues of the Law]. Tehran, (litho.), 1323-24/1905-7. 3 vols.

Combines the traditions of the four classical texts, with additional material from Sunnī collections. The work has been reprinted, latterly in 1956.

Title transliterated: Tafṣīl Wasā'il al-Shīᶜa..

D122
al-MAJLISĪ, Muḥammad Bāqir ibn Muḥammad Taqī (d. 1110-11/1698-1700).
[Oceans of Brightness]. بحار الانوار
Tehran, Matābiᶜ Mukhtalifa, 1301-10/1883-97. 25 vols.

The encyclopaedic collection of both Shīᶜite and Sunnī traditions by one of Shīᶜisms greatest scholars, left, however, incomplete by his death.

Title transliterated: Biḥār al-Anwār.

"Sayings of ᶜAlī"

D123
al-RAḌĪ, Muḥammad ibn al-Ḥusayn (d. 406/1015).
[Peak of Eloquence]. نهج البلاغة
Tabriz, (litho.), 1267/1851. 306 p.

The Sharīf al-Raḍī, whose father's name is given variously, was a descendant on both sides from ᶜAlī ibn abī Ṭālib and lived in Baghdad where he received his education. The *Nahj al-Balāgha* is a compilation, from diverse sources, of 245 *khutbas*, or sermons, of various lengths, 79 letters, and 208 sayings attributed to the fourth Caliph and first Imām of the Shīᶜites. The book has been lithographed and printed innumerable times and has had many commentaries written upon it.

Title transliterated: Nahj al-Balāgha.

Translations: Maulana Syed Mohammed Askari Jafery, *Nahjul Balagha of Hazrat Ali*, Hyderabad-Deccan, Seerat-uz-Zahra Committee, 1965. vi, [ii] + 560 p. The English translation contains four appendices of information regarding the sources of the book. This edition has been reprinted in Poona, India, and again in Tehran.

The Ministry of Islamic Guidance of the Government of Iran has reprinted from the translation, *Hazrat Ali's Letters and Sayings from the Nahj ul-Balagha (Peaks of Eloquence)* (Tehran, 1981. viii + 151 p.).

Continuations: Muḥammad Bāqir al-Maḥmūdī, [The Road of نهج السعادة فى مستدرك نهج البلاغة Happiness in Completion of the Peak of Eloquence]. Najaf, Maṭbaᶜa al-Nuᶜmān, 1965-73. 5 vols. A modern compilation.

Dictionaries

D124
IBN AL-ATHĪR, Al-Mubārak ibn Muḥammad (d. 606/1210).
[The Ultimate in النهاية فى غريب الحديث و الاثر Comprehending the Uncommon in the Narrative and the Tradition]. *Ed.* Ṭāhir Aḥmad al-Ẓawī *and* Maḥmūd Muḥammad al-Tanāhī. Cairo, ᶜĪsā al-Bābī al-Ḥalabī,

1963-66. 5 vols.

A dictionary of the less common words and unusual meanings in the prophetic traditions, in alphabetical order. Index.

Previously published in Tehran (1269/1852) and Cairo (1322/1904).

Title transliterated: Al-Nihāya fī Gharīb al-Ḥadīth wa al-Athar.

D125
al-ZAMAKHSHARĪ, Maḥmūd ibn ᶜUmar (d. 538/1144).
[The Superior Book كتاب الفائق فى غريب الحديث upon the Uncommon (Terms) in the Traditions]. *Ed.* Muḥammad al-Bajārī *and* Muḥammad abī al-Faḍl Ibrāhīm. Cairo, Dār Ihyāᵓ al-Kutub al- ᶜArabīya, 1364/1945. 2 vols.

Al-Zamakhsharī, an Arab born in Persia, was a noted grammarian and lexicographer. His is a dictionary of the peculiarities found in the language employed in the *ḥadīth* literature.

An earlier edition was published by the Majlis Dāᵓira al-Maᶜārif al-Niẓāmīya, Hyderabad-Deccan, 1324/1906, in two volumes (in 1).

Title transliterated: Kitāb al-Fāᵓiq fī Gharīb al-Ḥadīth.

¶ Another dictionary of obscure and difficult words in the traditions is that of Abū ᶜUbayd al-Harāwī [D68].

Indices & Concordances

Sunnī

D126
ᶜABD AL-BĀQĪ, Muḥammad Fuᵓād.
تيسير المنفعة بكتابى، مفتاح كنوز السنة و المعجم المفهرس لالفاظ الحديث النبوى
[The Facilitation in the Beneficial Use of My Book: Key of the Treasure of the Sunna and Dictionary Index to the Traditions of the Prophet]. Cairo, Maṭbaᶜa al-Manār, 1353/1935-39. 8 vols.

Detailed tables to facilitate research in the eight major Sunnī collections of traditions, setting forth in tabular form, the books and the chapters into which each is divided.

Title transliterated: Taysīr al-Manfaᶜa bi-Kitābī,...

D127
al-MIZZĪ, Yūsuf ibn al-Zakī (d. 742/1341).
Tuḥfatu'l-Ashrāf bi Maᶜrifat'l-Aṭrāf / تحفت الاشراف بمعرفة الاطراف: a concordance to the Musnads of the Companions of the Prophet & other narrators and a systematic codification of all the traditions in the six canonical books (the *Ṣiḥāḥ Sitta*). *Ed.* ᶜAbd al-Ṣamad Sharaf al-Dīn. Bombay, Dār al-Qayyima, 1965-83. 13 vols.

Index to the *isnāds* (chains of transmission) of the 19,595 traditions attributed to Muḥammad contained in the collections of Abū Daʾūd, Ibn Maja, al-Bukhārī, Mālik, Muslim, and al-Tirmidhī. Arranged alphabetically by first name (*ism*) of Muḥammad's Companions with the traditions they transmitted recorded, in abbreviated form, and the collections in which they appear, with complete *isnāds*. For most of the Companions their pupils are listed with the traditions they related and, sometimes, the names of their pupils and their traditions. All traditions quoted have been numbered consecutively. The work is supplemented with al-Asqalānī's النكت الظراف على الاطراف.

In his edition Sharaf al-Dīn has employed abbreviations and numberings for the books, chapters, and traditions of the six collections. As a result he published an index to the collections, *Al-Kashshāf 'an Abwāb Marāji'* Tuḥfatu'l-Ashrāf: *a masterguide to chapters of* Tuḥfatu'l-Ashrāf's *references: complete indices to headings of books & chapters of the six canonical works with their serial numbers, for locating the source of every tradition indexed by al-Mizzi in his concordance,* "Tuḥfatu'l-Ashrāf". Bombay, Al-Dār al-Qayyima, *2nd ed.*, 1981. xi + 551 p. This second edition contains a supplement to that published in 1966, which is available separately for those who have the first edition.

D128
al-NĀBULUSĪ, ᶜAbd al-Ghanī ibn Ismāᶜīl (d. 1143/1731). [The In- ذخائر المواريث فى الدلالة على مواضع الحديث herited Treasures in the Proofs of the Deposits of Tradition]. Cairo, Maṭbaᶜa Jamᶜa al-Nashr wa al-Taʾlīf al-Azharīya, 1352/1933-34. 4 pts. in 1 vol.

Index to the canonical books of al-Bukhārī, Muslim, Abū Daʾūd, al-Tirmidhī, al-Nasāʾī, Ibn Māja, and Mālik ibn Anas with the traditions cited under the names of the earliest transmitters arranged alphabetically within the seven classifications of reliability.

Title transliterated: Dhakhāʾir Mawārīth fī al-Dilāla ᶜalā Muwāḍī al-Ḥadīth.

D129
al-TŪQĀDĪ, Muḥammad al-Sharīf ibn Muṣṭafā. [Index to the Two مفتاح الصحيحين بخارى و مسلم Saḥīḥs of Bukharī and Muslim]. Istanbul, Al-Sharika al-Ṣiḥāfīya al-ᶜUthmānīya, 1313/1895-96. 10, 192 + 52 p.

Reprinted in Beirut in 1975.

Title transliterated: Miftāḥ al-Ṣaḥīḥayn Bukhārī wa Muslim.

D130
WENSINCK, A. J.
A Handbook of Early Muhammadan Tradition: alphabetically arranged. Leiden, E. J. Brill, 1927. XVIII + 268 p. [dbl. col.].

Subject index in English, with some Arabic terms in transliteration, without, unfortunately, adequate cross references, to the traditions contained in the six canonical collections, the *Musnad* of al-Dārimī, the *Muwaṭṭaʾ* of Mālik ibn Anas, the Zaydī collection of Zayd ibn ᶜAlī, Ibn Saᶜd's *Ṭabaqāt*, the *Musnad* of Aḥmad ibn Ḥanbal, the *Musnad* of al-Ṭayālisī, the *Sīra Rasūl Allāh* by Ibn Hishām, and al-Wāqidī's *Kitāb al-Maghāzī*. Provides a portion of the sentence in which the word or the subject appears and notations regarding the collection, etc., in which it is to be found. Frequently reprinted by the original publishers.

Translations: Muḥammad Rashīd Riḍḍā, مفتاح كنوز السنة. Cairo, Maṭbaᶜa Miṣr, 1934. 2, 21 + 544 p.

D131

---.

Concordance et Indices de la Tradition musulmane: les six livres, le *Musnad* d'al-Dārimī, le *Muwaṭṭaᵓ* de Mālik, le *Musnad* de Aḥmad ibn Ḥanbal. Leiden, E. J. Brill, 1933-69. 7 vols.

Complete concordance, in Arabic, to the important words found in all of the traditions recorded in the nine books mentioned. Each word is listed according to the form in which it appears, together with the entire, or a portion, of the tradition in which it is employed. A notation is provided in which of the collections that sentence is to be found and the book and chapter (according to arrangement) of that collection.

Shīᶜī

D132

al-KĀẒIMĪ, Muḥammad al-Mahdī.

[Key to the Four Books]. مفتاح الكتب الأربعة

Najaf, Maṭbaᶜa al-Ādāb, 1967- .

Index to the four canonical collections.

The author is variously listed under virtually any of his names: Muḥammad (or Maḥmūd) (ibn) al-Mahdī al-Mūwawī al-Dahsurkhī al-Iṣfahānī al-Kāẓimī.

Title transliterated: Miftāḥ al-Kutub al-Arbaᶜa.

Biographies of Traditionists

Sunnī

D133

al-ᶜASQALĀNĪ, Aḥmad ibn ᶜAlī ibn Ḥajar (d. 852/1449).

[Emendation تهذيب تهذيب الكمال فى معرفت الرجال of the Complete Emendation in the Knowledge of Men]. Hyderabad-Deccan, Dāᵓira Maᶜārif al-ᶜUthmānīya, 1325-28/1907-10. 12 vols.

Biographical dictionary of transmitters omitted by al-Dhahabī and al-Mizzī, arranged by *ism*.

Title transliterated: Tahdhīb Tahdhīb al-Kamāl fī Maᶜrifat al-Rijāl.

Continuations: Al-ᶜAsqalānī, تقريب التحذ يب Lucknow, (litho.), 1271-72/1865. 482 p.

D134

---.

[Classes of the Falsifiers]. طبقات المدلسين
Cairo, Maṭbaᶜa al-Ḥusaynīya, 1322/1904. 7 + 23 p.

Alphabetical lists of forgers of traditions, arranged into five classes. Also known as the تعريف احل التقديس.

Title transliterated: Ṭabaqāt al-Mudallisīn.

D135

---.

[Book of Attaining كتاب الاصابة فى تمييز الصحابة (Knowledge) in Distinguishing the Companions].
Ed. Alois Sprenger, *et. al.*, *A Biographical Dictionary of Persons Who Knew Muḥammad.* Calcutta, Asiatic Society of Bengal, 1856-88. 4 vols.

Bibliotheca Indica, Vol. XX.

Lives of the Companions and early ḥadīth transmitters.

Other editions have been printed in Cairo (1910 and 1939-40).

Title transliterated: Kitāb al-Iṣāba fī Tamyīz al-Ṣaḥāba.

D136

---.

[Book of the Balanced Tongue]. كتاب لسان الميزان
Hyderabad-Deccan, Dāɔira al-Maᶜārif alᶜUthmānīya, 1329-31/1911-13. 6 vols.

Biographies of weak traditionists and of those having tenuous connections with ḥadīth.

Title transliterated: Kitāb Lisān al-Mīzān.

D137

al-BUKHĀRĪ, Muḥammad ibn Ismāᶜīl (d. 256/870).
[Book of the Great History]. كتاب التأريخ الكبير
Ed. ᶜAbd al-Munᶜim Muḥammad al-Ḥasanayn. Hyderabad-Deccan, Maṭbaᶜa Jamᶜīya Dāɔira al-Maᶜārif al-ᶜUth-

mānīya, 1360-84/1941-64. 4 vols. in 8.

Dictionary of approximately 20,000 ḥadīth transmitters in alphabetical order by *ism*. The fourth (eighth) volume contains an index of *kunyas*.

Title transliterated: Kitāb al-Taʾrīkh al-Kabīr.

D138

al-DHAHABĪ, Muḥammad ibn ʿUthmān (d. 748/1348). [Book of Remembrance of the Transmitters]. كتاب تذكرة الحفاظ Hyderabad-Deccan, Maṭbaʿa Dāʾira al-Maʿārif al-Niẓāmīya, 1333-36/1915-18. 5 vols.

Biographical dictionary of traditionists.

An earlier edition was published by Ferdinand Wüstenfeld, *Liber Classium virorum qui Korani et Traditionum...*, Gottingen, 1833-34. 3 vols.

The dictionary had a number of continuations made to it: Muḥammad ibn ʿAlī al-Ḥusaynī (d. 765/1364), *Dhayl Tadhkira al-Huffāẓ*; Muḥammad ibn Muḥammad al-Makkī (d. 871/1466), *Laḥẓ al-Alḥāẓ*; ʿAbd al-Raḥmān ibn abī Bakr al-Suyūṭī (d. 911/1505), *Dhayl Ṭabaqāt al-Ḥuffāẓ*. These three have been edited, with notes, indices, and biographical materials about the authors by Muḥammad Zāhid al-Kawtharī, ذيل تذكرة الحفاظ . Damascus, Maṭbaʿa Ḥusam al-Dīn al-Qudsī, 1347/1928. iii + 454 p.

Title transliterated: Kitāb Tadhkira al-Ḥuffāẓ.

D139

---. [What is Revealing in the Knowledge of Those Who are Transmitters in the Six Books]. الكاشف فى معرفة من له رواية فى الكتب الستّة *Ed.* ʿIzzat ʿAlī ʿĪd ʿAtīya *and* Mūsā Muḥammad ʿAlī al-Mūshā. Cairo, Dār al-Kutub al-Ḥadītha, 1972. 3 vols.

Arranged alphabetically and based upon Jamāl al-Dīn al-Mizzī's *Taḥdhīb al-Kamāl*.

Title transliterated: Al-Kāshf fī Maʿrifa man lahu Rawāya fī al-Kutub al-Sitta.

D140

---. [The Balanced Scale in the Criticism of the Men]. ميزان الاعتدال في نقد الرجال *Ed.* ʿAlī Muḥammad al-Bajāwī. Cairo, ʿĪsā al-Bābī al-Ḥalabī, 1325/1963. 3

vols.

Biographical dictionary of those of doubtful authority, with brief remarks as to credibility.

Previously lithographed in Lucknow (1301/1884) and printed in Cairo (1325/1907-8) and Hyderabad-Deccan (1329-31/1911-13).

Title transliterated: Mīzān al-Iᶜtidāl fī Naqd al-Rijāl.

D141
IBN AL-ATHĪR, ᶜIzz al-Dīn abī al-Ḥasan Ali (d. 630/1233).
[Clearing of the Thicket in the Knowledge of the Companions]. اسد الغابة في معرفة الصحابة *Ed.* Shihāb al-Dīn al-Najafī. Tehran, Al-Maktaba al-Islāmīya, 1957. 5 vols.

Biographical dictionary of 7,500 Companions of the Prophet for the study of the traditions.

Other editions have been published in Cairo in 1280/1863 and in 1964.

Title transliterated: Usd al-Ghāba fī Maᶜrifa al-Ṣaḥāba.

D142
IBN ḤIBBĀN, Muḥammad al-Bustī (d. 354/965).
[Book of the Trustworthy]. كتاب الثقات Hyderabad-Deccan, Maṭbaᶜa Dāʾira al-Maᶜārif al-ᶜUthmānīya, 1973-80. 6 vols.

Alphabetical dictionary of trustworthy traditionists by a Persian born, hence al-Bustī, Arab scholar.

A short extract of the dictionary, كتاب الشاهر علماء الامصار has been edited by M. Fleischhammer (Wiesbaden, 1959).

Title transliterated: Kitāb al-Thaqāt.

D143
---.
[Book of Those Who are Invalidated Among the Traditionists]. كتاب المجروحين من المحدثين Hyderabad-Deccan, Maṭbaᶜa al-ᶜAzīzīya, 1970-73. 2 vols.

Brief biographical sketches of the transmitters whose testimony is invalid.

Title transliterated: Kitāb al-Majrūḥīn min al-Muḥaddithīn.

D144
IBN KHAYYĀṬ, Khalīfa (d. 240/854).
[Book of كتاب الطبقات عن ابى عمر و خليفة بن خياط Classes from Abī ᶜUmar and Khalīfa ibn Khayyāṭ]. *Ed.* Suhayl Zakkār. Damascus, Wizāra al-Thaqāfa wa al-Siyāḥa wa al-Irshād al-Qawmī, 1966. 2 vols.
Iḥyāɔ al-Turāth al-Qadīm, 14.

One of the oldest surviving biographical dictionaries of traditionists, containing some 3,375 sketches of men and women (in separate sections). Arranged according to the city or center in which they lived, beginning with the Prophet in Madina. An important element is the attention paid to their genealogies.

Title transliterated: Kitāb al-Ṭabaqāt ᶜan Abī ᶜUmar wa Khalīfa ibn Khayyāṭ.

D145
IBN SAᶜD, Muḥammad al-Ḥashimī (d. 230/845).
[Book of the Classes of the Great]. كتاب طبقات الكبير *Ed.* E. Sachau, *et. al. Biographien Muhammads, seiner gefährten und der spätern träger des Islāms bis zum jahre 230 der flucht.* Leiden, E. J. Brill, 1904-40. 9 vols.

One of the most important biographical dictionaries of transmitters arranged geographically and then chronologically within each region. Begins with an extensive life of the Prophet and of his Companions. Contains approximately 4,250 entries, including some 600 women. Volume IX, pt. 1 (1921) contains indices of names. Reprinted in 1967.

Other editions, without the indices, have been published in Cairo (1939) and Beirut (1958).

Translations: S. Moinul Haq *and* H. K. Ghazanfar. *Ibn Saᶜd's* Kitāb al-Ṭabaqāt al-Kabīr. Karachi, Pakistan Historical Society, 1967- . *Pakistan Historical Society Publication No. 46, 59.*

Title transliterated: Kitāb Ṭabaqāt al-Kabīr.

D146
al-RĀZĪ, ᶜAbd al-Raḥmān ibn abī Ḥātim (d. 327/939).
[Book of the Voiding (of Testimony) and the Setting Aright]. كتاب الجرح و التعديل Hyderabad-Deccan, Majlis Dāɔira al-Maᶜārif al-ᶜUthmānīya, 1952-53. 4 vols.

A dictionary regarded as particularly important for the details regarding reliability and for the quotations from earlier authorities.

Title transliterated: Kitāb al-Jarḥ wa al-Taᶜdīl.

D147

al-SAMᶜĀNĪ, ᶜAbd al-Karīm ibn Muḥammad (d. 562/1167). [Book of Lineages]. كتاب الانساب
Ed. D. S. Margoliouth. *The* Kitāb al-Ansāb *of al-Samᶜānī: reproduced in facsimile from the manuscript in the British Museum, Add. 23,355.* London, E. J. W. Gibb Memorial Series, 1912. 7 + 603 p.

Gibb Memorial Series, Vol. XX.

Primarily a biographical dictionary of the traditionists quoted in the six canonical books, arranged by *nisba*.

Another edition has been printed in Hyderabad-Deccan (1962).

Title transliterated: Kitāb al-Ansāb.

D148

al-SUYŪṬĪ, Jalāl al-Dīn ᶜabd al-Raḥmān (d. 911/1505). [Classes of the Transmitters]. طبقات الحفاظ
Ed. ᶜAlī Muḥammad ᶜAmr. Cairo, Maktaba Wahba, 1973. 14 + 717 p.

Brief biographical notes on 1,192 scholars of traditions and law to the mid-15th century.

Title transliterated: Ṭabaqāt al-Ḥuffāẓ.

Indices and Special Lists

D149

al-BAGHDĀDĪ, Aḥmad ibn ᶜAlī (d. 463/1071). [Book of Clearing كتاب موضح اوهام الجمع و التفريق the Guesswork in the Connections and the Distinctions]. *Ed.* ᶜAbd al-Raḥmān ibn Yaḥyā al-Muᶜallimī. Hyderabad-Deccan, Maṭbaᶜa Majlis Dāʾira al-Maᶜārif al-ᶜUthmānīya, 1959-60. 2 vols.

Dictionary of the similarities in the names of transmitters.

Title transliterated: Kitāb Mūḍiḥ Awhām al-Jamiᶜ wa al-Tafrīq.

D150

al-BAḤRĀNĪ, ᶜAbd al-Ghanī ibn Aḥmad (d. 1174/1761).
هذا كتاب قرة العين فى ضبط اسماء رجال الصحيحين
[This Book is a Delight to the Eye in Comprehending the Names of the Men in the Two *Ṣaḥīḥs*]. Hyderabad-Deccan, Maṭbaᶜa Majlis Dāʾira al-Maᶜārif al-Niẓāmīya, 1323/1905-6. 59 + 4 p.

A listing of the transmitters contained in the collections of al-Bukhārī and Muslim.

Title transliterated: Hādhā Kitāb Qurra al-ᶜAyn fī Ḍabṭ Asmāʾ Rijāl al-Ṣaḥīḥayn.

D151
IBN MĀKŪLĀ, ᶜAlī ibn Hibat Allāh (d. 487/1094).
الاكمال فى رفع الارتياب عن المؤتلف والامختلف من الاسماء و الكني و الانساب
[The Completion in Lifting the Doubt Regarding the Familiar and the Diverse Concerning the Names, *Kunyas*, and Lineage]. *Ed.* ᶜAbd al-Raḥmān ibn Yaḥya al-Muᶜalimī al-Yaᶜānī. Hyderabad-Deccan, Maṭbaᶜa Majlis Dāʾira al-Maᶜārif al-ᶜUthmānīya, 1962. 7 vols.

Al-Silsila al-Jadīda min al-Maṭbūᶜāt, 17.

A study of the names employed in the chains of transmitters of the Sunnī collections.

Title transliterated: Al-Ikmāl fī Rafᶜ al-Irtiyāb ᶜan al-Muʾtalaf...

D152
IBN QUNFUDH, Aḥmad ibn Ḥasan (d. 809-10/1406-7).
[Book of the Death Dates]. كتاب الوفيات
Ed. ᶜĀdil Nuwayhiḍ. Beirut, Manshūrāt al-Maktab al-Tijārī li-l-Ṭibāᶜa wa al-Nashr wa al-Tawzī, 1971. 394 p.

A simple chronological listing by death date of the names of the Companions and the transmitters of traditions. The editor has provided extensive annotations.

Title transliterated: Kitāb al-Wafayāt.

D153
al-NĀBULUSĪ, ᶜAbd al-Ghanī ibn Ismāᶜīl (d. 1143/1731).
ذخائر المواريث فى الدلالة علي مواضع الحديث
[Inherited Treasures in the Guidance Upon the Passing of Traditions]. Cairo, Maṭbaᶜa Jamᶜīya al-Nashr wa al-Taʾlīf al-Azharīya, 1352/1933-34. 4 pts.

Index to the transmitters contained in the six

canonical collections. The names of the transmitters are listed in alphabetical order and ranked within the seven classes of reliability.

Title transliterated: Dhakhāʾir al-Mawārīth fī al-Dalāla ʿalā Mawāḍiʿ al-Ḥadīth.

D154
al-NAWĀWĪ, Yaḥya ibn Sharaf (d. 676/1278).
[Instruction in the Names and the Language]. تهذيب الاسماء و اللغات *Ed.* Ferdinand Wüstenfeld. *The Biographical Dictionary of Illustrious Men, chiefly at the beginning of Islamism.* Göttingen, Society for the Publication of Oriental Texts, 1842-47. 9 pts.

A compilation of the names of the traditionists employed in the major collections to establish the correct orthography of their names.

Title transliterated: Tahdhīb al-Asmāʾ wa al-Lughāt.

Shīʿī

D155
al-BAḤRĀNĪ, Yūsuf ibn Aḥmad (d. 1189/1773).
لؤلؤة البحرين فى الاجازات و تراجم رجال الحديث
[The Pearls of Baḥrayn Regarding the Authorities and the Lives of the Transmitters of Traditions]. Najaf, Maṭbaʿa al-Nuʿmān, 1966. 461 p.

Title transliterated: Luʾluʾ al-Baḥrayn fī al-Ijāzāt wa Tarājim Rijāl al-Ḥadīth.

D156
al-KHWĀNSĀRĪ, Muḥammad Bāqir ibn Muḥammad (d. 1313/1895).
[Gardens روضات الجنات في احوال العلماء و السادات of Blessedness in the Lives of the Learned and the Sayyids]. *Ed.* Muḥammad ʿAlī Rawḍātī. Tehran, Dār al-Kutub al-Islāmī, 1327/1962. 748 p.

Title transliterated: Rawḍāt al-Jannāt fī Aḥwāl al-ʿUlamāʾ wa al-Sādāt.

D157
al-NAJĀSHĪ, Aḥmad ibn ʿAlī (d. 455/1063).
[Book of the Men]. كتاب الرجال
Bombay, (litho.), 1317/1899-1900. 340 p.

Biographical dictionary, in alphabetical order,

of the traditionists in the four canonical collections. *GAL*, SI, 256 has title: كتاب اسماء الرجال
Title transliterated: Kitāb al-Rijāl.

D158
al-ṬŪSĪ, Muḥammad ibn al-Ḥasan (d. 460/1068).
[The Men of al-Tusi]. رجال الطوسى
Ed. Muḥammad Sādiq Āl Baḥr al-ᶜUlūm. Najaf, Al-Maktaba wa al-Maṭbaᶜa al-Haydarīya, 1380/1961. 128, 535 + [i] p.
A classification of the Shīᶜite transmitters employed in all of the collections.
Title transliterated: Rijāl al-Ṭūsī.

SECTARIANISM

General

D159
TAQĪ, Muḥammad.
["Bibliography of Sects and Creeds"]. "كتابشناسى فرق و اديان" *Farhang-i Īrān Zamīn*, XII, 1343/1964, pp. 98-121.
Annotated title listing, in alphabetical order, of published and manuscript Arabic and Farsi writings on sectarianism.
Title transliterated: "Kitābshināsī Firaq wa Adyān".

Ibadīya

Bibliographies

D160
BAALI, A.
"Bibliographie ibadhite." *Revue Algérienne*, 1943-1945, Pt. 1, pp. 39-40.
Bare author listing of 50 (then) recent books and articles.

D161
al-DAMMARĪ, Abū al-Faḍl abī al-Qāsim ibn Ibrāhīm al-Barradī (d. *cir.* 850/1446).
[Untitled letter-catalogue]. [رسالة]
Trans. A. de C. Motylinski, "Bibliographie du Mzab: les livres de la secte abadhite." *Bulletin de Correspondance Africaine*, III, 1885, pp. 15-72 [16-29].

The introduction to the catalogue, as translated by Motylinski, states: "Lettre du cheikh Abou'l Qâsem ben Ibrahim el-Berrâdi ... contenant le catalogue des ouvrages composés par les campagnons de notre secte." (p. 16). Motylinski merely implies that he discovered it "au Mzab." *GAL*, II, 240 and SII, 339, provides no title. Incidentally, Sarkīs (I, 1141) spells the author's *nisba* "al-Barrāwī."

The catalogue, which occupies pp. 16-29, lists, with annotations, 82 Ibadite works from the earliest times of Islam to his own day by residence of author. The remainder of the article consists of detailed examinations of six historical and biographical texts, some not listed by al-Dammarī.

Biographies

D162

ABŪ ZAKARĪYĀ, Yaḥyā ibn abī Bakr al-Wārjalānī (d. 471/1078).

[Book of Biography and News of the Imāms]. كتاب السيرة و اخبار الائمّة

Translations: Trans. E. Masqueray, *Livres des Beni Mzab: chronique d'Abou Zakaria publiée pour la première fois traduite et commentée...* . Algiers, Imprimerie Ailland, 1878. lxxix + 413 p.

According to Motylinski [D161], p. 36, Masqueray's translation is of only slightly over half of the book. Motylinski provides on pages 36-38 a table of contents for the book based upon a manuscript in his possession.

Title transliterated: Kitāb al-Sīra wa Akhbār al-Aɔimma.

D163

al-SHAMMĀKHĪ, Aḥmad ibn abī ᶜUthmān (d. 928/1522).

[The Book of Biographies]. كتاب السير

Cairo, N.P., 1301/1883-84. 240 p.

Following a comparatively brief historical introduction of the Prophet and the early Caliphs, the author commences his biographical accounts of the Ibādī shaykhs of both the east and the west in more or less chronological order.

Motylinski [D161] states, on page 47, "Ce volumineux ouvrage est à la fois le résumé et le complément de la *Chronique d'Abou Zakarya*, du *Kitâb et-'T'abaqât* [of al-Darjīnī], du *Djaouâher el Montaqât* [of al-Dammarī] et d'un certain nombre de *Siar* d'importance secondaire dont les copies paraissent perdues."

Motylinski provides a fairly detailed table of contents of the book based upon a manuscript in his possession (pp. 47-65) and an "Index alphabétique des noms de lieux ou de tribus de l'Afrique relevés dans le *Kitâb es-Siar*" (pp. 66-70).

Title transliterated: Kitāb al-Siyār.

Ismāᶜīliya

Bibliographies

D164

FYZEE, A. A. A.

"Materials for an Ismaili Bibliography, 1920-1934." *Journal of the Bombay Branch of the Royal Asiatic Society, N.S.*, XI, 1935, pp. 59-65.

Author listing of 72 edited and translated texts and modern studies published during the period.

Supplements:

"Additional Notes for an Ismaili Bibliography." *JBBRAS,N.S.*, XII, 1936, pp. 107-109. Listing of materials published during 1934-36.

"Materials for an Ismaili Bibliography." *JBBRAS,N.S.*, XVI, 1940, pp. 99-101. Materials published during 1937-39.

D165

IVANOW, Vladimir.

Ismaili Literature: a bibliographical survey. *2nd ed.* Tehran, Ismaili Society, 1963. [viii] + 245 p.

The Ismaili Society Series A, No. 15.

Annotated bibliography of 863 Ismaili texts, mostly unpublished manuscripts. Revised and enlarged edition of his *A Guide to Ismaili Literature.* London, Royal Asiatic Society, 1933.

Contents: Part I. Fatimid and Mustaᶜlian Literature; Part II. Nizari Literature. Indices of authors, titles, places, technical terms, and subjects.

D166
POONAWALA, Ismail K.
Biobibliography of Ismāᶜīlī Literature. Malibu, California, Undena Publications, 1977. xix + 533 p.
Bibliographic survey of published and unpublished works by Ismāᶜīlī authors based upon the work of Ivanow.
Contents: Part One: Authors and Their Books; Part Two: Anonymous Works. Appendices, glossary, chronological list of authors, indices.

Biographies

D167
GHĀLIB, Muṣṭafā.
[Notices of the Ismāᶜīlīya]. اعلام الاسماعيلية
Beirut, Dār al-Yaqẓān al-ᶜArabīya, 1964. 624 p., tables.
A modern biographical dictionary of the learned and noted Ismāᶜīlīs from the classical period to the present. Five folding tables.
Title transliterated: Aᶜlām al-Ismāᶜīlīya.

Mahdīya

Bibliographies

D168
HOLT, Peter M.
"The Source Materials of the Sudanese Mahdiya." *St. Antony's Papers*, No. 4: *Middle Eastern Affairs*, No. 1, 1958, pp. 107-118.
Bibliographic survey of the available materials.

Muᶜtazilah

Biographies

D169
IBN AL-MURTAḌĀ, Aḥmad ibn Yaḥyā (d. 840/1437).
[Book كتاب المنية و الامل فى شرح كتاب الملل و النحل of Desire and Hope in Elucidating the Book of Beliefs and Sects].
Contains a brief biographical dictionary of the Muᶜtazilites which has been published twice: طبقات المعتزله [Classes of the Muᶜtazilah]. Beirut, Al-Maṭbaᶜa al-Kāthulīkīya, 1961. ii + 181 p.

(with German introduction), and again as the first part of فرق و طبقات المعتزله [Sects and Classes of the Muʿtazilah], edited with commentary by ʿAlī Sāmī al-Nashshar and ʿIsām al-Dīn Muḥammad ʿAlī. Alexandria, Dār al-Maṭbūʿāt al-Jāmʿī, 1972. 254 p.

The author was a Zaydī Imām of Yemen.

Title transliterated: Kitāb al-Munya wa al-Amal...

Qarmaṭīya

Bibliographies

D170

MASSIGNON, Louis.

"Esquisse d'une Bibliographie qarmate; avant-propos." T. W. Arnold *and* R. A. Nicholson, *eds. A Volume of Oriental Studies Presented to Edward G. Browne.* Cambridge, University Press, 1922. Pp. 329-38.

Classified listing of primary and secondary sources for the study of the Qarmaṭīya sect of the Shīʿites.

Contents: I. Textes doctrinaux; II. Textes historiques où légendaires; III. Etudes critiques des orientalistes.

Shīʿa

Bibliographies

D171

NAYSHABŪRĪ, Iʿjaz Ḥusayn ibn Muḥammad al-Kantūrī (d. 1282/1865).

كشف الحجب و الاستار عن اسماء الكتب و الاسفار

[Removing the Veils and Fetters from the Names of the Books and the Writings]. *Ed.* Muḥammad Hidāya Ḥusayn. *The Bibliography of Sheiʿa Literature.* Calcutta, Asiatic Society, 1912-35. 3 pts: [ii] + 118; [iii] + 607; [i], 5 + ii p.

Bibliotheca Indica, Vol. 203.

A bibliographical dictionary of Shīʿite books by an Indian scholar. The third part contains an index.

Title transliterated: Kashf al-Hujub wa al-Astār ʿan Asmāʾ...

D172
al-ṬIHRĀNĪ, Muḥammad Muḥsin Nazīl Sāmarrā.
[Access to the Literary الذريعة الى تصانيف الشيعة Works of the Shīᶜa]. Najaf, Maṭbaᶜa al-Gharī; Tehran, Maṭbaᶜa Majlis, 1355-99/1936-78. 25 vols. in 28 pts.

Listed by title, with annotations. A very important piece of work. The author is sometimes referred to as Āghā Buzurg. The first three volumes only were printed in Najaf, from volume four in Tehran.

Title transliterated: Al-Dharīᶜa ilā Taṣānīf al-Shīᶜa.

D173
al-ṬŪSĪ, Muḥammad ibn al-Ḥasan (d. 460/1068).
فهرست كتب الشيعة و نضد الأيضاح لعلم الهدى
[List of the Books of the Shīᶜa and Arrangement of the Explanations to the Right Guidance]. *Ed.* Muḥammad Ṣādiq Āl Baḥr al-ᶜUlūm. Najaf, Al-Maktaba al-Murtaḍawīya, 1356/1937. 20 + 196 p.

Lists 892 works by author in alphabetical order by *ism*.

A better known earlier edition is that of Alois Sprenger and Mawlawi ᶜAbd al-Haqq, Fihrist Kutub al-Shiʾa: *Tusy's list of Shyʾah books and ʾAlam al-Hoda's notes on Shyʾah biography*. Calcutta, Royal Asiatic Society of Bengal, 1853-55. 4 + 383 p. (*Bibliotheca Indica, XIX*).

Title transliterated: Fihrist Kutub al-Shīᶜa...

Supplements: Muḥammad ibn ᶜAlī ibn Shahrashub (d. 588/1192).
معالم العلماء فى فهرست كتب الشيعة و اسماء المصنفين منهم قديما و حديثا
Malim al-Ulama: *bibliography of the Shy'ahs (supplement to Tusy's* Fihrist *by Rashid ud-Din Muhammad ibn Ali ibn Shahrashub (died in 500* [sic] *H.)*. *Ed.* Al-Sayyid Muḥammad Ṣādiq Āl Baḥr al-ᶜUlūm. Najaf, Al-Maṭbaᶜa al-Ḥaydarīya, 1380/1961. 36 + 159 p.

Lists an additional 1,021 authors. An earlier edition by ᶜAbbās Iqbāl (Tehran, Maṭbaᶜa Fardīn, 1353/1934), apparently based upon an incomplete manuscript, listed only 990 authors.

Title transliterated: Maᶜālim al-ᶜUlamāʾ...

Biographies

D174
AMĪN, Muḥsin ʿAbd al-Karīm.
[Eyes upon the Shīʿa]. أعيان الشيعة
Beirut, Maṭbaʿa al-Inṣāf, 1951-60. 7 vols.
Modern biographical dictionary of Shīʿites. Reprinted numerous times.
Title transliterated: Aʿyān al-Shīʿa.

D175
al-KARKHĪ, Muḥammad ibn Muḥammad (d. 413/1022).
[Book كتاب الارشاد في معرفة حجج الله علي العباد of Guidance in the Knowledge of the Proofs of God for Mankind]. Najaf, Al-Maṭbaʿa al-Ḥusaydirīya wa Maktabaha, 1962. 368 p., illus.
The first part of the book is devoted to the life of ʿAlī, the second part contains the lives of the following eleven imāms.
Lithographed and printed numerous times. Mushār (V, 769-70) lists 12 printings between 1285 and 1377 in Iran alone.
Translations: Trans. I. K. A. Howard, Kitāb al-Irshād: *the book of guidance into the lives of the twelve Imams*. Elmhurst, New York, Tahrike Tarsile Qurʾan, Inc., 1981. xxxvii, iii + 616 p. The translator has provided a lengthy biographical-identification index.
Title transliteration: Kitāb al-Irshād fī Maʿrifa...

D176
al-KASHMĪRĪ, Muḥammad ibn Ṣādiq.
[Book of the Con- كتاب نجوم السماء فى تراجم العلماء stellations of the Heavens in the Biographies of the Learned]. Lucknow, (litho.), 1303/1886. 424 p.
Biographies of Shīʿite theologians of the 11th-13th/late 16th-19th centuries, arranged chronologically: 11th, pp. 4-157; 12th, pp. 157-312; 13th, pp. 313-424. No index.
Title transliterated: Kitāb Nujūm al-Samāʾ...

D177
SHŪSHTARĪ, Nūr Allāh ibn Sharīf (d. 1019/1610).
[Councils of the Faithful]. مجالس المومنين

Ed. Sayyid Ḥusayn. Tehran, (litho.), 1268/1852. 506 p.

Biographies of eminent Shīᶜites, completed in 1010/1602, divided into twelve chapters: "(1) places with Shīᶜite associations, (2) some Shīᶜite tribes and families, (3) Shīᶜite contemporaries of the Prophet, (4) Shīᶜites of the next generation, (5) Shīᶜite scholars of the succeeding generations, (6) Ṣūfīs, (7) philosophers, (8) Shīᶜite kings and 16 Shīᶜite dynasties, (9) governors, generals, etc., (10) wazīrs and calligraphists, (11) Arab poets, (12) Persian poets." Storey, I, pt. 2, pp. 1128-29.

Title transliterated: Majālis al-Muʾminīn.

D178
al-ṬABARSĪ, al-Faḍl ibn al-Ḥasan (d. 548/1153). [Information of the Men in the Guides of the Faith]. اعلام الورى بأعلام الهدى *Ed.* ᶜAlī Akbar al-Ghafārī. Beirut, Dār al-Maᶜrifa li-l-Ṭabāᶜa wa al-Nashr, 1979. 460 p.

Biographical dictionary of the Shīᶜite Imāms beginning with Muḥammad.

Title transliterated: Iᶜlām al-Warā bi-Aᶜlām al-Hudā.

Ṣūfīya

Biographies

D179
IBN AL-JAWZĪ, ᶜAbd al-Raḥmān ibn ᶜAlī (d. 597/1200). [Book of the Elite of the Elite]. كتاب صفة الصفوة Hyderabad-Deccan, Maṭbaᶜa Majlis Dāʾira al-Maᶜārif al-ᶜUthmānīya, 1968- .

Title transliterated: Kitāb Ṣifa al-Ṣafwa.

D180
al-IṢBAHĀNĪ, Aḥmad ibn ᶜAbd Allāh (d. 430/1038). [Ornament of the Saints and Classes of the Pure]. حلية الاولياء و طبقات الاصفياء Cairo, Maktaba al-Khanjī wa Maṭbaᶜa Miṣr, 1351-57/1932-38. 10 vols. in 5.

Completed eight years before his death this biographical dictionary of *Ṣūfīs* consists of the lives and sayings of 649 pious men and women beginning with the first caliph to his own time.

Preceded by a general description of Ṣūfism and the various etymologies of the term. *GAL*, I, 362, gives his patronymic as ᶜAlī. Reprinted in Beirut in 1967.

Title transliterated: Ḥilya al-Awlīyāɔ wa Ṭabaqāt al-Aṣfīyāɔ.

D181
al-SHAᶜRĀNĪ, ᶜAbd al-Wahhāb ibn Aḥmad (d. 973/1565).
[The Great Classes]. الطبقات الكبرى
Cairo, Maktaba al-Malījī, 1316/1898. 2 vols. in 1.

Sketches of the lives of famous mystics by an Egyptian *Ṣūfī*. Reprinted in Cairo in 1925 and translated into Urdu under the title طبقات الكبرى (Karachi, 1965).

Title transliterated: Al-Ṭabaqāt al-Kubrā.

D182
al-SULAMĪ, Muḥammad ibn al-Ḥusayn (d. 412/1021).
[Book of the Classes of the *Ṣūfīs*]. كتاب طبقات الصوفية *Ed.* J. Pederson, *Kitāb Ṭabaqāt al-Ṣufiyya*.
Leiden, E. J. Brill, 1960. x, 100, ii + 590 p.

Alphabetically arranged dictionary of 105 noted *Ṣūfīs* from the 2nd/7th through the 4th/9th century. Previously edited by Nūr al-Dīn Shurayba and printed in Cairo in 1953.

Title transliterated: Kitāb Ṭabaqāt al-Ṣūfīya.

Supplements:

ᶜAbd Allāh ibn Muḥammad Ansārī (d. 481/1089). [Classes of the Ṣūfīs]. طبقات الصوفية *Ed.* ᶜAbd al-Hayy Ḥabībī. Kabul, Wizāra Maᶜārif, 1341/1922-23. 2, 48 + 738 p. Provides the lives, in Farsi, of an additional 120 saints.

ᶜAbd al-Raḥmān ibn Aḥmad Jāmī (d. 898/1492). [The Breath of Divine Intimacy from the Excellencies of Sanctity]. نفحات الانس من حضرات القدس *Ed.* Mawlāna Ghulām ᶜĪsā ᶜAbd al-Ḥamīd *and* Mawlāna Kabīr al-Dīn Aḥmad, *The* Nafahtáal-Ons min Hadharát al-Qods, *or the lives of the Soofis, with a biographical sketch of the author, by W. Nassau Lees*. Calcutta, Lee's Persian Series, 1859. XX + 740 p. Chronological dictionary, in Farsi, of an additional 567 saints from the 2nd/8th century to the death of Qāsīm al-Anwār in 837/1433-34. Includes 34 female saints and 13 *Ṣūfī* poets. Reprinted in Cawnpore (1885), Lahore (1897), and Tehran (1957).

D183
al-YĀFIʿĪ, ʿAbd Allāh ibn Asʿad (d. 768/1367). [Book of the Meadow of the Breezes in the Narratives of the Good] كتاب روض الرياحين فى حكايات الصالحين. Bulaq, 1297/1880. xii + 356 p.

Collection of 500 biographies of saints and *Ṣūfīs* with pious narratives.

Alternate title: نزهة العيون النواظر .

Title transliterated: Kitāb Rawḍ al-Riyāḥīn fī Ḥikāyāt al-Ṣāliḥīn.

Dictionaries

D184
al-KĀSHĀNĪ, ʿAbd al-Razzāq ibn Aḥmad (d. 730/1329). [Book of the Technical Terms of the *Ṣūfīya*] كتاب الاصطلاحات الصوفية. *Ed.* Muḥammad Kamāl Ibrāhīm Jaʿfar. Cairo, Al-Hayʾa al-Miṣrīya al-ʿĀmma li-l-Kitāb, 1981. 207 p.

An earlier, perhaps better known, edition of the dictionary was that of Alois Sprenger, *ʾAbdu-r-razzāq's Dictionary of the Technical Terms of the Sufies*. Calcutta, Asiatic Society of Bengal, 1845. ix + 167 p. Sprenger's edition, however, comprises only half of the book.

A detailed analysis of the work was printed in the *Jahrbücher der Literature*, LXXXII, 1838, "Unzeige blatt für wissenschaft und kunst: Hammer-Purgstall's morgenländische handschriften, XXIV. Mystik," pp. 62-69.

Title transliterated: Kitāb al-Iṣṭilāḥāt al-Ṣūfīya.

LAW E

BIBLIOGRAPHY

E1
AGHNIDES, Nicolas P.
Mohammedan Theories of Finance With an Introduction to Mohammedan Law and a Bibliography. New York, Columbia University Press, 1916.

Studies in History, Economics and Public Law, Vol. LXX.

"Bibliography," pp. 157-96.

"The following bibliography is intended for use in the study of Mohammedan law directly from the Arabic sources, and, therefore, works on the subject written in European languages, as a rule, are not indicated, ..." The bibliography consists, for the most part, of Classical Arabic sources, *i.e.*, Qurʾān, *tafsīr*, *aḥādīth*, *fatāwa*, etc. with titles in transliteration.

E2
SPIES, O. *and* PRITSCH, E.
"Klassiches islamisches Recht." B. Spuler, *ed. Orientalisches Recht.* Leiden, E. J. Brill, 1964. Pp. 220-343.

Handbuch der Orientalistik. Erste Abteilung: Der Nahe und der Mittlere Osten: Ergänzungsband III.

This is undoubtedly the most complete bibliography published to date on Islamic jurisprudence as it includes both books and articles in oriental and western languages. The bibliography is preceded by a short (pp. 220-37) introduction to Islamic law.

Contents: III. Literarischer Überblick über die arabischen Rechts-werke, pp. 237-70 [lists 89 Arabic primary works with their commentaries or studies based upon them, arranged by school or sect]; IV. Bibliographie der Rechtsliteratur, pp. 270-343 [European language studies arranged into 12 subject headings]. Unfortunately, no index.

E5
STEIN, W. B.
"Bibliography of Mohammedan Law." *Law Library Journal*, XLIII, 1950, pp. 16-21.
Author listing of books and articles in western languages up to time of publication.

E4
KARAYALÇIN, Yaşar *and* MUMCU, Ahmet.
Türk Hukuk Bibliyografyası; Türk harflerinin kabulüne kadar yayınlanmuş kitap ve makaleler 1727-1928/ Bibliographie de Droit turc (1727-1928): livres et articles en caractères latins. Ankara, Ankara Üniversitesi, 1972. XIL + 355 p.
Banka ve Ticaret Hukuku Araştırma Enstitüsü, Yayın Nu: 101.
Detailed subject listing of 4,306 books and articles published in Ottoman Turkish from the introduction of printing into Turkey until the establishment of modern Turkish (1928). Authors and titles are given, however, in the Latin alphabet. Table of contents separately provided in Turkish and French. Author index.

E5
MALLAL, Bashir A.
"Malayan Legal Bibliography." *Majallah Perpustakan Singapura*, I, 1961, pp. 55-75.
A chronological listing, with annotations, of local publications, law compilations, and ordinances printed between 1807 and 1961. Lacks publication data.

ENCYCLOPAEDIAS

E6
Mawsūᶜa Jamāl ᶜAbd al-Nāṣir fī al-Fiqh al-Islāmī. موسوعة جمال عبد الناصر فى الفقه الاسلامي [Encyclopaedia "Jamāl ᶜAbd al-Nāṣir" on Islamic Law].Cairo, Al-Majlis al-Aᶜla li-l-Shuʾūn al-Islāmīya, 1386-/ 1966- .

Detailed encyclopaedia-dictionary of men and terms in Islamic law compiled, originally, in honor of the late President of Egypt.

¶ Also see appropriate articles in the various encyclopaedias and handbooks on Islam.

SPECIAL STUDIES

E7

ROBERTS, Robert.

The Social Laws of the Qorân: considered and compared with those of the Hebrew and other ancient codes. London, Williams and Norgate, Ltd., 1925. ix + 126 p.

Translation from the German of the author's doctoral dissertation submitted to the University of Leipzig, *cir*. 1905. Therefore, perhaps, somewhat dated, but the only study available.

Contents: A. Laws Concerning Marital Relations; B. Laws Concerning Slaves; C. Laws Concerning Inheritance; D. Laws Concerning Chastity; E. Laws Concerning Murder and Theft; F. Laws Relating to Commercial Matters; G. Laws Concerning Food, etc. Seven brief appendices on special studies. No index.

BIOGRAPHIES OF THE JURISCONSULTS

Sunnī

E8

al-WAQĪᶜ, Muḥammad ibn Khalaf (d. 306/918).

[History of the Judges]. اخبار القضاة

Ed. ᶜAbd al-ᶜAzīz Muṣṭafā al-Maraghī. Cairo, Maṭbaᶜa al-Istiqāma, 1947-55. 3 vols.

Al-Waqīᶜ, a *qāḍī* of Ahwāz, proposed to trace the history of the judiciary in the principle towns of the Islamic Empire, with those of Mecca and Madina listed first.

D. Sourdel, in "Les Cadis de Basra d'aprѐs Wakīᶜ." *Arabica*, II, 1955, pp. 111-14, lists those of that city, together with the volume and page numbers in which their names appear in this edition.

Title transliterated: Akhbār al-Quḍā.

Ḥanafī

E9
IBN QUṬLŪBUGHĀ, Qāsim (d. 879/1474).
[Crown of the Biographies in the Classes of the Ḥanafīya]. تاج التراجم فى طبقات الحنفية *Ed.* Gustav Flügel. *Die Krone der Lebensbeschreibungen Enthaltend die Classen der Hanefiten.* Leipzig, Deutsche Morgenländische Gesellschaft, 1862. xvi + 192 p.

Abhandlungen für die Kunde des Morgenländes, Bd. 2, no. 3.

Brief dictionary of the names of the Ḥanafite scholars to the author's own time. Reprinted in Baghdad in 1962.

Title transliterated: Tāj al-Tarājim fī Ṭabaqāt al-Ḥanafīya.

E10
al-LAKNAWĪ, ᶜAbd al-Ḥayy Muḥammad (d. 1304/1886).
[Radiant Benefits in the Biographies of the Ḥanafīya]. كتاب الفوائد النهية فى تراجم الحنفية Cairo, Aḥmad Nājī al-Jamālī wa Muḥammad Amīn al-Khanjī, 1324/1906. 249 + 13 p.

Title transliterated: Kitāb al-Fawāɔid al-Nihāya fī Tarājim al-Ḥanafīya.

E11
KEMĀL PASHA-ZĀDE, Aḥmad ibn Sulaymān (d. 940/1534).
[A Digest of the Classes of the Interpreters]. رسالة فى طبقات المجتهدين

A digest of this digest was published by Gustav Flügel, "Die Classen der hanefitischen Rectsgelehrten." *Königliche Sächsische Gesellschaft der Wissenschaften, Abhandlungen*, VIII, 1860, pp. 269-358.

Title transliterated: Risāla fī Ṭabaqāt al-Mujtahidīn.

E12
al-QURASHĪ, ᶜAbd al-Qādir ibn Muḥammad (d. 775/1373).
[The Bright Jewels in the Classes of the Ḥanafīya]. الجواهر المضيئة فى طبقات الحنفية Hyderabad-Deccan, Maṭbaᶜa Dāɔira al-Maᶜārif al-ᶜUthmānīya, 1332/1913-14. 2 vols.

Alphabetical dictionary of the Ḥanafite jurists

up to the second half of the 14th century.

Title transliterated: Al-Jawāhir al-Muḍīʾa fī Ṭabaqāt al-Ḥanafīya.

E13
TĀSHKŪBRĪZĀDA, Aḥmad ibn Muṣṭafā (d. 968/1561). [Classes of the Learned]. طبقات الفقهاء *Ed.* Aḥmad Nayl. Mosul, Maṭbaᶜa Naynuwī, 1954. 136 p.

A "bare bones" dictionary.

Title transliterated: Ṭabaqāt al-Fuqahāʾ.

Ḥanbalī

E14
IBN AL-FARRĀʾ, Muḥammad ibn Muḥammad (d. 526/1132). [Classes of the Ḥanābila]. طبقات الحنابلة *Ed.* Muḥammad Ḥamīd al-Fīkī. Cairo, Maṭbaᶜa al-Sana al-Muḥammadīya, 1371/1952. 2 vols.

Alphabetical dictionary of the Ḥanbalite traditionists and jurisconsults up to the beginning of the 6th/11th century. Entries cease with 512/1118.

Title transliterated: Ṭabaqāt al-Ḥanābila.

Abridgements: Muḥammad ibn ᶜAbd al-Qādir al-Nābulusī (d. 797/1395). [Book of the Abridgment]. كتاب اختصار *Ed.* Aḥmad ᶜUbayd. Damascus, N.P., 1350/1931-32. xii + 466 p.

Supplements: ᶜAbd al-Raḥmān ibn Aḥmad ibn Rajjab (d. 795/1392). كتاب الذيل على طبقات الحنابلة [Book of Continuation Upon the Classes of the Ḥanābila]. *Ed.* Muḥammad Ḥamīd al-Fīkī. Cairo, Maṭbaᶜa al-Sana al-Muḥammadīya, 1372/1953. 2 vols. Ibn Rajab began his notices with the colleagues of Ibn al-Farrāʾ and carried them to 750/1349, arranged by death date. Another, incomplete, edition was begun by Henri Laoust and Sāmī al-Dahhān, *Histoire des Ḥanbalites*, Damascus, 1951. One volume only published.

E15
al-SHAṬṬĪ, Jamīl ibn ᶜUmar. [Compendium of the Classes of the Ḥanābila]. مختصر طبقات الحنابلة Damascus, Ṭabaᶜ Mahfūza al-Muʾalim, 1339/1921. [iv] + 187 p.

Brief biographical sketches of Ḥanbalite juris-

consults to the beginning of the 20th century.
Title transliterated: Mukhtaṣar Ṭabaqāt al-Ḥanābila.

¶ Reference may also be made to the biographical work by Ibn al-ᶜImād, *Shadhrāt al-Dhahab fī Akhbār man Dhahab* [J95].

Malikī

E16
IBN FARḤŪN, Ibrāhīm ibn ᶜAlī al-Yaᶜmarī (d. 799/1397).
الديباج المذهب فى معرفة عيان علماء المذهب
[The Ornament of the Teaching in Knowing the Learned Sources of the Teaching]. Cairo, ᶜAbbās Shaqrūn, 1932. viii + 362 p.
Biographical dictionary of the Malikite jurisconsults, containing approximately 630 entries, up to his own time. This edition is printed with Aḥmad Bābā al-Takrūrī's (d. 1036/1627) supplement, [Attainment of Delight نيل الابتهاج بتطريز الديباج in Embroidering the Ornament]. An earlier edition of the combined dictionaries, bringing the entries down to 1596, was lithographed in Fez in 1317/1898-99.
Title transliterated: Al-Dībāj al-Madhhab fī Maᶜrifa ᶜIyān ᶜUlamāᵓ al-Madhhab.

E17
IBN MŪSĀ, ᶜIyād.
[Biographies of the Aghlabids]. تراجم أغلبية
Tunis, Al-Maṭbaᶜāt al-Rasmīya al-Tūnisīya, 1968. 568 p.
Biographical sketches of 173 Malikite jurists associated with the city of Tunis between 184-296/750-950.
Title transliterated: Tarājim Aghlabīya.

Shāfiᶜī

E18
al-ᶜABBĀDĪ, Muḥammad ibn Aḥmad (d. 458/1066).
[Classes of the Shāfiᶜite كتاب طبقات الفقهاء الشافعية Jurists]. *Ed.* Gösta Vitestam. Kitāb Ṭabaqāt al-Fuqahāᵓ aš-Šāfiᶜīya: *das klassenbuch der gelehrten Šafīᶜiten*. Leiden, E. J. Brill, 1964. X, 61 + 154 p., illus.

Very brief biographical sketches of Shāfiᶜite jurists, arranged by decades, up to the 5th/11th century by a jurist of Herat. This edition is illustrated with eight pages of manuscripts.

Title transliterated: Kitāb Ṭabaqāt al-Fuqahāʾ al-Shāfiᶜīya.

E19

al-ISNAWĪ, ᶜAbd al-Raḥīm ibn al-Ḥasan (d. 772/1370). [Classes of the Shāfiᶜīya]. طبقات الشافعية *Ed.* ᶜAbd Allāh al-Jabūrī. Baghdad, Riʾāsa Dīwān al-Awqāf, 1390-91/1970-71. 2 vols.

Iḥya al-Turāth al-Islāmī, Kitāb 1.

Arranged in alphabetical order by the names or surnames by which they were best known by an Egyptian scholar. The last entry died in 768/1367.

Title transliterated: Ṭabaqāt al-Shāfiᶜīya.

E20

al-SHĪRĀZĪ, Ibrāhīm ibn ᶜAlī (d. 476/1083-84). [Classes of the طبقات الفقهاء و يليه طبقات الشافعية Jurists and Classes of the Shāfiᶜīya]. *Ed.* Ihsān ᶜAbbās. Beirut, 1970. 231 p.

Brief biographical notices, listed according to town, of the jurisconsults down to his own time.

Previously printed in Baghdad, 1357/1938.

Title transliterated: Ṭabaqāt al-Fuqahāʾ...

E21

al-SUBKĪ, ᶜAbd al-Wahhāb ibn ᶜAlī (d. 771/1370). [Classes of the Shāfiᶜīya]. طبقات الشافعية الكبرى *Ed.* Maḥmūd Muḥammad al-Tanāḥī *and* ᶜAbd al-Fatāḥ Muḥammad al-Ḥalū. Cairo, ᶜĪsā al-Bābī al-Ḥalabī, 1383-94/1964-76. 10 vols.

Biographies of the Shāfiᶜite jurisconsults to the middle of the 8th/14th century arranged by decade. This edition contains notes and indices. An earlier edition was published in Cairo in 6 vols. in 1324-25/1906-7.

Title transliterated: Ṭabaqāt al-Shāfiᶜīya al-Kubrā.

Supplements: Abū Bakr ibn Hidāyat Allāh al-Muṣannif al-Kūrānī al-Kindī (d. 1014/1605). [Classes of the Shāfiᶜīya]. طبقات الشافعية

Baghdad, 1356/1937. 110 p. This brings al-Subkī's dictionary up to the beginning of the 11th/17th century.

Shīᶜī

E22
IBN SHAHRĀSHŪB, Muḥammad ibn ᶜAlī (d. 588/1192).
[Guideposts of the Learned]. معالم العلماء.
Ed. ᶜAbbās Eghbal. Tehran, N.P., 1353/1934. 142 p.
Short biographies of the Shīᶜite jurisconsults. Reprinted in Najaf in 1380/1960-61.
Title transliterated: Muᶜālim al-ᶜUlamāʾ.

E23
al-JAᶜDĪ, ᶜUmar ibn ᶜAlī ibn Samura (d. 586/1190).
طبقات فقهاء جبال اليمن و عيون من اخبار سادات , وساء و معرفة لسابهم و مبلغ أعمارهم ووقت و فاتهم و ميا ليهم
Les Générations des Jurisconsultes yéménites. *Ed.* Fuʾād Sayyid. Cairo, Maṭbaᶜa al-Sana al-Ḥamdīya, 1957. [xvi] + 327 p.
Al-Maktaba al-Yamanīya, 1.
The editor has simplified the title to: طبقات فقهاء اليمن. The French title appears only on the paper wrappers.
Title transliterated: Ṭabaqāt Fuqahāʾ Jibāl al-Yaman...

E24
al-KAẒIMĪ, Muḥammad Mahdī al-Mūsawī.
احسن الوديعة في تراجم مشاهير مجتهدى الشيعة
[The Most Beautiful Depository in the Biographies of Celebrated Shīᶜite Scholars]. Najaf, Al-Maṭbaᶜa al-Ḥaydarīya, 1968. 2 vols. in 1.
Biographical dictionary of approximately 100 Shīᶜite scholars who lived during the period 1750-1950 as a supplement to, and continuation of, al-Khwānsārī [D156]. Previously published in Baghdad, *cir.* 1930.
Title transliterated: Aḥsan al-Wadīᶜa fi Tarājim Mashāhīr Mujtahidī al-Shīᶜa.

LANGUAGE F

BIBLIOGRAPHY

Arabic

F1
BAKALLA, M. H.
Bibliography of Arabic Linguistics. London, Mansell Information/Publishing Ltd., 1975. xxxvii, 300 + 8 [Arabic text] p.

Author listings of a total of 2,018 books, articles, and dissertations on all aspects of the Arabic language in Arabic and European languages. Divided into an "Occidental Section" and an "Oriental Section." Six indices (General subject, Analytical subject, Co-authors and co-editors, Editors, Reviewers, and Arabic authors). See Addenda.

F2
KILLEAN, Carolyn G.
"Classical Arabic." *Ed.* Thomas A. Sebeok. *Current Trends in Linguistics*. Vol. 6: *Linguistics in South West Asia and North Africa*. The Hague, Mouton, 1970. Pp. 413-38.

Bibliography of modern studies on Classical and Modern Literary Arabic arranged in alphabetical order by author, in Arabic and European languages. The bibliography is preceded by a 12 page essay.

Panjabi

F3
GRIERSON, George A.
"A Bibliography of the Panjabi Language." *The Indian Antiquary: a journal of oriental research,* XXXV, 1906, pp. 65-72.

A listing of all works pertaining to Panjabi

known to the compiler.

Contents: I.- General; II.- Grammars, Dictionaries, and Aids to the Student, including collections of proverbs.

Persian

F4

LAZARD, Gilbert.

"Persian and Tajik." *Ed.* Thomas A. Sebeok. *Current Trends in Linguistics.* Vol. 6: *Linguistics in South West Asia and North Africa.* The Hague, Mouton, 1970. Pp. 64-96.

Particularly valuable for the many references to Persian studies.

F5

NAWABI, Y. M.

A Bibliography of Iran: a catalogue of books and articles on Iranian subjects, mainly in European languages. Tehran, Iranian Culture Foundation, 1969-71. 2 vols.

Publication nos. 53 & 106.

Classified listings by subject and then by author.

Contents: Vol. 2: Persian Language and Literature: I. Language [General Works; Chrestomathy; Dictionaries; Etymologies; Grammar; Proverbs; Wit and Humor; Writing and Calligraphy]. No index.

Turkish

F6

HAZAI, G.

"Turkish." *Ed.* Thomas A. Sebeok. *Current Trends in Linguistics.* Vol. 6: *Linguistics in South West Asia and North Africa.* The Hague, Mouton, 1970. Pp. 181-216.

Bibliography of modern studies on both the old and the new Turkish. Preceded by a lengthy summary.

BIOGRAPHIES OF THE GRAMMARIANS

F7

IBN AL-ANBĀRĪ, ʿAbd al-Raḥmān ibn Muḥammad (d. 577/1181).

[Book of the Pure- كتاب نزهت الالبّاء فى طبقات الادباء
ness of the Assiduous in the Classes of the Grammar-

ians]. *Ed.* Muḥammad abī al-Faḍl Ibrāhīm. Cairo, Dār Nahḍa Miṣr li-l-Tabaʿ wa al-Nashra, 1967. xii + 481 p.

Bio-bibliography of Arabic grammarians down to the author's own time, arranged chronologically. Previously printed in Cairo (1877), Baghdad (1960) and Stockholm (1963).

Title transliterated: Kitāb Nuzha al-Alibbāʾ fī Ṭabaqāt al-Udabāʾ.

F8

IBN QĀḌĪ SHUHBA, Abū Bakr ibn Muḥammad (d. 851/1448). [Classes of the Grammarians طبقات النحاة و اللغويين and Linguists]. *Ed.* Muḥsin Ghayaḍ. Najaf, Maṭbaʿa al-Nuʿmān, 1974. 317 p.

Title transliterated: Ṭabaqāt al-Nuḥā wa al-Lughawīyīn.

F9

al-LUGHAWĪ, ʿAbd al-Wāḥid ibn ʿAlī (d. 351/962). [Ranks of the Philologists]. مراتب النحويين *Ed.* Muḥammad abī al-Faḍl Ibrāhīm. Cairo, Maktaba Nahḍa Miṣr, 1955. ix + 140 p.

Title transliterated: Marātib al-Naḥwīyīn.

F10

al-QIFṬĪ, ʿAlī ibn Yūsuf (d. 646/1248). [Transmitter of Informa- انباه الرواة على انباه النحاة tion about the Knowledge of the Grammarians]. *Ed.* Muhammad abī al-Faḍl Ibrāhīm. Cairo, Maṭbaʿa Dār al-Kutub, 1369-70/1950-51. 3 vols.

Biographical dictionary of about 1,000 grammarians from the time of Abū al-Aswad al-Duʾālī to the beginning of the 7th/13th century.

Title transliterated: Inbāʾ al-Ruwā ʿala Anbāʾ al-Nuhā.

F11

al-SĪRĀFĪ, al-Ḥasan ibn ʿAbd Allāh (d. 368/979). *Biographies des Grammairiens* اخبار النحويين البصريين *de l'Ecole de Basra.* *Ed.* F. Krenkow. Paris, Paul Geuthner; Beirut, Imprimerie Catholique, 1936. ix + 116 p.

Bibliotheca Arabica, IX.

A facsimile edition published under the auspices of the Institut d'Etudes Orientales, Faculté des Lettres d'Alger. Reprinted in Baghdad in 1968.

Title transliterated: Akhbār al-Nahwiyīn al-Basriyīn.

F12
al-SUYŪṬĪ, ᶜAbd al-Raḥmān ibn Abī Bakr (d. 911/1505).
كتاب بغية الوعاة فى طبقات اللغويين و النحاة
[The Answer Book Regarding the Classes of the Lexicographers and the Grammarians]. *Ed.* Muḥammad abī al-Faḍl Ibrāhīm. Cairo, Maṭbaᶜa ᶜĪsā al-Ḥalabī, 1964. 2 vols.

Title transliterated: Kitāb Bughya al-Wuᶜā fī Ṭabaqāt al-Lughawīyīn wa al-Naḥā.

F13
al-ZUBAYDĪ, Muḥammad ibn al-Ḥasan (d. 379/989).
[Classes of the Grammar- طبقات النحويين و اللغويين ians and the Lexicographers]. *Ed.* Muḥammad abī al-Faḍl Ibrāhīm. *2nd ed.* Cairo, Dār al-Maᶜārif, 1973. 414 p.

Title transliterated: Ṭabaqāt al-Naḥwiyīn wa al-Lughawīyīn.

DICTIONARIES

Bibliographies

General

F14
ZAUNMÜLLER, Walfram.
Bibliographisches Handbuch der Sprachwörterbucher: ein internationales verzeichnis von 5600 wörterbücher der jahre 1460-1958 für mehr als 500 sprachen und dialekte/ A Critical Bibliography of Language Dictionaries. Stuttgart, Anton Hiersemann Verlag: New York/London, Hafner Publishing, 1958. XVI + 496 cols.

Arranged alphabetically by language with occasional brief explanatory notes. Index of languages by continent and index of personal names.

Arabic

F15
GHĀLĪ, Wajdī Rizq.
Arabic المعجمات العربية، بيليوجرافية شاملة مشروحة/

Dictionaries: an annotated comprehensive bibliography. Cairo, Al-Nāshr al-Hīyaɔ al-Miṣrīya al-ᶜĀmma li-l-Taɔlīf wa al-Nashr, 1391/1971. 253 + [iii] p.

Classified, annotated bibliography of 707 mono-, bi-, tri-, and multilingual Arabic dictionaries, lexicons, and phrase books.

"The bibliography is divided into three sections plus 2 appendices:

"1. Arabic general mono-lingual dictionaries (Arabic-Arabic). They are subdivided into: dictionaries of words, antonyms, synonyms, colloquial and foreign words, and subject dictionaries. Entries in each division are arranged alphabetically by authors.

"2. Bi-, tr-, and multilingual general dictionaries (Arabic-non-Arabic, and non-Arabic-Arabic dictionaries). This section is arranged alphabetically by foreign languages.

"3. Special Arabic dictionaries. This section is arranged alphabetically by subject headings.

"Appendix 1 includes a list of conversation and phrase books. It is arranged alphabetically by foreign languages. Appendix 2 includes special lists of terms. It is arranged alphabetically by subject headings." *[Intro.]*.

Author, title, subject, language, and chronological indices.

Supplements: Wajdī Rizq Ghālī. "Arabic Dictionaries: an annotated comprehensive bibliography. Supplement." *Mélanges de l'Institut Dominicain d'Etudes Orientales*, XII, 1974, pp. 243-87.

F16
QĀSIM, Nazār Muḥammad ᶜAlī.

المعاجم العربية فى العلوم و الفنون و اللغات: ترتيبها ، محتوياتها ، استعمالها على قاسم

[Arabic Dictionaries in the Sciences, Arts, and Languages: their order, contents, and use]. Baghdad, Al-Maktaba al-Markazīya, Jāmiᶜa Baghdād, [1967]. x + 192 p.

Classified, annotated listing of 333 monolingual Arabic dictionaries published since the introduction of printing to 1966.

Contents: 1. Al-Lughāt wa al-Ādāb; 2. Insāniyāt; 3. ᶜUlūm al-Baḥta wa al-Taṭbīqīya; 4. Al- ᶜUlūm al-Ijtimāᶜīya. Author and title indices.

Persian

¶ A bibliography of Persian language dictionaries is to be found in volume two (pages 45-60) of Y. M. Nawabi's *A Bibliography of Iran* [F5].

Reference Dictionaries

The following list of selected bi- and trilingual dictionaries are those most employed for reference purposes.

Arabic

F17
BLACHERE, R.; CHOUEMI, M. *and* DENIZEAU, Cl.
Dictionnaire Arabe-Français-Anglais (langue classique et modern). Paris, G. P. Maisonneuve & Larose, 1967- [in progress].

Important new trilingual dictionary issued in fascicules of approximately 64 pages each. Between four and six fasciculi are published each year with 12 comprising one volume.

Contents: I. أ ـ بقدوسد ; II. بقر ـ جزى ; III. جسأ ـ حدوى IV. حرث ـ

F18
KAZIMIRSKI, A. de Biberstein.
Dictionnaire Arabe-Français: contenant toutes les racines de la langue arabe, leurs dérivés, tout dans l'idiome vulgaire que dans l'idiome littéral, ainsi que les dialects d'Alger et de Maroc. Paris, G. P. Maisonneuve et Cie, 1860. 2 vols.

Reprinted in Cairo in 1875 in four volumes, and more recently in 1970 from the French edition.

F19
LANE, Edward William.
An Arabic-English Lexicon: derived from the best and the most copious eastern sources. London, Williams and Norgate, 1863-85. 8 vols.

The *Lexicon*, as envisaged by Lane was to consist of two parts, the first to comprise the most commonly used words, the second for those words either rarely used or not commonly known. The second part was never published. Lane, prior to his death in 1876, completed the *Lexicon* only through *qad*. The remainder was incompletely edited by his newphew, Stanley Lane-Poole, from Lane's notes. Has been reprinted in the original size in 1958 and again, in reduced format, in 1984.

Supplements:

R. P. A. Dozy. *Supplément aux Dictionnaires arabes*. *2nd ed*. Leiden, E. J. Brill, 1927. 2 vols. Supplemental words and meanings to the then available Arabic dictionaries, especially to Lane, derived from additional literary materials. Particularly valuable for the dialects of North Africa. Reprinted in 1967.

Anton Spitaler; Jörg Kraemer *and* Helmut Gätje. *Wörterbuch der klassischen Arabischen Sprache*. Wiesbaden, Otto Harrassowitz, 1957- [in progress]. Arabic-German-English lexicon based upon the notes of a number of German orientalists in continuation of Lane, beginning with the letter *kaf*. Issued irregularly in fasciculi, currently through volume II, part 7.

Persian

F20

STEINGASS, A.

A Comprehensive Persian-English Dictionary: including the Arabic words and phrases to be met with in Persian literature, being Johnson's and Richardson's Persian, Arabic and English dictionary rev., enl. and entirely reconstructed. London, Routledge and Kegan Paul, Ltd., 1892. 1539 p.

Turkish

F21

BARBIER DE MAYNARD, A. C.

Dictionnaire Turc-Français: supplément aux dictionnaires publiés jusqu'à ce jour renfermant 1° les mots d'origine turque, 2° les mots arabes et persans employés en osmanli avec leur signification particulière, 3° un grand nombre de proverbes et de locutions populaires, 4° un vocabulaire géographique de l'empire ottoman. Paris, Ernst Leroux, 1881-86. 2 vols.

Publications de l'Ecole des Langues Orientales Vivantes, II sèrie, Vol. IV-V.

F22
REDHOUSE, James W., *Sir.*
Turkish and English Lexicon: showing in English the significance of the Turkish forms. Constantinople, American Mission, 1890. 2224 p.
Regarded as the standard lexicon. A companion volume was previously published by Sir James, *English and Turkish Lexicon: showing in Turkish the literal, incidental, figurative and colloquial and technical significations of the English terms.* Oxford, University Press, 1884. 828 p.

F23
---.
Redhouse Yeni Türkçe-İngilize Sözlük/ New Redhouse Turkish-English Dictionary. *Rev. ed.* Istanbul, Redhouse Press, 1968. XXXII + 1292 p.
On the title page stated to be a "new" dictionary based upon Redhouse's 1890 edition. A standard work for both the old and the new literary language. Provides the modern spelling, the old Turkish script, and, of course, the English equivalents.

F24
TURKEY. Türk Dil Kurumu.
Onüçüncü [XIII] Yüzyıldan beri Türkiye Türkçesiyle Yazılmış Kitaplardan Toplanan Tanıkariyle Tarama Sözlüğü. [Research Dictionary of Thirteenth Century Turkish Writing]. Ankara, Türk Dil Kurumu, 1963- .
Historical dictionary of Turkish based upon some 225 early sources. Revised edition of TDK's *Türkiye Türkçesi Tarihî Sözlüğü Hazırlıklarından*, 1943-57. 4 vols.

Urdu

F25
PLATTS, John T.
A Dictionary of Urdu, Classical Hindi, and English. London, W. H. Allen & Co., 1884. viii + 1259 p.
Reprinted in Oxford in 1930.

LITERATURE G

GENERAL

Dictionaries

G1
PRUŠEK, Jaroslav, *ed.*
Dictionary of Oriental Literatures. London, George Allen & Unwin Ltd., 1974. 3 vols.

An international collaborative project to provide for the general reader and for students an alphabetical dictionary to the writers, genres, terms, and titles (in transliteration only) in the literature of Asia and North Africa. Each volume is according to region and language with the materials presented in alphabetical order according to the Latin alphabet. Articles are signed with some having brief bibliographies and all articles are quite short, none over a column in length.

Contents: Vol. I: East Asia [Chinese, Japanese, Korean, Mongolian, Tibetan]; Vol. II: South and South-East Asia [India, Pakistan and Bangladesh: Ancient Indian, Assamese, Baluchi, Bengali, Gujarati, Hindi, Indian literature written in English, Indo-Persian, Kannada, Kashmiri, Maithili, Malayalam, Marathi, Oriya, Panjabi, Pashto, Rajasthani, Sindhi, Tamil, Telugu, Urdu; Nepali; Sinhalese; South-East Asia: Burmese, Cambodian, Javanese, Malay and Indonesian, Philippines, Thai, Vietnamese]; Vol. III: West Asia and North Africa [Ancient Near East; Arab Countries: Classical Arabic, Algerian, Egyptian, Iraqi, Jordanian, Lebanese, Moroccan, Palestinian, Sudanese, Syrian, Tunisian; Turkey: Turkish, Turkic, Kurdish, Armenian; Iran: Ancient and Middle Persian, New Persian, Jewish-Persian, Kurdish, Armenian; Afghanistan:

Pashto, Dari; Soviet East: Abkhazian, Armenian, Avar, Azerbaijan, Chukot, Circassian, Darg, Georgian, Kazakh, Kirghiz, Kurdish, Lezgian, Ossetian, Tatar, Tajik, Turkic, Turkmen, Uzbek, Yakut].

¶ Detailed, scholarly articles on individual authors and genres will be found in the *Encyclopaedia of Islam* and its translations [C1].

Bio-bibliographies - General

G2

MUSHĀR, Khānbābā.

مؤلفین کتب چاپی فارسی و عربی ازآغاز چاپ تاکنون

[Authors of Printed Persian and Arabic Books from the Beginning of Printing to the Present]. Tehran, N.P., 1340-44/1961-65. 6 vols., illus.

Bio-bibliographical dictionary of classical and contemporary Arabic and Persian writers listed by *ism*. Provides brief bibliographical data, often illustrated with photographic or sketched portraits, and the titles of their works, with date and place of publication. No index. Stronger for Persian than for Arabic writers.

Title transliterated: Muʾallifīn Kutub Chāpī Fārsī wa ʿArabī...

Quotations

G3

AKSOY, Ömer Asim.

Atazözleri ve Deyimler [Proverbs and Sayings]. Ankara, Türk Dil Kurumu, 1965. 542 [ii] p.

Türk Dil Kurumu Yayınları: 238.

Lists 5,700 Turkish popular sayings and proverbs with introduction and bibliography.

G4

FIELD, Claude H. A. F.

Dictionary of Oriental Quotations (Arabic and Persian). London, Sonnenschein; New York, Macmillan, 1911. 351 p.

Brief quotations in transliteration and English translation from the works of 85 oriental authors, arranged alphabetically by first word. Indices of authors, subjects, and catchwords.

G5

GADEN, Henri.

Proverbes et Maximes Peuls et Toucouleurs: traduits, expliqués et annotés. Paris, Institut d'Ethnologie, 1931. XXXIII + 368 p.

Travaux et Mémoires de l'Institut d'Ethnologie, XVI.

ARABIC

Bibliographies

G6

ALTOMA, Salih J.

Modern Arabic Literature: a bibliography of articles, books, dissertations, and translations in English. Bloomington, Asian Studies Research Institute, Indiana University, 1975. [iv] + 73 p.

Occasional Papers No. 3.

Classified, unannotated listing of materials, in English, concerning Arabic literature since 1800. Consists of 850 items by author in each section. Does *not* provide name of publisher of books.

Contents: I. Bibliographies; II. Cultural Background; III. Modern Literature: general works; IV. Drama; V. Fiction; VI. Poetry; VII. Authors; VIII. Mahjarite (Syrian/Arab American) Writings; IX. North Africa Literature; X. Palestinian Themes and Arab-Jewish Relations; XI. Dissertations. Author index.

G7

MAKKĪ, Ṭāhir Aḥmad.

Des Sources bibliographiques /دراسة في مصادر الادب/ de la Littérature arabe. Cairo, Dār al-Maᶜārif, 1968- .

Title transliterated: Dirāsa fī Maṣādir al-Adab.

Bibliographies of Translations

G8

ANDERSON, Margaret.

Arabic Materials in English Translation: a bibliography of works from the pre-Islamic period to 1977. Boston, G. K. Hall & Co., 1980. xiii + 249 p.

Classified list of approximately 1,600 complete

and portions of works translated from the Arabic since the beginning of printing until 1977. Complete listings of translations of the Qur>ān and the *Thousand and One Nights* are not included. Author, translator, and title (both Arabic and English) index.

Contents: Anthologies of Classical and Pre-Islamic Materials; Anthologies of Materials Written or Collected after 1800; Documents Written before 1800; Documents Dating from 1800 to the 1970s; Islamic Studies; Philosophy; Music; Materials in the History of Science, Technology, and Medicine; History; Geography; Social Science Materials; Classical Arabic Literature; Modern Arabic Literature; Non-Islamic Religious Materials.

G9

KHOURY, R. G.

Bibliographie raisonnée des Traductions publiées au Liban à partir des Langues étrangers de 1840 à jusqu'aux environs de 1905. Paris, Faculté des Lettres et Sciences Humaines, Université de Paris, [1965]. 239 p.

Classified and annotated listings of 542 western European and Ottoman Turkish books translated into Arabic during this very formative period.

Contents: Première partie [bibliographie]: A- Sciences religieuses; B- Littérature; C- Histoire-géographie; D- Sciences; E- Institutions sociales. The second part is a brief essay, illustrated with graphs, on this translation activity. Indices of authors translated, names of translators, works translated and translation titles. No index of publishers, unfortunately.

G10

STEINSCHNEIDER, Moritz.

Die Europäischen Ubersetzungen aus dem Arabischen bis mitte 17. Jahrhunderts. Graz, Akademische Druck- u. Verlagsanstalt, 1956. XII, 84 + 108 p.

Reprinting of the author's two articles published in the *Sitzungsberichten der Kaiserlichen Akademie der Wissenschaften in Wien, philosophisch - historische Klasse*, CXLIX, 1904 and CLI, 1905.

Contents: A. Schriften bekannter Übersetzer; B.

Übersetzungen von Werken bekannter Autoren, deren Übersetzer unbekannt order unsicher sind; C. Anonyme Schriften oder von unsichere Autoren und Übersetzern. Index of personal names.

G11
WÜSTENFELD, Heinrich Ferdinand.
Die Übersetzungen arabischer Werke in das Lateinische seit dem XI. Jahrhundert. Göttingen, Dieterich'sche Verlags- buchhandlung, 1977. 1 + 133 p.

¶ Listings of translations into western languages from Arabic, Persian, and Ottoman Turkish are also to be found in Christian Schnurrer's *Bibliotheca Arabica* (1811) [A37], J. T. Zenker's *Bibliotheca Orientalis* (1846-61) [A16] , Victor Chauvin's *Bibliographie des Ouvrages arabes* (1810-85) [A37], and into English only in William T. DeBary and Ainslie Embree's *A Guide to Oriental Classics* (New York, Columbia University Press, 1964), "I. Classics of the Islamic Tradition" [compiled by Maan Z. Madina], pp. 11-33, and Salih Altoma's *Modern Arabic Literature* [G6].

Bio-bibliographies

G12
al-BAGHDĀTLĪ, Ismāᶜīl ibn Muḥammad.
[Gift of هدية العارفين اسماء المؤلفين و اثار المصنفين Acquaintance to the Names of the Authors and the Works of the Writers]. *Ed.* K. R. Bilge, M. K. İnal *and* A. Aktuç. Istanbul, Wizāra al-Maᶜārif, 1951-55. 2 vols.

Alphabetical dictionary of Muslim authors, with brief biographical notes and lists of their works, by the continuator of Kātib Čelebī.

Title transliterated: Hadīya al-ᶜĀrifīn Asmāɔ al-Muɔallifīn...

G13
BROCKELMANN, Carl.
Geschichte der arabischen Litteratur. Leiden, E. J. Brill, 1937-49. 5 vols.

Bio-bibliographical survey of Arabic literature from classical Islamic times to the outbreak of World War II. Provides a brief biographical notice on each author, bibliographical information on both the author and his works, and a listing of his extant works, with locations of manuscript copies and, if printed, publication details.

The original work, in two volumes, was printed in Weimar in 1898-1902 and reprinted, with corrections, in 1943-49. The pagination of the first and second editions differ. However, in the reprint the page numbers of the original are provided on the margins and it is to these that reference is made in the index and by others. Between 1937 and 1942 three supplementary volumes were issued. Author, title, and editor/translator indices are in the third supplementary volume. The entire work is currently being supplanted by Fuat Sezgin [G16].

Contents: B. I- Einleitung. 1. Buch - Die arabischen Nationallitterature; 2. Buch - Die islamische Litterature in arabischer Sprache. B. II: 3. Buch - Der Niedergang der islamischen Litterature. S. B. III: 4. Buch - Die moderne arabische Litterature. [The first two supplementary volumes are, respectively, to the first two original and have the same arrangement].

Translations: Trans. ᶜAbd al-Ḥalīm al-Najār. [Taʾrīkh al-Adab al-ᶜArabī]. تاريخ الادب العربي
Cairo, Dār al-Maᶜārif bi-Miṣr, 1962. 3 vols.

G14
DĀGHIR, Yūsuf Asᶜad.
مصادر الدراسة الادبية و فقا لمناهج التعليم الرسمية: لبنان، سوريا، العراق، مصر/
Elements de Bio-bibliographie de la Litterature arabe Conforme aux Programmes officiels de l'Enseignement: Liban, Syrie, Iraq, Egypte. Saida, Lebanon, Maṭbaᶜa Dayz al-Makhnās, 1950-56. 3 vols. in 4.

Authors are listed by year of death (hijra).

Title transliterated: Maṣādir al-Dirāsa al-Adabīya...

G15
al-IṢBAHĀNĪ, ᶜAlī ibn al-Ḥusayn (d. 356/967).
[Book of Songs]. كتاب الاغانى
Bulaq, 1285/1868-69. 20 vols.

Thesaurus of Arabic poetry set to music up to

the compiler's own time, with musical notes and biographies of poets, musicians, and singers.

An additional volume, edited by R. E. Brünnow, *The Twenty-first Volume of the* Kitâb al-Aghânî; *being a collection of biographies not contained in the edition of Bulak*. Leiden, E. J. Brill, 1888.

I. Guidi, with others, prepared an index to the full 21 volumes, *Tables alphabêtiques du* Kitâb al-Aghânî. Leiden, E. J. Brill, 1895-1900. 2 vols. I. Index des Poètes dont le *Kitâb* Cite des Vers; II. Index des Rimes; III. Index historique; IV. Index Géographique.

The Bulaq edition, together with Brünnow's additional volume and Guidi's index has been reprinted in Beirut *cir*. 1975. A new, vocalized, edition was begun by the Egyptian National Library in 1927 (Cairo, Matbaʿa Dār al-Kutub, 1927-54. 16 vols.). This edition was continued, volumes 17-24, by al-Hayʾa al-Miṣrīya al-ʿĀmma li-l-Taʾlīf wa al-Nashr (later, Al-Hayʾa al-Miṣrīya al-ʿĀmma li-l-Kitāb), 1970-74. Another printing, edited by ʿAbd al-Sattar Aḥmad Farraj, has been released by Dār al-Thaqafīya, 1955-73, in 25 volumes. The indices are in volumes 24 and 25.

Title transliterated: Kitāb al-Aghānī.

G16

SEZGIN, Fuat.

Geschichte des arabischen Schrifttums. Leiden, E. J. Brill, 1967- [in progress].

A reedition of Brockelmann's *GAL* [G13] providing the same information but in a different arrangement.

Contents (to date): B. I: Qurʾānwissenschaften, Hadīṯ, Geschichte, Fiqh, Dogmatik, Mystik - bis *ca*. 430 A.H. B. II: Poesie, Prosa, Philologie; Unterhaltungsliteratur und erbauliche Schriften - bis *ca*. 430 A.H. B. III: Medizin.

Translations: Trans. Fahmī abī al-Faḍl, تاريخ التراث العربي [History of the Arabic Legacy]. Cairo, Al-Hayʾa al-Miṣrīya al-ʿĀmma li-l-Taʾlīf wa al-Nashr, 1971- [in progress].

Iraq

G17
ᶜAWWĀD, Kūrkīs.
معجم المؤلفين العراقيين فى القرنين التاسع عشر و العشرين ١٨٠٠ - ١٩٦٩
A Dictionary of Iraqi Authors During the Nineteenth and Twentieth Centuries (1800-1969 A.D.). Baghdad, Maṭbaᶜa al-Irshād, 1969. 3 vols.

Alphabetical listing by *ism* of authors, their dates, the titles of their works, with publication dates, and the cities with which they are associated.

Title transliterated: Muᶜjam al-Muᵓallifīn al-ᶜIrāqiyīn...

Biographies

General

G18
KAḤḤĀLA, ᶜUmar Riḍā.
[Dictionary معجم المؤلفين تراجم مصنفي الكتب العربية of Authors: biographies of the writers of Arabic books]. Damascus, Maṭbaᶜa al-Turqī, 1376-81/1957-61. 15 vols. in 8.

A very useful modern dictionary of classical and modern Arabic writers in all fields, listed by *ism*. In addition to providing both the *hijra* and Christian dates of birth and death, and a brief account of his life, the primary bibliographical sources for each author are listed. Index of names in volumes 14 and 15.

Title transliterated: Muᶜjam al-Muᵓallifīn Tarājim Muṣannifī al-Kutub al-ᶜArabīya.

G19
al-TŪNKĪ, Maḥmūd Ḥasan.
[Dictionary of Writers]. معجم المصنفين
Beirut, Maṭbaᶜa wa Zinkūgharāf Ṭibāra, 1344/1925. 4 vols. in 2.

Another modern dictionary, but not as detailed as the preceding.

Title transliterated: Muᶜjam al-Muṣannifīn.

G20
ᶜUMARĪ, Muḥammad Yūsuf Kukan.
[Informa- اعلام النثر و الشعر فى العصر العربى الحديث

tion Regarding Prose and Poetry of the Arabs in the Modern Age]. Madras, Dār Ḥāfiẓa, 1980. 2 vols.

Biographical dictionary of Arabic writers of the 19th and 20th centuries.

Title transliterated: Iᶜlām al-Nathr wa al-Shiᶜr fī al-ᶜAṣr al-ᶜArabī al-Ḥadīth.

G21
YĀQŪT, Shihāb al-Dīn abī ᶜAbd Allāh (d. 626/1229).
معجم الادباء، المعروف بارشاد الاريب الى معرفة الاديب
[Dictionary of the Learned, known as the intelligent guidance to cultured knowledge]. *Ed.* D. S. Margoliouth. *Yâqût's Dictionary of Learned Men.* London, Luzac & Co./Leiden, E. J. Brill, 1907-13. 6 vols.

E. J. W. Gibb Memorial Series, VI.

Biographical dictionary of noted grammarians, philologists, calligraphers, poets, etc., arranged by *ism*.

Other editions have been published in Cairo (1925-27, 7 vols. and 1936-38, 20 vols.).

Title transliterated: Muᶜjam al-Udabāʾ...

Spain

G22
al-ANDALUSĪ, ᶜAlī ibn Bassām (d. 542/1147).
الذخيرة في محاسن اهل الجزيرة
[The Treasures in the Merits of the People of the West]. Cairo, Maṭbaᶜa Lajna al-Taʾlīf wa al-Tarjama wa al-Nashr, 1939-45. 3 vols.

Biographical dictionary and anthology of the writers and poets of Spain, primarily of his own generation. Organized by region: I. Cordova; II. Western Spain; III. Eastern Spain.

Title transliterated: Al-Dhakhīra fī Maḥāsin Ahl al-Jazīra.

Poets

G23
al-ĀMIDĪ, al-Ḥasan ibn Bishr (d. 371/987).
المؤتلف و المختلف فى اسماء الشعراء و كناهم و القابهم و انسابهم و بعض شعرهم
[The Similarities and the Diverse in the Names of the Poets: their *kunyas*, *laqabs*, and *nisbas* and portions of their poems]. *Ed.* F. Krenkow. Cairo, Maktaba al-Qudsī, 1354/1935.

556 p.

Brief notices of poets whose names are in part identical, in alphabetical order, together with short examples of their poetry.
Another edition, by ᶜAbd al-Sattār Aḥmad Farrāj, was published in Cairo in 1381/1961.

Title transliterated: Al-Muʾtalif wa al-Mukhtalif fī Asmāʾ al-Shuᶜarāʾ...

G24
al-AYYŪBĪ, Yāsīn.
[Dictionary of the Poets in the *Lisān al-ᶜArab*]. معجم الشعراء فى "لسان العرب" Beirut, Dār al-ᶜAlam li-l-Milāʾiyīn, 1980. 550 p.

Biographical dictionary, with cross-references, of the poets cited in the dictionary by Ibn Manẓūr.

Title transliterated: Muᶜjam al-Shuᶜarāʾ fī "Lisān al-ᶜArab".

G25
IBN AL-ABBĀR, Muḥammad ibn ᶜAbd Allāh (d. 658/1260).
[The Book Clothing the Poets]. كتاب الحلة السيراء Cairo, Al-Shirka al-ᶜArabīya li-l-Ṭibāᶜa wa al-Nashr, 1963. 2 vols.

A general biographical dictionary of poets by a Spanish Muslim scholar.

Title transliterated: Kitāb al-Ḥulla al-Siyarāʾ.

G26
IBN AL-MUᶜTAZZ, ᶜAbd Allāh (d. 296/908).
[Classes of the Modern Poets]. طبقات الشعراء المحدثين *Ed.* ᶜAbd al-Sattār Aḥmad Farrāj. Cairo, Dār al-Maᶜārif, 1956. 603 p.

Dhakhāʾir al-ᶜArab, 20.

Notices of the poets of the ᶜAbbāsid period, with extensive quotations from their poetry.

A facsimile edition of the manuscript in the Escorial library of Madrid was edited for the Gibb Memorial Series, N.S., XIII (London, 1939), by A. Eghbal.

Title transliterated: Ṭabaqāt al-Shuᶜāra al-Muḥdathīn.

G27

al-JADA, Aḥmad ᶜAbd al-Laṭīf.
[Poets of شعراء الدعوة الاسلامية فى العصر الحديث Islamic Themes in Modern Times]. Beirut, Muᵓassa al-Risāla, 1978- .

Biographical sketches, with examples of poetry, arranged by approximate date.

Title transliterated: Shuᶜarāᵓ al-Daᶜwa al-Islamīya fī al-ᶜAṣr al-Ḥadīth.

G28
al-JUMAḤĪ, Muḥammad ibn Sallām (d. 231/845).
[Classes of the طبقات الشعراء الجاهليين و الاسلاميين Pre-Islamic and Islamic Poets]. *Ed.* Maḥmūd M. Shākir, *Ṭabaqāt Fuḥūl al-Shuᶜarāᵓ*. Cairo, Dār al-Maᶜārif, 1952. 36 + 715 p.

Biographical index to the pre-Islamic and early Islamic poets with copious quotations from their poetry.

Both of the earlier editions (Leiden, 1916 and Aleppo, 1920) were incomplete.

Title transliterated: Ṭabaqāt al-Shuᶜarāᵓ al-Jāhiliyīn wa al-Islāmiyīn.

G29
al-MARZUBĀNĪ, Muḥammad ibn ᶜImrān (d. 384/994).
[Dictionary of the Poets]. معجم الشعراء *Ed.* F. Krenkow. Cairo, Maktaba al-Qudsī, 1354/1935.

This alphabetical dictionary of poets, with extracts from their poetry, occupies pages 199-556 of the edition of al-Āmidī [G23].

Another edition, prepared by ᶜAbd al-Sattār Aḥmad Farrāj, was published in Cairo in 1960.

Title transliterated: Muᶜjam al-Shuᶜarāᵓ.

G30
al-THAᶜĀLIBĪ, ᶜAbd al-Malik ibn Muḥammad (d. 439/1037).
[The Unique Pearl يتيمة الدهر في شعراء اهل العصر Concerning the Poetry of Contemporary People]. Cairo, ᶜAlī Muḥammad ᶜAbd al-Ṭayf, 1934. 4 vols.

Anthology of the poets of his time with biographical information, arranged into four geographical areas: Syria and al-Jazīra, Iraq, western Persia, and Khurasan and Transoxiana. The work has undergone numerous printings.

Oskar Rescher published an index to the 1887,

Damascus, edition, *Alfabetischer Index zur* Jêtima ed-Dahr *des Ta^câlibî*. Constantinople, Nefassel, 1914. ii + 38 p. Aḥmad al-Ḥaqq al-ᶜUthmānī prepared a detailed comprehensive index to the persons, places, books, etc. mentioned by al-Thaᶜālibī, كتاب فريدة العصر فى جداول يتيمة الدهر. Calcutta, Asiatic Society of Bengal, 1915. xv + 772 p. (*Bibliotheca Indica, N.S., No. 1215*).

Continuations:

Al-Thaᶜālibī. كتاب تتمة اليتيمة. *Ed.* ᶜAbbās Eghbal. *Tatimmat ul-Yatima, complément du Yatîmat*. Tehran, Maṭbaᶜa Fardīn, 1353/1934. 2 vols. in 1.

Muḥammad ibn Muḥammad al-Kātib al-Iṣfahānī [d. 597/1201]. حريدة القصر و جريدة العصر [Secluding the Shortcomings and Baring the Times]. This has been published in parts:

1. Syria: *Ed.* Shukrī Faysal. قسم شعراء الشام. Damascus, N.P., 1955-68.
2. Egypt: *Ed.* ᶜUmar al-Disūqī *and* ᶜAlī ᶜAbd al-ᶜAẓīm. القسم الرابع. Cairo, Dār al-Nahda Miṣr li-l-Ṭabaᶜ wa al-Nashr, 1964- .
3. North Africa: *Ed.* Muḥammad al-Marzūqī, Muḥammad al-ᶜArūsī al-Maṭwī *and* Al-Jīlānī ibn al-Ḥājj Yaḥyā. قسم شعراء المغرب. Tunis, Al-Dār al-Tūnisīa li-l-Nashr, 1966- .
4. Iraq: *Ed.* Muḥammad Bahja al-Athirī. القسم العراقى. Baghdad, Maṭbaᶜa al-Majmaᶜ al-ᶜIlmī al-ᶜIrāqī, [1955].

Indices to Biographies

G31

al-WAHHĀBĪ, Khaldūn.

[Biographical Source for Arab Writers]. مراجع تراجم الادباء العرب. Najaf, Al-Maṭbaᶜa al-Ḥaydarīya, 1376-82/1956-62. 4 vols.

An extremely useful index to the names of the classical and modern Arabic authors and the biographical dictionaries in which notices of them appear.

Title transliterated: Marājiᶜ Tarājim al-Udabāɔ al-ᶜArab.

Proverbs

General

G32
MONTET, Edouard.
Choix de Proverbes, Dictons, Maximes et Pensées de l'Islam. Paris, Librairie Orientale et Américaine, 1933. 205 p.

Short proverbs, sayings, etc. selected from the Qurʾān, classical authors, and locales presented in French translation, with occasional notes, and arranged by subject. Includes Arabic, Persian, and Turkish.

Contents: I. La Vie; II. La Morale; III. La Religion; IV. Proverbes, Dictons et Maximes d'un Caractère spécial.

Arabic

G33
BEN CHENEB, Mohammed.
Proverbes arabes de l'Algérie et du Maghreb: recueillis, traduits et commentés. Paris, Ernst Leroux, 1905-7. 3 vols.

Publications de l'Ecole des Lettres d'Alger. Bulletin de Correspondance Africaine, XXX-XXXII.

G34
BURCHHARDT, John Lewis.
Arabic Proverbs, or the Manners and Customs of the Modern Egyptians: illustrated from their proverbial sayings current at Cairo. *2nd ed.* London, B. Quaritch, 1875. [iii], viii + 283 p.

Collection of 782 proverbs, etc. of the 19th century arranged alphabetically by the letter of the Arabic alphabet. Each is given in the Arabic script and are provided with English translations. Most are accompanied by brief explanations. Reprinted in London in 1972.

G35
al-ḌABBĪ, ʿAmr ibn ʿImrān (d. 250/864-65).
[The Book of Proverbs]. كتاب الامثال
Ed. Ramadān ʿAbd al-Tawwāb. Damascus, Majmaʿ al-Lugha al-ʿArabīya bi-Dimashq, 1974. 188 p., illus.

Title transliterated: Kitāb al-Amthāl.

G36

GHABRIL, Jan.
Liban: proverbes et maximes. Beirut, Dār al-Kitāb al-Lubnān, 1972. 267 p.
Presented in the Arabic, with English, French, and Spanish translations.

G37
al-IṢFAHĀNĪ, Ḥamza ibn al-Ḥasan (d. 360/970)
[The Precious Pearl الدرة الفاخرة فى الامثال السائرة Regarding Current Proverbs]. *Ed.* ᶜAbd al-Majīd Qaṭāmish. Cairo, Dār al-Maᶜārif, 1971- .
Annotated dictionary of classical Arabic proverbs.
Title transliterated: Al-Durra al-Fākhira fī al-Amthāl al-Sāᵓira.

G38
JEWETT, James Richard.
"Arabic Proverbs and Proverbial Phrases: collected, translated, and annotated." *Journal of the American Oriental Society*, XV, 1893, pp. 28-120.
Publication of the author's doctoral dissertation presented to the Philosophical Faculty of the University of Stassburg in 1890. Comprises a selection of 291 proverbs and sayings collected in Syria in 1886 and presented in Arabic, with transliteration and translation, with explanatory notes.

G39
al-MAYDĀNĪ, Aḥmad ibn Muḥammad (d. 518/1124).
[Collection of Proverbs]. مجمع الامثال
Ed. Muḥammad abī al-Faḍl Ibrāhīm. Cairo, ᶜĪsā al-Bābī al-Ḥalabī, 1977-79. 4 vols.
This edition contains bibliographical references and indices. An earlier edition was published in Tehran in 1290/1873.
Title transliterated: Majmaᶜ al-Amthāl.
Translations: Trans. M. Quatremere. "Proverbes arabes de Meidani, publies et traduits." *Journal Asiatique*, IIIᵉ sèrie, IV, 1837, pp. 497-543; V, 1838, pp. 5-44, 209-258 [all published]. Published in Arabic script, French translation, and notes of 34 proverbs.
Trans. Gustav W. Freytag. *Arabum Proverbia Vo-*

calibus Instruxit. Bonn, A. Marcum, 1838-43. 3 vols. The third volume contains the commentary and indices. Reprinted in 1968.

G40
WESTERMARCK, Edward.
Wit and Wisdom in Morocco: a study of native proverbs. London, George Routledge & Sons, Ltd., 1930. xi + 448 p.

A collection of 2,013 proverbs, sayings, etc., presented in transliteration and translation, with explanatory notes, and arranged by subject. The Arabic text for each is presented in an appendix. Index of subjects.

G41
al-YŪSĪ, al-Ḥasan ibn Masʿūd (d. 1102/1691).
[Blossom of the Hill in Proverbs and Wisdom]. زهر الاكم في الامثال و الحكم *Ed.* Muḥammad al-Ḥajjī *and* Muḥammad al-Akhḍarī. [Rabat?], Dār al-Thaqāfa, 1981- .

Title transliterated: Zahr al-Akam fī al-Amthāl wa al-Ḥikam.

Preparation of Copy

G42
BLACHERE, R. *and* SAUVAGET, J.
Règles pour Editions et Traductions de Textes arabes. Paris, Société d'Edition "Les Belles Lettres", 1953. 42 p.

A booklet prepared for students at the Ecole des Hautes-Etudes by two noted French scholars for the preparation of Arabic texts and translations by them for submission of dissertations or of manuscripts for publication.

Contents: A. Dispositions Communes à la Partie arabe et à la Partie française; B. Partie arabe; C. Partie française.

PERSIAN

Bibliographies

G43
NAWABI, Y. M.
A Bibliography of Iran: a catalogue of books and articles on Iranian subjects, mainly in European languages. Tehran, Iranian Culture Foundation, 1969-71. 2 vols.

Iranian Culture Foundation, Nos. 53 & 106.

Volume two has as subtitle: *a list of books and articles...* .

Although claiming to be a general bibliography on Iran the two volumes are confined primarily to language and literature, although the bibliography is important on this count alone. Unfortunately the work often lacks important bibliographic details, *i.e.*, places and dates of publication, name of publisher, etc. Title also in Farsi.

Volume one is confined to pre-Islamic materials. Volume two, with 479 pages, is a bibliography of post-Islamic language and literature.

Contents (Vol. 2): I. Language; II. Literature-A. Literature [in general], B. Poets and Writers [in alphabetical order]. No index.

Bibliographies of Translations

G44
KARNEEV, S. B.
"Персидская Поэзия: материалы к библиографии Русских переводов" ["Persian Poetry: materials for a bibliography of Russian translations"]. *Bibliografiia͡ Vostoka*, X, 1936, pp. 101-10 [dbl. col.].

Listing by date from the seventeenth century to 1934 of 111 Russian translations. Index of authors.

Bio-bibliographies

G45
STOREY, Charles A.
Persian Literature: a bio-bibliographical survey. London, Luzac & Co., 1927- [in progress].

Detailed index to the classical and modern Persian authors and their works, both published and unpublished, providing printing data.

Contents: Vol. I: Qurʾānic Literature; History

and Biography - Part 1: Qurʾānic Literature; History; Part 2: Biography; Additions and Corrections; Indexes. Vol. II: Part I: A. Mathematics; B. Weights and Measures; C. Astronomy and Astrology; D. Geography; Part 2: E. Medicine; Part 3: F. Encyclopaedias and Miscellaneous; G. Arts and Crafts; H. Science; J. Occult Arts. See Addenda.

Translations: Trans. Yu. E. Bregel', *ed.* Yu. E. Borshchevskiĭ. **Персидская Литература: био-библиографческий обзор** [Persian Literature: bio-bibliographical survey]. Moscow, Glavnai͡a Redakt͡sii͡a Vostochnoĭ Literatury, 1972- [in progress?]. Translation with revisions, corrections, and additions. *Contents:* Vol. I: Qurʾānic Literature; General History; The Prophet and Early Islam. Vol. II: Special Histories of Persia, Kurdistan, Central Asia, Afghanistan, Turkey, Caucasia, Arab States, Europe and America, China and Japan. Vol. III: Addenda; Indices.

G46
HĀSHIMĪ, Aḥmad ʿAlī Khān.
تذكرة مخزن الغرائب [Biographies of the Store of Wonders]. Lahore, Oriental Publications Fund Committee, University of the Punjab, 1968- [in progress?].

Oriental Publications, Nos. 40- .

Biographical dictionary of Persian poets who lived between 874 and 1802 A.D., arranged alphabetically.

Title transliterated: Tadhkira Makhzan al-Gharāʾib.

G47
LĀHŪRĪ, Yamīn Khān.
تاريخ شعر و سخنوران فارسى در لاهور: از ظهور اسلام تاعصر شاهجهان [History of Farsi Poetry and Poetic Gifts of Lahore: from the appearance of Islām to the time of Shāhjahān]. Karachi, National Publishing House, 1971. 13 + 415 p.

Biographical dictionary and anthology of the poets of Lahore to the beginning of the 17th century.

Title transliterated: Taʾrīkh Shiʿr wa Sukhunwarān Fārsī dar Lāhūr...

G48
MUDARRIS, Muḥammad ᶜAlī, Tabrīzī.
ريحانة الادب در تراجم احوال معروفين نكنية و لقب
[Breath of Literature Regarding Biog- ياكنى و القاب
raphees Known by *Kunya* and *Laqab*]. *3rd ed.* Tehran, N.P., 1948-55. 8 vols.

Biographical dictionary of Persian literary figures listed by nickname or by-name. Not listed by Storey [G45] or Mushār [A38]. Kaḥḥāla [G18] (XI, 51) gives the title as: ريحانة الأدب فى تراجم المعرفين بالكنية او اللقب من العلماء و الحكماء و العرفاء و الشعراء.

Title transliterated: Rayḥāna al-Adab Dar Tarājim

G49
MUSHĀR, Khānbābā.
مؤلفين كتب چاپى فارسى و عربى از آغاز چاپ تاكنون
[Authors of Printed Persian and Arabic Books from the Beginning of Printing to the Present]. Tehran, N.P., 1340-44/1961-65. 6 vols.

Bio-bibliographical dictionary listing the authors by *ism*. Unfortunately, no index.

Title transliterated: Muᵓallifīn Kutub Chāpī Fārsī wa ᶜArabī...

G50
ᶜURŪJ, ᶜAbd al-Raᵓuf.
[Fārsī Although Urdū Poets]. فارسى كو شعرائ اردو
Karachi, National Publishing House, 1971. 4 + 230 p.

Biographical dictionary and anthology of Persian/Urdu poets of the Indian sub-continent from 1565 to 1917. In Urdu.

Proverbs

G51
ROEBUCK, Thomas.
A Collection of Proverbs, and Proverbial Sayings, in the Persian and Hindoostanee Languages. Calcutta, Printed at the Hindoostanee Press, 1824. xxi, 406 + 397 p.

Translations of proverbs collected primarily in the northern part of India.

¶ See also Edouard Montet, *Choix de Proverbes, ...* [G32].

TURKISH

Bio-bibliographies

G52
BURSALI, Mehmet Tahir.
[Ottoman Authors]. عثمانلی مؤلفلری
Istanbul, Maṭbaᶜa-i Āmīre, 1333-46/1915-24. 3 vols.

Bio-bibliographical dictionary of Ottoman Turkish writers up to *cir*. 1915, with lists of their works.

Translated into modern Turkish by A. Fikri Yavuz *and* İsmail Özen, *Osmanlı Müellifleri*. Istanbul, Meral Yayınevi, N.D. 3 vols.

An index was published by Aḥmed Remzī, مفتاح الکتب و اسامی مؤلفین فهرستی Istanbul, N.P., 1346/1928. 177 p.

The entire three volumes, including index, was reprinted in Farnborough, England, in 1971.

Title transliterated: Osmanlı Müellifleri.

G53
HOFMAN, H. F.
Turkish Literature: a bio-bibliographical survey. Section III: Moslim Central Asian Turkish literature. Utrecht, The Library of the University of Utrecht, 1969- [in progress?].

Introduction to the Turkish Chaghatay writers and their works providing the necessary biographical and bibliographical data.

Contents: Part I: Authors [6 vols. in 2 parts]. Lists the authors in alphabetical order.

Biographies

G54
SEHĪ, Edırneli. (d. 955/1548-49).
[Memorial of Sehi Eight Paradises]. تذکرهٔ سهی هشت بهشت *Ed*. Mehmed Süker. Istanbul, N.P., 1325, 1909. 144 p.

Biographical dictionary and anthology of 216 poets under eight headings or layers. The author is variously listed as Sehī Celebi or Sehī Bey.

Translations: Trans. Nedjati Hüsnü Lugal *and*

Oskar Rescher. *Sehi bey's* Tezkıre: *türkische dichterbiographien aus dem 16 jahr., nach dem druck 1325 H. (in teils freier, teils wörtlicher wiedergabe).* Istanbul, Universum-druckerei, 1942. vii + 142 p.

Title transliterated: Tadhkiraᵓ Sehī Hesht Bihisht.

Proverbs

G55

AKSOY, Ömer Asim.

Atasözleri ve Deyimler [Proverbs and Sayings]. Ankara, Türk Dil Kurumu, 1965. 542 + [ii] p.

Türk Dil Kurumu Yayınları: 238.

Provides 5,700 Turkish popular sayings and proverbs, with an introduction and bibliography. The bibliography (Chapter Four) is a classified listing of 431 Turkish and western language materials which are about or include samples of proverbs.

¶ See also Edouard Montet, *Choix de Proverbes*, [G32].

URDU

Bibliographies

G56

ᶜABD AL-ḤAQQ, *Mawlawi.*

[Bibliography of Urdū Books]. قاموس الکتب اردو Karachi, Anjuman Taraqqī Urdū Pākistān, 1961- [in progress?].

A classified listing of Urdu literature.

Title transliterated: Qāmūs al-Kutub Urdū.

PERFORMING ARTS H

DRAMA

Bibliographies

H1
ᶜAWWĀḌ, Ramsīs.
موسوعة المسرح المصرى البيليجرافية ١٩٠٠ ـ ١٩٣٠
[Encyclopaedia of the Egyptian Theatre: the bibliography 1900-1930]. Cairo, Al-Hayʾa al-Miṣrīya al-ᶜĀmma al-Kitāb, 1983. [ii] + 902 p. [dbl. col.].
Arranged by date.
Title transliterated: Mawsūᶜa al-Masraḥ al-Miṣrī: al-Bibliyujarāfīya 1900-1930.

H2
DĀGHIR, Yūsuf Asᶜad.
معجم المسرحيات العربية و المعربة، ١٨٤٨ ـ ١٩٧٥
[Dictionary of the Arab and Arabized Theatre, 1848-1975]. Baghdad, Al-Jumhūrīya al-ᶜIrāqīya, Wizāra al-Thaqāfa wa al-Fanūn, 1978. 723 p.
Bibliography of modern and contemporary drama and the theatre written in Arabic or translated into Arabic.
Title transliterated: Muᶜjam al-Masraḥiyat al-ᶜArabīya wa al-Muᶜarraba.

H3
LANDAU, Jacob M.
Studies in the Arab Theatre and Cinema. Philadelphia, University of Pennsylvania Press, 1968.
The appendix, pages 216-273, is "A List of Some Arabic Plays, 1848-1956" of approximately 225 plays under two separate headings: "I. Original Plays" and "II. Translated Plays."

H4

POYRAZ, Türkân *and* TUĞRUL, Nurnisa.

Tiyatro Bibliyografyası (1859-1928) [Bibliography of the Theatre (1859-1928)]. Ankara, Millî Kütüphane , 1967. XIV, [ii] + 288 p., illus.

Classified listing, with a few short annotations, of 2,488 books and articles in Ottoman Turkish on the theatre in Turkey. Authors and titles have been transliterated into modern Turkish. Author and title indices.

¶ For additional materials on the drama in Arabic and Persian, see Salih J. Altoma, *Modern Arabic Literature*, section "IV. Drama" [G6] and Y. M. Nawabi, *A Bibliography of Iran*, Vol. II: "Persian Language and Literature - Plays, Dramas & Theatre" [G43].

MUSIC

Bibliographies

H5

ARSEVEN, Veysel.

Açıklamalı Türk Halk Müziği Kitap ve Makaleler Bibliyografyası [Bibliography of Books and Articles on the Music of the Turkish People]. Istanbul, Millî Eğitim Basımevi, 1969. [vi] + 210 p.

Millî Folklor Enstitüsü Yayınları: 1.

Annotated listing of 177 books and 796 articles in modern Turkish in alphabetical order by author. Title and author indices.

H6

FARMER, Henry George.

The Sources of Arabian Music: an annotated bibliography of Arabic manuscripts which deal with the theory, practice, and history of Arabian music from the eighth to the seventeenth century. Leiden, E. J. Brill, 1965. XXVI + 71 p., illus.

Annotated, chronological listing of 353 published and unpublished manuscripts. Author and title index. An earlier edition of this bibliography printed in the *Records of the Glascow Bibliographic Society* (XIII, 1940, pp. 14-67) under the same title contained an index of subjects lacking in this current printing.

H7

WATERMAN, Richard A. *and* LICHTENWANGER, William. "Bibliography of Asiatic Musics." *Music Library Association Notes*, V, 1947, pp. 21-35, 178-186, 354-362, 549-562; VI, 1948, pp. 122-136, 281-296, 419-436, 570-583; VII, 1949, pp. 84-98, 265-279, 415-423, 613-621; VIII, 1950, pp. 100-118, 322-329.

Classified listings of books and articles in European languages on past and present musical theories and practice.

See esp.: II. Southwest Asia: Moslems - 1. General, VI, 1948, pp. 282-287 (nos. 1107-1220); 2. Arabic-speaking peoples, VI, 1948, pp. 288-296 (nos. 1221-1395); 3. Turkic-speaking peoples, VI, 1948, pp. 420-433 (nos. 1396-1631); 4. Iranians and others, VI, 1948, pp. 433-436 (nos. 1632-1699); and Addenda, VIII, 1950, pp. 325-329.

Glossaries

H8

al-FARUQI, Lois Ibsen.
An Annotated Glossary of Arabic Musical Terms. Westport, Connecticut, Greenwood Press, 1981. xxii + 511 p.

The terms are given in alphabetical order in transliteration according to the Latin alphabet. Each is provided with its Arabic root and English translation, often with short explanation. Includes names of individuals. Appendices: I: Index of English Musical Terms; II: Index of Arabic Roots [according to the Arabic alphabet]; III: Guide to Pronunciation and Transliteration; IV: List of Abbreviations; V: Authors and References Cited.

¶ For classical musical notation and biographies of musicians and singers consult al-Iṣbahānī's *Kitāb al-Aghānī* [G15].

I ART & ARCHITECTURE

GENERAL

Bibliographies

I1
CHANDRA, Jagdish.
Bibliography of Indian Art, History & Archaeology. Delhi, Delhi Printers Prakashan, 1978- [in progress?].

Subtitle: *Dr. Anand K. Coomaraswamy Memorial Volume.*

Vol. I (1978) is a classified listing of 8,329 books and articles in English.

Contents: Pt. I- Indian Art; Pt. II- Indian Architecture; Pt. III- Indian Sculpture; Pt. IV- Indian Painting; Pt. V- Handicraft (Minor arts); Pt. VI- Greater India. No index.

I2
CRESWELL, K. A. C.
A Bibliography of the Architecture, Arts and Crafts of Islam to 1st January 1960. London, American University at Cairo Press, 1961. xxiv p. + 1330 dbl. cols. + XXV p.

Annotated, classified listing of approximately 15,850 books, pamphlets, articles, albums, etc. on every aspect of Islamic monumental architecture and minor arts, excepting numismatics, from Spain to, and including, India. The work required nearly fifty years to compile by the master historian of Muslim architecture. Weak in Russian and oriental language materials.

Contents: Part I: Architecture [by country] ; Part II: Arts and Crafts [by subject]. Author index.

Supplements:

K. A. C. Creswell. *Supplement to the Bibliography of the Architecture, Arts and Crafts of Islam.* London, American University at Cairo Press, 1972. xiii + 366 dbl. cols. + IX p. The Russian language materials missing in the original volume have been included in this supplement.

At the time of compilation of this *Guide* a second supplement was in course of preparation under the general editorship of J. D. Pearson.

¶ For Arabic language works see section 2, "Insānīyāt" (pages 78-95) in Nazār Muḥammad ᶜAlī Qāsim's المعاجم العربية فى العلوم و الفنون و اللغات.... Baghdad, Al-Maktaba al-Markazīya, Jāmiᶜa Baghdād, 1967.

ARCHITECTURE

I3
MAYER, Louis A.
Islamic Architects and Their Works. Geneva, Albert Kundig, 1956. 183 p.

A chronological listing of 318 known Muslim architects, with short descriptions of their recorded and/or extant buildings.

CALLIGRAPHY

I4
HUART, Clément.
Les Calligraphes et les Miniaturists de l'Orient musulman. Paris, Ernst Leroux, 1908. 388 p., illus.

Detailed study of Arabic and Persian calligraphy and miniature painting with names of noted artists.

I5
SAFADI, Yasin Hamid.
Islamic Calligraphy. London, Thames & Hudson, 1978. 144 p., illus.

Twenty-four page historical essay on the development and styles of the Arabic script employed on paper, in architecture, and in the minor arts. Illustrated with 108 pages of plates.

COSTUME

I6
DOZY, Reinhard Pieter Anne.
Dictionnaire détaillé des Noms des Vêtements chez les Arabes. Jean Muller, 1845. viii + 446 p.

Dictionary according to the Arabic script of the terms for various parts of the dress of the Near East from earliest times to the middle of the nineteenth century. Each term in Arabic is fully vowelled, followed by detailed notes, including quotations from a variety of oriental authors.

Reprinted in Beirut in 1968 and again in Amsterdam in 1971, by Gé Nabrink & Son. That of Nabrink is of particular importance as it is a photographic reprint of the author's personal copy preserved in the University of Leiden library which contains numerous handwritten corrections, additions, and approximately 250 new articles. Full scholarly apparatus is by P. S. van Koningsveld.

I7
MAYER, Louis A.
Mameluk Costume: a survey. Geneva, Albert Kundig, 1952. 119 p., illus.

Descriptive text, with 20 illustrations, of the dress of the Mamluk rulers and soldiery of Egypt and Syria.

METALWORK

I8
---.
Islamic Metalworkers and Their Works. Geneva, Albert Kundig, 1959. 128 p., illus.

Important guide to the makers of metal utensils and their extant works and to incrustators and designers. Illustrated with 15 plates.

I9
---.
Islamic Armourers and Their Works. Geneva, Albert Kundig, 1962. 128 p., illus.

List of 225 swordsmiths and 34 cannonmakers

from the beginning of Islam to the early nineteenth century, with documentation of their known works and illustrated with 20 plates. In addition to editing this posthumous work Gaston Wiet prepared an additional note, "Répartition des armes par Musées et par Collections," pages 91-5.

Astrolabes

I10
ᶜAWWĀD, Kūrkīs.
الاسطرلاب و ماألف فيه من كتب و رسائل في العصور الاسلامية/
A Bibliography of Astrolabes During the Islamic Period. Baghdad, Maṭbaᶜa al-Rābiṭa, 1957. [26 p. dbl. col.].
Reprint of an article with the same title published in *Sumer*, XIII, 1957, pp. 154-78.
Annotated listing by author of 187 books, articles, and manuscripts in Arabic and western languages on astrolabes and their makers.

I11
MAYER, Louis A.
Islamic Astrolabists and Their Works. Geneva, Albert Kundig, 1956. 123 p., illus.
Names and details regarding known astrobabists and their extant works, illustrated with 26 plates.

TEXTILES

I12
BALDRY, John.
Textiles in Yemen: historical references to trade and commerce in textiles in Yemen from antiquity to modern times. London, British Museum, 1982. 107 p., illus., maps.
Occasional Paper 27.

WOODWORKING

I13
MAYER, Louis A.
Islamic Woodcarvers and Their Works. Geneva, Albert Kundig, 1958. 100 p., illus.
Chronological list of 163 known mastercraftsmen with descriptions of their extant works in the forms of *minbars*, doors, etc., illustrated with 12 plates.

J HISTORY

GUIDES & HANDBOOKS

Guides

General

J1
CAHEN, Claude.
Introduction à l'Histoire du Monde musulman médiéval XIIe - XVe Siècle: méthodologie et éléments de bibliographie. *3rd ed.* Paris, Librairie d'Amérique et d'Orient Adrien Maisonneuve, 1983. 216 p.

Initiation à l'Islam.

Revised edition of Jean Sauvaget and Claude Cahen's *Introduction à l'Histoire de l'Orient musulman: éléments de bibliographie. 2nd ed.* Paris, 1961.

Contents: I. Bibliographie générale des Outiles de Travail; II. Les Sources; III. Les Grands Aspects de l'Histoire musulmane; IV. Périodes historiques jusqu'au IVe Siècle; V. Temps Post-classiques; VI. L'Occident musulman. Author index.

J2
SAUVAGET, Jean *and* CAHEN, Claude.
Introduction to the History of the Muslim East: a bibliographical guide. Berkeley, University of California Press, 1965. xxi + 252 p.

Bibliographical essay on selected primary and secondary materials (books and articles) and reference sources for the study of Muslim history and culture from Muhammad to the dissolution of the Ottoman dynasty, excluding Muslim India. Basically a translation, with additions and corrections, of the authors' *Introduction à l'Histoire de l'Orient musulman:... . 2nd ed.* Paris, 1961. The translation retains many of its predecessor's errors and difficulties, including an inadequate author index. Its format precludes the use of the work for ready reference.

Contents: Part I. The Sources of Muslim History; Part II. Tools of Research and General Works; Part III. Historical Biography. Author index. No index of titles.

Africa

J3

DUIGNAN, Peter, *ed.*

Guide to Research and Reference Works on Sub-Saharan Africa. *Comps.* Helen F. Conover, Peter Duignan, *et. al.* Stanford, Hoover Institution Press, [1971]. xiii + 1,102 p.

Hoover Institution Bibliographical Series: XLVI.

An annotated listing of 3,127 entries covering virtually every conceivable subject on a large continent, excluding the northern tier of countries (Morocco, Algeria, Tunisia, Libya, and Egypt). Includes many works not generally regarded as reference materials. Includes only western European language works.

Contents: I. Guide to Research Organizations, Libraries and Archives, and the Book Trade; II. Bibliographies for Africa in General; III. Subject Guide in General; IV. Area Guide. Author, title, and subject index.

Iran

J4

AFSHĀR, Īraj.

A Directory for Iranian Studies. Tehran, Centre pour l'Etude et la Presentation de la Culture Iranienne, 1349/1970. 402 p. / راهنمای تحقیقات ایرانی

Publication No. 2.

A directory, primarily for Iranian students, to academic centers, research societies, scholars, journals, bookdealers, libraries, bibliographies, etc. of importance for the study of Iran from the most ancient past to the present. Foreign names are given in Latin letters and in Farsi transliteration. All annotations are in Farsi.

Title transliteration: Rāhnamā-i Taḥqīqāt Īrānī.

J5
---.
"A Bibliography of / "فهرستنامهٔ کتابشناسیهای ایران Bibliographies on Iranian Studies." *Īrānshināsī/ Iranica*, I, 1342/1963. 217 p.

An annotated, classified listing of 294 bibliographies, catalogues, journals, and other reference materials in Farsi and western European languages for the study of the ancient, classical Islamic, and modern periods of Iranian history and culture. Author and title indices.

Title transliterated: Fihristnāma Kitābshināsī-hā-i Īrān.

J6
ELWELL-SUTTON, L. P., *ed.*
Bibliographical Guide to Iran: the Middle East Library Committee Guide. Brighton, Sussex, The Harvester Press; Totowa, New Jersey, Barnes & Noble Books, 1983. xxv + 462 p.

A composite bibliography arranged by subject with contributions from 30 individuals with materials drawn from Farsi and western languages. Minimal bibliographic details and limited annotations. Internal organization makes the book difficult to use. There is an index of authors, but none of titles. Presumably replaces the editor's earlier *A Guide to Iranian Area Study* (Ann Arbor, 1952).

Turkey

J7
BIRGE, John Kingsley.
A Guide to Turkish Area Study. Washington, D.C., Committee on Near Eastern Studies, American Council of Learned Societies, 1949. xii + 240 p.

A bibliographical essay arranged by subject of 587 items in western European languages. Included is a genealogical table of the Ottoman Turks and a general chronology of Turkish history from 732 to 1945.

The *Guide* is now very much out of date, but has not been wholly replaced.

Contents: I. Sources of General Information; II. The Geography of Turkey; III. Population and Races of Turkey; IV. Language and Literature; V. History; VI. Political Structure of Turkey; VII. Social Organization in Turkey; VIII. Transportation and Communications in Turkey; IX. Finance, Industry, and Commerce; X. Education and Intellectual Life; XI. Religion; XII. Art; XIII. Music. Index.

J8
WERYHO, Jan W.
Guide to Turkish Sources. Montreal, The Library, Institute of Islamic Studies, McGill University, 1973. 24 p. [one side only].

A mimeographed list of works, arranged by subject, based primarily upon the holdings of the Institute.

"This bibliographic guide is concerned only with Turkey and the Turkish of Turkey, Ottoman and modern. Materials dealing with the Turkish-speaking world in general will be included, but no works about individual countries and languages other than Turkey and the Turkish of Turkey."

No index.

Handbooks

J9
BACHARACH, Jere L.
A Near East Studies Handbook. *3rd rev. ed.* Seattle, University of Washington Press, 1984. xiii + 168 p., charts, maps.

First published in 1974, this is a very useful historical handbook for students and the general public to the heartland of the Near East: the Arabian Peninsula, the Fertile Crescent, Iran, Turkey, and Egypt, 570-1983.

Contents: 1. Transliteration Systems; 2. Abbreviations: major periodicals and references; 3. Abbreviations: twentieth century social, political and economic groups; 4. Table of Dynasties; 5. Table of Rulers; 6. Genealogies; 7. Historical Atlas [31 line maps]; 8. Islamic Calendar; 9.

Glossary; 10. Chronology to October 1976; 11. Time Chart; 12. Semitic (Afro-Asiatic) Language Family; 13. Indo-European and Altaic Language Families; 14. Supplement: table of rulers [modern]; 15. Supplement: historical atlas [8 line maps]. General index and index to historical atlas.

BIBLIOGRAPHIES

The bibliographic listings which follow are necessarily limited to those on historical subjects and thus precluded are numerous excellent bibliographies on specific countries, areas, and regions which either have a section on history or contain citations of historical works.

General

J10
EGOROVA, D. N.
Библиография Востока. Вып. 1: Историы (1917-1925) [Bibliography of the East. Vol. 1: History (1917-1925)]. Moscow, Nauchnai͡a Assot͡siat͡sii͡a Vostokovedenii͡a pri TSK SSSR, 1928. 300 p. [all pub.].

Classified, annotated lists of 1,468 books and articles published in Russia during the period.

Contents: 1. Auxiliary Sciences. History of Science; 2. General Works; 3. Indo-Europeanic; 4. Egypt; 5. Babylonian Cultural Circle; 6. Hittites; 7. Ancient Iran; 8. Jews; 9. Jewish Culture; 10. Black Sea; 11. Hellenism; 12. Islam; 13. Arabs; 14. Persia; 15. Caucasus; 16. Oriental Peoples of Volga Area; 17. Turkey and Turks; 18. Arabia; 19. Central Asia; 20. Afghanistan; 21. Mongols and Mongolia; 22. Siberia; 23. Buddhism; 24. Japan; 25. China; 26. Tibet; 27. India; 28. Africa; 29. Indonesia, Australia, and Pacific Ocean; 30. Imperialism, Colonialism, and Nationalism; 31. Manuscripts; 32. Reports; 33. Study Institutions, Museums; 34. Lists of Scholarly Writings and Reviews; 35. Necrology. Indices.

Title transliterated: Bibliografii͡a Vostoka. Vyp. 1: Istoriy.

J11

SPULER, Bertold *and* FORRER, Ludwig.
Der vordere Orient in islamischer Zeit. Bern, A. Francke AG. Verlag, 1954. 248 p.

Classified bibliographical essay of the most important books and articles published between 1937 and 1953 on the Near East and North Africa, excluding India and Southeast Asia, from the time of Muhammad to the date of publication. Includes important materials in the languages of eastern Europe and in modern Turkish, but weak in Arabic and Persian publications. An excellent work despite these shortcomings, but method of presentation precludes its use for quick reference.

Contents: Der islamische vordere Orient mit Nordafrika, ohne Türkei [Bertold Spuler]: Einleitung; Geographie; Geschichte; Schöne Literature; Philosophie; Musik; Naturwissenschaften; Medizin; Wissenschaftsgeschichte; Neuerscheinungen. Das osmanische Reich und die Türkische Republik [Ludwig Forrer]: Reichsgeschichte; Provinzial- und Ortsgeschichte; Wirtschafts- und Socialgeschichte. General author index. No index of titles.

J12
WÜSTENFELD, Ferdinand.
Die Geschichtschreiber der Araber und ihre Werke: aus dem XXVIII und XXIX bande der *Abhandlungen der Königlichen Gesellschaft der Wissenschaften zu Göttingen*. Göttingen, Dieterische Verlags- Buchhandlung, 1882. [ii], viii + 307 p.

A chronological catalogue with an alphabetical index. Remains a useful compilation despite its age.

Crusades

J13
LAMONTE, John
"Bibliography of Works Relating to the Fiefs and Families of the Latin Crusading States in Syria, Palestine and Cyprus." *Bulletin of the International Committee of Historical Sciences*, IV, no. 15, 1932, pp. 308-18; VII, no. 26, 1935, pp. 42-55.

J14
MAYER, Hans Eberhard.

Bibliographie zur Geschichte der Krüzzuge. Hannover, Hahnsche Buchhandlung, 1960. xxii + 272 p.

Classified listing of 5,362 primary and secondary sources in western languages, including translations from the Arabic, on the history of the crusades and of the crusading states. Index of authors.

J15

MICHAUD, M.

Bibliographie des Croisades: contenant l'analyse de touts les chroniques d'orient et d'occident qui parlent des croisades. Paris, Anth^e. Boucher, MDCCCXXII. 2 vols.

"Eastern Question"

J16

BENGESCO, Georges.

Essai d'une Notice bibliographique sur la Question d'Orient: orient européen 1821-1897. Brussels, P. Lacomblez, Editeur; Paris, H. Le Soudier, Editeur, 1897. xiii, 327 + [i] p.

A chronological listing with brief annotations of 2,142 books and articles published in France and Belgium during the period. Indices of authors and anonymous works.

J17

JOVANOVIĆ, Vojislav.

Engleska Bibliografija o Istočnom Pitanju u Evropi [English Bibliography on the Eastern Question in Europe]. Belgrade, Državna Štamcarija Kraljevine Srbije, 1908. [ii] + 111 p. [dbl. col.].

Srpska Kraljevska Akademija Spomenik XLVIII: Drugi Razred 40.

Chronological listing, with occasional annotations, of 1,521 books and articles published between 1481 and 1905.

¶ Unfortunately, there are no modern continuations of these bibliographies.

Geographic

Africa

J18
MILI͡AVSKAI͡A, S. L. *and* SINIT͡SYNA, I. E.
Библиография Африки: дореволюционная и Советская литература на Русском языке оригинальная и лереводная [Bibliography of Africa: prerevolutionary and Soviet writings in Russian original and translations]. Moscow, Izdatel'stvo "Nauka", 1964. 276 p. [dbl. col.].

Classified listing of 2,506 books and articles published in Russia from the middle of the 18th century through 1961.

Contents: I. General Section; II. North Africa; III. Northeast Africa; IV. East Africa; V. South Africa; VI. West and Central Africa; Appendices: 1. Doctoral and Candidate Dissertations (1941-1961); 2. Africa in Artistic Literature; 3. List of Geographical Maps. Index of authors, editors, translators, reviewers, and titles.

Title transliterated: Bibliografii͡a Afriki...

North Africa

J19
TURBET-DELOF, Guy.
Bibliographie critique du Maghreb dans la Littérature française 1532-1715. Algiers, Bibliothèque Nationale, 1976. 299 p.

Bibliographies et Catalogues, 2.

Algeria

J20
PLAYFAIR, Robert L., *Sir.*
A Bibliography of Algeria: from the expedition of Charles V. in 1541 to 1887. *Royal Geographical Society Supplementary Papers*, II, 2, 1888, pp. 129-430.

A chronological list of 4,745 books, pamphlets, and articles in western languages, with author and subject indices.

Supplements: Sir Robert L. Playfair. *Supplement to the Bibliography of Algeria from the Earliest Times to 1895.* London, John Murray, 1898. iv + 321 p. Contains an additional 2,997 items with an appendix listing materials in the Public

Record Office and the Admiralty in London.

Both bibliographies, together with others on additional countries of North Africa by Sir Robert have been reprinted in two volumes by Gregg International Publishers Ltd., London, 1971.

Egypt

J21

GUEMARD, Gabriel.

Bibliographie critique de la Commission des Sciences et Arts de l'Institut d'Egypte. Cairo, Imprimérie Paul Barbey, 1936. 127 p.

Historical and bibliographical study of Napoleon Bonapart's famous scientific Commission and of the research institute he founded.

Contents: I.- Historique de la Commission des Sciences et Arts et de l'Institut d'Egypte; II.- Liste des Membres de la Commission; III.- Liste des Membres de l'Institut d'Egypte; IV.- Bibliographie: Classification générale et observations.

J22

IBRAHIM-HILMI, *Prince*.

The Literature of Egypt and the Soudan from the Earliest Times to the Year 1885 Inclusive: a bibliography comprising printed books, periodical writings, and papers of learned societies; maps and charts; ancient papyri, manuscripts, drawings, &c. London, Trübner and Co., 1886-88. 2 vols.

An attempt by the son of the Khedive Ismāʿīl during his exile in Europe to compile a complete bibliography of materials concerning Egypt in Arabic and western languages wherever printed. Placed in a single alphabetical order by title with no index. Vol. I. A-L; Vol. II. M-Z.

Reprinted by Kraus Reprint Ltd., Nendeln, Liechtenstein, 1966.

J23

MAUNIER, René.

Bibliographie économique, juridique et sociale de l'Egypte moderne (1798-1916). Cairo, Société Sultanieh d'Economie Politique, de Statistique et de Législation, 1918. XXXII + 372 p.

No. 1. Travaux spéciaux.

Classified listing of 6,695 books and articles in western languages published during the period. The bibliography is preceded by a "Liste chronologique des Revues publiées en Egypte de 1798 à 1916" which lists 64 European language journals.

Contents: I. Egypte en Générale; II. Economie égyptienne; III. Législation égyptienne; IV. Moeurs, Religions, Instruction publique. Author, subject, and personal name indices.

Supplements: G. Guémard. "Supplément à la Bibliographie économique, juridique et sociale de l'Egypte moderne (1798-1916) de M. René Maunier." *L'Egypte Contemporaine*, XVI, 1925, pp. 240-60.

Reprinted, without Guémard's corrections and addenda, New York, 1967.

J24
MUNIER, H.
Tables de la *Description de l'Egypte* suivies d'une Bibliographie sur l'Expédition française de Bonaparte. Cairo, Société Royale de Géographie d'Egypte, 1943. X + 380 p.

A very detailed study of the multi-volumed publication resulting from Bonaparte's Commission des Sciences et Arts and a classified bibliography containing 631 items written about the ill-fated expedition.

Cairo

J25
ZAKĪ, ʿAbd al-Raḥmān.
مراجع تاريخ القاهرة منذ انشائها الى اليوم / A Bibliography of the Literature of the City of Cairo [from its foundation to the present]. Cairo, Maṭbuʿāt al-Jamʿīya al-Jughrāfīya al-Miṣrīya, 1964. [ii], 19 [Arabic text], 21 + [ii] [European text] p.

Classified listings of books and articles about, or in which the city is mentioned. Bibliographic details are often lacking. No index.

Libya

J26
MINUTILLI, Frederico.
Bibliografia della Libia: catalogo alfabetico e metodico. Torino, Fratelli Bocca, 1903. viii + 136 p.

Classified listing of books and articles in western languages published through 1902.

Supplements: Ugo Ceccherini. *Bibliografia della Libia*. Rome, Tipografia Nazionale di G. Bertero e C., 1915. ix + 204 p. [dbl. col.]. Classified list of 3,041 books and articles supplementary to and in continuation of Minutilli, including publications 1903-14.

J27
PLAYFAIR, Robert L., *Sir*.
The Bibliography of the Barbary States. Part I: Tripoli and Cyrenaica. *Royal Geographical Society Supplementary Papers*, II, 4, 1889, pp. 557-614, with map.

Annotated, chronological listing of approximately 580 books, pamphlets, and articles written between 484 B.C. and 1889, with indices of authors and subjects. Includes a section on the materials in the Public Record Office. Reprinted in London in 1971.

Morocco

J28
IBN SŪDAH, ᶜAbd al-Salām ᶜAbd al-Qādir.
[Guide to the Historians of the Maghrib]. دليل مؤرخ المغرب Tetuan, Al-Maṭbaᶜa al-Ḥanīya, 1369/1949-50. 564 p.

Bio-bibliographical catalogue of the historians of Morocco and their works with 1,861 titles listed. Arranged into eight sections.

Title transliterated: Dalīl Muᵓarrikh al-Maghrib.

J29
MIEGE, Jean-Louis.
Le Maroc et l'Europe (1830-1894). Paris, Presses Universitaires de France, 1961. 2 vols.

The first volume, entitled "Sources - Bibliographie," is devoted exclusively to the published and unpublished books, articles, archival materials, official journals, newspapers, maps, etc. employed by the author for his history contained in the second volume. This comprises a fairly complete bibliography of the subject.

J30
LEVI-PROVENÇAL, E.
Les Historians des Chorfa: essai sur la littérature historique et bibliographique au Maroc du XVIe au XXe siècle. Paris, Emile Larose, Editeur, 1922. [vii] + 470 p.
Description of 500 works with author and title indices.

J31
MEKNASSI, A.
Sources et Bibliographie d'Histoire marocaine (du XVIe au premiere moitié du XXe siècle): étude bio-bibliographique. Tetuan, Al-Maṭbaᶜa al-Mahdīya, 1963. 59 + 164 [Arabic text] p.
The bibliography is to be found in the 59 pages of French text in which original works and translations are listed in alphabetical order by author without annotations or index.

J32
PLAYFAIR, Robert L., *Sir and* BROWN, Robert.
A Bibliography of Morocco from the Earliest Times to the End of 1891. *Royal Geographical Society Supplementary Papers*, III, 3, 1893, pp. 201-476, map.
Annotated, chronological listing of 2,243 books, pamphlets, and articles in western languages. Includes a section on the archival materials in the Public Record Office. Reprinted in London in 1971.

Tunisia

J33
ASHBEE, H. S. *and* GRAHAM, Alexander.
A Bibliography of Tunisia from the Earliest Times to the End of 1888: including Utica and Carthage, the Punic Wars, the Roman occupation, the Arab conquest, the expeditions of Louis IX. and Charles V. and the French protectorate. *Royal Geographical Society Supplementary Papers*, II, 4, 1889, pp. 1-144 [dbl. col.]., map.
An unnumbered listing of books, pamphlets, and articles in western languages by author. Reprinted in London in 1971.

Central Asia

J34
PIERCE, Richard A.

Soviet Central Asia: a bibliography. Berkeley, Center for Slavic and East European Studies, University of California, 1966. 3 pts. [189 pp. total].

Selected, classified listings of 2,009 books and articles in western and eastern European languages arranged by period. Author index in each part.

Contents: Pt. 1: 1558-1866. Bibliographies and Bibliographical Aids; Primary Sources; History; Administration; Trade; Military Operations; Journeys, Sojourns, and Expeditions. Pt. 2: 1867-1917. Bibliographies and Bibliographical Aids; History; Conquest and Annexation; Administration; Economy; Culture and Social Welfare; Ethnography; Native Law; Native Uprisings; World War I; The Revolutionary Movement; Comprehensive Accounts; Collections of Articles; Albums; Geography; Guidebooks, Directories, Almanacs; Description and Travel; Bukhara; Khiva; Serial Publications; Addenda. Pt. 3: 1917-1966. Bibliographies and Bibliographical Aids; History; Revolution; Civil War; Military Organization; Khiva and Bukhara; The Basmachi Movement; Party; Economy; Statistics; Population Trends; Culture; World War II; Post-War Developments; General Accounts; Ethnography; Geography; Collections of Articles; Guidebooks and Directories; Description and Travel, Memoires; The National and Colonial Question; Historiography; Some Essential Serial Publications.

Turkestan

J35
GORODET͡SKIĬ, V. D.

Библиография Туркестана [Bibliography of Turkestan]. Tashkent, Tipo-Litografiia V. M. Il'ina, 1913. [iv], II + 152 p. [dbl. col.] [all published].

Subject listing of 3,642 books and articles, primarily in Russian, but with some western European language materials. No index.

Contents: Geography; History; Minerology, Geology and Paleontology; Botony; Zoology; Meterology, Astronomy and Geodesy; Ethnography; Medicine, Veterinary, Physiology and Bacteriology; Rural

Economy; Books not Mentioned in the Preceding Sections; Appendix.

Title transliterated: Bibliografiia͡ Turkestana.

Europe

Albania

J36

LEGRAND, Emile *and* GÛYS, Henri.

Bibliographies albanaise: description raisonée des ouvrages publiés en Albanais ou relatifs à l'Albanie du quinzième siècle à l'année 1900. Paris, H. Welter, Editeur; Athens, Eleftheroudakis et Barth, 1912. VIII + 228 p.

Listing, with occasional annotations, of 724 books by date of publication from 1474. Indices of subjects, authors, booksellers and publishers, engravers, libraries, and proper names.

Spain

J37

BOĬKO, K. A.

Арабская Историческая Литература в Испании (8- первая треть 11 в.)[Arabic Historical Literature in Spain (8- first third of the 11 c.)]. Moscow, Izdatel'stvo "Nauka", 1977. 299 p.

Bio-bibliographical survey of Spanish-Arab historians to the end of the Umayyad Dynasty in Spain (1031 A.D.) based upon the works of Pons Boigues [J39], Brockelmann [G13], and Sezgin [G15]. An English abstract of the introduction is to be found on pages 226-30.

Title transliterated: Arabskaia͡ Istoricheskaia͡ Literatura v Ispanii...

J38

KAMPFFMEYER, Georg.

"Eine alte Liste arabischer Werke zur Geschichte spaniens und nordwest-africas." *Mitteilungen des Seminars für Orientalische Sprachen zu Berlin*, IX, Zweite Abteilung: "Westasiatische Studien," 1906, pp. 74-110.

A list of 153 works based upon an anonymous 14th century bibliography entitled فهرست كتب فى تاريخ الاندلس و المغرب.

J39
PONS BOIGUES, Francisco.
Ensayo Bio-bibliográfico sobre las Historiadores y Geógrafos arábigo-españoles. Madrid, San Francisco de Soles, 1898. [iv] + 514 p.

Listing of 303 authors and their works to the middle of the 11th century. Arabic index to titles and authors, Spanish index to authors alone.

J40
RODRIQUEZ, Carlos Joulia-Saint-Cyr.
Ensayo de Bibliografía Menor Hispano-musulmana (hojas y falletos impresos de los siglos XVI, XVII y XVIII). Madrid, Dirección General de Archivos y Bibliotecas, 1970. XIX + 377 p.

Chronological listing of 1,600 books in western languages, predominantly Spanish, printed between 1500 and 1800. Under each date the entries are listed by author or first word of title. Locations of copies are provided in nine libraries in Spain, Portugal, and Morocco.

J41
SÁNCHEZ ALONSO, Benito.
Fuentes de la Historia española e Hispano-americano: ensayo de bibliografía sistemática de impresos y manuscritos que ilustran la historia política de Españya y sus antiguas provincias de ultramar. *3rd ed*. Madrid, Consejo Superior de Investigaciones Cientificas, 1952. 3 vols.

Contains an important classified listing of European language materials on Muslim Spain in volume I, "Capitulo V: Periodo arabe - cristiana, hasta la venida a España de Carlos I (711-1517)", pp. 133-369.

Yugoslavia

J42
PÉTROVITCH, Nicolas S.
Essai de Bibliographie française sur les Serbes et

les Croates 1544-1900. Belgrad, Imprimerie de l'-Etat, 1900. XIV + 314 p.

Edition de l'Académie Royale de Serbie.

Listing by date of publication, without annotations, of 1,819 books and articles. Indices of authors and titles.

¶ For a bibliography of Bulgaria see N. V. Michoff, *Sources bibliographiques sur l'Histoire de la Turquie et la Bulgarie* [J55].

Near East

J43

BRYSON, Thomas A.

United States/Middle East Diplomatic Relations 1784-1978: an annotated bibliography. Metuchen, New Jersey, The Scarecrow Press, 1979. xiv + 205 p.

An annotated listing of 1,353 books, articles, and dissertations, confined to English, arranged by period.

Iran

J44

PIEMONTESE, A. M.

Bibliografia italiana dell'Iran, 1462-1982. Naples, Istituto Universitario Orientale, 1982. 947 p.

Istituto Universitario Orientale, Seminario di Studi Asiatici, Series Minor, 18.

Contents: 1. Bibliografia - Geografia - Viaggi e viaggiatori - Storia - Archeologia; 2. Arte - Lingua - Letteratura - Filosofia e Scienza - Religione - La Persia nella Letteratura italiana ed Europea.

J45

GUILLOU, André.

Essai bibliographique sur les Dynasties musulmanes de l'Iran. Madrid, Instituto Egipcio de Estudios Islámicos, 1957. 94 p.

Brief annotated listing, by dynasty, of the primary and secondary sources in western and oriental languages for the history of Muslim Iran.

J46

WICKENS, G. M. *and* SAVORY, R. M.

Persia in Islamic Times: a practical bibliography of its history, culture and language. Montreal, Institute of Islamic Studies, McGill University, 1964. 57 p.

A mimeographed selected and classified listing of 701 books in Farsi and western languages.

Iraq

Baghdad

J47
ᶜAWWĀD, Kūrkīs *and* al-ᶜALŪJĪ, ᶜAbd al-Ḥamīd.
جمهرة المراجع البغداد : فهرست شامل بما كتب عن
A Bibliography of بغداد منذ تاسيسها حتى الان /
Baghdad. Baghdad, Maṭbaᶜa al-Rābiṭa, 1962. 95 + 643 p.

Alphabetical author listings, with annotations, of 1,068 western and 5,357 Arabic language books and articles which deal wholly or in part on all aspects of the city from the time of its foundation. The Arabic section contains indices of authors, titles, and subjects for the materials in that language. None are provided, however, for the European section.

Title transliterated: Jamhara al-Marājiᶜ al-Baghdād:...

Najaf

J48
ᶜALĪ, ᶜAbd al-Raḥīm Muḥammad.
[The Origin of مصادر الدراسة عن مدينة النجف الاشرف
Study on the Noble City of Najaf]. Muḥammad Hādī al-Amīnī. مصادر الدراسة عن النجف و الشيخ الطوسي
Najaf, Maṭbaᶜa al-Najaf, 1382/1964, pp. 7-66.

An unannotated listing of 321 books and articles in Arabic in alphabetical order by title. No index.

Title transliterated: Maṣādir al-Dirāsa ᶜan Madīna al-Najaf al-Ashraf.

Syria

Damascus

J49
al-MUNAJJID, Ṣalāh al-Dīn.

المؤرخون الدمشقيون و آثارهم المخطوطة من القرن الثالث الهجرى الى نهاية القرن العاشر/ Les Historiens de Damas et Leurs Oeuvres du IXe jusqu'au XVIe Siècle. Cairo, Maṭbaᶜa Miṣr, 1956. 75 p., illus.

Annotated listing of 51 Arabic historians, illustrated with 20 reproductions of title pages. Also printed in *Majalla Maᶜhad al-Makhṭūṭāt*, II, 1956, pp. 63-145.

Title transliterated: Al-Muʾarrikhūn al-Dimashqīyūn...

Turkey

J50
BABINGER, Franz.
Die Geschichtschreiber der Osmanen und Ihre Werke. Leipzig, Otto Harrassowitz, 1927. vii + 477 p.

Bio-bibliographical survey of nearly 400 Ottoman Turkish historians with summaries of principal works, a list of manuscripts in European libraries, and a list of all Ottoman histories which have been edited and translated to 1927.

J51
BİNARK, İsmet.
Türk Sefer ve Zaferleri Bibliyografyası (İzahlı) [Turkish War and Peace Bibliography (Annotated)]. Ankara, Millî Kütüphane, 1969. XIV + 234 p., illus. *Millî Kütüphaneye Yardım Derneği Yayınları: 1.*

Classified, annotated listing of 585 books published since 1928 on Turkey's long history of conflict. Shelf numbers of Ankara libraries are provided. Illustrated with one colored plate.

Contents: I. Umumî Türk Zaferleri;II. Selçuklu-Türk Zaferleri;III. Osmanlı-Türk Zaferleri;IV. Millî Mücadele Yılları Zaferleri; V. Cumhuriyet Yılları Zaferleri; Ekler. Author and title indices.

J52
BOSTASHVILI, N. I.
Библиография Турции (истоия) [Bibliography of Turkey (history)]. Tbilisi, Izdatel'stvo "Metsniereba", 1971. 290 + [ii] p.

Classified listing of 1,963 books and journal and newspaper articles published in Georgian during the 19th and 20th centuries on the history of the Ottoman Empire and the Turkish Republic. The materials are given in Georgian with translation into Russian. No annotations. Indices of authors and subjects in both Georgian and Russian.

Contents: K. Marks and F. Engels on Turkey; V. I. Lenin on Turkey; Soviet System Statesmen on Turkey; Travels; Turkish Economic Condition and Workers-Peasants' Movements; Turkey in the Middle Ages; Turkey in Modern Times; Turkey and the First World War: Caucasian Front; Condition of the Balkan Peoples. National-liberation Movements. Balkan War; Turkey in Modern Times; U.S.S.R. and Turkey; Georgia and Turkey; Russia and Turkey; Russo-Turkish War 1877-78; National Issues. Appendices of books, collected works, journals, and newspapers.

Title transliterated: Bibliografii͡a Turtsii (istorii͡a).

J53
GÖLLNER, Carl.
Tvrcica: die europaischen Turkendrucke des XVI. jahrhunderts. Bucharest, Editura Academiei R.P.R.; Berlin, Akademie- Verlag G.M.B.H.; Baden-Baden, Verlag Librairie Heitz G.M.B.H., 1961-68. 2 vols., illus.

Annotated, chronological listing of 2,463 books published in Europe between 1501 and 1600 on the Turks and the Ottoman Empire. Indicates in which European library a copy is preserved, with catalogue number. Author, title, and library indices. An exceptionally fine example of rare book cataloging.

J54
KORAY, Enver.
Türkiye Tarih Yayınları Bibliyografyası 1729-1955 [Bibliography of Turkish Historical Publications 1729-1955]. *2nd ed.* Istanbul, Maarif Basımevi. XII + 680 p.

Classified bibliography of 4,791 books and articles printed in Turkey between 1729 and 1955 on history with emphasis on the history of the Turks, the Ottoman Empire, and republican Turkey.

Contents: Birenci Bölüm: 1729-1928 Arap Harfleriyle Baselmış Eserler: II- Muhtelif Milletler Tarihi - (25) Umumi Türk Tarihi; III- Çeşitli Konular - (1) Biyografi. İkinci Bölüm: 1928-1955 Türk Harfleriyle Baselmış Eserler: II- Muhtelif Milletler Tarihi - (37) Türk Tarihi; III- Çeşitli Konular - (6) Biyografi. Indices of authors and titles.

Continuations: Enver Koray. *Türkiye Tarih Yayınları Bibliyografyası II 1955-1968.* Istanbul, Millî Eğitim Basımevi, 1971. 510 + II p.

J55

MICHOFF, N. V.

Sources bibliographiques sur l'Histoire de la Turquie et la Bulgarie. Sofia, Imprimerie de l'Etat/ Imprimerie P. Glouchkoff, 1914-34. 4 vols.

The four volumes together list 1,585 books and articles published up to 1934. Each is in alphabetical order by author. Author and subject indices are in volume four.

J56

MORAN, Berna.

Türklerle ilgili İngilizce Yayınları Bibliyografyası [Bibliography of the Turks in English Publications]. Istanbul, İstanbul Matbaası, 1964. VI + 176 p., illus.

Listing, occasionally with lengthy annotations, 302 works printed between 1482 and 1699. Numbers 275-302 are English dramas which have as their subjects the Turks or other Near Eastern peoples.

J57

ROUILLARD, Clarence Dana.

The Turk in French History, Thought, and Literature (1520-1660). Paris, Boivin & Cie, Editeurs, [1941]. 700 p., illus.

Contents: Introduction- France and the Ottoman Turks before 1520; Pt. I- Historical Background and Official Relations Between France and the Ottoman Empire; Pt. II- The Portrayal of the Turk in French Geographical Literature; Pt. III- The Role of the Turk in the Development of Ideas in France; Pt. IV- The Turk in French Imaginative Literature; Appendices (I. A Bibliography of Pamphlets Relating to the Turks, 1481-1660 [by date of publication]. Index.

J58
SHIMIZU, Kosuke.
A Bibliography of Saljuq Studies. Tokyo, Institute for the Study of the Languages and Cultures of Asia and Africa, 1979. 71 p.

Studia Culturae Islamicae No. 12.

Classified listing of books and articles with emphasis upon those from Iran and Turkey. Supplements the bibliography published by the Millî Kütüphane of 1971 [J61].

J59
STURMINGER, Walter.
Bibliographie und Ikonographie der Türkenbelagerung Wiens 1529 und 1683. Graz, Verlag Hermann Böhlaus Nachf., 1955. XVI + 420 p., illus.

Author listing of 4,270 books, pamphlets, broadsides, and articles in European languages according to date of seige. Indices.

An earlier bibliography on the same subject was that of Heinrich Kábdebo, *Bibliographie zur Geschichte der Beiden Türkenbelagerungen Wien's 1529 und 1683.* Vienna, Verlag von Faesy & Frick, 1876.

In his review in the *Deutsche Literaturzeitung* (Jahrgang 78, Heft 5, Mai 1957, cols. 423-26) Otto Forst de Battaglia provides a lengthy list of additions to the bibliography, primarily Polish works.

J60
SVERCHEVSKAI͡A, A. K. *and* CHERMAN, T. P.
Библиография Турции (1713-1917) [Bibliography of Turkey (1713-1917)]. Moscow, Izdatel'stvo Vostochnoĭ Literatury, 1961. 266 + [i] p. [dbl. col.].

Classified listing of 5,116 books and articles published in Russian during the two centuries.

Contents: K. Marx and F. Engels on Turkey; V. I. Lenin on Turkey; General Works; Geography; Population. Ethnography; Journeys. Travel Guides; Economics; History; National Question; Position of Women; Political System. Legislation; Armed Forces; Philology; Religion. Islam; Education. Press; Art. Index of authors and titles.

Continuations: A. K. Sverchevskai͡a *and* T. P. Cherman. **Библиография Турции (1917-1958)** Moscow, Izdatel'stvo Vostochnoĭ Literatury, 1959. 190 p. [dbl. col.].

Title transliterated: Bibliografii͡a Turtsii...

J61
TURKEY. Millî Kütüphane.
Selçuklu Tarihi, Alparslan ve Malazgirt Bibliyografyası [Bibliography of the History of the Saljuks, Alp Arslan, and Manzikert]. Ankara, Millî Eğitim Basımevi, 1971. XIX, [iii] + 178 p.

Kültür Bakanlığı, Millî Kütüphane Yayınları: 1.

Secondary title: *"Malazgirt zaferinin 900. yıldönümü münasebetiyle hasırlanmış tarihi bir bibliyografya denemesi".*

Listing of 1,426 books and articles in western and oriental languages arranged by subject. Author and title indices.

Also see Kosuke Shimizu's *A Bibliography of Saljuk Studies* [J58].

J62
"Turkologischer Anzeiger" 1- , 1973- . *Weiner Zeitschrift für die Kunde des Morgenlandes*, 67- , 1975-.

Annual classified bibliography of books and articles on Turkish and Ottoman studies published in Turkish, western and eastern European languages. Index of authors, editors, etc. in each volume. An extremely detailed valuable bibliographic source.

Konya

J63
ERDOĞAN, Muzaffer.
İzahli Konya Bibliyografyası [Bibliography of Konya]. Istanbul, Anıl Matbaası, xiv + 99 p.

Yemen

J64
al-ḤABASHĪ, ᶜAbd Allāh Muḥammad.
[Sources for the History of Yemen]. مراجع تاريخ اليمن
Damascus, Manshūrāt Wizāra al-Thaqāfa, 1972. 384 p.

Alphabetical listing by title of printed and manuscript works in Arabic about Yemen or in which Yemenite historical materials are to be found. Author index.

Title transliterated: Marājiᶜ Taʾrīkh al-Yaman.

J65
SAYYID, Amīn Fuʾād.
Sources de l'- / مصادر تاريخ اليمن فى العصر الاسلامى
Histoire du Yémen à l'Epoque musulmane. Cairo, Institut Français d'Archéology Orientale du Caire, 1974. [xv], 504 [Arabic text] + XII p.

Textes et Traductions d'Auteurs Orientaux, T. VII.

Chronological listing of manuscript and printed materials in Arabic and western languages. Indices of titles and authors (incomplete). Unfortunately, filled with misprints.

Title transliterated: Maṣādir Taʾrīkh al-Yaman fī al-ᶜAṣr al-Islāmīya.

South & Southeast Asia

India

J66
CAMPBELL, Frank.
An Index-Catalogue of Bibliographical Works (chiefly in the English language) Relating to India: a study in bibliography. London, Library Supply Co., 1899. 99 p.

Despite its age this small volume remains a valuable guide to indices, bibliographies, and catalogues on both Hindu and Muslim India.

Contents: Sec. I. Asia and the East: general bibliographies; Sec. II. India: A. Periodical registers; B. Indian official publications; C. English Parliamentary Papers relating to India; D. General bibliographies; E. Special bibliographies [by subject]. No index.

Reprinted on microfich by Inter Documentation

Co., Zug, Switzerland, 1968.

J67
CASE, Margaret H.
South Asian History 1750-1950: a guide to periodicals, dissertations, and newspapers. Princeton, Princeton University Press, 1968. xiii + 561 p.

Classified listing of 5,411 articles from 351 periodicals and 26 *festschriften* published between 1800 and 1965, primarily in English, 650 doctoral dissertations presented to American, British, and Indian universities, and 341 English and bi-lingual English-Indian language and 251 Indian language newspapers, by place of publication. A very valuable reference work.

Contents: Pt. I- Articles: A. Areas not primarily under British control; B. Areas primarily under British control; C. Nationalism and politics; D. Economic history; E. Social history; F. Cultural history. Pt. II- Dissertations. Pt. III- Newspapers. Indices of authors, dissertations, and subjects.

J68
CHAUDHURI, Sashi Bhusan.
English Historical Writings on the Indian Mutiny 1857-1859. Calcutta, The World Press Private Ltd., 1979. 368 p.

The main body of this disappointing work is a bibliographic essay arranged into ten chapters. The "Appendix", pages 287-355, is a listing by author of 640 books in western languages and 78 books in various Indian languages. Also appended is a list of pamphlets, proclamations, and "notifications."

J69
DIVEKAR, V. D., *ed.*
Annotated Bibliography on the Economic History of India (1500 A.D. to 1947 A.D.). New Delhi, Gokhate Institute of Politics & Economics, Indian Institute of Social Science Research, 1977-80. 4 vols. in 5.

Includes only English language materials on the sub-continent (India, Pakistan, and Bangladesh). Arranged by types of records and then by subject, including theses. Each volume is separately indexed by author, subject, region, and, if appropriate, title.

J70
HASAN, Khan Bahadur Maulvi Zafar.
Bibliography of Indo-Moslem History, Excluding Provincial Monarchies. Calcutta, Government of India Central Publication Branch, 1932. iii, [i] + 42 p.
Memoires of the Archaeological Survey of India, No. 45.
A detailed list of 307 manuscripts of which, at the time of printing, only 53 had been published, arranged by title.

J71
LADENDORF, Janice M.
The Revolt in India 1857-58: an annotated bibliography of English language materials. Zug, Switzerland, Inter Documentation Company AG, 1966. v + 191 p.
Bibliotheca Asiatica 2.
Listing by type of material or by subject 985 books, articles, reports, memoires, etc., both published and unpublished, with indication of location. Not all of the English language materials published or held in India are included. Author index.

J72
MALIK, Ikram Ali.
A Bibliography of the Punjab and Its Dependencies (1849-1910). Lahore, Research Society of Pakistan, University of the Punjab, 1968. iii, [iii], 309 + [i] p.
Publication No. 8.
Lists a total of 2,259 books, reports, records, manuscripts, articles, and theses published or written about or during the period, arranged by type of material. Author and subject index.

J73
MARSHALL, D. N.
Mughals in India: a bibliographical survey. Bombay, Asia Publishing House, 1967- [in progress?].

Annotated author listing of the published and unpublished primary and secondary sources for the history of the Mughal Empire. Only volume one - manuscripts - has been published to date. Upon completion will supplant the earlier work by *Sri* Ram Sharma, *A Bibliography of Mughal India (1526-1707 A.D.)*, Bombay, Karnatak Publishing House, [1939].

Marshall's first volume lists over 2,100 manuscripts in western and oriental languages, discusses the contents, relative value, and location of each.

J74

--- *and* TARAPOREVALA, Vicaji D. B.

Mughal Bibliography: select Persian sources for the study of Mughals in India. Bombay, The New Book Co. Private Ltd., 1962. viii + 164 p.

A listing, with detailed annotations, 437 printed and manuscript sources.

Vincent A. Smith, in his *Akbar the Great Mogul 1542-1605, 2nd ed.*, Oxford, Oxford University Press, 1919, provided in Appendix D an excellent classified and annotated list of primary and secondary sources on the reign of that emperor.

Indonesia

J75

SOEDJATMOKO; ALI, Mohammad; RESINK, G. J. *and* KAHIN, G. McT., *eds.*

An Introduction to Indonesian Historiography. Ithaca, New York, Cornell University Press, 1965. xxviii + 427 p., maps.

A collection of 22 invited essays on various aspects of the subject.

Malaysia

J76

TREGONNING, K. G., *ed.*

Malaysian Historical Sources. Singapore, Department of History, University of Singapore, 1962. vi + 130 p., illus.

A collection of 18 bibliographical essays by 14

scholars. No index.

Far East

China

J77
CHANG, Hajji Yusuf.
A Bibliographical Study of the History of Islam in China. Montreal, Institute of Islamic Studies, McGill University, 1960. x + 208 p. [one side only].
An annotated listing of 857 books and articles in western languages and Chinese, with cross references. General, biographical, and geographical-racial indices.

J78
"Russian Materials on Islam in China: a preliminary bibliography." *Monumenta Serica*, XVI, 1957, pp. 449-479.
Classified listing of 142 books and articles.
Contents: I. Bibliographies; II. History; III. Economics; IV. Ethnography and Demography. Author, person, and subject index.

J79
PICKENS, Claude L., Jr.
Annotated Bibliography of Literature on Islam in China. Hankow, Society of Friends of the Moslems in China, 1950. [vi] + 72 p.
Subject listing of books and articles in Chinese and western languages.
Contents: I. General Sources; II. Introduction of Islam into China; III. History and Spread of Islam in China; Sects and Orders; V. Literature; VI. Indigenous Development; VII. Chinese-Muslim Terms; VIII. Statistics. Addenda and index of authors.

J80
PRATT, Mark Shrum.
Japanese Materials on Islam in China: a selected bibliography. Washington, D.C., Georgetown University, 1962. xix + 169 p. [one side only].
Classified listing, with occasional brief anno-

tations, of 780 books and articles published since the second quarter of the twentieth century. Not all items were personally examined by the compiler. Authors and titles are given in both Japanese characters and in transliteration. In addition, the titles are also translated.

Contents: I. Periodicals; II. Bibliographies; III. General Works; IV. History [from the T'ang to the present]; V. Ethnography; VI. Economics, Transportation and Communications; VII. Geography and Explorations; VIII. Religion and Islamic Law; IX. Arts and Sciences; X. Linguistics; XI. Translations into Japanese. General index.

BIOGRAPHIES

General

J81
al-DHAHABĪ, Muḥammad ibn ᶜUthmān (d. 748/1348). [The Importance in the News العبر في خبر من غبر from the Past]. *Ed.* Ṣalāḥ ad-Dīn al-Munajjid *and* Fuɔād Sayyid. Kuwait, Nāɔira al-Maṭbūᶜāt wa al-Nashr, 1960. 3 vols.

Al-Turāth al-ᶜArabī, 4.

Biographies of important men drawn from his large history of Islam.

Title transliterated: ᶜIbar fī Khabr min Ghabr.

J82
IBN KHALLIKĀN, Aḥmad ibn Muḥammad (d. 681/1282). [Book of the كتاب وفيات الاعيان و اتباء أبناء ازمان Death Dates of the Notables and Reports on the Sons of Time]. *Ed.* Ferdinand Wüstenfeld. *Ibn Challikani Vitae illustrium vivarum.* Göttingen, Dieterichschen Buchhandlung, 1835-50. 13 fasc.

Biographical dictionary by first name of 647 learned men, rulers (excluding caliphs), political figures, literati, etc., from the beginning of the caliphate to *cir.* 1256. Numerous other editions have been printed in Europe and the Near East.

Translations: Baron MacGuckin DeSlane. *Ibn Khallikan's Biographical Dictionary.* London, Oriental Translation Fund, 1842-71. 4 vols. Includes a lengthy introduction and copious notes derived from other Arabic sources. This translation has been reprinted photographically at least twice in New York, and reprinted from fresh type, with additions and corrections by S. Moinul Haq (Karachi, Pakistan Historical Society, 1961-65. 4 vols.). An earlier, Latin, translation was made by G. Pijnappel and printed in Amsterdam in 1845.

Title transliterated: Kitāb Wafayāt al-Aᶜyān...

Supplements & Continuations:

1. Ibn Shākir ibn Aḥmad al-Kutubī (d. 764/1362-63). كتاب فوات الوفيات [Omissions in the Wafayat]. *Ed.* Iḥsān ᶜAbbās. Beirut, Dār al-Thaqāfa, 1973-75. 5 vols. Provided with index. Additional material to many of the biographee's lifes and 483 new listings omitted by Ibn Khallikān or of those who died after him. Previously printed in Bulaq in 1283/1866-67 and 1299/1881-82, in two volumes.

2. Khalīl ibn Aybak al-Ṣafadi (d. 764/1362-63). كتاب الوافى بالوفيات [Book of the Ample in the Wafayat]. *Ed.* Sven Dedering, Helmut Ritter, *et. al. Das biographische Lexikon des ... as-Safadi.* Istanbul, Millî Eğitim Basımevi, 1949; Damascus, Al-Maṭbaᶜa al-Hāshimīya, 1953; Wiesbaden, Franz Steiner Verlag GMBH, 1959- [in progress]. An enormous supplement to the dictionaries of both Ibn Khallikān and al-Kutubī, containing short notices of approxminately 14,000 literati, jurisconsults, military and political leaders, etc. who lived during the first seven centuries of Islam. Arranged in alphabetical order by *ism* except that, as usual, all those named Muḥammad are listed first. Guiseppe Gabrieli has published an alphabetical list of the biographees in the dictionary, "Indice alfabetico di tutte le biografie contenute nel *Wafi bi-l-Wafayat* di al-Safadi nello esemplare fotografico dell'on Leone Caetani, principe di Teano (Roma)." *Atti dell' Academia dei Lincei*, Ser. VI, XXII, 1913, pp. 547-77, 580-620; XXIII, 1914, pp. 191-208, 217-65; XXIV, 1915, pp. 551-615; XXV, 1916, pp. 341-98.

3. Aḥmad ibn Muḥammad ibn al-Qāḍī (d. 1025/1616). درة الحجال في اسماء الرجال [Pearl of the Pavilions in the Names of the Men]. [J132].

J83
al-KHWĀNSĀRĪ, Muḥammad Bāqir.
الروضات الجنات فى احوال العلماء و السادات
[The Harvested Gardens Regarding the Positions of the Learned and the Sayyids]. Tehran, [litho.], 1306/1888. 779 p.

A ninetheenth century biographical dictionary of 713 learned Muslims, both Sunnīs and Shīᶜīs, of all periods and classes, theologians, mystics, poets, physicians, philosophers, etc., arranged alphabetically. Reprinted in Tehran in 1367/1948.

Title Transliterated: Al-Rawḍāt al-Janāt fī Aḥwāl al-ᶜUlamāʾ wa al-Sādāt.

J84
al-MARᶜASHĪ, Nūr Allāh ibn Sharīf (d. 1019/1610-11).
[Councils of the Faithful]. مجالس المؤمنين
Tehran, [litho.], 1268/1852. 259 p.

Biographical dictionary, in 12 chapters, of eminent Shīᶜites of all classes (not merely theologians). In Persian.

Title transliterated: Majālis al-Muʾminīn.

J85
al-ZIRIKLĪ, Khayr al-Dīn.
الاعلام : قاموس تراجم لاشهر الرجال و النساء من العرب و المستعربين و المستشرقين
[The Eminent Persons: a biographical dictionary of the better known Arabic men and women and of Arabists and Orientalists]. *2nd ed.* Beirut, Maṭbaᶜa Kūstamā Tasūmās wa Shirkahu, 1374/1955-56. 10 vols., illus.

General biographical dictionary of classical and modern Arab men and women of note, together with western Arabists and Orientalists. Provides brief biographical details, with sources, illustrated with photographs or drawings of the biographees or with photographs of manuscripts written by them. Listed by name by which best known. Index in volume 10.

Title transliterated: Al-Aᶜlām:...

Specialized

Blind

J86

al-ṢAFADĪ, Khalīl ibn Aybak (d. 764/1362-63).
[Interesting Jottings upon the Anecdotes of the Blind]. نكت الهميان فى نكت العميان *Ed.* Aḥmad Zakī Pashā. Cairo, Maṭbaᶜa al-Jamālīya, 1911. 16 + 320 p.

In alphabetical order. Reprinted in 1963.

Title transliterated: Nukat al-Humyān fī Nukat al-ᶜUmyān.

Reformers

J87
al-SAᶜĪDĪ, ᶜAbd al-Mutaᶜāl.
المجددون فى الاسلام من القرن الاول الى الرابع عشر: ١٠٠ هـ — ١٣٧٠ هـ
[Reformers of Islam from the First to the Fourteenth Century: 100 A.H. - 1370 A.H./600 A.D. - 1950-51 A.D.]. Cairo, Maktaba al-Ādāb, 1950. 636 p.

Title transliterated: Al-Mujaddidūn fī al-Islām...

J88
AMĪN, Aḥmad.
[Leaders of Reform in Modern Times]. زعماء الاصلاح في العصر الحديث Cairo, Maktaba al-Naḥḍa al-Miṣrīya, 1367/1948. 357 p.

Contents: Muḥammad ibn ᶜAbd al-Wahhāb; Midhat Pashā; Jamāl al-Dīn al-Afghānī; Aḥmad Khān; Amīr ᶜAlī; Khayr al-Dīn Pashā al-Tūnisī; ᶜAlī Pashā Mubārrak; ᶜAbd Allāh Nadīm; ᶜAbd al-Raḥmān al-Kawākabī; Muḥammad ᶜAbdū.

Title transliterated: Zuᶜamāɔ al-Iṣlāḥ fī al-ᶜAṣr al-Hadīth.

Shaykhs of al-Azhar

J89
ᶜABD AL-ᶜAẒĪM, ᶜAlī.
[The Shaykhs of al-Azhar from Its Foundation to the Present]. مشيخة الازهر منذ انشائها حتى الآن Cairo, Al-Hayɔa al-ᶜĀmma li-Shuɔūn al-Maṭbaᶜa al-Amīrīya, 1979-81. 2 vols.

Biographical dictionary of the leaders of the University of al-Azhar from 973 A.D.

Title transliterated: Mashyakha al-Azhar mundh Inshāɔihā ḥatta al-Ān.

Women

J90
al-BUSTĀNĪ, Karam.
[Arab Women in Culture, in Wealth, in War, in Prophecy]. النساء العربيات، في الادب، في الغناء، في الحرب، في الكهانة Beirut, Dār Sādir li-l-Ṭabāᶜ wa al-Nashr, 1964. 222 p.
Title transliterated: Al-Nisāʾ al-ᶜArabīya...

J91
KAḤḤĀLA, ᶜUmar Riḍā.
[Guide to Women among the Famous Arabs and Muslims]. اعلام في النساء في عالمي العرب و الاسلام *2nd ed.* Damascus, Al-Maṭbaᶜa al-Hāshimīya, 1959. 5 vols. in 3.
First published in three volumes in 1940.
Title transliterated: Aᶜlām fī al-Nisāʾ fī ᶜĀlamī al-ᶜArabī wa al-Islāmī.

J92
QADRĪYA ḤUSAYN, *Princess*.
[Celebrated Women in Islamic Learning]. شهيرات النساء في العالم الاسلامي Beirut, Dār al-Kātib al-ᶜArabī, 1965. 279 p.
Brief biographies of women scholars throughout Muslim history.
Title transliterated: Shahīrāt al-Nisāʾ fī al-ᶜĀlam al-Islāmī.

Chronological

1-700/622-1301

J93
al-DHAHABĪ, Muḥammad ibn ᶜUthmān (d. 748/1348).
[Biographies of Eminent Notables]. سير اعلام النبلاء Beirut, Muʾassasa al-Risāla, 1981- [in progress].
Dictionary of the important individuals, rulers, officials, scholars, etc. who died during the first seven centuries of Islam arranged in decades, extracted from his historical chronical, *Taʾrīkh al-Islām*.
Title transliterated: Siyar Aᶜlām al-Nubalāʾ.

1-750/622-1348-49

J94
al-YĀFIᶜĪ, ᶜAbd Allāh ibn Asᶜad (d. 768/1367).
مرآة الجنان و عبرة اليقظان فى معرفة حوادث الزمان
[The Mirror of the Heart and the Admonition of the Cautious in the Knowledge of the Events of Time]. Hyderabad-Deccan, Dāɔira al-Maᶜārif al-ᶜUthmānīya, 1337/1918-19. 4 vols.

Biographical dictionary of those who died during the period in each year, arranged by date of death.

Title transliterated: Mirɔā al-Janān...

1-1000/622-1592

J95
IBN AL-ᶜIMĀD, ᶜAbd al-Ḥayy ibn Aḥmad (d. 1089/1679). [Pieces of Gold شذرات الذهب فى اخبار من ذهب in Events of Old]. Cairo, Maktaba al-Qudsī, 1350-51/1931-33. 8 vols.

Biographical dictionary by a Syrian Ḥanbalī scholar chronologically arranged. No index, unfortunately. Transcribed from a manuscript in the Egyptian National Library.

Title transliterated: Shadhrāt al-Dhahab fī Akhbar man Dhahab.

7th-9th/13th-15th Centuries

J96
IBN TAGHRĪ BIRDĪ, Jamāl al-Dīn Yusuf (d. 874/1470). [The Pure Spring المنهل الصافي و المستوفى بعد الوافى and the Completion of the *Wafi*]. *Ed.* Aḥmad Yūsuf Najātī. Cairo, Dār al-Kutub al-Miṣrīya, 1956- .

Supplement to, and continuation of, al-Ṣafadī's biographical dictionary [J82], with notices of 2,798 sultans, amirs, and scholars who died between 1248 and 1458 listed alphabetically. Publication assumed by Al-Hayɔa al-Miṣrīya al-ᶜĀmma.

In 1932 Gaston Wiet published an index, with summaries, to the *Manhāl*, *Les Biographies du Manhal Safi*. Cairo, Imprimerie de l'Institut Français d'Archéologie Orientale. XV + 480 p. *Mémoires Présentés à l'Institut d'Egypte, T. 18.*

Title transliterated: Al-Manhal al-Ṣāfī...

7th-13th/13th-19th Centuries

J97
al-SHAWKĀNĪ, Muḥammad ibn ᶜAlī (d. 1250/1834-35).
البدر الطالع بمحاسن من القرن السابع، و يليه ملحق لزبارة اليمن
[The Rising of the Full Moon with Attractions from the Seventh Century, and Following It an Appendix by Zubāra of the Yemen]. Cairo, Maṭbaᶜa al-Saᶜāda, 1348/1929-30. 2 vols.

A biographical dictionary of learned men from the 7th century A.H. down to his own time, with an appendix of the biographies of 441 distinguished Yemenis of the 13th century A.H., compiled by Muḥammad ibn Muḥammad ibn Zubāra al-Ṣanᶜānī in 1348/1929-30, entitled قيل الوطر من تراجم رجال اليمن فى القرن الثالث عشر.

Title transliterated: Al-Badr al-Ṭāliᶜ...

8th/14th Century

J98
al-ᶜASQALĀNĪ, Aḥmad ibn ᶜAlī ibn Ḥajar (d. 852/1449).
الدرر الكامنة فى اعيان المائة الثامنة
[The Hidden Pearls in the Witnesses of the Eighth Century]. Hyderabad-Deccan, Dāᵓira al-Maᶜārif al-ᶜUthmānīya, 1348-50/1929-31. 4 vols.

Dictionary of rulers, officials, military officers, scholars, poets, merchants, chess-players, etc. who died during the 8th/14th century, arranged in alphabetical order.

Title transliterated: Al-Durar al-Kāmina fī Aᶜyān al-Māᵓa al-Thāmina.

9th/15th Century

J99
al-SAKHĀWĪ, Muḥammad ibn ᶜAbd al-Raḥmān (d. 902/1497).
الضؤ الامع لاهل القرن التاسع
[The Brilliant Light Upon the People of the Ninth Century]. Cairo, Maktaba al-Qudsī, 1353-55/1934-36. 12 vols.

A general biographical dictionary of those who died during the century, arranged alphabetically by *ism*. The eleventh volume contains an index of *kunyas*, the twelfth contains the biographies of women.

Title transliterated: Al-Ḍawᵓ al-Lāmiᶜ...

J100
al-SUYŪṬĪ, ᶜAbd al-Raḥmān ibn Abī Bakr (d. 911/1505).

[The Golden Order نظم العقيان فى عيان الاعيان
in Witnessing the Events]. *Ed.* Philip K. Hitti. *As-Suyuti's Who's Who in the Fifteenth Century.* New York, Syrian American Press, 1927. x, xvii, 179 + 15 p., illus.

General biographical dictionary by first name of 200 noted men and women who died during the 9th/15th century.

Title transliterated: Naẓm al-ᶜIqyān fī ᶜIyān al-Aᶜyān.

10th/15th-16th Century

J101
al-GHAZZĪ, Muḥammad ibn Muḥammad (d. 1061/1651).
[All of the Stars الكواكب السائرة باعيان المائة العاشرة
Who Witnessed the Tenth Century]. *Ed.* Jibrāᵓīl Sulaymān Jabbur. Beirut, American University of Beirut, 1945-59. 3 vols.

Dictionary of notable men and women who died during the century, arranged firstly into classes of 33 years, and within each class by first name, with all of the Muhammad's listed first. Reprinted in Beirut in 1979.

Title transliterated: Al-Kawākib al-Sāᵓira bi-Aᶜyān al-Māᵓa al-ᶜĀshira.

11th/16th-17th Century

J102
---.
لطف السمر و قطف الثمر (من تراجم اعيان الطبق الاولى من القرن الحادى عشر)
[Kindness of the Night and the Picking of the Fruit]. *Ed.* Maḥmūd al-Shaykh. Damascus, Wizāra al-Thaqāfa wa al-Irshād al-Qawmī, 1981- . Illus.

Al-Turāth al-ᶜArabī, 55.

Contains the lives of 300 eminent Muslims.

Title transliterated: Luṭf al-Samar wa Qaṭf al-Thamar...

J103
al-MUḤIBBĪ, Muḥammad Amīn ibn Faḍl Allāh (d. 1111/1699).
تاريخ خلاصة الاثر فى اعيان القرن الحادى عشر
[History in Tracking the Essence of the Notables of the Eleventh Century]. Cairo, Maṭbaᶜa al-Wahhabīya,

1284/1867-68. 4 vols.

Title transliterated: Taᵓrīkh Khulāṣa al-Athar fī Aᶜyān al-Qarn al-Ḥadī ᶜAshr.

12th/17th-18th Century

J104

al-JABARTĪ, ᶜAbd al-Raḥmān ibn Ḥasan (d. *cir.* 1241/1825-26).

[Wonderful Traces in عجائب الاثار فى التراجم و الاخبار Biographies and Events]. Bulaq, 1297/1879-80. 4 vols.

An important biographical and historical chronicle concentrating upon the 12th/18th century, with particular emphasis upon Egypt.

In 1954 Gaston Wiet published an Arabic index to the chronicle, *Index de Djabarti, merveilles biographiques et historiques*. Cairo, Dār al-Maᶜārif. I + 299 p.

Additional printings of the *ᶜAjāᵓib* have been made in Cairo (1884-85, 1904-5, and 1958-67 in 7 volumes). An undated recent edition has been published in Beirut.

Title transliterated: ᶜAjāᵓib al-Athār fī al-Tarājim wa al-Akhbār.

J105

al-MURĀDĪ, Muḥammad Khalīl ibn ᶜAlī (d. 1206/1791).

[Book of كتاب سلك الدر فى اعيان القرن الثانى عشر String of Pearls into the Eyes of the Twelfth Century]. Bulaq, 1291-1301/1874-83. 4 vols. in 2.

Alphabetically arranged by *ism*.

Title transliterated: Kitāb Silk al-Durr fī Aᶜyān al-Qarn al-Thānī ᶜAshr.

13th/18th-19th Century

J106

al-BAYṬĀR, ᶜAbd al-Razzaq ibn Ḥasan.

[Ornament of حلية البشر فى تاريخ القرن الثلث عشر Men in the History of the Thirteenth Century]. Damascus, N.P., 1961-63. 3 vols.

Maṭbuᶜāt al-Majmaᶜ al-ᶜIlmī al- ᶜArabī bi-Dimashq.

Title transliterated: Ḥilya al-Bashar fī Taᵓrīkh al-Qarn al-Thālith ᶜAshr.

J108
TAYMŪR, Aḥmad.
تراجم اعيان القرن الثالث عشر و اوائل الرابع عشر
[Biographies of the Eminent of the Thirteenth and Early Fourteenth Centuries]. Cairo, ᶜAbd al-Hamīd Aḥmad Haqqī, 1940. 164 p.
Title transliterated: Tarājim Aᶜyān al-Thālith ᶜAshr wa Awāʾil al-Rabiᶜ ᶜAshr.

14th/19th-20th Century
J109
MUJĀHID, Zakī Muḥammad.
الاعام الشرقية في المائة الرابعة عشرة الهجرية، من سنة
١٣٠١ الى ١٣٦٥/ سنة ١٨٨٣ الى ١٩٤٦/
Biographies of Famous Men of the Orient in the XIV Century Hijri, from 1301-1365 A.H., 1883-1946. Cairo, Dār al-Ṭibāᶜa al-Miṣrīya al-Ḥadītha, 1941-63. 4 vols.
Title transliterated: Al-Aᶜāmm al-Sharqīya fī al-Māʾa al-Rābiᶜa ᶜAshra al-Hijrīya,...

¶ Additional chronological biographical dictionaries for the centuries prior to the twentieth are to be found under individual countries. See especially J112, J124, J127, J133, J137, J143, J147, J159, and J160.

20th Century
J110
MANSOOR, Menahem.
Political and Diplomatic History of the Arab World 1900-1967: a biographical dictionary. Englewood, Colorado, Microcard Editions Books, 1974. xvi, [ii] + 144 p. [dbl. col.].
"This work is the eighth volume of a multivolume project entitled: *The Political and Diplomatic History of the Arab World: 1900-1967.*
"The purpose of this Biographical Dictionary is to describe, briefly, the political or diplomatic role of all persons who are mentioned either in the seven volumes of *The Political and Diplomatic*

History of the Arab World [chronology] ... or in *The Political and Diplomatic Documents of the Arab World: 1900-1967*... . The aim here is not to provide complete biographical data on the personalities under study but to provide basic information on the office and function of those personalities in a given year, provided these personalities played an important role in Arab political and diplomatic activities in or outside the Arab world."

Geographical

Algeria

J111
NUWAYHID, ᶜAdil.
معجم اعلام الجزائر من صدر الاسلام حتى منتصف القرن العشرين
[Dictionary of the Notables of Algeria from the Beginnings of Islam to the Middle of the Twentieth Century]. Beirut, Al-Maktaba al-Tijārī li-l-Ṭibāᶜa wa al-Nashr wa al-Tawzī , 1971. 271 p. [dbl. col.].

Title transliterated: Muᶜjam Aᶜlām al-Jazāʾir..

Bajāla [Bougie]

J112
al-GHUBRĪNĪ, Aḥmad ibn ᶜAbd Allāh (d. 714/1314).
عنوان الدراية فيمن من العلماء في المائة السابعة ببجاية
[The Book of Knowledge in What is Known of the Learned in the Seventh Century in Bajāla]. *Ed.* Muḥammad Ben Cheneb. Algiers, Al-Maṭbaᶜa al-Thaᶜālibīya, 1328/1910. 236 + 8 p.

Title transliterated: ᶜUnwān al-Dirāya fīman min al-ᶜUlamāʾ...

Tlemcen

J113
IBN MARYAM, Muḥammad ibn Muḥammad (d. 1014/1605).
البستان في ذكر الاولياء و العلماء بتلمسان
[The Garden of Remembrance Respecting the Saints and Learned of Tlemcen]. *Ed.* Muḥammad Ben Cheneb. Algiers, Maṭbaᶜa al-Thaᶜālibīya, 1326/1907. 315 + 65 p.

Title transliterated: Al-Bustān fī Dhikr al-ᶜAwlīyāʾ wa al-ᶜUlamāʾ bi-Tlimsān.

Arabia

J114
al-BAḤRĀNĪ, ᶜAlī ibn Ḥasan.
انوار البدرين في تراجم علماء القطيف و الاحساء و البحرين
[The Two Lights Upon the Learned of al-Qaṭīf, al-Aḥsāɔ, and al-Baḥrayn]. Najaf, Maṭbaᶜa al-Nuᶜmān, 1377/1957-58. 342 p.

Brief biographies of the learned, including Shīᶜites, who lived in or came from Qaṭīf, the Ḥasa Oasis of Arabia, and Bahrein.

Title transliterated: Anwār al-Badrayn fī Tarājim ᶜUlamāɔ...

Mecca

J115
al-FĀSĪ, Muḥammad ibn Aḥmad (d. 832/1429).
العقد الثمين في تاريخ البلد الامين
[The Precious Necklace in the History of the Sheltered Country]. *Eds.* Muḥammad Ḥāmid al-Fiqqī, Fuɔād Sayyid *and* Maḥmūd M. al-Ṭanāhī. Cairo, Maṭbaᶜa al-Sana al-Muḥammadīya, 1378-88/1959-69. 8 vols.

Biographical dictionary of those associated with the Holy City of Mecca, beginning, of course, with the Prophet, followed by others with the name of Muḥammad, and then in alphabetical order beginning with Aḥmad.

Title transliterated: Al-ᶜIqd al-Thamīn fī Taɔrīkh al-Balad al-Amīn.

Egypt

J116
al-KINDĪ, Muḥammad ibn Yūsuf (d. 350/961).
كتاب الولاة و كتاب القضاة
[The Book of the Governors and the Book of the Judges]. *Ed.* Rhuvon Guest. *The Governors and Judges of Egypt.* London, Luzac & Co., 1912. 72 + 686 p.

E. J. W. Gibb Memorial Series, Vol. 19.

Alphabetically arranged biographies of the governors and judges of Egypt from the Muslim conquest to 246/860. Also printed in Beirut in 1908.

Title transliterated: Kitāb al-Wulā wa Kitāb al-Quḍāɔ.

Continuations: Aḥmad ibn ᶜAlī ibn Ḥajar al-ᶜAsqalānī (d. 852/1449). رفع الاصر عن قضاة مصر

[Removing the Encumberances from the Judges of Egypt]. *Ed.* Ibrāhīm al-Ibyārī. Cairo, Al-Maṭbaᶜa al-Amīrīya, 1957-61. 2 vols. Biographical dictionary of the jurisconsults and judges of Egypt from 386/996 to his own day in alphabetical order in continuation of the apparently lost work of Ibn Zūlāk (d. 386/996) which itself was a continuation of al-Kindī.

India

J117

ᶜABD AL-RAZZĀQ IBN MĪR ḤASAN ᶜALĪ ḤUSAYNĪ (d. 1171/1758).

[Memorials of the Amirs]. مآثر الامرأ

Ed. Maulaví ɔAbdur-Rahím. Maásiru-l-Umara, *by Nawáb Samsámu-d-Daula Shah Nawáz Khan.* Calcutta, Asiatic Society of Bengal, 1888-91. 3 vols.

Bibliotheca Indica, 112.

Biographical dictionary of 730 high officials of the Mughals from the reign of Akbar to 1780, as completed by his son ᶜAbd al-Ḥayy. "... arranged in groups alphabetically according to the initial letter of the [official's] title and within these groups chronologically according to the dates of death,... ." [Storey, I, 1097]. Reprinted by Janaki Prakashan, Patna, 1979.

Title transliterated: Maɔāthir al-Umarāɔ.

Translations: Trans. Henry Beveridge *and* Baini Prashad. *The* Maathir-ul-Umara, *being biographies of the Muhammadan and Hindu officers of the Timurid sovereigns of India from 1500 to about 1780 A.D. 2nd ed.* Calcutta, Asiatic Society of Bengal, 1911-64. 3 vols. *Bibliotheca Indica, 202.* The two volumes of the translation were printed in 1911 and 1952. The third volume is the index and was printed in 1964.

J118

BEALE, Thomas William.

The Oriental Biographical Dictionary. *Rev. ed.* H. G. Keene. London, W. H. Allen & Co., 1894. vii + 431 p.

Contains approximately 6,000 biographies, almost entirely confined to Muslims in India. First published by the Asiatic Society of Bengal, 1881.

J119
al-ḤASANĪ, ᶜAbd al-Ḥayy ibn Fakhr al-Dīn.
نزهة الخواطر و بهجة المسامع و النواظر، يتضمن تراجم علماء الهند و اعيانها /
Nuzhatu'l-khawātir: biographies of scholars and eminent persons of India. Hyderabad-Deccan, Maṭbaᶜa Dāɔira al- Maᶜārif al-ᶜUthmānīya, 1962–70. 8 vols.

A modern biographical dictionary covering the period from the 1st/7th to the 14th/20th centuries up to the author's death in 1923. Vols. 1-7: 1st-13th; vol. 8: 14th.

Title transliterated: Nuzha al-Khawāṭir...

J120
BHAKKARĪ, Farīd (d. *cir.* 1062/1652).
[Treasury of the Disloyal]. ذخيرة الخوانين
Ed. Syed Moinul Haq. Dhakhirat al-Khawanin *of Shaykh Farid Bhakkari.* Karachi, Pakistan Historical Society, 1961. 3 vols.

Biographical dictionary in Persian of the courtiers and nobility of the Mughal period to 1061/1651 based, to a large degree, upon personal acquaintance with the persons mentioned.

Title transliterated: Dhakhīra al-Khawānīn.

J121
BUCKLAND, Charles Edward.
Dictionary of Indian Biography. London, Sonnenschein, 1906. 494 p.

Concise biographies of 2,600 English, Indian, and foreign individuals since 1750 of importance in the history, literature, science, etc. of India.

J122
LETHBRIDGE, Roper, *Sir.*
The Golden Book of India: a genealogical and biographical dictionary of the ruling princes, chiefs, nobles, and other personages, titled or decorated, of the Indian empire, with an appendix for Ceylon. London, S. Low, 1900. 366 p.

Useful for the latter part of the nineteenth century, with a large part of the material obtained from the biographees.

J123

Who's Who in India: containing lives and portraits of ruling chiefs, nobles, titled personages and other eminent Indians. Lucknow, Newul Kishore Press, 1911-14. 1610 p., illus.

Eight separate biographical lists by states or provinces arranged by order of precedence rather than alphabetically. Name index. Portraits of many biographees.

Iran

J124
BĀMDĀD, Mahdī.

شرح حال ایران در قرن ۱۲، ۱۳، ۱٤ هجری

[Description of the State of Iran in the 12th, 13th, and 14th Centuries of the Hijra]. Tehran, Chāpa-khānī Bānak, 1347-51/1966-72. 6 vols., illus.

General biographical dictionary of noted men of the 18th - 20th centuries A.D. in alphabetical order by first name. Many biographees have small portraits. Index in each volume. With volume five title changed to: تاریخ حال رجال ایران .

Title transliterated: Sharḥ Ḥāl Īrān...

Isfahan

J125
al-IṢBAHĀNĪ, Aḥmad ibn ᶜAbd Allāh (d. 430/1038).

[Book of Remembrance in the History of Isfahan]. كتاب ذكر اخبار اصبهان *Ed.* Sven Dedering. *Abū Nuᶜaim. Geschichte Iṣbahāns.* Leiden, E. J. Brill, 1931-34. 2 vols.

Following a brief history and topography of the city the work consists of biographies of scholars and others who had lived in or had connection with Isfahan.

Title transliterated: Kitāb Dhikr Akhbār Iṣbahān.

Qum

J126
RĀZĪ, Muḥammad

آثار الحجة، یا تاریخ و دائرة لمعارف حوزة علمیه قم

[The Signs of the Authorities: history and sphere to knowledge of the learned of Qum]. Qum, Kitābfarūshī Barqiᶜī, 1332-33/1954-55. 2 vols. in 1.

A modern biographical dictionary.

Title transliterated: Āthār al-Ḥujja:...

Iraq

Baghdad

J127

al-ALŪSĪ, ᶜAlī ᶜAlāᵓ al-Dīn

الدر المنتشر في رجال القرن الثاني عشر و الثالث عشر

[The Flowing Current Regarding Men of the 12th and 13th Centuries]. *Ed.* Jamāl al-Dīn al-Alūsī *and* ᶜAbd Allāh al-Jabūrī. Baghdad, Dār al-Jumhūrīya, 1967. 260 p., illus.

Biographical dictionary, illustrated with small portraits, of the learned of Baghdad who lived during the 17th - 18th centuries A.D. An incomplete compilation was previously published in Baghdad in 1930 as المسك الاذفر.

Title transliterated: Al-Durr al-Muntashar fī Rijāl...

J128

al-KHAṬĪB AL-BAGHDĀDĪ, Aḥmad ibn ᶜAlī (d. 463/1071). [History of Baghdad]. تاريخ بغداد

Cairo, Maktaba al-Khanjī, 1349/1931-32. 14 vols.

Biographical dictionary of over 7,800 scholars, poets, writers, and political figures, including women, who were born, lived in, or were otherwise associated with the city of Baghdad from the time of its foundation to the author's time. More or less arranged in alphabetical order by *ism*. Reprinted in Beirut in 1968.

J. P. Pascual published an *Index schématique du* Taᵓrīḫ Baghdad. Paris, Editions du Centre National de la Recherche Scientifique, 1971. vii + 104 p.

Continuations:

1. Muḥammad ibn Maḥmūd ibn Najjār (d. 643/1245). [Continuation of the ذيل تاريخ بغداد History of Baghdad]. Hyderabad-Deccan, Maṭbaᶜa Majlis Dāᵓira al-Maᶜārif al-ᶜUthmānīya, 1978- . Originally written in 30 volumes which brought the history down to his own time.

2. Muḥammad ibn Aḥmad al-Fāsī (d. 832/1429). [History تاريخ علماء بغداد المسمى منتخب المختار of the Learned of Baghdad, named the selected of the elected]. *Ed.* ᶜAbbās al-ᶜAzzāwī. Muntakhab al-Mukhtar: *choix historiques des ulemas de Bagh-*

dad. Baghdad, Maṭbaᶜa al-Ihālī, 1938. 286 p.
An abridgement of Muḥammad ibn Rāfī al-Sallāmī (d. 774/1372). المختار المذيل , a continuation of Ibn Najjār's continuation, containing 201 biographies alphabetically arranged.

Mosul

J129
al-ᶜUMARĪ, Muḥammad Amīn (d. 1203/1789).
منهل الاولياء و مشرب الاصفياء من سادات الموصل الحدباء
[Spring of the Helpers and Fountain of the Chosen Among the Sayyids of Mosul]. *Ed*. Saᶜīd al-Daywahshī. Mosul, Maṭbaᶜa al-Jumhūrīya, 1967-68. 2 vols., illus.

Title transliterated: Manhal al-Awlīya wa Mashrab al-Aṣfīya...

Lebanon

J130
al-SHADYĀQ, Tanūs ibn Yūsuf.
اخبار الاعيان في جبل لبنان
[News of Prominent People of the Mountain of Lebanon]. Beirut, Maktaba al-Irfān, 1954. 2 vols. in 1.

First printed in 1851.

Title transliterated: Akhbār al-Aᶜyān fī Jabal Lubnān.

Libya

Tripoli

J131
al-ZĀWĪ, Al-Ṭāhir Aḥmad.
ولاة طرابلس من بداية الفتح العربي الى نهاية العهد التركي
[Rulers of Tripoli From the Beginning of the Arab Conquest until the Termination of Turkish Rule]. Beirut, Dār al-Fatḥ li-l-Ṭabaᶜa wa al-Nashr, 1970. 295 p.

Covers the period 643-1911.

Title transliterated: Walā Ṭarābulus min Bidāya ...

Morocco

J132
IBN AL-QĀḌĪ, Aḥmad ibn Muḥammad al-Miknāsī (d. 1025/1616).

[Pearl of the Pavilions درة الحجال في اسماء الرجال in the Names of the Men]. *Ed.* I. S. Allouche. Durrat al-Hijal, *répertoire bibliographique d'Ahmad Ibn al-Qadi*. Rabat, Institut des Hautes-Etudes Marocaines, 1934-36. 2 vols.

Collection de Textes Arabes, IV-V.

Dictionary of the learned and famous of Morocco, including biographies of the illustrious jurisconsults of Islam omitted by Ibn Khallikān [J82]. Another edition was published by Muḥammad al-Aḥmadī Abī al-Nūr in Cairo in 1970-74, 3 vols.

Title transliterated: Durra al-Ḥijāl fī Asmāʾ al-Rijāl.

J133
al-IFRĀNĪ, Muḥammad ibn al-Ḥājj Muḥammad (d. 1156-57/1743-45).

كتاب صفوة من انتشر من اخبار صلحاء القرن الحادى عشر
[Book of the Choicest of What has been Written Regarding the News of the Righteous in the 11th Century]. Fez, [litho.], [N.D.]. 224, 5, [iii] + 4 p.

On the saints of Morocco of the 11th/17th century.

Title transliterated: Kitāb Ṣafwa man Intishar min Akhbār Ṣulaḥāʾ...

Fez

J134
IBN AL-QĀḌĪ, Aḥmad ibn Muḥammad al-Miknāsī (d. 1025/1616).

جذوة الاقتباس فيمن حل من الاعلام بمدينة فاس
[The Torch of Acquisition of Knowledge Concerning the Outstanding in the City of Fez]. Fez, [litho.], 1309/1892. 357 p.

Dictionary of the famous and learned who were born or lived in Fez, together with a topography of the city.

Title transliterated: Jadhwa al-Iqtibās fīman Ḥall min al-Aʿlām bi-Madīna Fās.

Oman

J135
al-SĀLIMĪ, ʿAbd Allāh ibn Ḥumayyd.

تحفة الاعيان بسيرة اهل عمان، للامام نور الدين عبد

[The Gift for the Eyes Regarding the Biographies of the People of Oman]. الله بن حميد السالمى Cairo, Dār al-Kutub al-ᶜArabī, 1961. 2 vols. in 1.

Title transliterated: Tuḥfat al-Aᶜyān bi-Sīra Ahl al-ᶜUmān,...

Spain

J136
al-ḌABBĪ, Aḥmad ibn Yaḥyā (d. 599/1202).
كتاب بغية الملتمس فى تاريخ رجال اهل الاندلس
[Book of Desire in Searching the History of the Men of Spain]. *Eds.* Francisco Codera *and* J. Ribera. *Desiderium Quaerentis Historiam Virorum Populi Andalusiae, dictionarium biographicum ab Adh-Dhabbi scriptum.* Matriti, A. J. de Rojas, 1885. XXV + 642 p.

Bibliotheca Arabico-hispana, III.

General biographical dictionary of famous men and women of Muslim Spain up to the close of the 12th century, accompanied by a history of the Islamic conquest and rule in the country to 1196. Reprinted photographically in Baghdad.

Title transliterated: Kitāb Bughya al-Multamas fī Taɔrīkh Rijāl Ahl al-Andalus.

J137
IBN AL-FARAḌĪ, ᶜAbd Allāh ibn Muḥammad (d. 403/1013).
[The Fixed in the الموصول فى تاريخ علماء الاندلس History of the Learned of Spain]. *Ed.* Francisco Codera. *Historia Virorum Doctorum Andalusiae.* Matriti, A. J. de Rojas, 1891-92. 2 vols.

Bibliotheca Arabico-hispana, VII-VIII.

Biographies of the religious leaders of Spain from the conquest to the end of the 4th/10th century. Re-edited by ᶜIzzat al-Aṭṭār under the title تاريخ العلماء و الرواة للعلم بلاندلس. Cairo, Maktaba al-Khanjī, 1954. 2 vols.

Title transliterated: Al-Mawṣūl fī Taɔrīkh ᶜUlamāɔ al-Andalus.

Continuations:

1. Khalaf ibn ᶜAbd al-Malik ibn Bashkuwāl (d. 578/1183). كتاب الصلة فى تاريخ ائمة الاندلس [The Link in the History of the Leaders of Spain]. *Ed.* Francisco Codera. *Aben-Pascualis* Assila *(dictionarium biographicum).* Matriti, A. J. de Rojas,

1882-83. 2 vols. in 1. *Bibliotheca Arabico-hispania, I-II*. Notices of approximately 1,400 men who lived during the 5th/11th and 6th/12 centuries. Re-edited by ᶜIzzat al- Aṭṭār (Cairo, 1955).

2. Muḥammad ibn ᶜAbd Allāh Ibn al-Abbār (d. 658/1260). كتاب التكملة لكتاب الصلة [Book of Completion of the Book of the Link]. *Ed.* Francisco Codera. *Complementum Libri* Assilah *(Aben Pascualis), dictionarium biographicum ab Aben al-Abbar scriptum*. Matriti, A. J. de Rojas, 1887-89. 2 vols. *Bibliotheca Arabico-hispana, V-VI*. Biographies of the religious leaders of Spain who died during the last quarter of the 6th/12th century and the first half of the 7th/13th century in continuation of Ibn Bashkuwāl's continuation of Ibn al-Faraḍī's dictionary. Supplemented and provided with indices by M. Alarcón and C. A. Gonzalez Palencia, "Apéndice a la Edición Codera de la 'Tecmila' de Aben al-Abbar." *Miscelánea de Estudios y Textos Árabes* (Madrid, Centro de Estudios Históricos), 1915, pp. 147-690.

J138
al-NUBĀHĪ, ᶜAlī ibn ᶜAbd Allāh (d. 713/1313-14). [History of the Judges of Spain]. تاريخ قضاة الاندلس *Ed.* E. Lévi-Provençal. *Histoire des Juges d'Andalousie, intitulée* Kitab al-Markaba al-ᶜUlya. Cairo, Dār al-Kitāb al-Miṣrī, 1948. x, 246 + x p.

Alternate title: كتاب المرقبة العليا فيمن يستحق القضاء و القتيا .

Title transliterated: Taʾrīkh Quḍā al-Andalus.

Cordoba

J139
al-KHUSHANĪ, Muḥammad ibn al-Ḥārith (d. 371/981?). [Book of the Judges of Cordoba]. كتاب قضاة قرطبة *Ed. & trans.* Julián Ribera. *Historia de los Jueces de Córdoba, por Aljoxaní*. Madrid, Imprim. Ibérica, 1914. xivi, 272 + 207 p.

Covers the period from the Muslim conquest to his own time. A new edition of the work has been published by Ibrāhīm al-Ibyārī (Cairo/Beirut, Dār al-Kutub al-Islāmī, 1982. 263 p.).

Title transliterated: Kitāb Quḍā Qurṭuba.

Granada

J140
IBN AL-KHAṬĪB, Muḥammad ibn ᶜAbd Allāh (d. 776/1375).
[The Encompassment in the History of Granada]. الاحاطة في اخبار غرناطة *Ed.* Muḥammad ᶜAbd Allāh ᶜAnān. Cairo, Maktaba al-Khanjī, 1973- .

The biographical dictionary of the celebrated men of the city of Granada is in the second part of his history.

Title transliterated: Al-Iḥāṭa fī Akhbār Gharnāṭa.

Sudan

J141
HILL, Richard
A Biographical Dictionary of the Sudan. *2nd ed.* London, Frank Cass and Co., Ltd., 1967. xvi + 409 p.

Primarily historical and literary personages of the Sudan, including Europeans, with less emphasis upon political figures. Does not include scientists.

J142
IBN ḌAYF ALLĀH, Muḥammad al-Nūr (d. 1224/1809-10).
كتاب الطبقات في خصوص الاولياء و الصالحين و العلماء و الشعراء في السودان
[The Book of the Classes Respecting the Saints, the Pious, the Learned, and the Poets of the Sudan]. *Ed.* Yūsuf Faḍl Ḥasan. Khartoum, Jāmiᶜa al-Kharṭūm, 1971. 23 + 422 p., illus.

Biographical dictionary of 270 Sudanese up to *cir.* 1800 A.D.

Title transliterated: Kitāb al-Ṭabaqāt fī Khuṣūṣ al-Awliyāɔ...

Syria

Aleppo

J143
IBN AL-ḤANBALĪ, Muḥammad ibn Ibrāhīm (d. 971/1563).
[Pearls of the Beloved in the History of the Notables of Aleppo]. در الحبب في تاريخ اعيان حلب *Ed.* Maḥmūd Aḥmad al-Fākhūrī. Damascus, Wizāra al-Thaqāfa wa al-Irshād al-Qawmī, 1972- .

Biographical dictionary of 637 learned and fam-

ous of Aleppo between 1450 and 1550 A.D.
Title transliterated: Durr al-Ḥabab fī Taʾrīkh Aʿyān Ḥalab.

Damascus

J144
IBNʿASĀKIR, ʿAlī ibn al-Ḥasan (d. 571/1176).
[History of the City of Damascus]. تاريخ مدينة دمشق
Ed. ʿAbd al-Qādir Badrān; Aḥmad ʿUbayd, *et. al.* *Tahdhīb Taʾrīkh Ibn ʿAsākir.* Damascus, Maṭbaʿa Rawḍa al-Shām, 1329-51/1911-32. 7 vols. [incomplete].
Biographies in alphabetical order of all "important" persons who were born, resided in, or visited Damascus from the time of the Muslim conquest up to the author's own time in 80 volumes. Also includes noted individuals who lived or were born in Aleppo, Baalbeck, Ramla, and Sayda. The publication of this lengthy work has had a checkered career because of the deaths of its various editors. The task has now been assumed by the Arab Academy of Damascus.
Title transliterated: Taʾrīkh Madīna Dimashq.

J145
IBN ṬŪLŪN, Muḥammad ibn ʿAlī (d. 953/1546).
قضاة دمشق ، الثغر البسام فى ذكر من ولى قضاة الشام
[Judges of Damascus: the smiling mouth in remembrance among the judges of Damascus]. *Ed.* Ṣalāh al-Dīn al-Munajjid. Damascus, Al-Majmuʿ al-ʿIlmī al-ʿArabīya, 1965. 16 + 418 p.
Title transliterated: Quḍā Dimashq,...

J146
LAOUST, Henri.
Les Gouverneurs de Damas sous les Mamlouks et les Premiers Ottomans (658-1156/1260-1744): traduction des annales d'Ibn Tûlûn et d'Ibn Gumʾa. Damascus, Institut Français de Damas, 1952. XIII + 289 p.

J147
al-SHAṬṬĪ, Muḥammad Jamīl.
روض البشر فى اعيان دمشق فى القرن الثالث عشر
[Exploration of the Men Among the Notables of Damas-

cus in the Thirteenth Century]. Damascus, Maṭbaᶜa Dār al-Yaqẓa al-ᶜArabīya, 1946. 270 p.

Title transliterated: Rawḍ al-Bashr fī Aᶜyān Dimashq...

Continuations: Muḥammad Jamīl al-Shaṭṭī. تراجم اعيام دمشق فى نصف القرن الرابع عشر الهجرى ١٣٠١ – ١٣٥٠ [Biographical Notices of the Notables of Damascus in the First Half of the Fourteenth Century, 1301-1350]. Damascus, Maṭbaᶜa Dār al-Yaqẓa al-ᶜArabīya, 1948. 123 p.

J148
al-ṢAFADĪ, Ṣalāh al-Dīn Khalīl ibn Aybak (d. 764/1362-63).
[Amirs of Damascus in Islam]. امراء دمشق فى الاسلام *Ed.* Ṣalāh al-Dīn al-Munajjid. Damascus, Al-Majmaᶜ al-ᶜIlmī, 1955, 15 + 221 p., illus.

Title transliterated: Umarāʾ Dimashq fī al-Islām.

Tunisia

Qayrawan

J149
al-DABBĀGH, ᶜAbd al-Raḥmān ibn Muḥammad (d. *cir.* 689/1290).
[The Reliable Guide for the Acquaintance of the People of Qayrawan]. معالم الايمان فى معرفة اهل القيروان *Ed.* Ibrāhīm Shabūh. Cairo, Maktaba al-Khanjī, 1968- .

Title transliterated: Maᶜālim al-Īmān fī Maᶜrifa Ahl al-Qayrawān.

J150
al-TAMMĀMĪ, Muḥammad ibn Aḥmad (d. 333/945).
[Classes of the Learned of Africa]. طبقات علماء افريقية *Ed & trans.* Muhammad Ben Cheneb. *Classes des Savants de l'Ifrīqīya.* Algiers, N.P., 1915-20. 2 vols.

Title transliterated: Ṭabaqāt ᶜUlamāʾ Ifrīqīya.

Also includes two additional works by Muḥammad ibn al-Ḥārith al-Khushanī (d. 361/971). طبقات علماء افريقية [Classes of the Learned of Africa], *and* al-Tammāmī. طبقات علماء تونس

[Classes of the Learned of Tunis].

The combined work thus provides biographies of the scholars of both Qayrawan and Tunis.

Tunis

J151

IBN MŪṢĀ, ᶜIyād.

[Biographies of the Aghlabids]. تراجم اغلبية

Tunis, Al-Maṭbaᶜa al-Rasmīya al-Tūnisīya, 1968. 568 p.

Biographical sketches by a modern writer of 173 Malikite jurisconsults associated with the city of Tunis between 184-296/750-950.

Turkey

J152

ALBAYRAK, Sadık.

Son Devir Osmalı Uleması (İlmiyeğ Ricalinin Teracim-i Ahvali) [Learned Men of the Late Ottoman Period]. Istanbul. Zafer Matbaası, 1980- , illus.

Biographical dictionary of the Ottoman religious leaders and jurists. Each entry is illustrated by a small photographic or sketched portrait and many are provided with illustrations of their handwriting (*fatāwas*, etc.).

J153

GÖVSA, İbrahim Alâettin, *ed.*

Türk Meshurları Ansiklopedisi: edebiyatta, sanatta, ılimde, harpte, politikada ve her sahada şöhret kazanmış olan Türklerin hayatları eserleri [Encyclopaedia of Famous Turks]. Istanbul, Yedigan Neşriyatı, 1946. [ii], 416 + [iv] p. [dbl. col.], illus.

Short biographical sketches of prominent men and women of the Ottoman period, most illustrated with photographic or sketched portraits.

J154

İNAL, Ibnülemin Mahmud Kemal.

Osmanlı Devrinde Son Sad Azamlar [Statesmen of the Last of the Ottoman Period]. Istanbul, Maarif Matbaası;Millî Eğitim Basımevi, 1940-53. 14 vols.

Volumes 1-5 published by the Maarif Mabaası, volumes 6-14 by the Millî Eğitim Basımevi.

J155
SĀMĪ, Shams al-Dīn (d. 1266/1850).
قاموس الاعلام، تاريخ و جغرافيا لغاتى و تعبير اصحله كافهٔ اسماء خاصه يى جامعدر
[Dictionary of Names, History, and Geography]. Istanbul, Mahran Maṭbaᶜa, 1306-16/1889-98. 6 vols.
Title transliterated: Qamūs al-Aᶜlām,...

J156
SÜREYYA, Mehmed.
سجل عثمانى ياخود تذكرهٔ مشاهير عثمانيه
[Ottoman Register, or biographies of the famous Ottomans]. Istanbul, Maṭbaᶜa-i Āmīre, 1308-11/1890-94. 4 vols.

Biographical dictionary of the entire period of Ottoman history to the date of publication of the sultans, noted officials, authors, soldiers, etc. In the fourth volume are lists of those related to the sultans and of those who filled important positions in the imperial household -- chamberlains, aghas, tutors, etc. The work was reprinted photographically in Farnborough, England in 1971.

Gültekin Oransay prepared a companion volume to the *Sicill-i, Osmanoğulları: Mehmed Süreyya Beğ'ın* Sicill-i Osmanî *birinci cild bab-ı evvelini düzeltilip genışletilmiş edimsel yenibasım biçiminde hazırlıyan.* Ankara, Küğ Yayım, 1969. 303 p. This contains 41 tables and genealogical charts, followed by a dictionary of names and terms found in the *Sicill-i.*

J157
ṬĀSHKUBRĪ-ZĀDAH, Aḥmad ibn Muṣṭafā (d. 968/1560).
الشقائق النعمانية فى علماء الدولة العثمانية
[The Red Anemones in the Learned of the Ottoman State]. Bulaq, 1299/1882. 2 vols.

Biographical dictionary, in Arabic, of 522 learned men, *ṣūfīs*, and physicians of the Ottoman Empire from the time of Uthman through the time of Sulayman I, *cir.* 1520. Arranged according to reign and then by first name. Printed on the margins of the Bulaq edition of Ibn Khallikān's biographical dictionary [J82].

Translations: Trans. Oskar Rescher. Eš-Šaqâ'iq en-Noᶜmânijje, *von Ṭašköprü-zâde.* Constantinople-

Galata, Buch- und steindruckerei Phoenix, 1927. 2, iv + 361 p.

Title transliterated: Al-Shaqāᵓiq al-Nuᶜmātīya fī ᶜUlamāᵓ al-Dawla al-ᶜUthmānīya.

Continuations:

1. ᶜAlī ibn Bālī Manq (d. 992/1584). [The Orderly Necklace العقد المنظوم فی ذكر افاضل الروم in Remembrance of the Best of the West]. Also printed on the margins of Ibn Khallikān. Biographies from Salīm I (1512) to *cir.* 1575. Translated by Oskar Rescher. *Ṭaşkoprüzade's "Eş-Şaqâᵓiq en-Noᶜmânijje" fortgesetzt von ᶜAlî Miniq...* . Stuttgart, N.P., 1934. [4] + 139 p.

2. ᶜAtāᵓ Allāh ibn Yaḥyā Newᶜī-zāde ᶜAtāᵓī (d. 1045/1637). حدائق الحقائق في تكميلة الشقائق [The Gardens of Truth in the Completion of the *Shaqāᵓiq*]. Istanbul, Dār al-Ṭabaᶜah al-ᶜĀmirah, 1268/1851. 771 p. Continuation in Turkish of the dictionary down to his own time, completed in the year before his death.

3. Ibrāhīm Ḥasib ᶜUshshāqī-zāde (d. 1137/1724). ذيل شقائق [Continuation of the *Shaqāᵓiq*]. *Ed.* H. J. Kissling. *Lebensbeschreibung berühmter Gelehrter und Gottesmänner des osmanischen Reiches im 17. Jahrhundert.* Weisbaden, Otto Harrassowitz, 1966. lix + 710 p., illus. A supplement to ᶜAtāᵓī's supplement in which, again in Turkish, he brings the dictionary down to his own time, adding nearly a hundred years.

Yemen

J158

al-MALIK AL-ASHRĀF ᶜUmar ibn Yūsuf ibn Rasūl (d. 696/1297).

[The Novel Companion in the Knowledge of the Lineages] طرفة الاصحاب في معرفة الانساب. *Ed.* K. W. Zettersteén. Damascus, Maṭbaᶜa al-Turqī, 1369/1949. 248 p.

Brief biographical and genealogical notices of famous personages connected with Yemen of all occupations up to the author's own time.

Title transliterated: Ṭurfa al-Aṣḥāb fī Maᶜrifa and Ansāb.

J159

al-ṢANᶜĀNĪ, Muḥammad ibn Muḥammad ibn Zubāra.
قيل الوطر من تراجم رجال اليمن فى القرن الثالث عشر
[Fulfilling the Desire (of knowing about) the Biographies of the Men of the Yemen in the Thirteenth Century].

Biographical dictionary of 441 learned men of the Yemen in the 13th/19th century compiled in 1348/1929-30. Published as an appendix to al-Shawkānī's *Al-Badr al-Ṭāliᶜ* [J97].

Title transliterated: Qayl al-Waṭar min Tarājim Rijāl al-Yaman...

J160
---.
[A Pleasurable نزهة النظر في رجال القرن الرابع عشر Glance into (the lives) of Men of the Fourteenth Century]. Ṣanᶜaɔ, Markaz al-Dirāsāt wa al-Abhāth al-Yamanīya, 1979. 2 vols. in 1.

Biographical dictionary of eminent Yemenis who died during the century, 1882-1979.

Title transliterated: Nuzha al-Naẓar fī Rijāl al-Qarn al-Rābiᶜ ᶜAshr.

GENEALOGY

History

J161
al-BALĀDHURĪ, Aḥmad ibn Yaḥyā (d. 279/892).
[Lineage of the Nobles]. انساب الاشراف

Detailed biographical history of the Arab tribes and of the Umayyad and Abbasid caliphs up to the reign of al-Manṣūr, 775 A.D.

The *Ansāb* has had a checkered publication history. The School of Oriental Studies, Hebrew University, issued two volumes in the early 1930's and then dropped the project. Volumes issued: *The* Ansāb al-Ashrāf *of al-Balādhurī*, vol. IVB, *ed.* Max Schloessinger [in three volumes: text, annotations, indices]. Jerusalem, Hebrew University Press, 1938-40; vol. V, *ed.* S. D. F. Goitein [in two volumes: text, annotations]. Jerusalem, Hebrew University Press, 1936.

In 1959 the Institute of Manuscripts of the League of Arab States began the republication beginning with volume one, *ed.* Muḥammad Ḥamīd Allāh.

Cairo, Dār al-Maᶜārif, 1959-. *Dhakhāʾir al-ᶜArab, 27-.*

A new edition has begun to appear in Wiesbaden in the series *Bibliotheca Islamica* (Franz Steiner Verlag). Vols. issued: III. *Ed.* ᶜAbdal-ᶜAzīz al-Dūrī, 1978. 383 p.; IV. *Ed.* Iḥsān ᶜAbbās, 1979. 730 p.

Title transliterated: Ansāb al-Ashrāf.

J162
IBN HAZAM, ᶜAlī ibn Aḥmad al-Andalusī (d. 456/1064). [News of the Names of the Arabs]. جمهرة انساب العرب *Ed.* E. Lévi-Provençal. Cairo, Dār al-Maᶜārif, 1948. 11, 524 + 11 p.

Dhakhāʾir al-ᶜArab, 2.

On the genealogies of the Arab and Berber families in Northwest Africa and Spain, with introductions in Arabic and French. A new edition by ᶜAbd al-Salām Muḥammad Hārūn, Cairo, 1968, in two volumes.

Title transliterated: Jamhara Ansāb al-ᶜArab.

J163
al-SAMᶜĀNĪ, ᶜAbd al-Karīm ibn Muḥammad (d. 562/1167). [Book of the Lineage]. كتاب الانساب *Ed.* ᶜAbd al-Raḥmān ibn Yaḥyā al-Maᶜalamī al-Yamanī. Hyderabad-Deccan, Majlis Dāʾira al-Maᶜārif al-ᶜUthmānīya, 1382-1402/1962-82. 13 vols.

Al-Silsila al-Jadīda min al-Maṭbūᶜāt, 19.

Genealogical work on the origins and relationships of the Arabs residing primarily in Iran and Transoxiana.

An earlier facsimili edition was edited by D. S. Margoliouth and published in the *Gibb Memorial Series*, Vol. 20 in 1920. A number of additional printings have been made in Baghdad (1970), Cairo (1971), and Beirut (1972).

Title transliterated: Kitāb al-Ansāb.

Abridgements:

1. ᶜAlī ibn Muḥammad ibn al-Athīr (d. 630/1283). اللباب فى تهذيب الانساب [The Quintessence in the Emendation of the Lineages]. *Ed.* Husām al-Dīn al-Qudsī. Cairo, Maktaba al-Qudsī, 1356/1937. 3 vols. in 2. An abridgement, with emendations, and reorganization into alphabetical order.

2. ᶜAbd al-Raḥmān ibn Abī Bakr al-Suyūtī (d. 911/1505). لب اللباب فى تحرير الأنساب [Essence of the Quintessence in the Redaction of the Lineages]. *Ed.* P. J. Veth. *Specimen e Litteris orientalibus, majorum partem libri as-Sojuti.* Leiden, S. & J. Luchtmans, 1840-42. 2 vols. in 1. An abridgement of Ibn al-Athīr's abridgement.

¶ In his *Ṭabaqāt* of traditionists Ibn Khayyāt [D144] enumerates the names of the Arab tribes and families who participated in the great migration of the 1st/7th century and the locations of the settlement of each.

Dictionaries

J164
ACCARDO, F.
Répertoire alphabétique des Tribus & Douars de l'Algérie: dresse d'après les documents officiels, sous la direction de M. Le Myre de Vilers. Algiers, Jules Carbonel, 1879. 2 vols.

J165
IBN ḤABĪB, Muḥammad al-Ḥasan (d. 779/1377).
[Book of the Various كتاب مختلف القبائل و مؤتلفها Tribes and Their Differences]. *Ed.* Ferdinand Wüstenfeld. *Muhammad Ben Habīb über die Gleichheit und Verschiedenheit der arabischen Stämmenamen.* Göttingen, Dieterich, 1850. viii + 52 p.

Title transliterated: Kitāb Mukhtalif al-Qabāʾil wa al-Mūʾtalifihā.

J166
KAḤḤĀLA, ᶜUmar Riḍā.
[Dictionary of معجم قبائل العرب: القديمة و الحديثة the Arab Tribes: old and new]. Damascus, Al-Maṭbaᶜa al-Yāshamīya, 1368-96/1949-76. 5 vols.

Modern alphabetical dictionary of the Arab tribes drawn from Arabic and European language sources. Provides derivations of tribal names and places of residences, with bibliographical notes. A very useful work on the subject.

Title transliterated: Muᶜjam Qabāʾil al-ᶜArab: al-Qadīma wa al-Hadītha.

J167
al-MALIK AL-ASHRĀF, ᶜUmar ibn Yūsuf ibn Rasūl (d.696/1296).
[The Novel Companion in the Knowledge of the Lineages]. طرفة الاصحاب في معرفة الانساب *Ed.* K. V. Zetterstéen. Damascus, Maṭbaᶜa al-Turqī, 1369/1949. 248 p.

An early Yemenite genealogical work which is of particular importance for the south Arabian tribes.

Also listed under biographical dictionaries [J158] because of its two-fold nature.

Title transliterated: Turfa al-Asḥāb fī Maᶜrifa al-Ansāb.

J168
al-MUGHĪRĪ, ᶜAbd al-Raḥmān ibn Ḥamad.
[The Select Book in Reporting the Arab Tribes]. الكتاب المنتخب فى ذكر قبائل العرب Cairo, Maṭbaᶜa al-Mughnī, 1962. vi + 182 p.

A modern work with compressed information.

Title transliterated: Al-Kitāb al-Muntakhab fī Dhikr Qabāᵓil al-ᶜArab.

J169
OPPENHEIM, Max A. S.
Die Beduinen. Leipzig/Wiesbaden, Otto Harrassowitz, 1939-68. 4 vols. in 5.

Contents: I. Die Beduinenstämme in Mesopotamien und Syrien; II. Die Beduinenstämme in Palästina, Transjordanien, Sinai, Hedjaz; III. Die Beduinenstämme in Nord- und Mittelarabien und in ᶜIrāk; IV. 1. Die arabischen Stamme in Chuzistān (Iran). Pariastamme in Arabien; IV. 2. Register und Literaturverzeichnis.

J170
al-QALQASHANDĪ, Aḥmad ibn ᶜAbd Allāh (d. 821/1418).
[The Completion of the Desire in the Knowledge of the Arab Lineages]. بهاية الارب فى معرفة انساب العرب *Ed.* ᶜAlī al-Khaqānī. Baghdad, N.P., 1378/1958. xxvii + 484 p.

Manshurāt Dār al-Bayān, 24.

An alphabetically arranged dictionary of the Arab tribes, with introduction into "science" of genealogy. Also edited by Ibrāhīm al-Ibyārī,

Cairo, 1959.
Supplements: Al-Qalqashandī. قلائد الجمان فى التعريف بقبائل عرب الزمان [Necklaces of Pearls in the Instruction of the Arab Tribes Through Time]. *Ed.* Ibrāhīm Ibyārī. Qalāʾid al-Djumān, *introducing Arab tribes through the ages.* Cairo, Dār al-Kutub al-Ḥadītha, 1963. 16 + 259 p.

Tables

J171
al-KALBĪ, Hishām ibn Muḥammad (d. 204/819).
[Multitude of the Lineages]. جمهرة الانساب
Ed. Werner Caskel *and* Gert Strenziok. Ǧamharat an-Nasab: *das geneologisch werk des Hišam ibn Muḥammad al-Kalbī.* Leiden, E. J. Brill, 1966. 2 vols.

One of the earliest and best genealogical works on the tribes of the Arabian Peninsula during the classical period. The edition is provided with 334 tables arranged by tribal stem. Index of names in volume two.

Title transliterated: Jamhara al-Ansāb.

J172
al-SUWAYDĪ, Muḥammad Amīn.
[Ingots of Gold سبائك الذهب فى معرفة قبائل العرب in the Knowledge of the Arab Tribes]. Baghdad, N.P., 1280/1863-64. 118 p.

Tabulation of the Arabic tribes from the time of Muḥammad to the beginning of the 19th century, based upon al-Qalqashandī's *Nihāya* and other materials. The compiler died in 1830. Reprinted numerous times in both Baghdad and Cairo.

Title transliterated: Sabāʾik al-Dhahab fī Maʿrifa Qabāʾil al-ʿArab.

J173
WÜSTENFELD, Ferdinand.
Genealogische Tabellen der arabischen Stämme und Familien. Göttingen, Dieterichschen Buchhandlung, 1852-53. 2 vols.

Detailed genealogical tables of the southern and northern tribes of the Arabian Peninsula during the classical period, based upon original sources.

Contents: I. Pt. 1: Die jemenischen Stämme

[tables 1-22]; Pt. 2: Die ismâᶜîlitischen Stämme [tables A-Z]; II. Register zu den genealogischen tabellen.

HERALDRY

J174
MAYER, Louis A.
Saracenic Heraldry; a survey. Oxford, Clarendon Press, 1933. xvi + 302 p., illus.

A full examination into the heraldry of the Mamluk sultanate of Egypt and Syria. Illustrated with 71 plates of designs.

J175
TAYMŪR, Aḥmad
رسالة لغوية عن الرتب و الالقاب المصرية لرجال الجيش و الهيئات العلمية و القلمية منذ عهد امير المؤمنين عمر الفاروق
[A Philological Note on Egyptian Ranks and Titles of the Men of the Army and Forms and Styles of Badges from the Time of the Caliph ᶜUmar al-Fārūk]. Cairo, Lajna Nashr al-Muʾallifāt al-Taymūrīya, 1950. 98 p.

Title transliterated: Risāla Lughawīya ᶜan al-Rutab wa al-Alqāb al-Miṣrīya...

NAMES

¶ The classical Muslim name, which was, and still is, adopted by all converts to Islam, was generally composed of five parts:

Kunya - the name by which a father or mother quite often came to be known following the birth of the first son (Abū=father, Umm=mother), hence, Abū Aḥmad.

Ism - the personal name of an individual, *e.g.*, Aḥmad, Fāṭima.

Abnāʾ - the patronymic indicating relationship with the father (Ibn=son of, Bint=daughter of), therefore, Aḥmad ibn Manṣūr.

Nisba - indication of origin, province, town, tribe, sect, etc. (ending with long "ī"), al-Baghdādī.

Laqab - often a nickname indicating a special characteristic (the lame), occupation (the writer), etc., beginning with the definite article "al-", and placed at the end of the total name, al-Kātib. May also be a title of honor often associated with the faith or the state and then placed before the name, Sayf al-Dīn ("Sword of the Faith").

The total name could thus read: Abū Aḥmad Maḥmūd ibn Manṣūr ibn ᶜAlī al-Baghdādī al-Kātib.

J176
al-ASQALĀNĪ, Aḥmad ibn ᶜAlī ibn Ḥajar (d. 852/1449).
[The Understanding of the تبصير المنتبه بتحرير المشتبه Prudent in Comprehending the Obscure]. *Ed.* ᶜAlī Muḥammad al-Bujāwī. Cairo, Al-Dār al-Miṣrīya li-l-Tāʾlif wa al-Tarjama, 1964-67. 4 vols.
Title transliterated: Tabṣīr al-Muntabih bi-Taḥrīr al-Mushtabih.

J177
AYALON, David.
"Names, Titles and 'Nisbas' of the Mamluks." *Israel Oriental Studies*, V, 1975, pp. 189-232.

J178
BARBIER DE MEYNARD, A. C.
"Surnoms et Sobriquets dans la Littérature arabe." *Journal Asiatique*, Sér. 10, IX, 1897, pp. 173-244, 365-428; X, 1897, pp. 55-118, 193-273.
Also indicates the titles of the works in which they have been found.

J179
al-BĀSHĀ, Ḥasan.
الالقاب الاسلامية فى التاريخ و الوثائق و الاثار
[Islamic Laqabs in History, Documents, and Monuments]. Cairo, Al-Nahḍa, 1957. 577 p.
Title transliterated: Al-Aqlāb al-Islāmīya fī al-Taʾrīkh...

J180
CAETANI, Leone *and* GABRIELLI, Guiseppe.
Onomasticon arabicum; ossia repertorio alfabetico dei nomi di persona e di luogo contenuti nelle principali opere storiche, biografiche e geografiche

stampate e manuscritte, relative all'Islam. Rome, Casa Editrice Italiana, 1915. 2 vols. [all published].

An attempt to provide a listing of the names of all persons listed in the original sources in a single alphabetical order, with bibliographical notes regarding the works in which they appear.

Contents: Vol. I: Fonti, Introduzione; Vol. II: Aabil - Abdallah.

J181
GARCIN DE TASSY, Joseph-Héliodore *and* RENAN, Z. "Mémoire sur les Noms propres et les Titres musulmans." *Journal Asiatique*, Sér. 5, 1854, pp. 422-510.

Also printed separately by the Imprimerie Imperiale, Paris, 1854, 93 p.

J182
IBN AL-ATHĪR, Al-Mubārak ibn Muḥammad (d. 606/1210). [Book of Ornamentation]. كتاب المرصع
Ed. C. F. Seybold. *Ibn al-Atîr's (Maǵd alDîn alMubarak) Kunja Wörterbuch, betitelt* Kitâb al-Muraṣṣaᶜ. Weimar, E. Felber, 1896. xviii + 267 p.

Ergängzungshefte zur Zeitschrift für Assyriologie.

An incomplete edition.

Title transliterated: Kitāb al-Muraṣṣaᶜ.

J183
IBN DURAYD, Muḥammad ibn al-Ḥasan (d. 321/933). [Book of Derivation]. كتاب الاشتقاق
Ed. Ferdinand Wüstenfeld. *Abu Bekr Muhammad ben el-Hasan Ibn Doreid's Genealogisch-Etymologisches Handbuch.* Göttingen, Dieterichschen Buchhandlung, 1854. viii + 370 p.

Etymological dictionary of Arabic names, arranged according to genealogical stem.

This edition reprinted in Leipzig in 1900. A new edition was published by ᶜAbd al-Salām Muḥammad Hārūn in Cairo, 1958.

Title transliterated: Kitāb al-Ishtiqāq.

J184
al-JA'FARI, Fatima Suzan.

Muslim Names. N.P., American Trust Publications, 1977. 46 p.

Very useful, though incomplete, listings of female and male names, each list in alphabetical order according to the Latin alphabet. Each name is given in a well-written Arabic, in transliteration, and in English translation.

J185
JUSTI, Ferdinand.
Iranisches Namenbuch. Marburg, N. G. Elwert, 1895. XXVIII + 526 p.

Alphabetical dictionary of Iranian personal names of both the pre-Islamic and Muslim periods derived from original sources. Genealogical tables of the ancient and Islamic Iranian dynasties are to be found on pages 390-479.

Photographically reprinted in Hildesheim in 1963.

J186
MARTY, Paul.
"Folklore tunisien: l'onomastique des noms propres de personne." *Revue des Etudes Islamiques*, X, 1936, pp. 363-434.

J187
NAIMUR-REHMAN, M.
"The Kunya-names in Arabic." *Allahabad University Studies*, V, 1929, pp. 341-442; VI, 1930, pp. 751-883.

J188
Onomasticon Arabicum.

An international enterprise to classify and index on computer the names and biographical data of all persons during the classical period who appear in the biographical dictionaries, historical texts, geographical gazetteers and "route books", and epigraphical remains. The ultimate purpose is to allow any scholar to obtain almost instantaneously, in abbreviated form, a surprising amount of information about anyone mentioned in any of the sources.

An introduction to the project is to be found

in Fedwa Malti Douglas and Geneviève Fourcade, *Serie Onomasticon Arabicum, 6, The Treatment by Computer of Medieval Arabic Biographical Data: an introduction and guide to the Onomasticum arabicum.* Paris, Editions du Centre National de la Recherche Scientifique, 1972. xii + 138 p.

J189
al-QUMMĪ, ᶜAbbās ibn Muḥammad Riḍā.
[Kunyas and Laqabs]. الكنى و الالقاب
Najaf, Al-Maṭbaᶜa al-Ḥaydarīya, 1356/1957. 3 vols.
Title transliterated: Al-Kunā wa al-Alqāb.

J190
RINGEL, Heinrich.
Die Frauennamen in der arabisch-islamischen Liebesdichtung: ein beitrag zur problem der ost-westlichen literaturübertragung. Leipzig, G. Kreysing, 1938. 133 p.

J191
al-SAMARRĀᵓĪ, Ibrāhīm.
Al-Aᶜlām al-ᶜArabīya, etude de nomes [*sic*] der [*sic*] personnes. الاعلام العربية، دراسة لغوية اجتماعية/
Baghdad, Al-Maktaba al-Ahlīya, 1964. 94 p.
A list of personal names.
Title transliterated: Al-Aᶜlām al-ᶜArabīya...

J192
SAUVAGET, Jean.
"Noms et Surnoms de Mamelouks." *Journal Asiatique*, 238, 1950, pp. 31-58.
Alphabetical listing in Arabic of 209 Arabic and Turkish names and titles of the Mamluks, with explanations as to meanings. Derived from original sources.

J193
TABRĪZĪ, Muḥammad ᶜAlī Mudarris.
ريحانة الادب فى تراجم المعروفين بالكنية و اللقب
ياكنى و اللقاب
[Essence of Culture in the Knowledge of the Kunyas and Laqabs]. Tabriz, Chāpkhāna-ī Shafiq, 1349/1970. 8 vols.
Biographical dictionary of famous persons arranged by their *kunyas* and *laqabs* in alphabetical

order.

Title transliterated: Rīḥāna al-Adab fī Tarājim al-Maᶜrūfīn...

J194
VROONEN, Eugène.
Les Noms de Personnes en Orient et Spécialement en Egypte. Noms musulmans: arabes, turcs. Noms chrétiens: arméniens, coptes, grecs, libanais et syriens, maltais. Noms israélites. Cairo, Le Scribe Egyptien, 1946. xvi + 191 p.

Lists of personal names.

Homonyms

J195
al-AZDĪ, ᶜAbd al-Ghanī ibn Saᶜīd al-Miṣrī (d. 409/1019).
[Book of the كتاب المؤتلف و المختلف فى اسماء الرجال Familiar and the Differences in the Names of Men]. Allahabad, [litho.], 1327/1909. 2 vols.

Dictionary of similar, although distinct, names of the traditionists, each with a biographical sketch. Printed together with his مشتبه النسبه [Similar Nisbas]. A dictionary of *nisbas* of traditionists which, because of their similarities, may lead to confusion between them. Also see [D96].

Title transliterated: Kitāb al-Muↄtalif wa al-Mukhtalif fī Asmāↄ al-Rijāl.

J196
al-HAMDĀNĪ, Al-Ḥasan ibn Aḥmad (d. 334/945).
[The Iklīl: first book]. الاكليل : الجزء الاول
Ed. Oscar Löfgren. *Südarabisches Muštabih: verzeichnis homönymer und homographer eigennamen.* Uppsala, Almqvist & Wiksells Boktryckeri AB, 1953. 86 + [i] p.

Bibliotheca Ekmaniana. Universitatis Regiae Upsaliensis 57.

A dictionary of South Arabian homonyms and homographs of personal names, extracted from a unique manuscript in Berlin.

Title transliterated: Al-Iklīl: al-juzↄ al-awal.

J197
IBN AL-QAYSARĀNĪ, Muḥammad ibn Ṭāhir (d. 507/1113).

كتاب الانساب المتفقة فى الخط المتماثلة فى النقط و الضبط
[Book of Names Conforming in Similar Letters, Pointing, and Vowelization]. *Ed.* P. de Jong. *Homonyma inter Nomina relativa,...* . Leiden, E. J. Brill, 1865. xix + 229 p., illus.

With an appendix, pp. 167-224, by Muḥammad ibn ᶜUmar al-Iṣbahānī (d. 581/1185).

Title transliterated: Kitāb al-Ansāb al-Muttafiqa fī al-Khaṭṭ...

OCCUPATIONS

Dictionaries

J198
al-BĀSHĀ, Ḥasan.
الفنون الاسلامية و الوظائف على الاثار [Islamic Occupations and Positions of Employment]. Cairo, Dār al-Nahḍa al-ᶜArabīya, 1965-66. 3 vols.

Title transliterated: Al-Funūn al-Islāmīya wa al-Waẓāᵓif ᶜalā al-Athār.

HISTORICAL DICTIONARIES

J199
ANTHONY, John Duke; PETERSON, John Everett *and* ABELSON, Donald Sean.
Historical and Cultural Dictionary of the Sultanate of Oman and the Emirates of Eastern Arabia. Metuchen, New Jersey, Scarecrow Press, 1976. vii + 128 p.

Historical and Cultural Dictionaries of Asia, 9.

J200
HANIFI, Mohammed Jamil.
Historical and Cultural Dictionary of Afghanistan. Metuchen, New Jersey, Scarecrow Press, 1976. viii + 141 p.

Historical and Cultural Dictionaries of Asia, 5.

J201
Iran-shahr: a survey of Iran's land, people, ايرانشهر / culture, government and economy. Tehran, Chāpakhāna

Dānishkā-hi, 1362-63/1963-64. 2 vols., illus., maps.
Articles in Farsi on all aspects of Iran's history and present, illustrated with charts, photographs, and folding maps.
Title transliterated: Īrānshahr.

J202
RILEY, Carroll L.
Historical and Cultural Dictionary of Saudi Arabia. Metuchen, New Jersey, Scarecrow Press, 1972. vi + 133 p.
Historical and Cultural Dictionaries of Asia, 1.

J203
SPENCER, William.
Historical Dictionary of Morocco. Metuchen, New Jersey, Scarecrow Press, 1980. xliv + 152 p.
African Historical Dictionaries, 24.
Includes lists of Moroccan Dynasties, high commissioners of the Spanish Protectorate, resident-generals of the French Protectorate, a glossary of terms, chronology, and bibliography.

CHRONOLOGIES & DYNASTIC TABLES

Chronologies

J204
CAETANI, Leone.
Annali dell'Islam. Milan, U. Hopli, 1905-26. 10 vols., illus., maps [all published].
Detailed chronology of Islamic history arranged by year (only completed to 660 A.D.) and then by region, based upon original published and manuscript sources. The materials for each event are translated into Italian and critically examined. Volume six contains a complete index to the first five; the remaining four have no index. Reprinted in Hildesheim in 1972.
Translations: Trans. Hüseyin Cahit. *İslâm Tarihi.* Istanbul, Tanin-Vatan Matbaası, 1924-27, 10 vols.

J205
---.

Chronographia islamica; ossio riassunto chronologico della storia di tutti poppli musulmani dall'anno 1 all'anno 922 della higrah (622 - 1517 dell'era volgare). Paris, Librairie Paul Geuthner, 1912. 5 vols. [all published].

Brief chronology of the important events in Islamic history arranged by year and then by region. Each event has appended a short bibliography of original literary sources. Ceases with the fall of the Umayyad dynasty.

J206

---.

Cronografia generale del Bacino mediterraneo e dell' Oriente musulmano dal 622 al 1517 dell'era völgare. Rome, Fondazione Caetani, Reale Accademia Nazionale dei Lincei, 1923. VII + 327 p. [all published].

Meant to serve as the continuation of his *Chronographia islamica* with the same format. Only fascicule I: 133 - 144 A.H. [750 - 762 E.V.] published. Prince Leone was an excellent scholar with fine ideas for reference books, but each was too much for one man to attempt to complete.

J207

DANİŞMEND, İsmail Hami.

İzahli Osmanlı Tarihi Kronolojisi [Explanation of Ottoman Historical Chronology]. Istanbul, Türkiye Basımevi, 1950-71. 5 vols.

Detailed chronology of events from the Mongol conquest of Baghdad to the abolition of the Caliphate presented in both the Muslim and Christian calendars. The fifth volume, *Osmanlı Devlet Erkânı* [Ottoman State Officials] consists of lists of viziers, shaykhs al-Islam, ulama, etc.

Contents: Vol. I: 656-918/1258-1512; Vol. II: 919-981/1513-1573; Vol. III: 982-1115/1574-1703; Vol. IV: 1115-1342/1708-1924.

J208

GROHMANN, Adolf.

Arabische Chronologie und arabische Papyruskunde. Leiden, E. J. Brill, 1966. xii + 118 p., illus., table, maps.

Handbuch der Orientalistik, Ergängzungsband II,

1. Halbband.

J209
SAUVAGET, Jean.
Memento chronologique d'Histoire musulmane. Paris, Adrien-Maisonneuve, 1950. 22 p.
Initiation à l'Islam, No. 4.
A very brief and general comparative table of events in the Muslim world and in Europe from the birth of Muhammad to 1948.

China

J210
PILLSBURY, Barbara L. K.
"Muslim History in China: a 1300-year chronology." *Journal Institute of Muslim Minority Affairs*, III, 2, 1981, pp. 10-29.
Short comparative chronology extending from *cir.* 1100 B.C. to 1980 A.D. divided into two columns - "Important Events Outside China" and "Events in China." Contains some surprising errors. Useful because Muslim history within China is seldom mentioned in the standard histories and not included within any of the available chronologies.

India

J211
BURGESS, James.
The Chronology of Modern India: for four hundred years from the close of the fifteenth century A.D., 1494-1894. Edinburgh, John Grant, 1913. vii + 483 p.
Annual chronology and, where known or merited, by month and day. Important index of proper names and subjects. Reprinted in Dublin in 1973.

J212
DUFF, C. Mabel.
The Chronology of Indian History from the Earliest Times to the Beginning of the 16th Century. London, Constable, 1899. xi + 409 p.
An interesting departure of this chronology is that the events are not only listed according to the Gregorian calendar, but also by that of the

action or people concerned, *i.e.*, Hindu, Muslim, etc. An appendix provides dynastic tables for the various rulers of India. Index of proper names and subjects.

The book is often listed under the compiler's married name - Rickness - although the title page states Duff. Reprinted in Delhi in 1972.

J213
SHARMA, J. S.
India Since the Advent of the British: a descriptive chronology, from 1600 to Oct. 2, 1969. Delhi, S. Chand & Co., 1970. xxx + 817 p.

An annual chronology of events within the entire Indian sub-continent by year and day according to the Christian calendar. Arranged into six parts: I: 1600-1895; II: 1896-1905; III: 1906-1918; IV: 1919-1935; V: 1936-1947; VI: 1948-1969.

Chronological Charts

J214
GOMAA, I.
A Historical Chart of the Muslim World. Leiden, E. J. Brill, 1971.

Handbuch der Orientalistik, Abteilung I: Ergänzungsband VII.

Large colored chronological chart of Islamic history from 600 A.D. to the present.

Dynastic Tables

J215
LANE-POOLE, Stanley.
The Mohammedan Dynasties: chronological and genealogical tables with historical introductions. London, Constable and Sons, 1893. xxviii + 361 p.

Publication of Lane-Poole's notes based upon his numismatic studies in the British Museum and the Egyptian National Library. Contains numerous genealogical tables, many folding, and two colored historical charts of the dynasties. Arranged by region and then by dynasty, with an index to rulers. Has been repeatedly reprinted.

Translations:

1. V. V. Bartol'd. **Мусульманские Династии.** St. Petersbourg, 1899. XV + 344 p.

With additions and corrections.

2. Halil Eldem. دولى اسلامى • Istanbul, 1345/1927. 640 p. Translation into Ottoman Turkish with corrections, particularly regarding Asia Minor.

3. Aḥmad al-Saᶜīd Sulaymān. تاريخ الدول الاسلامية و معجم الاسر الحاكمة • Cairo, Dār al-Maᶜarif, 1972. 2 vols. A new Arabic translation incorporating the corrections of both Bartol'd and Edhem, with additional material by the translator.

C. E. Bosworth has published a new edition, under his own name, with corrections and additions and a greatly enlarged index of personal names, dynasties, peoples, and tribes. *The Islamic Dynasties: a chronological and genealogical handbook. 2nd ed.* Edinburgh, University Press, 1980. xviii + 245 p.

J216

ZAMBAUR, Edouard de.

Manuel de Généologie et de Chronologie pour l'Histoire de l'Islam. Hanover, Librairie Orientaliste Heinz Lafaire, 1927. 2 vols., maps.

Detailed genealogical tables and chronological lists of caliphs, sultans, vizirs, and provincial governors from Spain to India and from the time of Muhammad to the first quarter of the 20th century. Weak on fringe dynasties. Volume one contains the lists, volume two contains 20 genealogical tables and five maps.

Translations: معجم الانساب و الاسرات الحكمة فى التاريخ الاسلامى • Cairo, Fuad I University, 1951. 2 vols. An Arabic translation *without* corrections, tables, or maps.

Ottomans

J217

ALDERSON, A. D.

The Structure of the Ottoman Dynasty. Oxford, Clarendon Press, 1956. xvi + 186 p.

Detailed discussions, illustrated with 63 genealogical tables, of the Ottoman royal house from its beginnings to the dissolution of the caliphate in 1924.

¶ Also for the Ottoman Dynasty see appendices three and four in B. G. Spiridonakis, *Empire ottoman* [J242]. III. "Tableau chronologique des Sultans ottomans," pp. 461-62; IV. "Liste chronologique des Grands Vizirs ottomans depuis 855/1451 jusqu'en 1341/1922," pp. 463-470.

Tables of the Iranian dynasties are also to be found in Ferdinand Justi's *Iranisches Namenbuch* [J185], pp. 390-479.

Governors

J218

HENIGE, David P.

Colonial Governors From the Fifteenth Century to the Present: a comprehensive list. Madison, University of Wisconsin Press, 1970. xx + 461 p.

"The purpose of this work, which is intended as a work of reference and makes no pretense whatever to any broader aim, is to present lists of the governors of the European colonies from 1415 when the Portuguese occupied Ceuta, to the present time.

"... I have adopted an alphabetical arrangement within each imperial system [Belgium, Denmark, France, Germany Great Britain, Italy, Japan, Netherlands, Portugal, Russia, Spain, Sweden, United States]."

General index and index of governor's names. Each section is followed by a selective bibliography.

¶ For the high-commissioners and resident-generals of the former Spanish and French Protectorates of Morocco see William Spencer, *Historical Dictionary of Morocco* [J203].

The Records of the British Residency and Agencies in the Persian Gulf by Penelope Tuson [J253], contains an appendix listing the names of the British Residents and Agents in the Persian/Arabian Gulf from 1763 to 1948.

CALENDARS & COMPARATIVE DATES

Introductions

J219

GROHMANN, Adolf.
I. Arabische Chronologie; II. Arabische Papyruskunde. Leiden, E. J. Brill, 1966, XI + 118 p., illus.

Handbuch der Orientalistik: Erste Abteilung: Der Nahe und der Mittlere Osten - Ergänzungband II.

I. Arabische Chronologie, which occupies pages 1-48, is an introduction to the subject of pre-Islamic and Islamic chronology. Contains no conversion tables.

J220
TAQIZADEH, S. H.
"Various Eras and Calendars Used in the Countries of Islam." *Bulletin of the School of Oriental and African Studies*, IX, 1938, pp. 903-22; X, 1939, pp. 107-32.

Discussion and explanation of the 21 eras and calendars, both lunar and solar, used during the classical and modern periods.

Conversion Tables

J221
BANERJEE, Amulya Chandra.
Chronological Tables: shewing the dates of Bengali, Sakha, Mughee, Mulki, Tipperah, Burmese, Sakabda, Bhelaity or Amli, Fusli, Sambat or Hindee and Hijree eras corresponding with those of English era current in India from 1800-1912. Calcutta,

J222
al-BUNDĀQ, Muḥammad Ṣāliḥ.
التقويم الهاوى: دراسة علمية و تاريخية عن التقاويم
جداول موافقة التاريخين الهجرى و الميلادى لمدة
١٦٤٠ عام هجرى تقديم يومى لمدة ٢٧٥ سنة ميلادية
كيفية البحث عن اسم اليوم لتاريخ معين مع مجموعة
نصوص و مستندات و فتاوى حول التقويم الهجرى و
الحساب الفلكى/

Guiding Calendar: a scientific and historical study of calendars, tables of parallel of hijrah and Christian dates comprising 1640 hijrah years, a daily calendar of 275 Christian years, how to find the name of a day for a specific date, texts, documents, fatwas about the Hijrah calendar and the

astronomical calculations. Beirut, Dār al-Afāq al-Jadīda, 1400/1980. 252 p.
Title transliterated: Al-Taqwīm al-Hāwī:...

J223
CATTENOZ, H. G.
Tables de Concordance des Eres chrétienne et hégirienne. *2nd ed.* Casablanca, Editions Techniques Nord-Africaines, 1954. pp. unnumbered.
Simplified tables for the conversion of the days of the Muslim lunar calendar into those of the Gregorian with no mathematical computation required. Each table covers five years of both calendars and the 12 months of the Muslim year. Begins with the year 1 A.H. (622 A.D.) to 1400 A.H. (1981 A.D.).

J224
FREEMAN-GRENVILLE, G. S. P.
The Muslim and Christian Calendars: being tables for conversion of Muslim and Christian dates from the Hijra to the year A.D. 2000. Oxford, University Press, 1963. vii + 87 p.
Handbook for the conversion of dates by means of a mathematical computation. Includes short lists of the principal Muslim and Christian festivals.

J225
GRUMEL, V.
Traité d'Etudes byzantines: I. La Chronologie. Paris, Presses Universitaires de France, 1958. XII + 487 p.
Bibliothèque Byzantine.
Comprehensive handbook of the various calendars employed during the "mediaeval" period in Europe and the Near East, together with data on comets, eclipses, earthquakes, etc., to 1453.
Troisième partie: Tableaux chronologiques - No. III. Concordance entre les anneés de l'Hégire et les anneés de l'ère chrétienne; No. IV. Calendriers liturgiques: VI. Principales fêtes musulmanes. [Also attached is an historical list of rulers].

J226
HAIG, Wolseley, *Sir*.
Comparative Tables of Muhammadan and Christian Dates: enabling one to find the exact equivalent of any day in any month from the beginning of the Muhammadan era. London, Luzac & Co., 1932. 32 p.

Pocket-sized handbook for the conversion of dates by a specially devised formula from 622-2000 A.D. Small errata slip pasted in.

J227
SWAMIKANNU PILLAI, Lewis Dominic.
An Indian Ephemeris, A.D. 700 to A.D. 1799: showing the daily solar and lunar reckoning according to the principal systems current in India, with their English equivalents, also the ending moments of tithis and nakshatras and the years in different eras, A.D., Hijra, Saka, Vikrama, Kaliyuga, Kallam, etc., with a perpetual planetary almanac and other auxiliary tables. Delhi, Agam, 1928. 7 vols.

J228
TSYBULSKY, V. V.
Calendars of Middle Eastern Countries: conversion tables and explanatory notes. Moscow, "Nauka" Publishing House, 1979. 55 p.

A very useful conversion book covering not only the lunar Hijra calendar, but also the various calendars of Turkey, Iran, Afghanistan, Israel, the Copts, Mongols, and others.

Translation of the compiler's earlier (1977) work, Современные Календари Станжнего и Среднего Востока... .

J229
UNAT, Faik Reşit.
Hicrî Tarihleri Milâdî Tarihe Çevirme Kılavuzu [Conversion Guide for Muslim-Christian History]. Ankara, Türk Tarih Kurumu Basımevi, 1959. XVI + 175 p.

Türk Tarih Kurumu Yayını, VII Seri, No. 37.

Tables for the conversion of dates in the Muslim era and the Ottoman financial calendar (*mālī*) into Christian dates, pages 99-143. The *mālī* calendar was employed by the Ottoman Government from 1676 to 1925.

J230
WÜSTENFELD, Ferdinand *and* MAHLER, Edvard.
Wüstenfeld - Mahler'sche Vergleichungstabellen zur muslimischen und iranischen Zeitrechnung mit Tafeln zur Umrechnung orient-christlicher ären. *3rd ed.* Wiesbaden, Deutsche Morgenländsche Gesellschaft, 1961. 90 p.

Oversize tables for the conversion of the Muslim, Iranian, Turkish, Syriac, etc., etc. calendars to the Julian and Gregorian Christian calendars from 622 to 2076 A.D. by means of an ingenious enclosed slide-rule. Directions for use are in German, English, French, and Russian. Greatly expanded from the tables first published by Wüstenfeld in 1854.

¶ Conversion tables for the Ottoman *mālī* calendar are also to be found in the appendix by Joachim Mayr, "Anhang osmanische Zeitrechnungen - umrechnung der malijjedaten," in Franz Babinger's *Die Geschichtschreiber der Osmanen...* [J50], pages 424-25.

NATURAL PHENOMENA

Earthquakes

J231
AMIRAN, D. H. Kallner.
"A Revised Earthquake-catalogue of Palestine." *Israel Exploration Journal*, I, 1950-51, pp. 223-46; II, 1952, pp. 48-65.

A chronological listing of the earthquakes in the greater Palestine area from 64 B.C. to 1951 A.D., with locale, extent, if known, and damage. The list is contained in the first part, together with topographical index and bibliography.

J232
ERGİN, Kâzım; GÜÇLÜ, Uğur *and* UZ, Zeki.
Türkiye ve Civarının Deprem Kataloğu (milâttan soma 11 yılından 1964 sonuna kadar)/A Catalog of Earthquakes for Turkey and Surrounding Area (11 A.D. to 1964 A.D.). Istanbul, İstanbul Teknik Üniversitesi, [viii] + 169 p.

Arz Fiziği Enstitüsü Yayınları No: 24.

The major part of the work is a tabulation of 2,204 earthquakes to December 31, 1964, providing date, time of origin (if known), macroseismic data, instrument data, brief remarks, and source of information. The tabulation is followed by a description of the damage caused by the major quakes from that of 17 A.D. to that of October 6, 1964. Numerous isoseismal maps are also provided. The entire work is bi-lingual in Turkish and English.

For the period 11 A.D. to 1903 A.D. it is based, with additional seismic information, upon the work of N. Pinar and E. Lahn, *Türkiye Depremleri İzahlı Kataloğu*. Ankara, Bayındırlık Bakanlığı, 1952. *Yapı ve İmar İşleri Reisliği Yayınları Serı 6, Sayı 36*. This latter includes historical data.

J233
al-SUYŪṬĪ, ᶜAbd al-Raḥmān ibn Abī Bakr (d. 911/1505).
[Uncovering the Rattling on the Description of Earthquakes]. كشف الصلصلة عن وصف الزلزلة

Translations:

1. *Trans.* Alois Sprenger. "As-Soyuti's Work on Earthquakes." *Journal of the Royal Asiatic Society of Bengal*, XII, 1843, pp. 741-49. An incomplete translation based upon a corrupt manuscript.

2. *Trans.* Saïd Nejjar. Kashf aç-Çalçala 'an Waçf az-Zalzala *(traité du tremblement de terre)*. Rabat, Cahiers du Centre Universitaire de la Recherche Scientifique, 1973-74. Num. 3. XXVI. [ii] + 106 p. A French translation with notes of al-Suyūṭī's study of earthquakes from the earliest (?) times to 996/1588, in chronological order. Nejjar's translation goes beyond the original author's death.

Title transliterated: Kashf al-Ṣalṣala ᶜan Waṣaf al-Zalzala.

Floods

J234
SŪSĀ, Aḥmad.
The Floods of Baghdad in History. / فيضانات بغداد فى التاريخ Baghdad, Maṭbaᶜa al-Adīb, 1965. 2 vols., illus.

A very detailed examination of the nature and

extent of the flooding of the city and its environs to which it is susceptible from ancient times to 1963, with numerous maps, charts, and graphs.

¶ See also V. Grumel, *Traité d'Etudes byzantines* [J225]. The third part, "VII.- Phénomènes naturels," contains lists and tables of solar and lunar eclipses in Asia Minor and the Near East from 285-1500 A.D., comets 300-1462 A.D., and earthquakes.

DOCUMENTS

Handbooks

J235
GROHMANN, Adolf.
Einführung und Chrestomathie zur arabischen Papyruskunde. Prague, Státní Pedagogické Nakladatelství, 1954. 2 vols. in 1 [single pagination], illus.
Československý Ústov Orientální v Praze; Monografie Archivu Orientálního, Vol. XIII.

J236
---.
From the World of Arabic Papyri. Cairo, Royal Society of Historical Studies, 1952. XXII + 262 p., illus.
General introduction to the materials and methods of study of Arabic papyri by the leading authority in the field, with examples of texts. More general than the above, but an excellent beginning for the subject.
Contents: 1. The Importance and Value of Arabic Papyri; 2. The Finds and the Finding Places; 3. The Writing Material; 4. The Writing Instrument; 5. The Ink; 6. The Writing; 7. The Language of the Papyri; 8. Some Rules Should be Followed in the Editing of Arabic Papyri.

J237
HAMŪDĀ, Maḥmūd ʿAbbās.
[Introduction to المدخل الى دراسة الوثائق العربية the Study of Arabic Archives]. Cairo, Dār al-Thaqāfa li-l-Ṭabāʿa wa al-Nashr, 1980. 7 + 467 p., illus.
Title transliterated: Al-Madkhal ilā Dirāsa al-

Wathāʾiq al-ʿArabīya.

¶ In the second part of his handbook *I. Arabische Chronologie;...* Professor Grohmann [J219] has presented another introduction to Arabic papyri, "II. Arabische Papyruskunde" occupies pages 50-118.

Guides & Inventories

Europe

Europe (in general)

J238
DÜSTER, Joachim.
Oman Treaty Index: index to sources for treaties and other international acts relating to the Sultanate of Oman. Pforzheim, Germany, Oman Studies, 1980. 20 p.

J239
FEDERLEY, Berndt L.
Sources of the History of North Africa, Asia and Oceania in Finland, Norway and Sweden: the national archives of Finland, the national archives of Norway, the national archives of Sweden. Munich, K. G. Saur, 1981. 233 p.
Guides to the Sources for the History of Nations: 3rd series North Africa, Asia and Oceania; vol. 3, Sources for the History of North Africa, Asia and Oceania in Scandinavia, part 2, Finland, Norway, Sweden.
Translations from the Finnish, Norwegian, and Swedish, with index.

J240
Guide to Materials for West African History in European Archives [series]:
No. 1- Carson, Patricia. *Materials for West African History in the Archives of Belgium and Holland.* London, The Athlone Press, 1962. 86 p.
No. 2- Ryder, A. F. C. *Materials for West African History in Portuguese Archives.* London, The

Athlone Press, 1965. vi + 92 p.

No. 3- Gray, J. R. *and* Chambers, D. S. *Materials for West African History in Italian Archives.* London, The Athlone Press, 1965. viii + 104 p.

No. 4- Carson, Patricia. *Materials for West African History in French Archives.* London, The Athlone Press, 1968. viii + 170 p.

No. 5- Matthews, Noel. *Materials for West African History in the Archives of the United Kingdom.* London, The Athlone Press, 1973. 225 p.

J241

THOMAS, Daniel H. *and* CASE, Lynn M., *eds.*

The New Guide to the Diplomatic Archives of Western Europe. *2nd ed.* Philadelphia, University of Pennsylvania Press, 1975. xi + 441 p.

Contains 18 chapters on the archives of Austria, Belgium, Denmark, Finland, France, Germany, Great Britain, Greece, Italy,Luxemburg, The Netherlands, Norway, Portugal, Spain, Sweden, Switzerland, Vatican City, and the United Nations and other international organizations, each written by a specialist on the subject. Each chapter contains four categories of information: a history of the principal depositories; a description of the organization, arrangement, and classification of the records; administration of the depositories, hours, regulations, etc.; a bibliography of the principal collections published documents and of the most useful printed guides and inventories. Fortunately, there is a general index covering all of the depositories.

France

J242

SPIRIDONAKIS, B. G.

Empire ottoman: inventaire des mémoires et documents aux archives du Ministère des affaires Etrangères de France. Thessaloniki, Institute for Balkan Studies, 1973. 536 p.

Detailed catalogue of the documents concerning Turkey and France and Franco-Turkish relations between 1451 and 1814 contained within 132 of the 136 volumes entitled "Memoires et documents - fonds divers: Turquie" in the archives of the

French foreign ministry. Provides the number of the document, the number of the pages of each, and its title or description. Index of proper names, but none of subjects.

Appendices: I. Liste chronologique des Ministres des affaires Etrangères, 1589-1898; II. Liste des Ambassadeurs, Ministres, Chargés d'Affaires et Envoyés en Missions spéciales de France auprès de la Porte ottomane de 1525 à 1898; III. Tableau chronologique des Sultans ottomans; IV. Liste chronologique des Grands Vizirs ottomans depuis 855/1451 jusqu'en 1341/1922.

Great Britain

J243

ASHTIANY, Julia.

The Arabic Documents in the Archives of the British Political Agency: Kuwait 1904-1949. London, The British Library, 1982. 373 p.

An index to, and summary of, the documents from the Agency now housed in the India Office Library.

J244

BARRIER, N. Gerald.

Punjab History in Printed British Documents: a bibliographic guide to Parliamentary Papers and select, nonserial publications, 1843-1947. Columbia, Missouri, University of Missouri Press, 1969. [vi] + 108 p.

University of Missouri Studies, Vol. L.

Classified listing, with an excellent introduction to the subject and detailed annotations, of 488 House of Commons papers and official materials of diverse nature printed in India. Provides locations of holding libraries.

Contents: Pt. I: Parliamentary Papers on the Punjab; Pt. II: Nonserial Publications on the Punjab. General index.

J245

FOSTER, William, *Sir.*

The English Factories in India, 1618-69: a calendar of documents in the India Office, British Museum, and Public Record Office. Oxford, Oxford University Press, 1906-27. 13 vols.

Supplements: Sir Charles Fawcett. *The English Factories in India (New Series).* Oxford, Clarendon Press, 1936-55. 4 vols. Covers the years 1670-84.

J246
GRIMWOOD-JONES, Diana.
Sources for the History of the British in the Middle East, 1800-1978: a catalogue of the Private Papers Collection in the Middle East Centre, St. Antony's College, Oxford. London, Mansell Publishing Ltd., 1979. 22 fiches, with booklet.

Microfiche reproduction of the card index to the personal and official papers of those involved in Near Eastern affairs during the period.

J247
HALL, L.
A Brief Guide to Sources for the Study of Afghanistan in the India Office Records. London, India Office Library and Records, 1981. 60 p.

Provides a list of the materials about the country from 1600-1948, mainly accounts and records of British relations.

J248
JONES, Philip.
Britain and Palestine 1914-1948: archival sources for the history of the British mandate. Oxford, Oxford University Press, 1979. x + 256 p. [dbl. col.].

Published for The British Academy.

"The project has conducted a survey to locate and list briefly the unpublished papers and records of those individuals and organisations, whose base was in Britain, that had involvement or interest in events in Palestine during the first half of this century." [*Intro.*].

Contents: Personal Papers [listed in alphabetical order by person]; Records of Selected Organisations and Societies in Britain; Official Archives in Britain; Archives Outside Britain; Guide to Selected Libraries and Record Offices in Britain; Appendix to Personal Names.

J249
KHAN, Shafaat Ahmad, *Sir.*
Sources for the History of British India in the Seventeenth Century. London, Oxford University Press, 1926. viii + 395 p.
Allahabad University Series in History, Vol. IV.
A guide to the documents and manuscripts in libraries and archives in Great Britain and India.

J250
MATTHEWS, Noel *and* WAINWRIGHT, M. Doreen.
A Guide to Manuscripts and Documents in the British Isles Relating to Africa. London, Oxford University Press, 1971. XVI + 321 p.
The second in a series of guides published under the auspices of the School of Oriental and African Studies, University of London. As with the first this includes materials in public, official, institutional, corporate, university, and private libraries within the United Kingdom and the Republic of Ireland, for all of Africa south of the Sahara.

J251
---.
A Guide to Manuscripts and Documents in the British Isles Relating to the Middle East and North Africa. London, Oxford University Press, 1980. xvii + 482 p. [dbl. col.].
"The area covered here encompases the Arab countries of the Middle East and North Africa, Israel, Cyprus, Turkey, Iran and certain regions of the Caucasus, Central Asia and the Crimea." [*Intro.*].

J252
SAINSBURY, Ethel Bruce.
A Calendar of the Court Minutes, etc., of the East India Company, 1635 [-79]. Oxford, Clarendon Press, 1907-38. 11 vols.

J253
TUSON, Penelope.
The Records of the British Residency and Agencies in

the Persian Gulf. IOR R/15. London, India Office Library and Records, 1979. xix + 188 p., illus.

India Office and Records: Guides to Archive Groups.

Guide to the 3,500 files and volumes of correspondence and papers from the British Political Residency at Bushire and from the British Agencies at Bahrayn, Kuwait, Muscat, and Sharjah, 1763-1947, and to the 11,500 files from the Political Agent's Courts at Bahrayn, 1924-48. Appendices describe the East India Company's "factories" in Iran and the Gulf, 1616-1763, British representation in Ottoman controlled western Arabia and Iraq, 1635-1932, and a roster of British Residents and Agents in the Gulf, 1763-1948.

J254

WAINWRIGHT, M. Doreen *and* MATTHEWS, Noel.

A Guide to Western Manuscripts and Documents in the British Isles Relating to South and South East Asia. London, Oxford University Press, 1965. xix + 532 p.

The first in a series of guides published under the auspices of the School of Oriental and African Studies, University of London, which provide detailed information about the holdings of both private papers and government documents in public, official, institutional, corporate, university, and private libraries in England, Scotland, Wales, Northern Ireland, and the Republic of Ireland. Does not include the Public Record Office in London. A supplement is currently under preparation by J. D. Pearson.

Italy

J255

GIGLIO, Carlo.

Inventario delle Fonti manoscritti Relative alla Storio dell'Africa de Nord esistenti in Italia. Leiden, E. J. Brill, 1971- [in progress?].

Detailed inventories of the archival materials contained in the various Italian ministries and in private collections regarding North Africa up to 1922. Each volume includes complete indices. Published under the auspices of the Istituto di

Storia ed Istituzioni dei Paesi Afro-Asiatici, Università de Pavia.

Contents: Vol. I. *Gli Archivi storici del soppresso Ministero dell'Africa italiana e del Ministero degli Affari esteri dalle origini al 1922.* 1971. xxxii + 534 p., with 6 folding chronological tables. Vol. II. *Gli Archivi storici del Ministero della Difesa (esercito - marina - aeronautica) dalle origini al 1922.* 1972. xviii + 307 p.

Spain

J256

LABARTA, A.

"Inventario de los Documentos árabes contenidos en Procesos inquisitoriales contra Moriscos valencianos Conservados en el Archivo Histórico Nacional de Madrid (legajos 548-556)." *Al-Qantara*, I, 1980, pp. 115-64.

United States of America

J257

KAGANOFF, Nathan M.

Guide to America-Holy Land Studies. New York, Arno Press, 1980- [in progress].

"A Joint Project of the American Jewish Historical Society and the Institute of Contemporary Jewry, The Hebrew University of Jerusalem."

"... a projected series of volumes designed to provide the serious student and scholar with a guide to primary source material reflecting the relationship of the United States and the Holy Land from the early 19th century until 1948." [*Preface*].

J258

UNITED STATES. Library of Congress.

Government Publications: a guide to bibliographic tools. *4th ed. Ed.* Vladimir M. Palic. Washington, D.C., Library of Congress, 1975. ix + 441 p.

"This guide outlines bibliographic aids in the field of official publications issued by the United States, foreign countries, and international organizations." [*Preface*].

Contents: Part I- United States of America (Federal government; states, territories, and local governments); Part II- International Governmental Organizations; Part III- Foreign Countries.

J259

---. ---, General Reference and Bibliography Division. The United States and Africa: guide to U.S. official documents and government-sponsored publications on Africa, 1785-1975. *Comp.* Julian W. Witherell. Washington, D.C., Library of Congress, 1978. xix + 949 p. [dbl. col.].

"A selection of publications on Africa issued by or for the U.S. government from the late eighteenth century to September 1975 is recorded in this guide. Except for publications specifically on Egypt, all of Africa is covered, including the islands of the southeastern Atlantic and western Indian oceans. ... Only unclassified material is recorded here. Titles marked *restricted*, *confidential*, or *official use only*, with no indication that they were subsequently declassified, are not included. ... Entries are grouped into five chronological sections [1785-1819, 1820-1862, 1863-1920, 1921-1951, 1952-1975] subdivided by region or country. ... the first four are limited primarily to congressional and presidential documents, commercial reports, diplomatic papers, and treaties,... ." [*Preface*]. Very detailed index.

J260

---. National Archives, National Archives and Records Service.
Materials in the National Archives Relating to the Middle East. Washington, D.C., The National Archives, 1955. 96 p.

"This reference information paper discusses records in the National Archives relating to Iran and the following parts of the old Ottoman Empire: Arabia, Iraq, Lebanon, Palestine, Syria, and Turkey. The material is organized by subject and thereunder by country, with a general section on the Middle East for most subjects. ... Materials relating to the Middle East have been identified in 67 record groups in the National Archives, representing records of the legislative branch and every executive department of the Government except the Post Office Department. Records of the Congress noted in this paper are mainly manuscript records." [*Intro.*].

Africa

Africa and the Near East (in general)

J261
UNITED STATES. Library of Congress, Center for the Coordination of Foreign Manuscript Copying.
"A Preliminary Listing of Published Materials Relating to Archives and Manuscript Collections in Africa and the Near East." *News from the Center*, No. 3, Spring 1968, pp. 20-33.

Author listing without annotations. Contains a number of errors.

Contents: I. Books and Pamphlets; II. Articles.

Supplements: Roderic H. Davison. "Archives in the Near East, with special reference to Ottoman history." No. 4, Fall 1968, pp. 2-11.

This informative and important publication ceased after the appearance of No. 7, Spring 1970, because of insufficient support from The Library of Congress.

J262
---. ---, General Reference and Bibliography Division, Reference Department.
French-speaking West Africa: a guide to official publications. *Comp.* Julian W. Witherell, African Section. Washington, D.C., Reference Department, General Reference and Bibliography Division, Library of Congress, 1967. xii + 201 p. [dbl. col.].

"This guide to official publications of French-speaking West Africa lists as comprehensively as possible the published government records from the mid-19th century to the present date. It includes publications of the federation of French West Africa, its eight component colonies (later territories), the French administration in the mandated territory (later trust territory) of Togo, and documents of the autonomous and national governments of each state. ... This bibliography is arranged in four main parts. The first records publications of the federation of French West Africa (1895-1959), and the second includes documents of the French administrations and later of the autonomous and national governments in Dahomey, Guinea, Ivory Coast, Mali Federation (1959-60), Mali Republic, Mauritania, Niger, Senegal, Togo, and Upper Volta. ... A third part covers selected publications issued by the metropolitan government in Paris,... ." [*Preface*].

J263
---. ---.
Spanish-speaking Africa: a guide to official publications. *Comp.* Susan Knoke Rishworth, African Section. Washington, D.C., Reference Department, General Reference and Bibliography Division, Library of Congress, 1973. xiii + 66 p. [dbl. col.].

"..., this guide lists published official records of Spanish-speaking Africa from the 19th century to the present, including publications issued by the Spanish Government about or on behalf of its African territories. For the purpose of this bibliography, Spanish-speaking Africa will include Equatorial Guinea, Spanish Sahara, Ifni, and that part of northern Morocco known as the Spanish Zone until it was united with the rest of the country when Morocco became independent from France in 1956. The Spanish islands situated off the coast of northern Morocco, ..., have been excluded from this guide... ." [*Preface*].

Algeria

J264
BOURGIN, Georges.
"Les Documents de l'Algérie Conservés aux Archives nationales." *Revue Africaine*, L, 1906, pp. 157-84.

J265
ESQUER, Gabriel.
"Les Sources de l'Histoire de l'Algérie." *Histoire et Historiens de l'Algérie*. Paris, Libraire Félix

Alcan, MCMXXXI. Chap. XV, pp. 381-424.
Collection du Centenaire de l'Algérie (1830-1930).
A useful discussion of the archival and other primary source materials available in Algeria and in France.

J266
FRANC, Julien.
L'Histoire de la Colonisation de l'Algérie: les sources d'archives. Algiers, Imp. Pfeiffer et Assant, 1928. 167 + [ii]. p.
Contents: I. Coup d'oeil sur l'Histoire de la Colonisation de l'Algérie; II. Sources imprimées; III. Sources d'Archives [in Algeria]; IV. Archives départementales; V. Archives de France; Conclusion.

J267
TAMĪMĪ, ᶜAbd al-Jalīl.
Sommaire des Registres arabes et turcs d'Alger. Tunis, Revue d'Histoire Maghrebine, 1979. 115 p., illus.
Publications de la Revue d'Histoire Maghrebine, Vol. 2.
Originally published as "Inventaire sommaire des Registres arabes et turcs d'Alger" in *Revue d'Histoire Maghrebine*, I, 1974, pp. 83-96.

Egypt

J268
AMĪN, Muḥammad Muḥammad.
فهرست وثائق القاهرة حتى نهاية عصر سلاطين المماليك (٢٣٩ ـ ٩٢٢هـ/٨٥٣ ـ ١٥١٦م) : مع نشر و تحقيق تسعة نماذج /
Catalogue des Documents d'Archives du Caire de 239/853 à 922/1516 (depuis le IIIe/IXe siècle jusqu'à la fin de l'époque mamlouke): suive de l'édition critique de neuf documents. Cairo, Institut Français d'Archéologie Orientale du Caire, 1981. 564 [Arabic] + XVI p., illus.
Textes Arabes et Etudes Islamiques, Tome XVI.
Detailed catalogue of private papers in the national archives in the citadel, in the Ministry of Waqfs, the archives of the Coptic Patriarchate,

and the national archives and library. Index of proper names and a concordance.

Title transliterated: Fihrist Wathāʾiq al-Qāhira...

J269
DENY, Jean.
Sommaire des Archives turques du Caire. Cairo, Société Royale de Géographie d'Egypte, 1930. viii + 638 p., illus.

Extensive guide to the archives of Cairo, primarily for the period of Muḥammad ʿAlī and his successors by a former librarian of the royal palace library.

J270
EGYPT. Al-Hayʾa al-ʿĀmma li-Shuʾūn al-Maṭbaʿa al-Amiriya.
[Index to فهرست التشريعات المصرية، ١٨٦٤ ـ ١٩٧١ Egyptian Legislation, 1864 - 1971]. Cairo, Al-Hayʾa al-ʿĀmma li-Shuʾūn al-Maṭbaʿa al-Amīrīya, 1972. 11 + 1234 p.

Important index to the statutes, decrees, ordinances, etc., issued by the rulers and official governing bodies of Egypt since the reign of Ismāʿīl.

Title transliterated: Fihrist al-Tashriʿāt al-Miṣriya,...

J271
RIVLIN, Helen Anne B.
The Dār al-Wathāʾiq in ʿAbdīn Palace at Cairo as a Source for the Study of the Modernization of Egypt in the Nineteenth Century. Leiden, E. J. Brill, 1970. VI + 134 p.

An inventory of the Arabic, Ottoman Turkish, and European language documents and registers then located in these special archives at the former royal palace. A ten page introduction precedes the nine appendices which tabulate this very important collection.

J272
SHAW, Stanford J.
"Cairo's Archives and the History of Ottoman Egypt."

Report on Current Research on the Middle East, 1956, pp. 59-72. Washington, D.C., The Middle East Institute, 1956.

Detailed information concerning the Egyptian national archives and the archives of the Court of Personal Status for material on the history of Egypt under the Ottomans.

Morocco

J273
MIEGE, Jean-Louis.
Le Maroc et l'Europe (1830-1894). Paris, Presses Universitaires de France, 1961. 2 vols.

The first volume (234 pp.) is devoted exclusively to a detailed listing of the primary, published and unpublished, and secondary sources employed by the author in the writing of his history contained in the second volume. It is a valuable introduction to the archival materials for a history of French colonization during the period. Unfortunately, there is neither a table of contents nor an index.

Contents: Les Sources: I.- Sources manuscrits [archival materials]; II.- Sources imprimées [published archival materials, official gazettes, etc.]; III.- Les Sources cartographiques; Bibliographie: I.- Ouvrages parus entre 1830 et 1904; II.- Ouvrages et études sur le Maroc posterieurs à 1904; III.- Ouvrages et articles generaux. Each section is in alphabetical order by author.

J274
RABAT. League of Arab States. Bureau Permanent de Coordination de l'Arabisation dans le Monde Arabe. Encyclopédie du Maghreb arabe (section marocaine). Première partie: Bibliothèque Général de Rabat. Rabat, League of Arab States, Bureau Permanent de Coordination de l'Arabisation dans le Monde Arabe, N. D.

Issued in fasciculus by language:

Bibliographie des archives et documents allemands. 27 p. 201 entries.

Bibliographie des archives et documents anglais. 33 p. 438 entries.

J275
ROUARD DE CARD, Edgard M. M.
Les Traités de Commerce Conclus par le Maroc avec les Puissances étrangères. Toulouse, E. Privat, 1907. 86 p.

Tunisia

J276
MANTRAN, Robert.
Inventaire des Documents d'Archives turcs du Dar el-Bey, Tunis. Paris, Presses Universitaires de France, 1961. XLIV + 135 p.
Université de Tunis. Publications de la Faculté des Lettres, 5e serie: Sources de l'Histoire tunisienne, 1.

Near East

Iran

J277
FRAGNER, Bert G.
Repertorium persischer Herrschaftsurkunden: publizierte originalurkunden (bis 1848). Freiburg in Breisgau, Klaus Schwarz, 1980. ix + 389 p.
Islamkundliche Materialien, 4.
A chronological listing of 868 published Persian royal edicts written on paper and inscribed on buildings. Provides full bibliographical references to articles and reproductions. Indices of proper names, place names, technical terms, and authors cited.

J278
SCHIMKOREIT, Renate.
Regesten Publizierter safawidischer Herrscherurkunden: erlasse und staatsschreiben der frühen neuzeit Irans. Berlin, Klaus Schwarz Verlag, 1982. 552 p.
Inventory of 537 published documents of the Safawid period arranged chronologically from 1501, and then arranged by subject. Five indices.

Syria

J279
MANDAVILLE, Jon E.
"The Ottoman Court Records of Syria and Jordan." *Journal of the American Oriental Society*, 86, 1966, pp. 311-19.

A brief introduction to and indications of the availability of the Sharīᶜa court records for the Ottoman period in Aleppo, Damascus, Homs, and Jerusalem.

J280
RUSTUM, Asad.
A Calendar of State Papers from the Royal Archives of Egypt Relating to the Affairs of Syria. Beirut, American University Press, 1940-43. 4 vols.

A register, with summaries, and often publication of the full text, of materials contained within the Abdin Palace archives during the reign of Muḥammad ᶜAlī.

Turkey

J281
ÇETİN, Atillâ.
Başbakanlik Arşivi Kılavuzu [Guide to the Prime Ministry Archives]. Istanbul, Enderun Kitabevi, 1980. xvi + 171 p.

Descriptions of the categories of the documents with indications of which have been catalogued and those open for research. Includes a brief survey of other archives in Turkey.

A previous guide to these archives was that by Mitat Sertoğlu, *Muhteva Bakımından Başvekâlet Arşivi* (Ankara, 1955).

J282
DUMAN, Hasan.
Osmanlı Yıllıkları (Salnameler ve Nevsaller): bibliografya ve bazı İstanbul kütüphanelerine göre bir katalog denemesi/Ottoman Year-Books (Salname and Nevsal): a bibliograph [*sic*] and a union catalogue with reference to Istanbul libraries. Istanbul, İslâm Konferansı Teşkilâtı, İslâm Tarih, Sanat ve Kültürü Araştırma Merkezi (IRCICA), 1402/1982. 135 + [vi Arabic text] p.

Title also in Arabic. Introduction in Turkish, English, French, and Arabic.

"The publication of the salnames by the Ottoman State started just after the Tanzimat period (1263 AH/1847 AC) and continued till the end of the First World War. (The last issue being in 68th year, 1333-34 R/1918 AC). Provincial salnames were also published during this period. ... State salnames contained general information; provincial salnames contained specific information about a wide geographical area; i.e. the whole Arabian peninsula, Iraq (Baghdad, Basra and Mosul), Syria and Palestine, Anatolia, East and West Thrace, Albania, Yugoslavia, Bulgaria, North East Africa (Egypt, Tripoli), part of the Mediterranean islands and even Acaristan which is situated to the East of the Black Sea." [*Preface*].

J283
ERTUĞ, H. R.
"Osmanlı Devrinde Salnameler"[Yearbooks in the Ottoman Period]. *Hayat Tarih Mecmuası,* IX (7), no. 103, 1973, pp. 15-22; IX (8), no. 104, 1973, pp. 10-16.

A listing of all Ottoman yearbooks published.

J284
SHAW, Stanford J.
"Archival Sources for Ottoman History: the archives of Turkey." *Journal of the American Oriental Society*, 80, 1960, pp. 1-12.

Extensive and detailed information concerning four major archival depositories in Istanbul and Ankara, six other official archives, and three personal and family archives in Istanbul.

J285
---.
"Ottoman Archival Materials for the Nineteenth and Early Twentieth Centuries: the archives of Istanbul." *International Journal of Middle East Studies*, 6, 1975, pp. 94-114.

An important description of the archival materials in the four categories of basic laws and regulations, administrative records and regulations, records of sultans and statesmen, and judicial records.

J286
---.
"Turkish Source Materials for Egyptian History." *Ed.* P. M. Holt. *Political and Social Change in Modern Egypt.* London, Oxford University Press, 1968, pp. 28-48.

J287
ZAJĄCZKOWSKI, Ananiasz *and* REYCHMAN, Jan.
Handbook of Ottoman-Turkish Diplomatics. *Trans.* Andrew S. Ehrenkreutz. The Hague, Mouton & Co., 1968. 232 p., charts.

Revised and expanded edition of *Zarys Dyplomatyki Osmánsko-Tureckiej* (1968).

Bibliographies and introduction in detail to the intricacies of the Ottoman diplomatic records.

South & Southeast Asia

India

J288
CHAUDHRY, Nazir Ahmad.
Calendar of Persian Correspondence: collection of treaties, *sanads*, letters, etc., which passed between the East India Company, Sikhs, Afghans and other notables. Lahore, Superintendent, Government Printing, Punjab, 1972- [in progress].

Contents: Vol. I. *A Collection of Treaties,* Sanads, *and General Correspondence Dating Between 1785 and 1836 Housed in the Punjab Record Office and Translated from the Persian into Urdu and then into English.* Contains a total of 1,110 items either published or calendared. Glossary of terms and index of proper names.

J289
INDIA. Andhra Pradesh Archives.
Mughal Documents: catalogue of Aurangzeb's reign. *Ed. & comp.* M. A. Nayeem. Hyderabad-Deccan, State Archives, Gov't. of Andhra Pradesh, 1980- [in progress].

Projected to be completed in 10 volumes.

Contents: Vol. I: 1648-1663 A.D.

J290
---. Bombay. Directorate of Archives.
Bombay Records Series, Descriptive Catalogue. Bombay, Government Central Press, 1954- [in progress].
Contents: Vol. I. *Descriptive Catalogue of the Secret & Political Department Series, 1755-1820. Comp.* V. G. Dighe. viii + 652 p. Guide to the papers of the Bombay Presidency of the East India Company regarding its relations with neighboring states.

J291
---. Rajasthan State Archives.
A Descriptive List of the Arzdhashts (Persian) Addressed by the Various Officials to the Rulers of Jaipur, 1658-1707. Bikaner, Rajasthan State Archives, [1981]. 98 p.
With summaries.

J292
---. ---.
A Descriptive List of the Bikaner Makhmakhas, English Record, 1896-1914. Bikaner, Rajasthan State Archives, [1980]. ii, 80 + 69 p.

J293
---. ---.
A List of the English Records of the Ajmer Commissioner, 1818-1899. Bikaner, Rajasthan State Archives, [1980?]. ii + 126 p.

J294
LOW, D. A.
Government Archives in South Asia: a guide to national and state archives in Ceylon, India and Pakistan. Cambridge, Cambridge University Press, 1969. xii + 355 p., chart.
An inventory, with emphasis upon the national archives of India. Unfortunatelv, no index.

J295
RIAZUL ISLAM.
A Calendar of Documents on Indo-Pakistan Relations

1500-1750. Karachi, Bunyad-i Farhang Iran/Institute of Central and West Asian Studies, University of Karachi, 1979-82. 2 vols.

Detailed register, by ruler, of the diplomatic correspondence of the Mughal and other Muslim rulers of India with the Safawids of Persia, the Ottoman Empire, and the Uzbek Khans of Central Asia.

J296
SARAN, P.
Descriptive Catalogue of Non-Persian Sources of Medieval Indian History (covering Rajasthan and adjacent regions). New York [Delhi], Asia Publishing House, 1965. xi, [iii] + 234 p.

A survey of slightly over 200 documents in Rajasthani located in various public and private libraries of importance for the history of Muslim and Hindu rule of the area, 800-1800. In English and the Devanagri script.

Indonesia

J297
VAN NIEL, Robert.
A Survey of Historical Source Materials in Java and Manila. Honolulu, University of Hawaii Press, 1970. [iv] + 255 p.

Contents: 1. The Indonesian National Archives; 2. Archive of the Indonesian Department of Internal Affairs; 3. Local Government Archives in Java; 5. Manuscript Collections in Indonesian Libraries; 6. Private Archives in Indonesia; 7. The Philippine National Archives; 8. Manuscript Collections in Philippine Libraries; 9. Religious Archives in the Philippines.

Useful general accounts rather than registers.

Collections

Africa & Asia (General)

In general the following collections of documents do not include those pertaining to a single event nor to those of one ruler.

J298
BOURNE, Kenneth *and* WATT, Cameron, *eds*.
British Documents on Foreign Affairs: reports and papers from the Foreign Office Confidential Print. Frederick, Maryland, University Publications of America, 1983-88. 420 vols. [projected].

"The Confidential Print comprises diplomatic despatches and other papers [from the middle of the 19th century to World War II] which, ..., were printed for limited circulation within the British Government." [*Brochure*].

Divided into two parts chronologically and within each part by country or area: Part I: *From the Mid-Nineteenth Century to the First World War - The Near and Middle East, 1856-1914* (*Ed*. David Gillard. 20 vols. 1984); *Asia* (30 vols. 1985-86); *Africa* (25 vols. 1986-87). Part II: *From the First to the Second World War - Turkey, Iran, and the Middle East, 1919-1938* (*Ed*. Robin Bidwell. 35 vols. 1984-85); *Asia* (50 vols. 1985-88); *Africa* (30 vols. 1987-88).

J299
CHARRIERE, Ernest.
Négociations de la France Dans le Levant: ou, correspondances, mémoires et actes diplomatiques des ambassadeurs de France à Constantinople et des ambassadeurs, envoyés ou résidents à divers titres à Venise, Rome, Matte et Jérusalem, en Turquie, Perse, Géorgie, Crimée, Syrie, Egypte, etc., et dans les états de Tunis, d'Alger et du Maroc; publiés pour la première fois par... . Paris, Imprimerie Nationale/Imprimerie Impériale. 1848-60. 4 vols.

Collection de Documents Inédites sur l'Histoire de France, Publiés par les Soins du Ministre de l'Instruction publique. 1. série. Histoire politique.

Contents: I. 1515-1547; II. 1547-1566; III. 1567-1580; IV. 1581-1589.

J300
HUREWITZ, J. C.
The Middle East and North Africa in World Politics: a documentary record. *2nd ed*. New Haven, Connecticut, Yale University Press, 1975. 3 vols.

Revised and greatly enlarged edition of the compiler's *Diplomacy in the Near and Middle East* (1956).

Collection of numerous documents, many published in English for the first time, on the history of the area from Afghanistan to Morocco, 1535-1975.

Contents: I. *European Expansion, 1535-1914;* II. *British-French Supremacy, 1914-1945;* III. *British-French Withdrawal and Soviet-American Rivalry, 1945-1975.*

J301
PARIS. Société d'Histoire generale et d'Histoire diplomatique.
Archives diplomatiques: recueil international de diplomatie et d'histoire. Paris, Société d'Histoire generale et d'Histoire diplomatique, 1861-1914. 131 vols.

Publication of more than 100,000 documents exchanged between all nations concerning matters of international affairs and politics during the period 1861-1914. There is a general index covering only the first 46 volumes in volume 46.

Photographically reprinted in Nendeln, Liechtenstein.

Africa

North Africa - General

J302
HOPKINS, J. F. P.
Letters from Barbary, 1576-1774: Arabic documents in the Public Record Office. Oxford, Oxford University Press, 1982. xviii + 112 p.

Oriental Documents VI.

Translations, with annotations, of Arabic and Turkish letters sent from the rulers of Morocco, Tunis, and Tripoli to the English sovereigns and other high officials from the time of Elizabeth I to George III (1558-1820).

J303
MAS-LATRIE, Louis de, *Comte.*
Traités de Paix et de Commerce et Documents Divers

Concernant les Relations des Chrétiens avec les Arabes de l'Afrique septentrionale au Moyen Age; recueilles par l'ordre de l'Empereur et publiés avec une introduction historique. Paris, H. Plon, 1865-68. 2 vols.

The first volume is comprised exclusively of the historical introduction and a chronological table. The second volume contains the original texts of commercial and political agreements dating from the 12th through the 15th centuries.

Supplements: Louis de Mas-Latrie. *Traitès de Paix et de Commerce...* . Paris, J. Baur et Détaille, 1872. II + 119 p.

J304
ROUARD DE CARD, Edgard.
Traités de la France avec les Pays d'Afrique de Nord, Algérie, Tunisie, Tripolitaine, Maroc. Paris, A. Pedone, Editeur, 1906. XV + 422 p.

Treaties, accords, diplomatic notes, etc., concluded during the 17th-19th centuries, not only between France and the North African states, but also between France and other European nations about North Africa. Basically commercial and concessionary treaties.

J305
TAMĪMĪ, ʿAbd al-Jalīl [Abdeljelil Temimi].
Recherches et Documents d'Histoire maghrebine: l'Algérie, la Tunisie et la Tripolitine (1816-1871). *2nd ed.* Tunis, Revue d'Histoire Maghrebine, 1980. 206 p., illus.

Publications de la Revue d'Histoire Maghrebine, vol. 3.

Contains six short *études* and 55 documents in French, either original or translations from the Arabic or Turkish. First edition published by the Université de Tunis in 1971.

J306
TILLOY, René.
Repertoire Tilloy: répertoire alphabétique de jurisprudence, de doctrine et de législation algérienne, tunisienne et musulmane. *2nd rev. ed. Ed.* Louis Milliot *and* Georges Rectenwald. Algiers, P. & G.

Soubiron/Paris, Juris-classeurs Editions Godde, 1930-35. 7 vols.

Algeria

J307

BUGEAUD DE LA PICONNERIE, Thomas Robert, *le Maréchal, Duc d'Isly.*

Le Maréchal Bugeaud, d'après sa correspondance intime et des documents inédits 1784-1849. *Ed. Comte* H. d'Ideville. Paris, Librairie de Firmin-Didot et Cie., 1881-82. 3 vols.

The most important single collection of basic source materials on the campaigns and administration of Marshal Bugeaud in Algeria establishing French authority in that country, from 1836-46. Appointed governor-general of French Algeria in 1840, a post which he retained until his resignation in July 1846.

Translations: Trans. & ed. Charlotte Mary Yonge. *Memoirs of Marshal Bugeaud, from his private correspondence and original documents, 1784-1849.* London, Hurst and Blackett, 1884. 2 vols.

Supplements: Capitaine Tattet. *Lettres Inédites du Maréchal Bugeaud, Duc d'Isley (1808-1849), colliegées et annotées par M. le Capitaine Tattet.* Paris, Emile-Paul Frères, 1922. 413 p. Contains previously unpublished letters written between 1836 and 1849 treating with his campaigns and his rôle as governor-general.

J308

LA MARTINIERE, Maximillien A. D. H. P de *and* LACROIX, N.

Documents pour Servir à l'Etude du Nord Ouest africain. Algiers, Gouvernement Général de l'Algérie, Service des Affaires Indigènes, 1894-97. 4 vols., illus.

J309

PLANTET, Eugène.

Correspondance des Deys d'Alger avec la Cour de France, 1579-1833, recueille dans les dépôts d'archives des Affaires étrangères, de la Marine, des Colonies et de la Chambre de Commerce de Marseille.

Paris, F. Alcan, 1889. 2 vols.
Contents: Vol. I. 1579-1700; Vol. II. 1700-1833.

J310
YVER, Georges.
Correspondance du Général Damrémmot, Gouverneur Général des Possessions française dans le Nord de l'Afrique (1837). Paris, H. Champion, 1927. xxvi, [iii] + 798 p.

Gouvernement Général de l'Algérie, Collection de Documents inédits sur l'Histoire de l'Algérie après 1830. Ire Serie, Correspondance Général, IV.

Contains 381 documents, primarily concerning the French invasion and occupation, with annotations and cross-indices.

¶ For additional documents on Algeria see the preceding section on North Africa - general.

Egypt

J311
FRANCE. Ministère des Affaires Etrangères.
Documents diplomatiques. Accords conclus, le 8 Avril 1904 entre la France et l'Angleterre au sujet du Maroc, de l'Egypte, de Terre-Neuve, etc. Paris, Imprimerie Nationale, 1904. 47 p., maps.

J312
---. ---.
Documents diplomatiques: affaire du canal de Suez. Dècembre 1875. Paris, Imprimerie Nationale, 1875. 205 p.

Correspondence, documents, etc., covering the period 22 March 1872 - 27 November 1875.

Supplements:

1. *Documents diplomatiques. Commission internationale pour le libre usage du canal de Suez. Avril - novembre, 1885.* Paris, Imprimerie Nationale, 1885. vi + 243 p.

2. *Documents diplomatiques. Négociations relatives au règlement international pour le libre usage du canal de Suez. 1886-1887.* Paris, Im-

primerie Nationale, 1887. viii + 119 p.

J313
---. ---.
Documents diplomatiques: affaires d'Egypte. Paris, Imprimerie Nationale, 1880-85. 19 vols. [published separately over the period].

Correspondence and documents concerning the foreign debt of Egypt and events leading up to, and including, the British occupation in 1882.

Contents: [i]: *1878-1879.* 1880. 384 p.; [ii]: *1880.* 1881. 6 + 160 p.; [iii]: *1880-82.* 1882. 5 vols. in 1; [iv]: *1881.* 1882. vii + 72 p.; [v]: *1881-1882.* 1882. viii + 158 p. [15 Nov. 1881 - 11 March 1882]; [vi]: *1882.* 1882. 2 vols. in 1 [12 March - 2 June 1882]; [vii]: *1882-1883.* 1883. viii + 134 p.; [viii]: *Indemnités égyptienne, 1882 - 1883, et exposé de la situation présenté aux Chambres le 15 jan. 1883 avec un recueil de documents.* 1883. 3 vol. in 1.; [ix]: *Institution d'une commission mixte pour l'examen des réclamations résultant des derniers événements d'Eypte. 1882-1883.* 1883. vii + 94 p.; [x]: *1884.* 1884. 32 p.; [xi]: *1884-1893.* 1893. xxvi + 536 p.; [xii]: *8 janvier - 21 mars 1885.* 1885. viii + 53 p.

J314
---. ---.
Documents diplomatiques. Negociations relatives a la reforme judiciaire en Egypte. Janvier 1875 [et novembre 1875]. Paris, Imprimerie Nationale, 1875. 2 vols.

J315
GROHMANN, Adolf.
Arabic Papyri in the Egyptian National Library. Cairo, National Library, 1934-63. 6 vols.

Photographic reproductions, transcriptions into the cursive script, English translations, and detailed notes on the early Muslim Egyptian materials written on papyrus.

J316
NĀHUM, Hāyyīm.

Recueil de Firmans impériaux ottomans Adressés aux Valis et aux Khédives d'Egypte, 1006 H. - 1322 H. (1597 J.C. - 1904 J.C.). Cairo, Administration des Biens Privés et des Palais Royaux, 1934. xlvii + 366 p.

French summaries with notes.

Libya

J317

al-DAJJĀNĪ, Aḥmad Ṣidqī *and* ADHAM, ᶜAbd al-Salām.

وثائق تاريخ ليبيا الحديث: الوثائق العثمانية، ١٨٨١ - ١٩١١

[Documents on the Modern History of Libya: Ottoman documents 1881-1911]. Benghazi, Manshūrāt Jāmiᵓa Binghāzī, 1974. 309 + 18 p., illus.

Collection with introductions and translations into Arabic.

Title transliterated: Wathāᵓiq Taᵓrīkh Lībyā al-Ḥadīth:...

Morocco

J318

BECKER Y GONZALES, D. Jerónimo.

Tratados, Convenios y Acuerdos Referentes á Marruecos y la Guinea Española. Madrid, Impr. del Patronato de Huérfanos de Intendencia é Intervencion Militores, 1918. 333 p.

Publicaciones de la Liga Africanista Española.

Texts, with explanatory notes, of 18 documents of the 19th century to 1894.

J319

CAGIGAS, Isidro de las.

Tratados y Convenios Referentes á Marruecos. Madrid, Instituto de Estudios Africanos, 1952. 506 p.

Publication, without commentary, of the texts of 94 treaties and conventions of diverse nature beginning with the Spanish-Moroccan treaty of 1767.

J320

CAILLE, J. *and* LA VERONNE, Chantal de.

"Sur les Recueils d'Actes internationaux Relatifs au Maroc." *Hespéris*, XLVI, 1959, pp. 73-85.

A study of the published document collections.

J321
CASTRIES, Henri Marie de la Croix, *Comte*, *et. al*.
Les Sources Inédites de l'Histoire du Maroc de 1530 à 1845. Paris, Ernst Leroux, 1905-60. 27 vols.

Publication of archival materials in France, The Netherlands, the United Kingdom, Spain, and Portugal concerning the Muslim dynasties of northwest Africa to the French conquest.

Contents: I[e] série - *Dynastie saadienne: 1530-1660*. I. *Archives et Bibliothèques de France* [+ index. *Ed*. Henri Castries. 4 vols.]; II. *Archives et Bibliothèques des Pays-Bas* [*Ed*. Henri Castries. 6 vols.]; III. *Archives et Bibliothèques d'Angleterre* [*Eds*. Henri Castries, Pierre de Cenival *and* Phillipe de Cossé-Brissac. 3 vols.]; IV. *Archives et Bibliothèques d'Espagne* [*Eds*. Henri Castries, Robert Ricard *and* Chantal de la Véronne. 2 vols.]; V. *Archives et Bibliothèques de Portugal* [*Eds*. Pierre de Cenival, David Lopes *and* Robert Ricard. 5 vols.]. IIe série - *Dynastie filalienne* [1663-1845]. I. *Archives et Bibliothèques de France* [*Eds*. Henri Castries, Pierre de Cenival *and* Phillipe de Cossé-Brissac. 6 vols. + index].

J322
FRANCE. Ministère des Affaires Etrangères.
Documents diplomatiques. Accords conclus, le 8 avril 1904 entre la France et l'Angleterre au sujet du Maroc, de l'Egypte, de Terre-Neuve, etc. Paris, Imprimerie Nationale, 1904. 47 p., maps.

J323
---. ---.
Documents diplomatiques. Affaires du Maroc. Paris, Imprimerie Nationale, 1880-1912. 7 vols. [published separately over the period].

Contain altogether more than 1,500 documents pertaining to French diplomatic actions in her expansion into Morocco.

Contents: [i]: *Question de la Protection diplomatique et consulaire au Maroc*. 1880. 278 p.; [ii]: *1901-1905*. 1905. xvii + 320 p.; [iii]; *1906*. *Fascicule no. i, Affaires du Maroc; ii. Protocoles et Comptes rendus de la Conférence d'Al-*

gésiras. Pour suite à "Affaires du Maroc 1901-1905." 1906. ix + 296 p.; [iv]: *1906-1907. Pour faire suite à "Affaires du Maroc 1901-1905" et Protocoles et Comptes rendus de la Conférence d'Algésiras."* 1907. xix + 405 p.; [v]: *1907-1908. Pour faire suite à "Affaires du Maroc iii 1906-1907."* 1908. xvii + 394 p.; [vi]: *1908-1910. Pour faire suite à "Affaires du Maroc iv 1907-1908."* 1912. xvi + 397 p.; [vii]: *1910-1912. Pour faire suite à "Affaires du Maroc v 1908-1910."* 1912. xxii + 671 p.

J324
IBN AZZUZ, Mohammad.
Compendio de los Pactos internacionales de Marruecos (indice de los tratados ajustados por Marruecos (1092-1354 - 1681-1935) y de otros documentos internacionales). Tetwan, Editora Marroquí, 1949. 145 p.

Instituto General Franco de Estudios e Investigación Hispano-Arabe. Publicaciones Fuera de Serie.

J325
MIEGE, Jean-Louis.
Documents d'Histoire économique et sociale marocaine au XIXe siècle. Paris, Centre National de la Recherche Scientifique, 1969. 359 + [iv] p.

A selection of fifty documents either written originally in French or translated into French from the Arabic, together with numerous tables and charts drawn from the documents. Index of all names found in the documents.

J326
MILLIOT, Louis.
Recueil de Jurisprudence chérifienne. Tribunal du ministre chérifien de la justice et conseil supérieur d'ouléma (Medjlès al-Istinâf). Paris, E. Leroux, 1920-24. 2 vols.

J327
RIVIERE, Paul Louis.
Table générale analytique et raisonnée des Traités, Codes, Lois et Règlements du Maroc (dahirs, arrêtés

viziriels et résidentials, ordres, ordonnances, circulaires, instructions et avis), Accompangnés des Lois et Décrits français Concernant le Maroc. Paris, L. Tenin, 1923-25. 4 vols.

J328
---.
Traités, Codes, et Lois du Maroc. Paris, Société du Recueil Sirey, 1924-25. 3 vols.
Covers the period 1767 to 1923.

J329
ROUARD DE CARD, Edgard M. M.
Documents diplomatiques pour Servir à l'Etude de la Question marocaine. Paris, A. Pedone, 1911. 159 p., maps.
Contents: Sec. I. Traités et Accords Conclus par la France avec le Maroc; Sec. II. Accord entre la France et Divers Etats au Sujet de Maroc; Sec. III. Conventions internationales Relatives au Maroc.

J330
---.
Traités et Accords Concernant le Protectorat de la France au Maroc. Paris, A. Pedone, 1914. viii + 123 p., maps.

¶ For additional collections of documents concerning Morocco see above section - North Africa - General and item number J311.

Sudan

J331
MUSᶜAD, Muṣṭafā Muḥammad.
المكتبة السودانية العربية، مجموعة النصوص والوثائق العربية الخاصة بتاريخ السودان فى العصور الوسطى /
Bibliothèque soudano-arabe; recueil de textes et de documents arabe relatifs à l'histoire du Soudan au moyen-age. Cairo, Dār al-Ittiḥād al-ᶜArabī, 1972. 16 + 452 p.
Title transliterated: Al-Maktaba al-Sūdānīya al-ᶜArabīya, ...

Tunisia

J332
FRANCE. Ministère des Affaires Etrangères.
Documents diplomatiques. Affaires de Tunisie, avec une carte de la régence. 1870-1881 [with supplément]. Paris, Imprimerie Nationale, 1881. xxiv, 312, v + 74 p., map.

Supplements:

1. *Documents diplomatiques. Revision des traités tunisiens. 1881-1897.* 1897. 87 p.
2. *Documents diplomatiques. Revision des traités tunisiens. 1896-janvier 1897.* 1897. 55 p.
3. *Documents officiels Relatifs à l'Organisation du Protectorat français en Tunisie.* 1886. 19 p.

J333
PLANTET, Eugène.
Correspondance des Beys de Tunis et des Consuls de France avec la Cour, 1577-1830. Paris, F. Alcan, 1893-99. 3 vols.

Contents: Vol. I. 1577-1700; Vol. II. 1700-1770; Vol. III. 1770-1830.

¶ For additional documents see above section North Africa - General.

Near East

Near East - General

J334
ANDERSON, M. S.
The Great Powers and the Near East 1774-1923. London, Edward Arnold, 1970. viii + [ii], 181 + [i] p.

Selection of treaties, reports, memoranda, etc. to illustrate the history of the relations. Each is preceded by a brief introduction.

Contents: I. The Rise of Russian Power and the French Invasion of Egypt; II. The Napoleonic Wars; III. The Greek War of Independence; IV. The Mehmet Ali Crises, 1832-41; V. The Struggle for Internal Reform in the Ottoman Empire; VI. The Crimean War; VII. The Eastern Crisis of 1875-8; VIII.

The Eastern Question, 1878-1914; IX. European Economic Activity in the Ottoman Empire in the Later Nineteenth and Early Twentieth Centuries; X. The Growth of Nationalism in the Near East in the Early Twentieth Century; XI. The First World War and the Peace Settlement, 1914-23. Glossary. No index.

J335
BIDWELL, Robin.
Foreign Office Confidential Print. London, Frank Cass & Co., Ltd., 1971- .

Facsimile reprinting of the written and telegraphic reports received by the British Foreign Office, and the replies sent, which were issued for limited distribution within the Government. The facsimile consists of basic raw material regarding events in Arabia and Turkey.

Contents: The Affairs of Kuwait 1896-1905 [2 vols.]; The Affairs of Arabia 1905-1906 [2 vols.]; The Affairs of Asiatic Turkey and Arabia 1906-1913 [8 vols.].

J336
ḤAMĀDA, Muḥammad Māhir.
الوثائق السياسية و الادارية العائدة للعصر الأموى
٤٠ ـ ١٣٢هـ، ٦٦١ ـ ٧٥٠م
[Political and Administrative Documents of the Umayyad Period, 40-132 A.H. 661-750 A.D.]. Beirut, Muʾassa al-Risāla/Dār al-Nafāʾis, 1981. 613 p.

Collected texts from diverse sources.

Title transliterated: Wathāʾiq al-Siyāsīya wa al-Idārīya al-ʿĀʾida li-l-ʿAsr al-Umawī...

J337
ISMAIL, Adel.
Documents diplomatiques et consulaires Relatifs à l'Histoire du Liban et des Pays du Proche-orient du XVII siècle á nos Jours: documents recueilles sous l'égide de l'Emire Maurice Chéhab Directeur Général des Antiquités du Liban. Beirut, Editions des Oeuvres Politiques et Historiques, 1975- [in progress].

A multi-volumed collection of French documents.

J338

ROSSI, Ettore.
Documenti sull'Origine e gli Sviluppi della Questione Araba (1875-1944). Rome, Istituto per l'Oriente, 1944. [v], lvi + 251 p., maps.
Well annotated collection of documents in French and Italian.

J339
TUSON, Penelope.
British Policy in Asia: India Office Memoranda. Vol. I: The Middle East 1856-1947. London, Mansell Publishing Ltd., 1980. 39 fiches, with booklet.
Reproduction on microfiche of the texts of memoranda produced or collected by the India Office Political and Secret Department.

Iran

J340
ALEXANDER, Yonah *and* NANES, Allan.
The United States and Iran: a documentary history. Frederick, Maryland, University Publications of America, 1983. 524 p.
Publication of previously published and unpublished official documents illustrative of the relations between the two countries since the first Treaty of Friendship and Commerce of 1856.

J341
HERTSLET, Edward, *Sir*.
Treaties, &c. Concluded Between Great Britain and Persia, and Between Persia and Other Foreign Powers, Wholly or Partially in Force on the 1st April, 1891. London, Butterworth's, 1891. xii + 239 p., maps.

J342
RIAZUL ISLAM.
A Calendar of Documents on Indo-Persian Relations (1500-1750). Tehran, Iranian Culture Foundation/ Karachi, Institute of Central and West Asian Studies, 1979- .

Lebanon

J343

NAWWĀR, ᶜAbd al-Azīz Sulaymān.
وثائق اساسية من تاريخ لبنان الحديث،١٥١٧-١٩٢٠/
Basic Documents for the Modern History of Lebanon, 1517-1920. Beirut, Jāmiᶟa Bayrūt al-ᶜArabīya, 1974. 596 p., maps.
Title transliterated: Wathāᶟiq Asāsīya min Taᶟrīkh Lubnān al-Ḥadīth,...

¶ For additional documents on Lebanon since the 17th century see Adel Ismail, *Documents diplomatiques et consulaires*... [J337].

Muscat

J344
FRANCE. Ministère des Affaires Etrangères.
Documents diplomatiques. Affaires de Mascate. Commerce des armes à Mascate, 1912-1914. Paris, Imprimerie Nationale, 1914. vi + 63 p.

Oman

J345
PORTER, J. D.
Oman and the Persian Gulf, 1835-1949. Salisbury, North Carolina, Documentary Publications, 1982. 90 p., maps.
Letters, reports, and documents from the archives of the United States.

Syria

J346
RUSTUM, Asad.
Materials for a Corpus of Arabic Documents Relating to the History of Syria under Mehmet Ali Pasha. Beirut, American University Press, 1930-34. 5 vols. in 4.
Publication of original archival materials of court and public records preserved in private collections.

Turkey

J347

ARISTARCHES, Gregorios.
Législation ottomane, ou recueil des lois, réglements, ordonnances, traités, capitulations, et autres documents officiels de l'Empire ottoman. Constantinople, Frère Nicolaïdes, 1873-88. 7 vols.

J348
FRANCE. Ministère des Affaires Etrangères.
Documents diplomatiques. Affaires arméniennes. Projets de réformes dans l'Empire ottoman, 1893-1897. Paris, Imprimerie Nationale, 1897. xix + 371 p.
Supplements: 1895-1896. 1897. xv + 124 p.

J349
---. ---.
Documents diplomatiques. Affairs d'Orient. Paris, Imprimerie Nationale, 1877-98. 10 vols. [published separately during the period].
Contents: [i]: *1875-1876-1877*. 1877. 2 + 377 p.; [ii]: *Congrès de Berlin, 1878*. 1878. 316 p., maps; [iii]: *Affaire de Crète. Conflit gréco-turc. Situation de l'Empire ottoman, février - mai 1897*. 1897. xxxii + 373 p.; [iv]: *Affaire de Crète, juin 1894 - février 1897*. 1897. xxv + 350 p.; [v]: *Autonomie crétoise, mai - décembre 1897*. 1898. vii + 35 p.; [vi]: *Autonomie crètoise, janvier - octobre 1898*. 1898. xvi + 196 p.; [vii]: *Emprunt de l'indemnité de guerre hellénique. Evacuation de la Thessalie, janvier - juin 1898*. 1898. x + 109 p.; [viii]: *Evacuation de la Crète par les troupes ottomanes. Installation d'un haut commissaire, octobre - novembre 1898*. 1898. 53 p.; [ix]: *Mai 1897 - oct. 1898*. 1898. 4 vols. in 1; [x]: *Négociations pour la paix. Traité gréco-turc, mai - décembre 1897*. 1898. ix + 92 p., map.

J350
---. ---.
Documents diplomatiques. Affaires de Turquie, 1900-1901. Paris, Imprimerie Nationale, 1902. viii + 70 p.

J351
GALANTE, Abraham.

Documents officiels turcs Concernant les Juifs de Turquie: recueil des 114 lois, règlements, firmans, bérats, ordres et décisions de tribunaux. Traduction française avec résumes historiques, annotations et un appendice avec sept autres documents. Istanbul, Haim, Rozio, 1931. 254 p.

Supplements: Istanbul, Impr. Hüsnütabiat, 1941. 46 p.

J352
GEVAY, Anton von.

Urkunden und Aktenstücke zur Geschichte der Verhältnisse Zwischen Österreich, Ungern und der Pforte im xvi und xvii Jahrhunderte: gesandtschaften König Ferdinands I. an Sultan Suleiman I. Vienna, Aufkosten des Herausgebers, 1838-42. 3 vols. [all published].

Issued in eleven unnumbered parts, each with separate paginations.

Contents: B. I. 1527-32; B. II. 1532-36; B. III. 1536-41.

J353
GIANNINI, Amedeo.

Documenti per la Storia della Pace orientale, 1915-1932. *3rd ed.* Rome, Istituto per l'Oriente, 1933. 392 p.

With extensive materials in French and Italian on the treaties of Sèvres and Lausanne.

J354
HERTSLET, Lewis.

Treaties &c Between Turkey and Foreign Powers, 1535-1855. London, Harrison & Sons, 1855. xv + 788 p.

Collection of texts in western languages by the then Keeper of [British] State Papers, published on behalf of H.M. Stationery Office.

J355
NORADOUNGHIAN, Gabriel.

Recueil d'Actes internationaux de l'Empire ottoman: 1300-1902. Paris, F. Pichon, 1897-1903. 4 vols. in 3.

Collection of treaties, conventions, arrangements, declarations, protocols, berats, etc. with foreign powers.

Reprinted on both paper and on microfiche in 1978.

J356
TESTA, Ignaz von, *Freiherr*.
Recueil des Traités de la Porte ottoman avec les Puissances étrangères Depuis le Premier Traité Conclu, en 1536, entre Suléyman I et François I Jusqu'à Nos Jours. Paris, Amyot/Muzard/ Ernest Leroux, 1864-1911. 11 vols.

Primarily texts of the treaties between France, Austria, and Turkey. Volumes IV-XI continued by his sons Alfred de Testa and Leopold de Testa. Each treaty is followed by an appendix of documents giving the textual diplomatic history of its subject matter. "Table analytique" in front and "Table chronologique" at the end of each volume.

Contents: France: I. 1536-1775; II. 1775-1863; III. 1841-53; IV. 1458-1853; Appendice, 1853-55; V. 1392-1868; VI. 1858-70; VII. 1862-74; VIII. 1869-94. Autriche: IX. 1606-1857; X. 1718-1868; XI. "Conventions télégraphiques et postales," 1857-1910.

Reprinted on microfiche in Wiesbaden.

J357
YOUNG, George, *Sir*.
Corps de Droit ottoman: recueil des codes, lois, règlements, ordonnances et actes les plus importants du droit intérieur, et d'études sur le droit coutumier de l'Empire ottoman. Oxford, Clarendon Press, 1905-6. 7 vols.

Yemen

J358
al-ḤIWĀLĪ, Muḥammad ibn ᶜAlī al-Akwaᵓ.
الوثائق السياسية اليمنية من قبيل الاسلام الى سنة ٣٣٢هـ
[Yemeni Diplomatic Documents from Pre-Islam to 332 A.H. (943-44 A.D.)]. Baghdad, Dār al-Harīya li-l-Ṭabāᶜa, 1396/1976. 317 p., illus.

Title transliterated: Al-Wathāᵓiq al-Siyāsīya al-Yamanīya...

J359
SALIM, Sayyid Muṣṭafā.
[Yemenite Documents: a study of historical documents]. وثائق يمنية، دراسة و ثائقية تاريخية Cairo, Al-Maṭbaᶜa al-Fanīya, 1982. 504 + i p., illus.

A collection of 52 documents of various types extending in date from 1045/1635 to 1337/1919. Each is given in a photographic copy, transcription, and detailed notes.

Title transliterated: Wathāʾiq Yamanīya,...

¶ Additional documents pertaining to the Near East are to be found in volumes XI and XIII of Charles Aitchison's *A Collection of Treaties,...* [J360].

South & Southeast Asia

South & Southeast Asia - General

J360
AITCHISON, Charles Umpherston, *Sir*.
A Collection of Treaties, Engagements, and Sanads Relating to India and Neighbouring Countries. *5th ed.* Calcutta, Government of India Central Publication Branch, 1929-33. 14 vols.

A valuable collection of primarily British documents for the history of Southeast Asia, the Near East, and parts of Central Asia up to nearly the time of printing.

Contents: Vol. I. Punjab, Punjab States and Delhi; Vol. II. United Provinces of Agra and Oudh, Bengal, Bihar, Orissa and The Central Provinces; Vol. III. Rajputana; Vol. IV. Central India Agency, Bhopal Agency and Southern States of Central and Malwa Agency; Vol. V. Central India (Bundelkhand and Baghelkhand and Gwalior); Vol. VI. Western India States and Baroda; Vol. VII. Bombay - Part I: The Peshwa, The Mahi Kantha Agency and The Rewa Khantha Agency; Vol. VIII. Bombay - Part II: Kaira Agency, Surat Agency, Thana Agency, Kolaba Agency, Shalapur Agency, Poona Agency, Satara Agency, Bijapur Agency, Belgaum Agency, Dharwar Agency, Nasik Agency, Kolhapur Residency and Southern Mahratra Country States Agency and The

Lapsed States; Vol. IX. Hyderabad, Mysore and Coorg; Vol. X. Madras and The Madras States; Vol. XI. Aden and The South Western Coast of Arabia, The Arab Principalities in the Persian Gulf, Muscat (Oman), Baluchistan and The Northwest Frontier Province; Vol. XII. Jammu and Kashmir, Sikkim, Assam and Burma; Vol. XIII. Persia and Afghanistan; XIV. Eastern Turkistan, Tibet, Nepal, Bhutan and Siam.

Photographically reprinted in Delhi in 1983.

India

J361
FOSTER, William, *Sir*.
The English Factories in India, 1618-[1669]: a calendar of documents in the India Office, British Museum and Public Record Office. Oxford, The Clarendon Press, 1906-[27]. 13 vols.

Each volume covers a specific period and was published independently. Of utmost importance for the study of English East India Company relations with not only the Muslim rulers of India, but also for its relations with those enroute.

J362
KHAN, Yusuf Husain.
Farmans and Sanads of فرامين و اسناد سلاطين دكن/ the Deccan Sultans. Hyderabad-Deccan, Central Records Office, Government of Andhra Pradesh, 1963. 43 + 39 p., illus.

Title transliterated: Farāmīn va Asnād Salaṭīn-i Dakkan.

J363
---.
Selected Documents of Aurangzeb's Reign, 1659-1706 A.D. Hyderabad-Deccan, Central Records Office, Government of Andhra Pradesh, 1958. xv, 243 + 18 p., illus.

J364
---.
Selected Waqai of the Deccan, 1660-1671 A.D. Hyderabad-Deccan, Central Records Office, Hyderabad Gov-

ernment, 1953.

J365
SHAN MOHAMMAD.
The Aligarh Movement: basic documents (1864-1898). Meerut, Meenakshi Prakashan, 1983. 3 vols.

J366
---.
The Indian Muslims: a documentary record, 1900-1947. Meerut, Meenakshi Prakashan, 1980- .

Volumes issued to date: I. Founding of the Muslim League; II. Separate Electorates; III. The Tripoli and Balkan Wars; IV. Mosque Incident & Communal Harmony; V. Interest in First World War; VI & VII. Khilafat Movement.

Indonesia

J367
CHIJS, Jacobus A. van der.
Nederlandsch-Indisch Plakaatboek, 1602-1811. Batavia, Landsdrukkerij, 1885-1900. 17 vols.

Bataviaasch Genootschap van Kunsten en Wetenschappen.

Collection of all government publications on the East Indies from 1602 to 1811. Vol. XVII: "Systematisch register."

J368
HEERES, Jan E. *and* STAPEL, Frederik W.
Corpus diplomaticum Neerlando-Indicum: verzameling van politieke contracten en verdere verdragen door de Nederlanders in het Oosten gesloten, van privilegebrieven aan hen verleend, enz. The Hague, Martinus Nijhoff, 1907-55. 6 vols.

J369
JONGE, Johan K. J. de *and* DEVENTER, Marinus L. van.
De Opkomst van het Nederlandsch Gezag in Oost-Indië: verzameling van onuitgegeven stukken uit het Oud-Koloniaal Archief. 's-Granvenhage-Amsterdam, Martinus Nijhoff, 1862-88. 13 vols.

Collection of source materials on the Dutch East India Company from 1595 to 1811, principally concerning Java. The first three volumes cover the years 1595-1610 in general. Volumes IV-XIII deal with Dutch rule over Java. An index for volumes I-VII was prepared by J. Neinsma ('s-Gravenhage-Amsterdam, 1875) and a complete index for all 13 volumes by J. W. G. van Haarst ('s-Gravenhage, 1888).

J370
TIELE, Pieter A. *and* HEERES, Jan E.
Die Opkomst van het Nederlandsch Gezag in Oost-Indië: bouwstoffen voor de geschiedenis der Nederlanders in den Maleischen Archipel. The Hague, Martinus Nijhoff, 1886-95. 3 vols.
Extension of Jonge and Deventer to cover the islands outside Java.

Europe

Serbia

J371
ELEZOVIĆ, Gliša.
Турски Споменици [Turkish Documents]. Belgrade, Srpska Kralevska Akademija, 1940-52. 2 vols.
Zbornik za Istočnjačku Istorisku.
Reproductions, with Serbian translations and French summaries, of 178 Ottoman documents pertaining to the Serbian province of the Empire preserved in the archives of the city of Dubrovnik and in the library of the Serbian Academy.
Title transliterated: Turski Spomenici.

Sicily

J372
CUSA, Salvatore.
I Diplomi greci ed arabi di Sicilia Pubblicati nel Testo originale. Palermo, Stabilmento Tipografia Lao, 1868-82. 1 vol. in 2, illus.
Editions and translations, illustrated with reproductions, of documents contained in the Sicilian archives. Only the first of the two projected volumes was published. Part two of the first volume was published in 1882.

Spain

J373
ALARCÓN Y SANTÓN, Maximiliano *and* GARCIA DE LINORES, Ramon.
Los Documents árabes diplomáticos del Archivo de la Córona de Aragón. Madrid, Escuela de Estudios Arabes, 1940. xi + 438 p.
Collection of edited and translated documents from the second half of the 13th to the first half of the 15th century preserved in the archives of Barcelona.

J374
SECO DE LUCENA, L.
Documentos arábigo-granadinos: edición critica del texto árabe y traducción al español con introducción, notas, glosarios e indices. Madrid, Instituto de Estudios Islámicos, 1961. L, 192, [iv], 8 plates + 189 p. Arabic text

Terms

J375
PAKALIN, Mehmet Zeki.
Osmanlı Tarıh Deyimleri ve Terimleri Sözlüğü. [Dictionary of Ottoman Historical Phrases and Technical Terms]. Istanbul, Millî Eğitim Basımevı, 1946-56. 3 vols.
Ottoman administrative terms and usages derived from materials within the Ottoman archives. Each term is given in both the Arabic script and in modern Turkish.

Statistics

J376
McCARTHY, Justin.
The Arab World, Turkey, and the Balkans 1878-1914: a handbook of historical statistics. Boston, G. K. Hall, 1982. XXX + 309 p.
Statistical tables translated from Ottoman Government publications and from the Ottoman archives.
Contents: I. Administrative Subdivisions; II. Climate; III. Population; IV. Medical; V. Education; VI. Justice; VII. Money; VIII. Government Income; IX. Government Expenditures; X. Manufacturing; XI. Transportation; XII. Foreign Trade;

XIII. Minerals; XIV. Agriculture; XV. Animal Husbandry.

EPIGRAPHY

General

J377

COMBE, Etienne; SAUVAGET, Jean; WIET, Gaston, *et. al.* Répertoire chronologique d'Epigraphie arabe. Cairo, Institut Français d'Archéologie Orientale, 1931- .

An attempt to compile a catalogue of all of the Arabic inscriptions of the classical period from Spain to India in a single chronological order. Includes those previously published and some not published but communicated to the compilers.

Each inscription is presented in the Arabic script and in French translation. Brief annotations provide provence, purpose, style of writing, and a bibliography.

Contents [to date]: T. I. 22-243 A.H.; T. II. 243-285 A. H.; T. III. 285-320 A.H.; T. IV. 320-354 A.H.; T. V. 354-386 A.H.; T. VI. 386-425 A.H.; T. VII. 425-485 A.H.; T. VIII. 485-550 A.H.; T. IX. 550-601 A.H.; T. X. 601-626 A.H.; T. XI. 626-653 A.H.; T. XII. 653-680 A.H.; T. XIII. 680-705 A.H.; T. XIV. 706-731 A.H.; T. XV. 731-746 A.H.; T. XVI. 746-764 A.H.; T. XVII. 762-783 A.H.

Monik Kervran, Solange Ory *and* Madeleine Schneider have compiled a very useful geographical index to the *RCEA*. *Index géographique du Répertoire chronologique d'Epigraphie arabe (Tomes I à XVI)*. Cairo, Institut Français d'Archéologie Orientale du Caire, 1975. XVI + 164 p. [dbl. col.]. *Bibliothèque d'Etude, T. LXVIII*. Published under the auspices of the Centre d'Epigraphie arabe de l'Ecole pratique des Hautes etudes (IVe section) in Paris. Employing both classical and modern sources each geographical name found in the inscriptions published in the *RCEA* through volume XVI has been identified and notation is given in which inscription(s) the name is to be found.

J378

DODD, Erica Cruikshank *and* KHAIRALLAH, Shereen. The Image of the Word: a study of Quranic verses in

Islamic architecture. Beirut, American University of Beirut Press, 1981. 2 vols.

Volume two consists of three indices to the Qur>ānic inscriptions employed in public buildings constructed during the classical period: 1) Index of Qur>ānic Verses Employed; 2) Geographical Location of Monument; 3) Location of Inscription Within the Structure.

Algeria

J379

COLIN, G. *and* MERCIER, G.

Corpus des Inscriptions arabes et turques de l'Algérie. Paris, Leroux, 1901-2. 2 vols., illus.

Publication of the inscriptions with detailed annotations.

Contents: T.I. Département d'Alger [by G. Colin]; T.II. Département de Constantine [by G. Mercier].

Egypt

J380

BERCHEM, Max van *and* WIET, Gaston.

Matériaux pour un Corpus inscriptionum arabicorum. Paris, Leroux/Cairo, Institut Français d'Archéologie Orientale, 1894-1930. 2 vols., illus.

Compilation of the inscriptions of Cairo with detailed annotations. Issued in fasciculus.

Contents: Ire pt. Egypte: I. Le Caire [by Max van Berchem, 1894-1903]; II. Supplément [by Gaston Wiet, 1929-30].

India

J381

AHMAD, Qeyamuddin.

Corpus of Arabic and Persian Inscriptions of Bihar (A.H. 640-1200). Patna, K. P. Jayaswal Research Institute, 1973. xxxiii, 418 + 77 p., illus.

Historical Research Series, Vol. X.

Very detailed examination of 196 epigraphs found in the modern state of Bihar dating between July 1242 and 1786 A.D. Only religious texts without dates and inscriptions on moveable objects have been omitted. Each is presented with introductory notes, transcription, and transliteration and reproduced photographically.

J382
AHMED, Shamsud Din.
Inscriptions of Bengal. Rajshahi, Varendra Research Museum, 1960. 338 p.

J383
BHAVNAGAR. Antiquarian Department.
Corpus inscriptionum Bhavnagari: being a selection of Arabic and Persian inscriptions collected by the Antiquarian Department, Bhavnagar State. Bombay, Printed at the Education Society's Steam Press, Byculla, 1889. 57 p.

J384
CALCUTTA. Indian Museum.
الفهرست الجامع للنقوش العربية و الفارسية فى المتحف الهندى، كلكتة / Catalogue of Arabic and Persian Inscriptions in the Indian Museum, Calcutta. *Comp.* Chinmoy Dutt. Calcutta, Indian Museum, 1967. 72 p., illus.

Monograph No. 2.

Twenty-one plates illustrating the inscriptions, accompanied by the texts in Arabic script with English translations, with bibliography.

J385
CHAUDHURI, Sibadas.
Bibliography of Studies in Indian Epigraphy (1926-50). Baroda, Oriental Institute, 1966. x + 113 p.

Author listing of published books and articles on the Hindu, Buddhist, and Muslim inscriptions of the entire Indian sub-continent. Subject index.

J386
DANI, Ahmad Hasan.
Bibliography of the Muslim Inscriptions of Bengal (down to A.D. 1538). Dacca, Asiatic Society of Bengal, 1957. ix + 147 p.

A *répertoir*, rather than a bibliography, of the inscriptions arranged by rulers. Issued as an appendix to the *Journal of the Asiatic Society of Bengal*.

Contents: Sec. A- Analysis of the Inscriptions;

Sec. B- Study of the Inscriptions; Sec. C- Muslim Sultans in Sanscrit Sources.

J387
DENISON-ROSS, E.; HOROWITZ, J. *and* YAZDANI, G.
Epigraphia indo-moslemica. Calcutta, Superintendent Government Printing, 1908-54. 18 vols., illus.

Publication of the Persian Muslim inscriptions of India in specialized, detailed, illustrated articles. Issued as an irregular supplement to *Epigraphia indica.*

Issuance: 1907-8 (1908); 1909-10 (1912); 1911-12 (1914); 1913-14 (1917); 1915-16 (1919); 1917-18 (1921); 1919-20 (1924); 1921-22 (N.D.); 1923-24 (N.D.); 1925-26 (N.D.); 1927-28 (1931); 1929-30 (1932); 1931-32 (1935); 1933-34 (1935); 1935-36 (1939); 1937-38 (1941); 1939-40 (1950); 1949-50 (1954).

A partial index to the inscriptions published is by V. S. Bendrey. *A Study of Muslim Inscriptions, with special reference to the inscriptions published in the* Epigraphia indo-moslemica, *1907-1938, together with summaries of inscriptions chronologically arranged.* Bombay, Karnatak Publishing House, [1944]. [vii] + 197 p.

Since 1956 published as *Epigraphia indica, Arabic and Persian Supplement.* New Delhi, Department of Archaeology, 1956- . Volumes issued: 1951-52 (1956); 1953-54 (1957); 1957-58 (1961); 1959-60 (1962)

Iran

J388
Corpus inscriptionum iranicarum.
London, Lund Humphries, 1977- .

An ambitious attempt to publish in portfolio and text volumes, issued irregularly, all of the inscriptions on stone, etc., from the earliest times by locale. For the Islamic inscriptions the following volumes have been issued to date: Part 4: Persian Inscriptions Down to the Early Safavid Period: Vol. II: Korasan Province - Pt. 1, ed. by W. L. Hanaway. 1977. 24 plates. Vol. VI: Mazandaran Province - Pt. 1: Eastern Mazandaran, ed. by A. D. H. Bivar and Ehsan Yarshater. 1978.

72 plates.

¶ For additional inscriptions in Farsi see Bert G. Fragner, *Repertorium persischer Herrschaftsurkunden:...* [J277].

Morocco

J389
BEL, Alfred.
Inscriptions arabes de Fès. Paris, Leroux, 1919. 3, 1 + 420 p., illus.
Survey of the Arabic inscriptions of Fez, with necessary annotations on each. Illustrated with 82 plates. Previously published in parts in the *Journal Asiatique*, 11me sèr., IX, X, XII, XIII, and XV (1917-19).

J390
DEVERDUN, Gaston.
Inscriptions arabes de Marrakech. Rabat, Editorial Techniques Nord-Africaines, 1956. XXXVI + 296 p., illus.
Publication of the classical Arabic inscriptions with French translations and annotations. Illustrated with 25 plates.

Spain

J391
LEVI-PROVENÇAL, E.
Inscriptions arabes d'Espagne. Leiden, E. J. Brill/ Paris, Larose, 1931. 2 vols., illus.
Important collection of the Arabic inscriptions of Muslim Spain from the conquest to 1492, arranged by province. Each inscription is printed in the Arabic script, with a French translation, and provided with notes giving provence, purpose, style of writing, size, date, and material. The second volume contains 44 plates illustrating the more important of the inscriptions described.

Syria & Palestine

J392
BERCHEM, Max van; HERZFELD, Ernst E. *and* SOBERNHEIM, Moritz.
Matériaux pour un Corpus inscriptionum arabicorum.

Cairo, Institut Français d'Archéologie Orientale, 1909-56. 5 vols., illus.

Compilation of the inscriptions of the important Muslim cities of Syria and Palestine, with detailed annotations.

Contents: IIme pt. Syrie du Nord: [I] Akkar, Hisn al-Akrad, Tripoli [by Moritz Sobernhem. 1909]; [II] Inscriptions et Monuments d'Alep [2 vols. by Ernst E. Herzfeld. 1954-56]; Syrie du Sud: I. Jérusalem (ville), II. Jérusalem (haram), III. Jérusalem [2 vols. by Max van Berchem. 1920-27].

J393
MOAZ, Khaled *and* ORY, Solange.
Inscriptions arabes de Damas: les stèles funéraires. Damascus, Institut Français d'Etudes Arabes de Damas, 1977- .

Contents: T.I- Cimetière d'Al-Bab al-Sagir.

Tunisia

J394
ROY, Bernard *and* POINSSOT, Paule.
Inscriptions arabes de Kairouan. Paris, Klincksiech, 1950-58. 624 p., illus.

Collection of the Arabic inscriptions, with translations, annotations, and 98 illustrations. Issued in parts as a publication of the Institut des Hautes études de Tunis.

J395
ZBISS, Slimane Mostafa.
Corpus des Inscriptions arabes de Tunisie. Tunis, Imprimerie S.A.P.I., 1955- .

Publication, with annotations and illustrations, of the important Muslim centers of Tunisia. A publication of the Direction des Antiquities et Arts de Tunisie.

Contents: I. pt. 1. Inscriptions de Tunis et sa Banlieue (1955); pt. 2. Inscriptions du Garjani (1962); II. Inscriptions de Monastir (1960).

Turkey

J396
BERCHEM, Max van *and* EDHEM, Halil.

Matériaux pour un Corpus inscriptionum arabicorum. Cairo, Institut Français d'Archéologie Orientale, 1910. viii + 110 p., illus.

Annotated and illustrated compilation of the Arabic inscriptions of Sivas and Divrigi.

Contents: IIIme pt. Asie mineure.

J397
HUART, Clement.
"Epigraphie arabe d'Asie mineure." *Revue Semitique*, II, 1894, pp. 61-75, 120-34, 235-41, 324-32; III, 1895, pp. 73-85, 175-82, 214-18, 344-71.

J398
MANTRAN, Robert.
"Les Inscriptions arabes de Brousse." *Bulletin d'Etudes Orientales*, XIV, 1954, pp. 87-114.

Detailed discussion of 48 Arabic inscriptions found in Brusa.

PALAEOGRAPHY

J399
ABBOTT, Nabia.
The Rise of the North Arabian Script and Its Kurɔānic Development, with a full description of the Kurɔān manuscripts in the Oriental Institute. Chicago, University of Chicago Press, 1939. xxii + 103 p.

Oriental Institute Publications, L.

Contents: 1- Rise and Development of the North Arabian Script; 2- Development of Specific Scripts.

J400
ARBERRY, Arthur John.
Specimens of Arabic and Persian Palaeography, selected and annotated. London, India Office, 1939. viii p. + 48 plates.

Selected from among the manuscripts in the India Office Library.

J401
FEKETE, Lajos.
Die Siyāqat-schrift in der türkischen Finanzverwalt: beitrage zur türkischen paläographie mit 104 tafeln. *Trans.* A. Jacobi. Budapest, Akadémiai Kiadó, 1955. 2 vols.

Manual for the script employed in the Ottoman financial records, with numerous examples of documents and notes.

Contents: B. 1- Einleitung. Textproben; B. 2- Faksimiles.

J402
GROHMANN, Adolf.
Arabische Paläographie. Vienna, Hermann Böhlaus Nachf., 1967-71. 2 vols., illus.

Österreichische Akademie der Wissenschaften, Philosophische-Historische Klasse: Denkschriften, 94. Band, 1 & 2 Abhandlung. Forschungen zur Islamischen Philologie und Kulturgeschichte, Bd. I & II.

The most detailed study yet published on Arabic palaeography and calligraphy.

Contents: B. I: I. Einleitung; II. Beschreibstoffe; III. Die Schreibgeräte; Die Tinte. Indices. B. II: Das Schriftwesen. Die Lapidarschrift: I. Einleitung; II. Die Lapidarschrift. Indices.

J403
HAZAI, Georg.
Einführung in die persische Paläographie: 101 persische dokumente. Budapest, Akadémiai Kiadó, 1977. 594 p., illus.

A detailled discussion of Persian diplomatics and palaeography with the documents presented in facsimili, in Arabic script and German translation. Illustrated with 242 examples.

J404
MORITZ, Bernard.
Arabic Palaeography: a collection of Arabic texts from the first century of the Hidjra till the year 1000. Cairo, National Press, 1905. 188 plates.

Publications of the Khedivial Library, 16.

Examples of Arabic calligraphic styles as illustrated in the papyri and manuscript collections of the Egyptian National Library. No text.

J405
SCHIMMEL, Annemarie.

Islamic Calligraphy. Leiden, E. J. Brill, 1970. xi + 31 p., illus.

Scholarly discussion of the history of the Arabic script, its multitude of styles, and its place as an art form. Illustrated with 48 plates and 76 figures.

J406

STOJANOW, Valery.

Die Entstehung und Entwicklung der osmanisch-türkischen Paläographie und Diplomatik, mit einer bibliographie. Berlin, Klaus Schwarz Verlag, 1983. v + 332 p.

Islamkundliche Untersuchungen, Bd. 76.

Summarization of the major handbooks and articles on the subject, together with an extensive bibliography. Additional bibliographic items in Turkish have been provided by Suraiya Faroqhi in her review published in the *International Journal of Middle East Studies*, 16, 1984, pp. 436-37.

J407

VAJDA, Georges.

Album de Paléographie arabe. Paris, Adrien-Maisonneuve, 1958. 94 plates.

Examples of the various styles and development of Arabic calligraphy as represented in the manuscript collection of the Bibliothèque Nationale in Paris. No descriptive text.

Contents: I. Coufique; II. Syrie; III. Iraq; IV. Egypte; V. Espagne; VI. Afrique du Nord; VII. Soudan; VIII. Iran; IX. Turquie, Anatolie; X. Transoxiane; XI. Yemen; XII. Indes.

NUMISMATICS

J408

CODRINGTON, Oliver.

Manual of Musulman Numismatics. London, Royal Asiatic Society, 1904. viii + 239 p.

Royal Asiatic Society Monograph No. 7.

Although inadequate and now out-of-date remains the only introduction to a difficult subject.

J409

MAYER, Louis A.

Bibliography of Moslem Numismatics, India excepted. *2nd ed.* London, Royal Asiatic Society, 1954. IX + 283 p.

Oriental Translation Fund, XXXV.

Author listing of 2,092 books and articles on the coinages and weights of the classical Islamic world from Spain through Afghanistan. Index of dynasties, subjects, and rulers.

Additions and corrections by A. Kmietowicz, "Supplement to L. Mayer's *Bibliography of Moslem Numismatics*," *Folia Orientalia*, II, 1960, pp. 259-75.

J410

SCHAENDLINGER, Anton C.

Osmanische Numismatik von den Anfängen des osmanischen Reiches bis zu Seiner auflösung 1922. Braunschweig, Klinkhardt & Biermann, 1973. 178 p., illus.

Illustrated with 17 plates of coins.

J411

SINGHAL, C. R.

Bibliography of Indian Coins: Part II (Muhammadan and Later Series). Bombay, The Numismatic Society of India, 1952. vi + 218 p.

This work thus contains the material not included in Mayer.

Contents: (A) Sulṭāns of Delhī; (B) Kings of Bengal; (C) Kashmir; (D) The Bahmanīs; (E) Sulṭāns of Jaunpur; (F) Sulṭāns of Gujarāt; (G) Sulṭāns of Mālwa; (H) ᶜĀdil Shāhi Dynasty of Bījāpur; (I) Niāẓm Shāhi Dynasty of Aḥmednagar; (Ia) Quṭb-Shāhi Dynasty of Golconda; (J) Barid Shāhi Dynasty of Bidar; (K) Fārūqi Kings of Khandish; (L) Sulṭāns of Maᶜbar; (M) Muhammadan (miscellaneous); (N) Mughal Emperors of India; (O) Governors of Sind; (P) Durrānis; (Q) Native States of India; (R) Sikhs; (S) Nawābs of Awadh; (T) Coins of Mysore; (U) East India Company; (V) Indo-Portuguese; (W) Indo-Danish; (X) Coins of Malay; (Y) Andaman Islands; (Z) Māldīves Islands; Sāssanian Coins. Bibliography of Reference Books. Indices of authors, rulers and dynasties, and mints.

J412

---.
Mint-towns of the Mughal Emperors of India. Bombay, Numismatic Society of India, 1953. iii + 51 p.

A detailed list of the mint-towns of India in alphabetical order employed by the Mughals. Based upon a thorough study of the coinage the author is enabled to provide the dates each town was employed and the types of coins struck in each by the individual emperors.

J413
ZAMBAUR, Edward Karl Max von.
Die Münzprägungen des Islams: zeitlich und örtlich geordnet. *Ed.* P. Jaeckel. Wiesbaden, F. Steiner Verlag, 1968- .

Reference guide to all known mint towns of the classical Islamic world.

Contents: B. I. Der Westen und Osten bis zum Indus, mit synoptischen tabellen.

GEOGRAPHY K

BIBLIOGRAPHIES

Egypt

K1
LORIN, Henri, *ed.*
Bibliographie géographique de l'Egypte. Cairo, Société Royale de Géographie d'Egypte, 1928-29. 2 vols.
Classified listings of a total of 8,841 books, articles, reports, pamphlets, etc., on the land and people of Egypt from the most ancient times to the first quarter of the 20th century. Author and title index in each volume. A valuable compilation.
Contents: T. I: Géographie physique et Géographie humaine [*Comps*. Henriette Agrel, Georges Hug, Jean Lazach *and* René Morin]; T. II: Géographie historique [*Comp*. Henri Munier].

Iran

K2
GANJĪ, Muḥammad Ḥasan.
[Index of Articles on Geography]. فهرست مقالات جغرافیای Tehran, Danishkad-a Adabiyāt, 1341-/1962- .
Listing by country, region, province, or city of 9,243 Farsi language articles published from the beginning of printing in that language to *cir.* 1960-61. Indices of authors, titles, and places. Consists primarily of materials on Iranian geography.
Title transliterated: Fihrist-i Maqālāt Jughrāfīyā-ī.

K3
PETROV, M. P.

Библиография по Географии Ирана: указатель литературы на Русском языке (1720-1954). [Bibliography of Iranian Geography: a guide to literature in the Russian language (1720-1954)]. Ashkhabad, Izdatel'stvo Akademii Nauk Turkmenskoi, SSR, 1955. 234 + [iii]p., illus., maps.

Title also in Turkic in transliteration.

Annotated, alphabetical listing of 960 books and articles published during the period. Indices of proper names, subjects, and locations of publication. The illustrations are photographs of texts or title pages. The maps are folded in end pocket.

Title transliterated: Bibliografii͡a po Geografii Irana:...

Iraq

K4
ᶜAWWĀD, Kūrkīs.
["What Has "ما طبع عن بلدان العراق باللغة العربية" Been Printed on the Country of Iraq in the Arabic Language."]. *Sumer*, IX, 1953, pp. 63-97; X, 1954, pp. 40-72.

Bibliography of books and articles on the geography, particularly historical, of Iraq listed by towns and cities.

Title transliterated: Mā Tabᶜᶜan Buldān al-ᶜIrāq bi-l-Lugha al-ᶜArabīya.

Turkey

K5
TRAK, Selçuk.
Türkiye Coğrafya Eserleri: genel bibliyografyası [Geographical Works on Turkey]. Ankara, Uzluk Basımevi, 1942. 272 p.

List of works in Ottoman and modern Turkish and in western languages on the geography of Turkey printed between 1595 and 1941. Arranged by subject and by district of contemporary Turkey.

K6
TÜRKAY, Cevdet.
İstanbul Kütüphanelerinde Osmanlı'lar Devrine aid Türkçe - Arapca - Farsça Yazma ve Basma Coğrafya Eserleri Bibliyoğrafyası [Bibliography of Turkish,

Arabic, and Persian Manuscript and Printed Works of the Ottoman Period on Geography in the Libraries of Istanbul]. Istanbul, Maarif Basımevi, 1958. [ii] + 94 p.

Listed according to the library in which they are housed. No index.

ATLASES & CHARTS

Atlases & Maps

Bibliographies

General

K7

HALE, Gerry A.

"Maps and Atlases of the Middle East." *Middle East Studies Association Bulletin*, III, 3, Oct. 1969, pp. 17-39.

Although now dated this comparatively brief article is a good introduction to the subject both in the availability, and non-availability, of maps. Included is a very useful list of "Addresses of Mapping Agencies" in the United States, Europe, the Middle East, and North Africa.

Arabian Peninsula

K8

TIBBETTS, G. R.

Arabia in Early Maps: a bibliography of maps covering the Peninsula of Arabia printed in western Europe from the invention of printing to the year 1751. Naples, The Falcon Press/London, The Oleander Press, 1978. 175 p., illus.

Provides full details of 281 maps listed by date of publication. Illustrated with 22 reproductions in color and sepia.

Palestine

K9

RÖRICHT, REINHOLD.

Bibliotheca geographica Palaestinae: chronologisches verzeichniss der auf die geographie des heiligen landes bezüglichen literature von 333 bis 1878 und versuch einer cartographie. Berlin, H. Reuther's

Verlagsbuchhandlung, 1890. XX + 742 p.

In addition to a bibliography of traveler's accounts the work lists 747 maps of Palestine made during the period.

Atlases

General

K10

BRICE, William C.

Historical Atlas of Islam. Leiden, E. J. Brill, 1981. 71 p., maps.

Atlas volume containing 70 colored maps to accompany the second edition of the *Encyclopaedia of Islam* illustrating the historical development of the faith. Index.

K11

CORNU, Georgette.

Atlas du Monde arabo-islamique à l'Epoque classique IXe - Xe siécles: repertoires des toponymes des cartes I à VI. Leiden, E. J. Brill, 1983. xiv + 92 p., maps.

Historical gazetteer of the names of the provinces, their subdivisions, cities and towns, and natural features as they are given in the volumes of the Arabic geographers and travelers published in the series *Bibliotheca Geographorum Arabicorum*, *i.e.*, al-Iṣṭakhrī, Ibn Ḥawqāl, Muqaddasī, Ibn al-Faqīh, Ibn Khurdadhbih, Qudāma, Ibn Rustah, Yaᶜqūbī, and al-Masᶜūdī. All places are located on the six folding maps and references are made to the appropriate volumes in the *BGA*, to Yāqūt's *Muᶜjam al-Buldān* and to the *Encyclopaedia of Islam*.

K12

HAZARD, Harry W.; COOKE, H. Lester, Jr. *and* SMILEY, J. McA.

Atlas of Islamic History. Princeton, New Jersey, Princeton University Press, 1951. 49 p., maps.

Princeton Oriental Series, Vol. 12.

One of the first historical atlases of Islam covering the period from the 1st/7th - 13th/20th century. The same basic map is used throughout extending from Iran to Spain with line and color changes to indicate variations in historical context. Map and text on opposing pages. Two pages of maps (four total) illustrate Islam in India and the Far East. Conversion table for dates and geographical index. Pages measure 28x 36 cm.

K13
KINGSBURY, Robert C. *and* POUNDS, Norman J. G.
An Atlas of Middle Eastern Affairs. London, Methuen & Co., Ltd., 1964. vi, [ii] + 117 p.
Treatment of the historical, geographical, economic, national and cultural trends within the Near East from ancient times to the present in both text and 58 line maps. Pages measure 20½x 12½ cm.

K14
McEVEDY, Colin.
The Penguin Atlas of Medieval History. Harmondsworth, Penguin Books Ltd., 1961. 96 p., maps.
A relatively inexpensive handbook for students consisting of 38 black, white, and blue maps, each measuring 14x19 cm., illustrating the political, religious, and economic history of Europe, North Africa, and the Near East from 362 - 1478 A. D. Each map is accompanied by a brief historical introduction.

K15
REICHERT, Rolf.
Atlas histórico regional do Mundo árabe (mapas e resumo cronológico)/A Historical and Regional Atlas of the Arabic World (maps and chronological survey). Salvador, Brazil, Universidade Federal de Bahia, Centro de Estudios Afro-Orientais, [1969]. 204 p., maps.
Outline historical maps for the Fertile Crescent, the Arabian Peninsula, and North Africa. Each is prefaced by an introductory historial text and with genealogical tables. No index.

K16
ROBINSON, Francis.
Atlas of the Islamic World Since 1500. Oxford,

Phaidon Press/New York, Facts on File, 1982. 240 p., maps, illus.

With 47 maps and *cir.* 400 illustrations, with historical text.

K17
ROOLVINK, R.
Historical Atlas of the Muslim Peoples. Amsterdam, Djambatan, 1957. X + 38 p. of maps.

Small format atlas of colored maps illustrating Muslim history from 612 B.C. to the 20th century.

Africa

K18
FAGE, J. D.
An Atlas of African History. *2nd ed.* London, Edward Arnold (Publishers) Ltd., 1963. 64 p.

A student's atlas of 62 line maps illustrating the political and economic history of the African continent from the earliest times to the present. No index.

K19
KLEMP, Egon.
Africa on Maps Dating from the Twelfth to the Eighteenth Century. Leipzig, Edition Leipzig, 1968. 77 plates.

Published on behalf of the Deutsche Staatsbibliothek Berlin.

Reproductions in color and half-tone with separate booklet of descriptions. Large folio volume.

K20
GAILEY, Harry A., Jr.
The History of Africa in Maps. Chicago, Denoyer-Geppert Co., 1967. 96 p.

Forty-six black and white outline maps of the history of Africa south of the Sahara from prehistory to 1967. Includes climatic, botanical, sociological, and linguistic maps.

India

K21
DAVIES, C. Collin.
An Historical Atlas of the Indian Peninsula. *2nd ed.* Madras, Oxford University Press, 1959. 97 p.
Physical, economic, political, and historical atlas of the Indian sub-continent from *cir.* 500 B.C. to 1947. Consists of 48 black and white line maps (each 15x20 cm.), with accompanying one page texts and brief bibliographies. Map nos. 15, 16, 17, 18, 19, 20, 21, 22, 24, 25, 26, 27, 28, 29, 32, 34, 35, and 48 are useful for the study of Muslim India through partition.

K22
GOLE, Susan.
India Within the Ganges. New Delhi, Jaya Prints, 1983. 239 p., maps.
A detailed discussion of the maps of India from 1477 to 1800, *i.e.*, up to the accurate surveys, illustrated with 125 pages of maps, some in color. Index and bibliography.

K23
HABIB, Irfan.
Atlas of the Mughal Empire: political and economic maps with detailed notes, bibliography and index. New Delhi, Oxford University Press, 1982. 184 p., maps.
Excellently produced 32 detailed black and white line maps in fairly large format with 70 pages of notes and an extensive name and subject index. A very useful volume for the study.

K24
SCHWARTZBURG, Joseph E.
An Historical Atlas of South Asia. Chicago, University of Chicago Press, 1978. xxxix + 352 p., maps.
The Association for Asian Studies, Reference Series No. 2.
A misnomer for a very handsome and useful folio volume on the political and economic history of the Indian sub-continent from pre-history to the present. The numerous colored maps are very detailed and include maps of towns and cities. The historical text occupies pages 151-352 in triple

column.

A beautiful example of atlas production.

Indonesia

K25

AMSTERDAM. Nederlandsch Aardrijkskundig Genootschap. Atlas van Tropisch Nederland. Batavia, Reproductiebedrijf van den Topografischen Dienst in Ned.-Indië, 1938. 37 maps.

Geographical, political, and historical atlas of the Indonesian archipelago.

Iran

K26

NAṢR, Seyyid Hossein; MOSTOFI, Aḥmad *and* ZARYAH, Abbās, *eds.*

Historical Atlas of Iran. Tehran, Tehran University, 1350/1971. [63] p., maps.

Issued in commemoration of the 2,500th anniversary of Iran the 27 colored maps (two folding) provide the names of the major cities, many minor ones, political boundaries, provinces, etc., in Farsi and English or French. Each map has introductory historical text in Farsi, English and French. Index of place names.

Iraq

K27

SŪSA, Aḥmad.

[Atlas of Baghdad: اطلس بغداد : تاريخي و جغرافي historical and geographical]. Baghdad, Maṭbaᶜa al-Musāḥa, 1952. 32 p.

With line maps and descriptive text.

Title transliterated: Aṭlas Baghdād: taʾrīkhī wa jughrāfī.

Ottoman Empire

K28

PITCHER, Donald Edgar.

An Historical Geography of the Ottoman Empire from Earliest Times to the End of the Sixteenth Century. Leiden, E. J. Brill, 1973. 171 p., maps.

Detailed historical narrative of the expansion of the Turks in Asia Minor, Europe, and the Near East to 1606 with 36 colored large-scale maps and

29 pull-outs of the regions and on important smaller areas. Index of all geographical names with their equivalents in the local languages.

Contents: I. Historical Background; II. Foundation of the Ottoman Empire; III. Conquests of Murad I and Bayezid I (1362-1402); IV. Recovery after Ankara (1402-1451); V. Second Period of Expansion (1451-1502); VI. From Sultanate to Empire (1503-1520); VII. Climax and Breakdown of the Imperial Achievement (1520-1606); VIII. Political Geography of the Imperial Administration; IX. Ottoman Provinces in the 16th Century.

GAZETTEERS & DICTIONARIES

General

K29
BAHJAT, ᶜAlī.
قاموس الامكنة و البقاع التي يرد ذكرها في كتب الفتوح
[Lexicon of the Places and Sites Mentioned in the Books of the Conquests]. Cairo, Sharka Ṭabaᶜ al-Kutub al-ᶜArabīya, 1956. 3 + 216 p.

Gazetteer of the Islamic Empire based primarily upon al-Balādhurī's *Futūḥ al-Buldān*.

Title transliterated: Qamūs al-Amkina wa al-Biqāᶜ...

K30
al-BAGHDĀDĪ, ᶜAbd al-Muʾmin ibn ᶜAbd al-Ḥaqq (d. 739/1338-39).
[The Examining مراصد الاطلاع على اسماء الامكنة و البقاع Observatory upon the Names of Places and Locations]. *Ed.* ᶜAlī Muḥammad al-Bijāwī. Cairo, Dār Akhyāʾī al-Kutub al-ᶜArabīya, [1957]. 3 vols.

Abridgement of Yāqūt's *Muᶜjam al-Buldān* with many of the geographic and historical explanations omitted.

An earlier edition, by T. G. J. Juynboll, *Lexicon geographicum* (Leiden, 1860-64), in six volumes, was based upon a defective manuscript. F. Wüstenfeld provided, in his edition of Yāqūt (volume V, pp. 11-32), some additions to Juynboll's text from another manuscript. The Cairo edition is based upon a more complete text.

Title transliterated: Marāṣid al-Iṭṭilāᶜ ᶜala Asmāɔ al-Amkina wa al-Biqāᶜ.

K31
al-BAKRĪ, ᶜAbd Allāh ibn ᶜAbd al-ᶜAzīz (d. 487/1094). [Dictionary معجم الاستعجم من اسماء البلاد و المواضع of the Confusion in the Names of Countries and Places]. *Ed.* Muṣṭafā al-Saqā. Cairo, Maṭbaᶜa Lajna al-Tālīf wa al-Tarjama wa al-Nashr, 1364-71/1945-51. 4 vols.

Geographical dictionary of the Islamic Empire with short descriptions of each location, city, and town, by a Spanish Muslim geographer. Provides detailed explanations regarding pronunciation of proper names.

Title transliterated: Muᶜjam al-Istaᶜjam min Asmāɔ al-Bilād wa al-Mawāḍī .

K32
al-HIMYARĪ, Muḥammad ibn ᶜAbd al-Munᶜim (d. 900/1494). كتاب الروض المعطار فى خبر الاقطار (معجم جغرافى مع مسرد عام) [Book of the Perfumed Gardens in the Names of the Regions]. *Ed.* Iḥsān ᶜAbbās. Beirut, Maktaba Lubnān, 1975. 18, [ii] + 745 p. [dbl. col.].

Provides the names of the locales with short topographical information. Indices.

Title transliterated: Kitāb al-Rawḍ al-Miᶜṭār fī Khabar al-Aqṭār.

K33
YĀQŪT, Shihāb al-Dīn abī ᶜAbd Allāh (d. 626/1229). [Dictionary of the Countries]. معجم البلدان *Ed.* Ferdinand Wüstenfeld. *Jacut's geographisches Wörterbuch.* Leipzig, Otto Harrassowitz, 1866-73. 6 vols.

The most important of the classical geographical dictionaries with often lengthy descriptions of the regions, towns, and cities, including historical details.

A subject index to the work has been published by Oskar Rescher, *Sachindex zu Wüstenfeld's Ausgabe von Jâqûts* "Muᶜǧam el-Buldân" *nebst einem verzeichnis der darin angeführten werke* (Stuttgart, 1928).

Reprinted in Beirut, 1955-57, in 5 volumes.

Title transliterated: Muᶜjam al-Buldān.

K34
al-ZAMAKHSHARĪ, Maḥmūd ibn ᶜUmar (d. 538/1144).
[Book of Mountains, Places, كتاب الجبال و الامكنة والمياه and Waters]. *Ed.* Salverda de Grave. *Specimen e Literis orientalibus,...* . Leiden, E. J. Brill, 1856. 31 + 201 p.

A "bare bones" lexicon with limited information.

Reprinted in Najaf in 1938 and again in 1962.

Title transliterated: Kitāb al-Jibāl wa al-Amkina wa al-Miyāh.

Afghanistan

K35
ADAMEC, Ludwig W.
Historical and Political Gazetteer of Afghanistan. Graz, Akademische Druck- u. Verlagsamstalt, 1972- .

Re-edition of the British, formerly secret, *Gazetteer of Afghanistan*, with additional new material to 1970. Illustrated with numerous maps and genealogical tables.

Contents [to date]: Vol. I- Badakshan Province and Northeastern Afghanistan [1972]; Vol. II- Farah and Southwestern Afghanistan [1973]; Vol. III- Herat and Northwestern Afghanistan [1975]; Vol. IV- Mazar-i-Sharif and North-central Afghanistan [1979]; Vol. V- Kandahar and South-central Afghanistan [1980].

Arabian Peninsula

K36
al-ᶜAQĪLĪ, Muḥammad ibn Aḥmad ᶜĪsā.
[Geographical Dictionary of the Country of Saᶜūdī Arabia]. المعجم الجغرافي للبلاد العربية السعودية Riyad, Dār al-Yamāma al-Baḥth wa al-Tarjama wa al-Nashr, 1969. 2 vols.

Title transliterated: Al-Muᶜjam al-Jughrāfī li-l-Bilād al-ᶜArabīya al-Saᶜūdīya.

K37
al-JĀSIR, Ḥamad.
المعجم الجغرافى للبلاد العربية السعودية: شمال المملكة: امارات حايل والجوف وتبوك وعرعر والقريات
[Geographical Dictionary of the Country of Saᶜūdī Arabia:...]. Riyad, Dār al-Yamāma li-l-Baḥath wa

al-Tarjama wa al-Nashr, 1977- .

K38
LORIMER, J. G.
Gazetteer of the Persian Gulf, ᵓOmān, and Central Arabia. Calcutta, Superintendent Government Printing, 1908-15. 2 vols., maps.

Originally printed as a secret government document for use by officials of the Government of India. Reprinted in England in 1970 in six volumes.

Contents: Vol. I. Historical; Vol. II. Geographical and Statistical.

K39
SCOVILLE, S. A.
Gazetteer of Arabia: a geographical and tribal history of the Arabian Peninsula. Graz, Akademische Druck- u. Verlagsamstalt, 1979- .

Lists in alphabetical order the geographical features, cities, towns, and tribes of the Peninsula and gives a history and description of each entry. To be completed in four volumes. Regarded as out-dated and incomplete by some scholars.

Contents [to date]: Vol. I: A-E.

Egypt

K40
MASPERO, Jean *and* WIET, Gaston.
Matériaux pour Servir à la Géographie de l'Egypte: liste des provinces, villes et villages d'Egypte cités dans les tomes I et II des *Khitat* de Maqrîzî. Cairo, Institut Français d'Archéologie Orientale, 1914-19. VIII + 283 p.

Geographical dictionary in Arabic alphabetical order with names in Arabic script and French transliteration. Details for each location are derived from Arabic, Greek, and western sources.

Detailed indices: I.- Index geographique: A.- Arabe; B.- Français, Grec, Copte. II.- Index historique: A.- Arabe; B.- Français, Grec, Copte. III.- Index des Noms communs: A.- Arabe; B.- Français, Grec, Copte. IV.- Index chronologique: A.- Ere de l'Hégire; B.- Ere chrètienne.

K41
RAMZĪ, Muḥammad
القاموس الجغرافي البلاد المصرية، من عهد قدماء المصريين الى سنة ١٩٤٥
[Geographical Dictionary of the Country of Egypt: from the earliest times of Egypt until 1945]. Cairo, Maṭbaᶜa Dār al-Kutub al-Miṣrīya, 1953-63. 4 pts. in 2 vols.

Title transliterated: Al-Qāmūs al-Jughrāfī al-Bilād al-Miṣrīya:...

India

K42
DEY, Nundo Lal.
The Geographical Dictionary of Ancient and Medieval India. *2nd ed.* London, Luzac & Co., 1927. x + 262 p., line map.

Calcutta Oriental Series, No. 21.

A brief gazetteer of the towns, rivers, etc., of India in historical times in a single alphabetical order, with brief historical and geographical notes drawn from past and current authors. Descriptions are brief, albeit often interesting, but no attempt has been made to indicate position on the single map. Several reprints.

K43
MILBURN, William.
Oriental Commerce: a geographical description of the principal places in the East Indies, China, and Japan with their produce, manufactures and trade. *2nd ed.* Thomas Thornton. London, Kingsbury, l'Arbury and Allen, 1825. 3, 1 + 586 p., maps.

Twenty historical maps provide details. First printed in 1813.

K44
THORNTON, Edward.
A Gazetteer of the Territories Under the Government of the Viceroy of India. *Rev. & ed.* Sir Roper Lethbridge *and* Arthur N. Wollaston. London, W. H. Allen & Co., 1886. 2, 1 [vii] + 1070 p.

Records location, with latitude and longitude, of cities, towns, and villages.

Iran

K45
ADAMEC, Ludwig W.
Historical Gazetteer of Iran. Graz, Akademische Druck- u. Verlagsamstalt, 1976- .

Re-edition, with new material, of the formerly secret archival material compiled by the General Staff of British India. Illustrated with numerous maps.

Contents [to date]: Vol. I. Tehran and Northwestern Iran [1976]; Vol. II. Meshed and Northeastern Iran [1981].

K46
BARBIER DE MAYNARD, Charles A. C.
Dictionnaire géographique, historique et littéraire de la Perse et des Contrées adjacentes. Paris, Imprimerie Nationale/B. Duprat, 1861. xxi + 640 p.

Translations of the relevant articles in Yāqūt's *Muᶜjam al-Buldān* with additional material from later Muslim geographers. Arranged in Arabic alphabetical order.

Reprinted in Amsterdam in 1971.

K47
IRAN. Sitād-i Artish. Dāyirah-i Jughrāfiyā-ī.
[Geographical Dictionary of Iran, Its Villages]. فرهنگ جغرافيائي ايران، آباديها Tehran, Dayirah-i Jughrafiyā-ī, Sitād-i Artish, 1949-54. 10 vols., illus., maps.

Gazetteer of all the cities, towns, and villages of Iran, with detailed information about religion, language, people, and products. Prepared by the geographical section of the Iranian army general staff. Volumes one to nine edited by Ḥusayn ᶜAlī Razmara.

Title transliterated: Farhang Jughrāfīyā-ī Īrān, Ābādīhā.

K48
SCHWARZ, Paul von.
"Iran in Mittelalter nach den arabischen Geographen." *Quellen und Forschungen zur Erd- und Kulturkunde*. Leipzig, Heims, 1921. Vol. IV, pp. 289-511.

Arranged in alphabetical order.

K49
TOMASCHEK, Wilhelm.
Zur historischen Topographie von Persien. Osnabrück, Biblio- Verlag, 1972. 180 p., map.

Reprinted from *Sitzungsberichte der Philosophisch- Historischen Classe der Kaiserlichen Akademie der Wissenschaften zu Wien*, B. 102, 1883, pp. 145-211; B. 108, 1885, pp. 561-652.

Lebanon

K50
FURAYḤA, Anīs.
معجم اسماء المدن و القرى اللبنانية و تفسير معانيها، دراسة لغوية
[Dictionary of the Names of the Towns and Villages of Lebanon, with an explanation of the meaning of (their names), a lexicographical study]. *2nd ed.* Beirut, Maktaba Lubnān, 1972. xlii + 189 p.

Each name is fully vocalized and transliterated into the Latin alphabet.

Title transliterated: Muᶜjam Asmāɔ al-Mudun wa al-Qurā al-Lubnānīya...

K51
ḤANNĀ, Wadīᶜ Niqūlā.
قاموس لبنان، يشتمل على اسماء مدن و قرى جمهورية لبنان مرتبا بشكل قاموس مع تفصيل واف عن عدد سكان كل واحدة منها ولاية مديرية و محافظة تتبع مع وصف معاهدها و تجارتها و حاصلاتها و من اشتهر منها رجلا و نساء
[Gazetteer of Lebanon...]. Beirut, Maṭbaᶜa al-Salām, 1927. 8 + 263 p.

Title transliterated: Qāmūs Lubnān,...

Libya

K52
al-ZĀWĪ, Al-Ṭāhir Aḥmad.
معجم البلدان الليبية
[Dictionary of the Country of Libya]. Tripoli, Maktaba al-Nūr, 1968. 292 p., illus.

Title transliterated: Muᶜjam al-Buldān al-Lībīya.

Morocco

K53
BANᶜID ALLĀH, ᶜAbd al-ᶜAzīz.

الموسوعة المغربية للاعلام البشرية و الحضارية:
Villes et Tribus. معلمة المدن و القبائل/
Muhammadiya, Morocco, Maṭbaᶜa Faḍāla, 1397/1977.
389 p. [dbl. col.].

Alphabetical dictionary of the tribes and towns of Morocco and Muslim Spain based upon classical Arabic and modern sources.

Title transliterated: Al-Mawsūᶜa al-Maghribīya li-l-ᶜAlām al-Bashrīya wa al-Ḥaḍarīya:...

Palestine

K54

MARMARDJI, A. S.

Textes géographiques arabes sur la Palestine; recueillis, mis en ordre alphabetique et traduits en Français. Paris, Librairie Lecoffre J. Gabalda et Cie., 1951. XVII + 267 p.

Descriptions of the provinces, cities, and towns of greater Palestine, in Arabic alphabetical order, as they existed in the classical Islamic period. Translated from the works of 28 Arabic geographers and historians writing between 864 and 1730.

Syria

K55

DUSSAUD, René.

Topographie historique de la Syrie antique et médiévale. Paris, Paul Geuthner, 1927. lii + 632 p., illus.

Geographical and historical dictionary of the provinces, cities, and towns of Syria based upon original sources and illustrated wtih 16 folding maps.

K56

LeSTRANGE, Guy.

Palestine Under the Moslems; a description of Syria and the Holy Land from A.D. 650 to 1500. London, Palestine Pilgrims Text Society, 1890. XVI + 604 p.

Geographical and historical description of Islamic Syria and Palestine derived from contemporary sources. Reprinted in Beirut in 1965 with an introduction by Walid Khalidy.

Turkey

K57
MOSTRAS, C.
Dictionnaire géographique de l'Empire ottoman. St. Petersbourg, Academia Scientiarum Imperialis, 1873. xii + 241 p.
Drawn from the sources of the time.

K58
RIFAᶜT, Aḥmad.
لغات تاريخيه و جغرافيه· حروف هجا ترتيبى اوزره
[Dictionary of History and Geography]. Istanbul, Maḥmūd Maṭbaᶜa, 1299-1300/1881-82. 7 vols.
Title transliterated: Lughāt Taʾrīkhīye ve Coğrāfıye...

¶ A geographical vocabulary on the Ottoman Empire is also to be found in Barbier de Meynard's *Dictionnaire turc-français* [E21]. Also see Shams al-Dīn Sāmī's *Qāmūs al-Aᶜlām* [J155].

¶¶ For the historical geography of Muslim Spain see Banᶜid Allāh's *Al-Mawsūᶜa al-Maghrabīya* [K53].

HOMONYMS

K59
YAQŪT, Shihāb al-Dīn abī ᶜAbd Allāh (d. 626/1229).
كتاب المشترك وضعا و المفترق صقعا
[Book of the Similarly Written and the Separation of the Locales]. *Ed.* Ferdinand Wüstenfeld. *Jacut's* Moschtarik, *das ist, lexicon geographischer homonyma.* Göttingen, Druck und Verlag der Dieterischen Buchhandlung, 1846. xviii + 45 + 475 p.
Dictionary of the cities, towns, etc., within the classical empire having the same name but different locations. Reprinted in Baghdad in 1963.
Title transliterated: Kitāb al-Mushtarik Waḍᶜā wa al-Muftariq Ṣaqᶜā.

TOPONYMS

K60
GROOM, Nigel.
A Dictionary of Arabic Topography and Place Names;

transliterated Arabic-English with an Arabic glossary. Harrow, England, Longman, 1983. 369 p.

Listed in accordance with the Arabic alphabet are the terms employed in Arabic geographical names based upon the classical lexicographers and geographers. Each term is given in transliteration, in the Arabic script, and an English translation.

K61
GEORGACAS, Demetrius J.
The Names for the Asia Minor Peninsula and a Register of Surviving Anatolian Pre-Turkish Placenames. Heidelberg, Carl Winter Universitätsverlag, 1971. 136 p.

Beiträge zur Namenforschung, Neue Folge, Beiheft 8.

Contents: I. Bibliography; II. The Anatolian Peninsula; III. The Names Designating the Peninsula (A. Ancient Names; B. Post-classical, Byzantine, and later names; Latin, western European, Slavic, Arabic and Turkish names); IV. Appendices: 1: Turkish placenames in Asia Minor continuing names of Greek or other origin; 2: Rumili, Rumeli, Rumelia; 3: Türkmen; Osmanli; V. Index.

K62
SECO DE LUCENA, Luis.
Topónimos árabes Identificados. Granada, Universidad de Granada, 1974. viii + 83 p.

Anejos de Miscelánea de Estudios Árabes y Hebraicos, Ser. A; III. Series: Bibliotheca Orientalista Granadina.

Toponyms of locales in the district of Granada.

DESCRIPTIONS

Near East (General)

K63
LeSTRANGE, Guy.
The Lands of the Eastern Caliphate: Mesopotamia, Persia, and Central Asia from the Moslem conquest to the time of Timur. Cambridge, University Press, 1905. xvii + 536 p.

Geography and history of the eastern portion of

the empire by province based upon the works of 24 Muslim geographers dating from 864 to 1604. Illustrated with 10 folding maps.

Reprinted by the same press in 1930 with a list of emendations.

K64
SPRENGER, Alois.
Die Post- und Reiserouten des Orients. Leipzig, F. A. Brockhaus, 1864. XXVI, [ii] + 159 p., maps. [all published].

Abhandlungen der Deutschen Morgenländischen Gesellschaft, III. Bd. No. 3.

In this comparatively brief book Sprenger attempted to describe the routes of the eastern portion of the empire which were employed by the *Barīd* (postal service) on official business and by ordinary travelers. Based upon original sources with liberal use of the Arabic, in that script. The 16 large separate maps are particularly detailed. The first ten pages are devoted to a detailed description of the postal service. No index, which, presumably, was to be included in the second volume. Reprinted in Amsterdam in 1972.

Syria

K65
GAUDEFROY-DEMOMBYNES, Maurice.
La Syrie à l'Epoque des Mamelouks d'aprés les Auteurs arabes: description géographique, economique et administrative précédée d'une introduction sur l'organisation gouvernmentale. Paris, Librairie Orientaliste Paul Geuthner, 1923. CXI + 288 p.

Haut-Commissariat de la République Français en Syrie et au Liban, Service des Antiquités et des Beaux-Arts: Bibliothèque Archéologique & Historique, T. III.

Contents: Introduction; Première partie: Description géographique de la Syrie; Deuxième partie: Organisation administrative de la Syrie. Seven appendices and three indices.

K66
IBN SHADDĀD, Muḥammad ibn ᶜAlī (d. 684/1285).
الاعلاق الخطيرة فى ذكر امراء الشام و الجزيرة

[The Importance of Remembering the Amirs of Syria and the Jazira].

A large historical topography written while resident in Egypt between 1272 and 1281. Only the following portions of the work have been edited to date:

1. Dominique Sourdel. *La Description d'Alep d'Ibn Šaddād.* Damascus, Institut Français d'Etudes Arabes de Damas, 1953. xxxii + 231 p.

2. Sāmī al-Dahhān. *La Description de Damas d'Ibn Šaddād.* Damascus, Institut Français d'Etudes Arabes de Damas, 1956. lvi + 473 p.

3. Sāmī al-Dahhān. *Liban, Jordanie, Palestine, Topographie historique d'Ibn Šaddād,...* . Damascus, Institut Français d'Etudes Arabes de Damas, 1963. xxv + 347 p., illus.

Title transliterated: Al-Aᶜlāq al-Khaṭīra fī Dhikr Umarāᵓ al-Shām wa al-Jazīra.

K67
al-MUNAJJID, Ṣalāh al-Dīn.

مدينة دمشق عند الجغرافيين و الرحالين المسلمين

Damas; vue par les géographes et les voyageurs musulmans. Beirut, Dār al-Kitāb al-Jadīd, 1968. 350 p.

Title transliterated: Madīna Dimashq ᶜinda al-Jughrāfīyīn wa al-Raḥḥālīn al-Muslimīn.

Turkey

K68
TAESCHNER, Franz G.

Das anatolische Wegenetz nach osmanischen Quellen. Leipzig, Mayer & Müller, G.m.B.H., 1924. xvi, 246 + 12 p., illus.

Tuerkische Bibliothek, Bd. 22.

Description of the road system and places of Anatolia under the Ottomans based upon Muslim geographers and travelers and western travel books.

Yemen

K69
al-SULĀMĪ, ᶜArrām ibn al-Asbagh (d. 275/888).

كتاب اسماء جبال تهامة و سكانها و ما فيها من القرى
و ما يتبت عليها من الاشجار و ما فيها من المياه

[Book of the Names of the Mountains of the Tihāma

and of their Residents and What is in Them of Villages, Trees, and Water]. Cairo, Maktaba al-Khanjī bi-Miṣr, 1374/1955. [(ii), 131 + (iii)], p.

Published as number eight in the series *Nawādir al-Makhṭūṭāt* with continuous pagination.

A brief explication of the topography of the seacoast region of the Yemen, with indices.

Title transliterated: Kitāb Asmāʾ Jibāl Tihāma ...

TRAVELS

Bibliographies

General

K70

COX, Edward Godfrey.

A Reference Guide to the Literature of Travel; including voyages, geographical descriptions, adventures, shipwrecks and expeditions. Seattle, University of Washington, 1935-38. 2 vols.

University of Washington Publications in Language and Literature, Vol. 9.

Despite its age and general character this bibliography of travel literature is included because it is a veritable mine of information and is often overlooked. Unfortunately, there is no index.

Material is arranged geographically and within each section chronologically. Covers the literature from the 16th into the 20th century.

Travel accounts for the Muslim world are to be found in Vol. I- The Old World: VIII. Near East; IX. Central Asia; X. East Indies; XIII. Africa (pp. 201-318 and 354-401).

K71

ATKINSON, Geoffroy.

La Littérature géographique française de la Renaissance; description de 524 impressions d'ouvrages publiés en Français avant 1610, et traitant des pays et des peuples non Europeéns, que l'on trouve dans les principales bibliothèques de France et de l'Europe occidentale. Paris, Editions Auguste Ricard, 1927. 563 p., illus.

Chronological inventory of the travel accounts of Frenchmen in the whole of the Orient to 1610, illustrated with reproductions of 300 title pages.

K72
LEVAL, André.
Voyages en Levant pendant les XVIe, XVIIe et XVIIIe Siècles; essai de bibliographie. Budapest, Singer et Wolfner, 1897. 30 p.
Author listing with titles of their accounts.

K73
PERES, Henri.
"Voyageurs musulmans en Europe aux XIXe et XXe Siècles: notes bibliographiques." *Mémoires de l'Institut Français d'Archéologie Orientale du Caire*, LXVIII, 1935, pp. 185-95.
Subtitle: Mélanges Maspero III.
Published and unpublished works listed by date from 1826 to 1934.

K74
WEBER, Shirley Howard.
Voyages and Travels in the Near East Made During the XIX Century: being a part of a larger catalogue of works on geography, cartography, voyages and travels, in the Gennedius Library in Athens. Princeton, The American School of Classical Studies at Athens, 1952. x + 252 p.
Arranged by date of publication between 1798 and 1900 and then by author.

K75
---.
Voyages and Travels in Greece, the Near East and Adjacent Regions Made Previous to the Year 1801: being part of a larger catalogue of works on geography, cartography, voyages and travels, in the Gennadius Library in Athens. Princeton, The American School of Classical Studies at Athens, 1953. VII + 208 p.
Catalogues of the Gennedius Library, II.
II. Travelers in the Near East and Adjacent Regions, arranged chronologically by the date of the journey, where known (589 items); V. Proskynetaria (24 items).

Iran

K76
IRAN. Kitābkhāna Millī.
فهرست توصیفی سفرنامه هلی آلمانی موجود در کتابخانه ملی ایران/
Katalog der Deutschsprachigen Reisebeschreibungen in der Iranischen Staatsbibliothek. *Comp.* Shahla Babazadeh. Tehran, Kitābkhāna Millī, 2537/1978. [vi] + 123 p., illus.

Annotated catalogue of 23 books of German travel literature respecting Iran. Listed in alphabetical order with full bibliographical details in German and Farsi. Lengthy annotations exclusively in Farsi. Indices.

Title transliterated: Fihrist Tawṣīfī Safarnāmah Halī Alamānī...

K77
---. ---.
فهرست توصیفی سفرنامه هلی انکلیسی موجود در کتابخانه ملی ایران/
Descriptive Catalogue of the English Itineraries in the National Library of Iran. *Comp.* Muḥammad Jaktājī. Tehran, Kitābkhāna Millī, 2535/1976. [v], 264 + [iii] p.

Annotated catalogue of 88 books of travel literature in English, not all by the travelers themselves, which have, at least in part, descriptions of Iran. Listed in alphabetical order according to the Arabic script into which the names have been transliterated. Each is listed first in English with full bibliographical details and then in Farsi. The annotations, often quite lengthy, are solely in Farsi. Indices.

Title transliterated: Fihrist Tawṣīfī Safarnāmah Halī Inglīsī...

K78
---. ---.
فهرست توصیفی سفرنامه هلی فرانسوی موجود در کتابخانه ملی ایران/
Catalogue descriptif des Récits de Voyages en Langue française Conservés à la Bibliothèque nationale d'Iran. *Comp.* Muḥammad Jaktājī. Tehran, Kitābkhāna Millī, 2535/1977. [xii], 244 + 10 p., illus.

Alphabetical listing by author in Arabic script of 44 works in French regarding travels, even by

Arabs, in Iran. Titles, with full bibliographic details, are provided in French, followed by their translation into Farsi. Lengthy annotations and illustrations of title pages. Indices.

Iraq

K79

ᶜAWWĀD, Kūrkīs.

"العرّب من كتب الرجلات الاجنبية الى العراق"

[Arabization of the Books of Foreign Travelers to Iraq] *Al-Aqlām*, I, 1384/1963, pp. 54-74.

A bibliographical essay in three parts of travel accounts from the earliest times to 1937. Firstly, a brief synopsis of the accounts of 21 travelers; secondly, a chronological listing of the names of travelers in both Latin and Arabic scripts, and, finally, a bibliographical listing of 51 travel accounts in western European languages and Arabic.

Title transliterated: Al-ᶜArrab min Kutub al-Rujlāt al-Ajnabīya ilā al-ᶜIrāq.

Palestine

K80

SCHUR, Nathan.

Jerusalem in Pilgrims and Travelers' Accounts: a thematic bibliography of western Christian itineraries 1300 - 1917. Jerusalem, Ariel Publishing House, 1980. 151 + [vi Hebrew text] p.

Not a bibliography, but rather a concordance to Jerusalem as described by these travelers. As the title indicates travel accounts by Eastern Christians, Muslims, and Jews are not included. Provides the year for each traveler, his name, and the page numbers for his description of the subject. All published copies of the book are imperfect.

Contents: Section I - Sites; Section II - The Jews; Section III - The Christians; Section IV - The Moslems; Section V - General; Section VI - Indexes.

¶ Reinhold Röhricht's *Bibliotheca geographica palaestina* [K9] contains a list of 3,515 travelers and studies of travels arranged in chronological order.

¶¶ For a bibliographic list of travelers in the Arabian Peninsula consult pages 33-63 of the American Geographical Society's *Bibliography of the Arabian Peninsula* (New Haven, Connecticut, Human Relations Area Files, 1956).

Those for Central Asia are to be found in each chronological division of *Soviet Central Asia* by Richard A. Pierce [J34].

Henri Lorin's *Bibliographie géographique de l'Egypte* [K1] contains two subsections on travelers in Egypt: T. I- II. Relations de Voyages et Ouvrages de Caractère historique [732 items]; T. II- III. Relations de Voyage [457 items].

For travelers in Turkey and the Ottoman Empire a bibliography of their accounts is to be found primarily on pages 30-57 in *Türkiye Coğrafya Eserleri* by Selçuk Trak [K5].

L SCIENCE

GENERAL

Bibliographies

General

L1
KAZANCIGİL, Aykut *and* SOLOK, Vural.
Türk Bilim Tarihi Bibliyografyası (1850-1981) [Bibliography of Turkish Writings on the History of Science (1850-1981)]. Istanbul, İstanbul Matbaası, 1981. XXIII + 328 p.

İstanbul Üniversitesi Cerrahpaşa Tıp Fakültesi Atatürk'ün Yüzüncü Doğum Yılmı Kutlama Yayınları, Özel Seri 1.

Listing by author, in modern Turkish only, of 1,143 books and articles. Author, title, and subject indices.

L2
NAṢR, Sayyid Ḥusayn *and* CHITTICK, William C.
کتابشناسی توصیفی منابع تاریخ علوم اسلامی / An Annotated Bibliography of Islamic Science. Tehran, Imperial Academy of Philosophy, 1975-78. 2 vols. [all published].

Publications Nos. 1 & 36.

Two volumes of a projected five volume catalogue of books and articles in western European languages, with occasional annotations in English and Farsi. Publication interrupted by the Iranian revolution. The two volumes contain a total of 4,341 items. Author index in each volume. Publication details often incomplete.

Contents: Vol. I: I. General Works; II. Biographical and Bibliographical Studies of Muslim Men of Science. Vol. II: III. Sciences Influential in the Formation of the Islamic Sciences; IV. Translation of Scientific Texts into Islamic Languages; V. Classification of the Sciences, Scientific Encyclopedias and Bio-bibliographies; VI. Cosmology and Cosmography; VII. Logic.

Title transliterated: Kitābshināsī Tawṣīfī Manābīᶜ Taʾrīkh ᶜUlūm Islāmī.

India

L3

RAHMAN, Abdur.

Science and Technology in Medieval India: a bibliography of source materials in Sanscrit, Arabic, and Persian. New Delhi, Indian National Science Academy, 1982. xxxi + 179 p.

"Published for the National Committee for the Compilation of History of Sciences in India."

Yemen

L4

al-HABASHĪ, ᶜAbd Allāh Muḥammad.

[Sources of مصادر الفكر العربى الاسلامي فى اليمن Arabic Islamic Thought in Yemen]. Ṣanᶜāʾ, Markaz al-Dirāsāt al-Yamanīya, [1978]. 682 p.

A bio-bibliographical survey of Yemeni writers in the Islamic sciences.

Title transliterated: Maṣādir al-Fikr al-ᶜArabī al-Islāmī fī al-Yaman.

¶ For a bibliography of Arabic works on science see pages 97-129 in Nazār Qāsim, *Al-Muᶜājim al-ᶜArabīya fī al-ᶜUlūm...* [F16].

Biographies

L5

al-DUJAYLĪ, ᶜAbd al-Ṣāḥib ibn ᶜImrān.

[Arab Personages اعلام العرب فى العلوم و الفنون in the Sciences and Arts]. *2nd ed.* Najaf, Maṭbaᶜa al-Nuᶜmān, 1966. 3 vols.

Chronological biographical dictionary of 380 scientists and artists who lived between the 7th and the 18th centuries A.D.

Title transliterated: Aᶜlām al-ᶜArab fī al-ᶜUlūm wa al-Funūn.

L6

al-QIFṬĪ, ᶜAlī ibn Yūsuf (d. 646/1248).

[Book of the News of كتاب اخبار العلماء باخبار الحكماء the Learned in the History of the Philosophers]. *Ed.* Julius Lippert. Tarih al-Hukama, *oder Gelehrtenlexicon des Ibn al-Qifty's, Arabischer Gelehrter und Staatsbeamter, 568-646 A.H. (1172-1248 A.D.).* Leipzig, Dietrich'sche Verlagsbuchhandlung, 1903. XXII + 496 p.

Biographical dictionary of 414 Greek, Syrian and Muslim physicians, astronomers, and philosophers in a synopsis by al-Zawzanī. Another edition, by Muḥammad Amīn al-Khanjī, was published in Cairo in 1326/1908.

Reprinted in Amsterdam in 1971.

Dictionaries

L7
GHĀLIB, Idwār.

Dictionnaire des Sciences / الموسوعة فى علوم الطبيعة de la Nature. Beirut, Al-Maṭbaᶜa al-Kāthulīkīya, 1965-66. 3 vols., illus.

A polyglot dictionary of 24,871 Arabic terms in all aspects of the natural sciences with their equivalents in Latin, French, English, German, and Italian. The first two volumes are in alphabetical order (Arabic script) (I- *alif-sīn*; II- *shīn-yā*), the third places the terms in alphabetical order in each of the five other languages.

Title transliterated: Al-Mūsūᶜa fī ᶜUlūm al-Tibīᶜa.

L8
al-TAHĀNAWĪ, Muḥammad Aᶜlā ibn ᶜAlī (*fl.* 1158/1745).

[Discoverer of the Technical كشّاف اصطلاحات الفنون Terms of the Sciences]. *Ed.* Mohammad Wajib, ᶜAbd al-Haqq *and* Ghalam Kadir. *A Dictionary of the Technical Terms Used in the Sciences of the Musulmans.* Calcutta, Royal Asiatic Society of Bengal, 1853-62. 2 vols.

Bibliotheca Indica, XVII & XXIII.

Supplement: Ed. & trans. A. Sprenger. *First Appendix to the Dictionary ..., Containing the Logic of the Arabians, with an English translation.* Calcutta, Royal Asiatic Society of Bengal, 1854. 36 + 29 p. *Bibliotheca Indica, XXIII.*

The three volumes were reprinted in two in 1980.

ASTRONOMY

Bibliographies

L9
CARMODY, Francis J.
Arabic Astronomical and Astrological Sciences in Translation: a critical bibliography. Berkeley, University of California Press, 1956. vi + 193 p.
Detailed bibliography of the translations arranged by Arabic author.

L10
SUTER, Heinrich.
"Die Mathematiker und Astonomer der Araber und Ihre Werke." *Zeitschrift für Mathematik und Physik; Abhandlung zur Geschichte der Mathematischen Wissenschaften*, X, 1900, IX + 277 p.
Alphabetical list of 528 Muslim mathematicians and astronomers with the titles of their works. Provides details regarding printed editions (up to 1900) and translations available. Although out-of-date has not been entirely superceded.

Tables

L11
GOLDSTINE, Herman H.
New and Full Moons 1001 B.C. to A.D. 1651. Philadelphia, American Philosophical Society, 1973. 229 p.
Memoirs of The American Philosophical Society, Vol. 94.
Tables for the times, dates, and lunar longitudes of all lunar syzygies during the period. Of value for Islamic studies because of astronomical and astrological references in the texts.

L12
TUCKERMAN, Bryant.
Planetary, Lunar, and Solar Positions at Five-day and Ten-day Intervals. Philadelphia, The American Philosophical Society, 1962-64. 2 vols.
Memoirs of The American Philosophical Society, Vols. 56 & 59.
Tables providing the positions of the sun, moon, and visible planets for the years 601 B.C. to A.D. 1649. Vol. I: 601 B.C. - A.D. 1; Vol. II: A.D. 2

- A.D. 1649.

¶ For solar and lunar eclipses see V. Grumel's *Traité d'Etudes byzantines* [J225], of which the third part, VII.- Phénomènes naturels, contains tables of solar and lunar eclipses in Asia Minor and the Near East from 285 to 1500 A.D., and comets from 300 to 1462 A.D.

MEDICINE

Bibliographies

L13
AGHA, Zouhir M.
Bibliography of Islamic Medicine and Pharmacy/Bibliographie der islamischen Medizin und Pharmazie. Leiden, E. J. Brill, 1983. xii + 108 p.

Annotated listing of 698 items of scholars from *all* parts of the Muslim world, including the Indian sub-continent.

L14
EBIED, R. Y.
Bibliography of Mediaeval Arabic and Jewish Medicine and Allied Sciences. London, Wellcome Institute of the History of Medicine, 1971. 150 p.

Bibliography of over 1,972 Arabic, Hebrew, and western European books and articles. Those in oriental languages are in those scripts with English translation.

Contents: Sec. I: General Works Which Have a Bearing on Relevant Topics; Sec. II: Writings of Arab and Jewish Physicians and Critical Writings About Them.

L15
HAMARNEH, Sami.
Bibliography on Medicine and Pharmacy in Medieval Islam. Stuttgart, Wissenschaftliche Verlagsgesellschaft m.b.h., 1964. 204 p., illus.

Contents: I. Books on Medicine and Pharmacy; II. Relevant and Useful Books on the History of Islamic Civilization; III. Reference Books, Bibliographies and Dictionaries; IV. Current Periodicals. General index.

Section one is an author, editor, and translator listing of books in Arabic and western languages, with occasional annotations, on the history of Muslim medicine between the 9th and 14th centuries from Spain to Pakistan. The remaining bibliographies are a hodge-podge without internal organization.

Additions and corrections have been published by Otto Spies, "Beitrage zur medizinisch-pharmazentischen Bibliographie des Islams," *Der Islam*, XVIX, 1968, pp. 138-71.

Biographies

L16
IBN ABĪ UṢAYBIᶜA, Aḥmad ibn al-Qāsim (d. 668/1270). [Book of Sources كتاب عيون الانباء في طبقات الاطباء of Information on the Classes of the Physicians]. *Ed.* August Müller. *Ibn Abi Useibia*. Cairo/Königsberg i. Pr., [selbstverlag], 1882-84. 2 vols.

Biographical dictionary of over 600 Muslim physicians arranged in chronological order. Reprinted in 1971 in one volume. See Addenda.

L17
IBN JULJUL, Sulaymān ibn Ḥasan (d. *cir.* 384/994). [Classes of the Physicians طبقات الاطباء و الحكما and the Learned]. *Ed.* Fuᵓād Sayyid. *Les Générations des Médecins et des Sages*. Cairo, Institut Français d'Archéologie Orientale du Caire, 1955. 48, 138 + 10 p.

Textes et Traductions d'Auteurs Orientaux, T. 10.

¶ For additional biographies see al-Qifṭī, *Kitāb Akhbār al-ᶜUlamāᵓ* [L6].

Glossaries

L18
FONAHAN, Adolf M.
Arabic and Latin Anatomical Terminology, chiefly from the Middle Ages. Kristiana, J. Dybwad, 1922. [iv] + 174 p.

Skrifter Utgit av Videnskapaselskapets i Christiania 1921, II. Historisk-filosofisk Klasse, 2 Bind, No. 7.

The terms are listed in Arabic alphabetical order, in that script, with Latin translations.

Encyclopaedias & Dictionaries

L19
KAMAL, Hassan.
Encyclopaedia of Islamic Medicine, with a Greaco-Roman background. Cairo, General Egyptian Book Organization, 1975. 864 p., illus.

Contains, in addition, three appendices: I. Dictionary of Islamic Materia Medica: Latin-Arabic; II. Dictionary of Islamic Materia Medica: [Arabic-Latin]; III. Dictionary of Chief Medical Terms.

L20
al-QŪṢŪNĪ, Madyan ibn ᶜAbd al-Raḥmān (d. 1044/1634).
[Dictionary of the قاموس الاطبّاء و ناموس الالبّاء Physicians and Confidant of the Assiduous]. Damascus, Majmuᶜ al-Lugha al-ᶜArabīya bi-Dimashq, 1979- .

Dictionary of classical medical and pharmacological terms. Reproduction of a manuscript copy. *Title transliterated:* Qāmūs al-Aṭibbāʾ...

WEIGHTS & MEASURES

L21
HINZ, Walther.
Islamische Masse und Gewichte Umgerechnet ins metrische System. Leiden, E. J. Brill, 1955. VIII + 68 p.

Handbuch der Orientalistik, Supplement Band I.

Brief introduction to the maze of Islamic weights, measures, and land distances with useful tables for their conversion into the modern metric system. Reprinted by the original publishers in 1970.

Translations: *Trans.* I͡u. Z. Bregeli͡a. **Мусульманские Мерыивеса с Пореводом в Метриуескую Систему.** Moscow, Izdatel'stvo "Nauka", 1970, pp. 9-74. Included within the book is a study by E. A. Davidovich. **Материалы по Метрологии Средневековый Средней Азии** [Materials on Medieval Central Asian Metrology], pp. 75-143.

L22
WRIGHT, H. Nelson.
The Coinage and Metrology of the Sultans of Delhi. Delhi, Manager of Publications, 1936. xx + 432 p.

¶ Books and articles published on Islamic weights and measures are included in L. A. Mayer, *Bibliography of Moslem Numismatics* [J409].

M SOCIAL SCIENCES

ECONOMICS

Bibliographies

M1
KHAN, Muhammad Akram.
Islamic Economics: annotated sources in English and Urdu. Leicester, The Islamic Foundation, 1983. 221 p.
Islamic Economics Series - 7.
Classified, annotated listing of books and articles in the two languages on classical and contemporary economics under Islam. Very selective with emphasis upon comparatively recent literature. Urdu titles are in transliteration only. Author and subject indices.

M2
NIENHAUS, Volker.
Literature on Islamic Economics in English and German/Literatur zur islamischen Ökonomik in Englisch und Deutsch. Cologne, Al-Kitab Verlag, 1982. XI + 149 p.
Forschungsberichte Islamische Wirtschaft.
Subject listing of books and articles on classical and contemporary Islamic thought and practice.

M3
SIDDIQI, Muhammad Nejatullah.
Contemporary Literature on Islamic Economics: a select classified bibliography of works in English, Arabic and Urdu up to 1975. Leicester, The Islamic Foundation, 1978. 69 p.
International Centre for Research on Islamic

Economics - Research Report No. 1.

A bibliography of 700 books and articles on Islamic economic thought. Does not include materials on the economic history of Islam.

SOCIOLOGY & ETHNOGRAPHY

Bibliographies

General

M4
ᶜABD AL-HĀDĪ, Muḥammad Fatḥī.
الدليل الببليوجرافى للانتاج الفكرى العربى فى العلوم
الاجتماعية : علم الاجتماع و الانثروبولوجيا و الفولكلور
[Bibliographic Guide to Arabic Intellectual Production in the Social Sciences: sociology, anthropology, and folklore]. Cairo, Idāra al-Tawthīq wa al-Maᶜlūmāt, 1979. 18 + 760 p.

Books and articles by Arab authors or published in Arabic.

Title transliterated: Al-Dalīl al-Bibliyūjrāfī li-l-Intāj al-Fikrī al-ᶜArabī fī al-ᶜUlūm al-Ijtimāᶜīya:...

M5
BEIRUT. Université de St-Joseph, Centre d'Etudes pour le Monde Arabe Moderne.
Arab Culture and Society in Change: a partially annotated bibliography of books and articles in English, French, German, and Italian. Beirut, Dar el-Mashreq Publishers, 1973. XLI + 318 p. [dbl. col.].

Lists a total of 4,954 books and articles published, and theses presented, between World War I and December 1971.

Contents: I. Acculturation in General; II. Townsmen, Countrymen and Nomads; III. Cultural Reaction to Economic Change; IV. Condition of Women; V. Marriage and Family; VI. Youth; VII. Education; VIII. The Arabic Language; IX. Pluralism, Ethnic and Religious; X. Political Ideology; XI. Islam and Modern Thought; XII. Islam in Modern Society; XIII. Islam and the State; XIV. Islam and Modern Law; XV. Supplementary. Indices.

M6
TEZCAN, Mahmut.
Türk Sosyoloji Bibliyografyası 1928-1968 [Turkish Sociology Bibliography 1928-1968]. Ankara, Başnur Matbaası, 1969.

Ankara Ünıversitesi Eğitim Fakültesi Yayınları: 6; Eğitim ve Toplum Araştırmaları Enstitüsü Yayınları: 1.

Unannotated, classified listing of 6,255 books and articles on sociology, etc., published in modern Turkish only.

Contents: I. Toplumsal Bilimler Metodolojisi ve Araşsırma Teknikleri; II. Sosyoloji Tarihi Kuramlar ve Genel Sosyoloji; III. Toplumsal Psikoloji; IV. Irk ve Toplumsal Yönleri; V. Kültür, Toplumsal Yapı ve Uygarlık Sosyolojisi; VI. Karmaşik Yapilar; VII. Toplumsal Değişme, Ekonomik Kalkinma ve Ekonomik Sosyoloji; VIII. Kütle Olayı; IX. Siyasal Etkileşim, Siyaset Bilimi ve Siyaset Sosyolojisi; X. Toplumsol Farklilaşma; XI. Köy Sosyolojisi, Toplum Kalkınması ve Bolğe Sosyolojisi; XII. Şehir Sosyolojisi; XIII. Sanat ve Ahlâk Sosyolojisi; XIV. Eğitim Sosyolojisi; XV. Din Sosyolojisi; XVI. Hukuk Sosyolojisi; XVII. Bilim Sosyolojisi ve Teknoloji; XVIII. Nüfus Sosyolojisi; XIX. Aile Sosyolojisi; XX. Tıp Sosyolojisi; XXI. Toplumsal Sorunlar ve Toplumsal Refah; Ekler. Author index.

¶ For Turkish publications on ethnology see, Millî Folklor Enstitüsü, *Türk Folklor ve Etnografya Bibliyografyası* [D37].

Egypt

M7
COULT, Lyman H., Jr.
An Annotated Bibliography of the Egyptian Fellah. Coral Gables, Florida, University of Miami Press, 1958. v + 144 p., map.

Title on fly-leaf: *An Annotated Research Bibliography of Studies in Arabic, English, and French of the Fellah of the Egyptian Nile 1798-1955.*

With 831 titles fully annotated. Those in Arabic are presented in transliteration and translation. Compiled in Egypt.

Contents: General Reference Works; Secondary Analyses; Travel and Description; Records of Professionals Serving the Village; Autobiographical Accounts; Reports by Trained Egyptians; Short Field Trips; Advanced Studies. Author and title indices. Glossary.

Morocco

M8

ADAM, André.

Bibliographie critique de Sociologie, d'Ethnologie et de Géographie humaine du Maroc: travaux de langues anglaise, arabe, espagnole et française, arrêtée au 31 décembre 1965. Algiers, Centre de Recherches Anthropologiques, Préhistoriques et Ethnographiques, 1972. 353 p.

Mémoires XX.

Annotated author listing of 2,198 books and articles. Those in Arabic are given in transliteration with French translations. Subject index.

M9

WEEKES, Richard V., *ed.*

Muslim Peoples: a world ethnographic survey. *2nd ed.* Westport, Connecticut, Greenwood Press, 1984. 2 vols., tables, maps.

An alphabetically arranged dictionary of 198 ethnic groups of Muslims throughout the world in signed articles of varying length, each with a short bibliography, written by a number of specialists. Although principally concerned with the contemporary scene the work also has relevance for the study of these peoples in the past.

ADDENDA

BIBLIOGRAPHY • General Works

A16a
EDE, David; LIBRANDE, Leonard; LITTLE, Donald P.; RIPPIN, Andrew; TIMMS, Richard *and* WERYHO, Jan.
Guide to Islam. Boston, G. K. Hall & Co., 1983. xxiv, [ii] + 261 p. [dbl. col.].
The Asian Philosophies and Religions Resource Guide.
A selective, classified, and annotated bibliography of 2,962 books and articles, primarily in English, published through 1967, on the faith, history, and culture of Islam from Muhammad to modern times, and from Spain to China. Author and subject indices. A bibliography particularly useful to English-speaking students.

Newspapers & Periodicals

A56a
UNITED STATES. Library of Congress.
African Newspapers in the Library of Congress. Washington, D.C., Library of Congress, 1984. 144 p.
Comp. John Pluge, Jr.
An updating of the list published in 1977 with 931 titles (original and on microfilm) listed by country in alphabetical order and then arranged by city.

A56ab
---. ---.
African Newspapers Available on Microfilm. Washington, D.C., Photoduplication Service, Library of Congress, February 1984. 27 p.
Primarily contemporary newspapers with a few, mainly from Egypt, dating prior to 1924. Arranged by country, city, and title, with dates, on microfilm and number of reels.

LIBRARIES & ARCHIVES • Directories

B1a
PARIS. Institut du Monde Arabe, Centre de Documentation, Bibliothèque.
Répertoire des Bibliothèques et des Organismes de Documentation sur le Monde arabe. Paris, Institut du Monde Arabe, 1984. 150 p.
RIMA
An attempt to list, with full details, all of the libraries throughout the world which have an interest in the Arab world, both classical and contemporary. Based as it is upon a questionnaire it is, unfortunately, incomplete. Index of personal names only.

ENCYCLOPAEDIAS

C10a
STRAYER, Joseph R., *ed.*
Dictionary of the Middle Ages. New York, Charles Scribner's Sons, 1982- [in progress].
In reality an encyclopaedia in 13 volumes [projected] with articles of various lengths by a wide variety of, primarily, American scholars. Each article is followed by a brief bibliography and cross-referenced to other articles. Fortunately, includes many articles on the classical Muslim world and Islam. The thirteenth volume is to be a general index.

RELIGION & PHILOSOPHY • Qurᵓān • *Dictionaries*

D58a
NAṢṢĀR, Ḥusnī.
التيسير فى تفسير الفاظ القرآن الكريم : القاموس القرآني
[Facilitation in Explaining the Terms of the Qurᵓān: Qurᵓānic dictionary]. Alexandria, Manshāᵓa Anwār al-Maᶜrifa, 1979. 286 p.
A dictionary of the difficult words in the Qurᵓān, arranged by *Sūra*.
Title transliterated: Al-Taysīr fī Tafsīr Alfāẓ al-Qurᵓān al-Karīm:...

D72a
IBN AL-JAWZĪ, ᶜAbd al-Raḥmān ibn ᶜAlī (d. 597/1200).
منتخب قرة عيون النواظر فى الوجوه و النظائر فى القرآن الكريم
[Selected Pleasures for the Eyes Regarding the Synonyms and Antonyms in the Holy Qurᵓān]. *Ed.* Muḥammad al-Sayyid al-Ṣifṭāwī *and* Fuᵓād ᶜAbd al-Minᶜam Aḥmad. Alexandria, Munshaᵓa al-Maᶜārif, [1979]. 324 p., illus.

An abridgement of his نزهة العيون النواظر, a dictionary of the synonyms and antonyms.

Title transliterated: Muntakhab Qurra ᶜUyūn al-Nawāẓir fī al-Wujūh wa al-Naẓāᵓir fī al-Qurᵓān al-Karīm.

Philosophy • *Dictionaries*

D91a
EGYPT. Majmaᶜ al-Lugha al-ᶜArabīya.
[Dictionary of Philosophy]. المعجم الفلسفى
Cairo, Al-Hayᵓa al-ᶜĀmma li-Shuᶜūn al-Maṭbaᶜa al-Amirīya, 1979. 5 + 326 p.

Title transliterated: Al-Muᶜjam al-Falsafā.

D91ab
WAHBA, Murād.
Vocabulairs philosophique arabe. المعجم الفلسفى
Cairo, Dār al-Thaqāfa al-Jadīda, 1979. 476 + 49 p.

An Arabic, English, and French dictionary of philosophical terms.

Title transliterated: Al-Muᶜjam al-Falsafā.

Traditions • *Collections*

D103a
ABŪ DAᵓŪD, Sulaymān ibn al-Ashᶜath.

Translations: Trans. Ahmad Hassan. *Sunan Abu Dawud: translated into English with explanatory notes & an introduction.* Lahore, Sh. Muhammad Ashraf, 1984. 3 vols.

Sectarianism • *Ṣūfīya*

D183a
ḤILMĪ, Muṣṭafā.
الزهاد الاوائل : دراسة فى الحياة الروحية الخالصة

[The First Ascetics: a study in فى القرون الاولى the pure spiritual life of the early centuries]. Alexandria, Dār al-Daᶜū, 1979. 223 p.

Biographical sketches of the earliest *Ṣūfīs*.

Title transliterated: Al-Zuhhād al-Awāʾil:...

LANGUAGE • Arabic • *Bibliographies*

F1a

BAKALLA, M. H.

Arabic Linguistics: an introduction and bibliography. London, Mansell Information/Publishing, 1983. lxx + 741 p.

A revised and greatly enlarged edition of his *Bibliography of Arabic Linguistics* with contributions by Peter Abboud, B. Ingham, T. Prochazka, and Kh. Semaan and more than doubling the number of entries.

LITERATURE • Arabic • *Biographies*

G17a

MAḤFŪZ, Muḥammad.

[Biographies of Tunisian تراجم المؤلفين التونسيين Authors]. Beirut, Dār al-Gharb al-Islāmī, 1982. 2 vols.

Biographical dictionary of classical and modern authors coming from or resident in Tunisia.

Title transliterated: Tarājim al-Muʾallifīn al-Tūnisīyīn.

Arabic • *Dictionaries*

G31a

WAHBA, Majdī.

معجم المصطلحات العربية فى اللغة و الادب/

A Dictionary of Arabic Literary & Linguistic Terms. Beirut, Maktaba Lubnān, 1979. 272 p.

Includes a seventeen page "English-Arabic Glossary".

Title transliterated: Muᶜjam al-Muṣṭalaḥāt al-ᶜArabīya fī al-Lugha wa al-Adab.

Arabic • *Proverbs*

G41a
LUNDE, Paul *and* WINTLE, Justin.
A Dictionary of Arabic and Islamic Proverbs. London, Routledge & Kegan Paul, 1984. 200 p.
Translations, with index.

Persian • *Bio-bibliographies*

G45a
STOREY, Charles A.
Persian Literature: a bio-bibliographical survey.
Contents: Vol. III - Part 1 [1984]: A. Lexicography; B. Grammar; C. Prosody and Poetics.

ART & ARCHITECTURE • Architects

I3a
TAYMŪR, Aḥmad.
[Architects in Islamic Times]. المهندسون في العصر الاسلامى *2nd ed.* Cairo, Dār Nahda Miṣr li-l-Ṭabaᶜ wa al-Nashr, 1979. 147 p.
Biographical dictionary of Islamic architects and their works. First published in 1957 under the title: اعلام المهندسين فى الاسلام
Title transliterated: Al-Muhandasūn fī al-ᶜAṣr al-Islāmī.

Painting • *Bibliography*

I14a
ROHANI, Nasrin.
A bibliography of Persian Miniature Painting. Cambridge, Massachusetts, The Aga Khan Program for Islamic Architecture, 1982. vi + 158 p.

HISTORY • Biographies • *Geographical*

J116a
al-ḤANBALĪ, Aḥmad ibn Ibrāhīm (d. 875/1471).
[The Easing of the Mind Regarding the Exploits of the Banū Ayyūb]. شفاء القلوب في مناقب بنى أيوب *Ed.*

Nāẓim Rashīd. Baghdad, Wizāra al-Thaqāfa wa al-Funūn, Tawzīᶜ al-Dār al-Waṭanīya li-l-Tawzi wa al-Aᶜlām, 1978. 494 p.

Silsila Kutub al-Turāth, 65.

History and biographical dictionary of the Ayyūbids.

Title transliterated: Shifāɔ al-Qulūb fī Manāqib Banī Ayyūb.

J123a

JAIN, Naresh Kumar.

Muslims in India: a biographical dictionary. New Delhi, Manohar, 1979-82. 2 vols.

Contains biographies of approximately 1,200 Indian Muslims who lived or were active between 1857 and the late 1970s.

Contents: Vol. I: A-J; vol. II: K-Z.

J157a

PAKALIN, Mehmet Zeki.

Türkiye Teracimi Ahval Ansiklopedisi/Encyclopédie biographique de Turquie. Istanbul, Ekspress Matbaası, 1929. cxxxv + 608 p., illus.

A who's who and who was who in Turkish and French, illustrated with miniature portraits of the biographees.

Chronologies & Dynastic Tables

J213a

PANHWAR, Muhammad Hussain.

Chronologial *[sic]* Dictionary of Sind (from geological times to 1539 A.D.). Jamshoro, Pakistan, Institute of Sindhology, University of Sind, 1983. xxvii, 395, 66 + 70 p., illus., maps.

Institute of Sindhology Publications: No. 99.

Calendars & Comparative Dates

J230a

MUKHTĀR, Muḥammad.

كتاب التوفيقات الالهامية في مقارنة التواريخ الهجرية
بالسنين الافرنكية و القبطية [Book of Knowledge of Adaptations in the Comparative Datings of the Hijra, Gregorian, and Coptic Years]. Beirut, Al-Muɔassasa

al-ᶜArabīya li-l-Dirāsāt wa al-Nashr, 1980. 2 vols.
Includes a chronology of the major events in Islamic history.
Contents: Vol. I: 1-750A.H./622-1350A.D.; vol. II: 751-1500A.H./1350-2077A.D.
Title transliterated: Kitāb al-Tawfīqāt al-Ilhāmīya fī Muqārana al-Tawārīkh al-Hijrīya bi-al-Sinīn al-Ifrankīya wa al-Qubṭīya.

Natural Phenomena

J234a
DEV, Jarnail Singh.
Natural Calamities in Jammu and Kashmir. New Delhi, Ariana Publishing House, 1983. vi + 161 p.
An examination of the various calamities, particularly floods and epidemics, which befell the former princely state between 1846 and 1925.

Documents • *Guides & Inventories*

J241a
BONO, Salvatore.
"Documentazione sulla Libia nell'Archivo del Ministero degli Esteri a Bruxelles (1850-1950)." *Africa: revista trimestrale de studi e documentazione*, XXXVIII, 1983, pp. 415-422.
A useful, detailed survey of the archival materials.

Documents • *Collections*

J330a
ḤAKĪM, Muḥammad ibn ᶜAzūz.
[Documents وثائق الحركة الوطنية في شمال المغرب on the National Movement in Northern Morocco]. Tetwan, Muɔassasa ᶜAbd al-Khāli al-Ṭarīsī li-l-Thaqāfa wa al-Fikr, 1980- [in progress].
Selected and annotated documents on the national movement between 1916 and 1936.
Title transliterated: Wathāɔiq al-Ḥaraka al-Waṭanīya fī Shamāl al-Maghrib.

J336a
ḤAMĀDĀ, Muḥammad Māhir.

الوثائق السياسة و الادارية العائدة للعصور العباسية المتابعة ٢٤٧ ـ ٦٥٦ هـ / ٨٦١ ـ ١٢٥٨ م: دراسة و نصوص

[Political and Administrative Documents Belonging to the ᶜAbbāsid Period Between 247-656 A. H./861-1258 A.D.]. Beirut, Muᶜassa al-Risāla, 1978. 517 p.

Silsila Wathāᵓiq al-Islāmī, 3.

Collected from diverse sources.

Title transliterated: Al-Wathāᵓiq al-Siyāsa wa al-Idārīya al- ᶜAᵓida li-l-ᶜUṣūr al-ᶜAbbāsīya...

J346a

al-KHĀZZAN, Fīlīb *and* Farīd, *trans.*

مجموعة المحررات السياسية و المفاوضات الد ولية عن سوريا و لبنان من سنة ١٨٤٠ الى سنة ١٩١٠

[Collection of Administrative Documents and International Negotiations on Syria and Lebanon from 1840 to 1910]. Al-Hazamiya, Lebanon, Dār al-Rāᵓid al-Lubnānī, 1983- [in progress].

Translations from the English and French.

Title transliterated: Majmūᶜa al-Muḫarrirāt al-Siyāsīya wa al-Mufāwaḍāt al-Dawlīya ᶜan Sūrīyā wa Lubnān...

J366a

ANSARI, Mohammad Azhar.

Administrative Documents of Mughal India. Delhi, B. R. Publishing Corp., 1984. 78 + 41 p., illus.

Persian court documents for the period 1563-1858 in English translation, with 13 pages of facsimili.

J366ab

PRAKASH, Om.

The Dutch Factories in India, 1617-1623: a collection of Dutch East India Company documents pertaining to India. New Delhi, Munshiram Manoharlal, 1984. xxiv + 332 p., illus., map.

Translations, with annotations, of documents contained within the Algemeen Rijksarchief, The Hague.

GEOGRAPHY • Atlases • *General*

K17a
al-ᶜATTĀR, ᶜAdnān.
[Histor- الاطلس التاريخي للعالمين العربى و الاسلامى ical Atlas of the Arabic and Islamic Worlds]. Damascus, Manshūrāt Saᶜd al-Dīn, 1979. 88 p., maps.
Title transliterated: Al-Aṭlas al-Taʾrīkhī li-l- ᶜĀlamayn al-ᶜArabī wa al-Islāmī.

Gazetteers & Dictionaries • *Iran*

K49a
BARTOL'D, V. V.
Историко-географическкий Обзоръ Ирана [Historical-geographical Survey of Iran]. St. Petersbourgh, Tip. V. Kirshbachma, 1903. 176 p., map.
Derived, by this master Russian scholar, from original sources.
Title transliterated: Istoriko-geografisheskīī Obzor' Irana.
Translations: Trans. Svat Soucek. *Historical Geography of Iran.* Princeton, Princeton University Press, 1984. 275 p., map. *Modern Classics in Near Eastern Studies.*

SCIENCE • Medicine • *Biographies*

L16a
IBN ABĪ UṢAYBIᶜA, Aḥmad ibn al-Qāsim.
Continuations: Aḥmad ᶜĪsā. معجم الاطباء من سنة ٦٥٠ هـ الى يومنا هذا: ذيل عيون الانباء فى طبقات الاطباء لابن ابى اصيبعة [Dictionary of Physicians, from the year 650 A.H. to the present day: continuation of *Sources of Information on the Classes of Physicians* by Ibn abī Uṣaybiᶜa]. Cairo, Jāmiᶜa Fuʾād al-Awwal, Kullīya al-Ṭibb, 1942. 527 p.

INDEX

In this index all definite and indefinite articles preceding proper names and titles have been omitted for simplification, irregardless of language. All books and articles are given in short-title only unless the full title is necessary for comprehension of the subject matter. The letter "a" following an entry number signifies that that entry is to be located in the Addenda; the letter "n" indicates that the entry is found in the note(s) following that entry number (preceded by the sign ¶).